SHORT-TERM PSYCHOTHERAPIES FOR DEPRESSION

Behavioral, Interpersonal, Cognitive, and Psychodynamic Approaches

Edited by

A. JOHN RUSH

University of Texas Health Science Center at Dallas

THE GUILFORD PRESS

New York London

A Division of Guilford Publications, Inc.
200 Park Avenue South, New York, N.Y. 10003

Printed in the United States of America

LIBRARY OF CONGRESS CATALOGING IN PUBLICATION DATA

Main entry under title:

Short-term psychotherapies for depression.

Includes bibliographies and indexes.

1. Depression, Mental. 2. Psychotherapy, Brief.
I. Rush, A. John. [DNLM: 1. Depression—Therapy.
2. Psychotherapy, Brief. WM 171 S559]
RC537.S5 616.85′2706 81-7058
ISBN 0-89862-615-3 AACR2

CONTRIBUTORS

Janis L. Anderson, MA, Department of Psychology, Vanderbilt University, Nashville, Tennessee

Aaron T. Beck, MD, Center for Cognitive Therapy, University of Pennsylvania, Philadelphia, Pennsylvania

Eve Chevron, PhD, Department of Psychiatry, Yale University School of Medicine, New Haven, Connecticut; Connecticut Mental Health Center, New Haven, Connecticut

Donna E. Giles, MA, Department of Psychiatry, University of Texas Health Science Center at Dallas, Dallas, Texas

Sally J. Grosscup, PhD, Department of Psychology, University of Oregon, Eugene, Oregon

Gerald L. Klerman, MD, Psychiatric Service, Massachusetts General Hospital, Boston, Massachusetts

Peter M. Lewinsohn, PhD, Department of Psychology, University of Oregon, Eugene, Oregon

Peter McLean, PhD, Department of Psychiatry, University of British Columbia, Vancouver, British Columbia

Stephanie Samples O'Malley, MA, Department of Psychology, Vanderbilt University, Nashville, Tennessee

Bruce J. Rounsaville, MD, Department of Psychiatry, Yale University School of Medicine, New Haven, Connecticut; Connecticut Mental Health Center, New Haven, Connecticut

A. John Rush, MD, Department of Psychiatry, University of Texas Health Science Center at Dallas, Dallas, Texas

Anthony Ryle, DM FRCPsych, University Health Service, The University of Sussex, Falmer, Brighton, Sussex, England

Janet A. Sandell, PhD, Department of Psychology, Vanderbilt University, Nashville, Tennessee

Hans H. Strupp, PhD, Department of Psychology, Vanderbilt University, Nashville, Tennessee

J. Michael Sullivan, PhD, Department of Psychology, University of Oregon, Eugene, Oregon

Gloria Jennings Waterhouse, PhD, Department of Psychology, Vanderbilt University, Nashville, Tennessee

Myrna M. Weissman, PhD, Department of Psychiatry, Yale University School of Medicine, New Haven, Connecticut; Connecticut Mental Health Center, New Haven, Connecticut

Jeffrey E. Young, PhD, Center for Cognitive Therapy, University of Pennsylvania, Philadelphia, Pennsylvania

Joseph Zaiden, MD,* Clinton County Mental Health Center, Shelby, North Carolina; private practice of short-term psychotherapy, Shelby, North Carolina

*Deceased.

PREFACE

Recent years have witnessed the gradual development of various short-term psychological approaches to psychopathology. Behavioral, interpersonal, cognitive, and psychodynamic theories have been sharpened, refined, and focused. Short-term psychotherapy methods have now been derived from each of these perspectives. Recently, clinical trials of these various therapies have become much more common. To the surprise of many researchers, evidence for the efficacy of a number of these treatments has been accrued.

This volume is an attempt to bring together and examine these four major approaches from two different but related viewpoints: the theoretical–empirical and the clinical–applied perspectives. As such, it is hoped that this book will provide new insights to both researchers and practitioners.

The affective disorders or depressions are heterogeneous with regard to biology, genetics, and treatment response, as Chapter 1 makes clear in detail. Therapists wishing to treat patients with a particular short-term psychotherapy must carefully select those patients who are most suitable for and most likely to respond to the psychotherapy. Further suggestions for selecting patients for each approach are provided in the clinically oriented chapters that follow. Furthermore, problems, reasons for failure, and technical suggestions are provided in the chapters that describe the clinical applications of behavioral, interpersonal, cognitive, and psychodynamic therapies for depression.

The theoretical–research chapters that introduce each of these four approaches review the theoretical model, the studies that attempt to test the assumptions in each model, and the available studies that have tested the efficacy of the treatment in depressed patients.

By placing these four approaches side by side, the reader may hope to develop a clearer picture of the commonalities and differences among these theories and treatments. Whether there are actual differences either in terms of overall effect or outcome, or in terms of the patients or the depressions for which each treatment is suited, is still unclear. The question of whether there are essential elements common to all psychotherapies is described by Ryle in Chapter 10.

The era of designing specific psychotherapeutic techniques for particular clinical problems is just beginning. The field is still grappling with questions of how best to match patients with the treatments available. Further evidence for the efficacy of various therapies is called for. Do these treatments differ in their ability to reduce symptoms, their ability to provide prophylaxis, or both? Does the personality of the patient dictate which treatment is most acceptable? Answers to these questions and others will come from clinical hunches and experiences that are tested with scientific methods.

In the past, psychotherapy researchers have been quick to lament the large gap between research findings and actual clinical practice. However, this gap, I believe, is beginning to close as the relevance of theoretical and research findings to clinical problems increases, and as clinicians are trained in the theory and conduct of more than one psychotherapy.

Since final answers with regard to the causes and treatments for the depressions are still far from clear, it would behoove both practitioners and researchers of varying theoretical persuasions to continue to share their experiences, ideas, and data. While both clinical and research work are likely to benefit from such cross-fertilization, let us hope that our patients obtain the greatest benefits of all.

A. John Rush
Dallas, Texas

CONTENTS

⁜ 1 ⁜

DIAGNOSING DEPRESSIONS

A. JOHN RUSH

INTRODUCTION

It is appropriate for a volume dealing with various psychotherapeutic treatments for the affective disorders to begin with a chapter on differential diagnosis of the depressions. Depressions are a particularly common set of disorders. Lehmann (1971) has estimated that one in five depressed persons receives treatment, that one in 50 is hospitalized, and that one in 200 may commit suicide. Furthermore, the lifetime expectancy of an affective disorder is on the order of 10% to 15%. This expectancy appears to be higher in women than in men. In addition, recent reports indicate a rising incidence of suicide, particularly among adolescents. In fact, suicide is now the second most common cause of death in this age group, while accidents are the most common cause of death. Suicides are largely manifestations of depressive disorders. Thus, depressive disorders are the most frequently seen, and perhaps the most lethal, of the psychiatric disorders.

While the affective disorders have been conceptualized from many points of view (biological, psychodynamic, behavioral, and cognitive), many of these conceptualizations suffered until recently from an underlying assumption that appears more and more clearly to be invalid: namely, that the affective disorders are homogeneous with regard to etiology and treatment response. Recent biological investigations, as well as psychotherapeutic and pharmacological outcome studies, have shown rather clearly that the affective disorders are indeed heterogeneous with regard both to biology and to treatment response. Given this heterogeneity, as well as the wide range of available psychotherapeutic and biological treatments, the clinician is confronted with the problem of how to select the most effective treatment for an individual patient.

A. John Rush. Department of Psychiatry, University of Texas Health Science Center at Dallas, Dallas, Texas.

Since the affective disorders are heterogeneous with regard to treatment response, the clinician must clearly evaluate each patient in hopes of finding some indicators or contraindicators for selecting particular treatments, particularly psychosocial or psychotherapeutic modalities. Current ability to identify those patients or disorders that are most effectively treated by psychotherapy is clearly limited; however, some suggestions can be gleaned from both clinical experience and research data that bear on this important clinical decision.

Furthermore, once treatment has been chosen and applied, it is absolutely essential for the clinician to conduct careful and repeated reevaluations to determine that the patient is, in fact, responding as expected to the treatment selected, whether it is medication or psychotherapy. If the initially prescribed treatment is not effective, the clinician should consider either restructuring the approach or changing to a different method of treatment altogether. This judgment often requires a new medical and psychiatric evaluation. Thus, full collaboration between biologically oriented and psychotherapeutically oriented practitioners is essential.

To illustrate the point, there is no evidence to date that manic–depressive or bipolar depressions respond to behavioral, cognitive, or other psychotherapeutic maneuvers. Rather, lithium or antidepressant medications provide both symptom relief and prophylaxis in the majority of these disorders. Without a careful evaluation, manic–depressive or bipolar disorder may be misdiagnosed as depressive neurosis or nonendogenous major depressive disorder and may be thought to be responsive to psychotherapeutic methods used alone. If the therapist does not recognize his or her error in the course of the patient's failure to respond to the treatment selected, the patient may be labeled "resistant," and referral for pharmacological treatment will not ensue.

While some depressions may respond little, if at all, to psychotherapeutic endeavors, other depressions may be effectively treated by such methods. The fact that affective disorders are differentially responsive to the psychotherapies suggests strongly that there are both specific and unique effects obtained in psychotherapy that are not obtained by other treatments. If psychotherapeutic methods were equivalently effective across all subtypes of depression, clinicians might wonder whether any specific, active ingredients are included in such psychosocial interventions.

DIAGNOSIS

A diagnosis ("to know through") is, in fact, simply a working hypothesis. This hypothesis is the clinician's best judgment as to what the ailment is, and, in some instances, as to how it may have come about. Specifically, diagnosis focuses on the nature of the pathological processes and the malfunctions that are present. Diagnosis, therefore, involves both *classification* and some hypothesis with regard to an *explanation* for the disorder.

A diagnosis serves several purposes: (1) simplification of complex data; (2) simplification of communication between professionals; (3) improved prognostic judgments; (4) assistance in selection of appropriate treatments; and (5) improvements in clinical research strategies. On the other hand, critics of the diagnostic process argue that (1) diagnoses lack reliability; (2) diagnoses do not produce useful definition of the problems to which therapy must be addressed; and (3) diagnosis represents a labeling process making an "illness" out of a "problem in living."

These misconceptions should be corrected at the outset. Descriptive diagnosis as currently practiced, utilizing criterion-based systems such as the third edition of the *Diagnostic and Statistical Manual of Mental Disorders* (DSM-III) (American Psychiatric Association, 1980) or the Research Diagnostic Criteria (RDC) (Spitzer, Endicott, & Robins, 1978), are in fact highly reliable. Interrater reliability for major categories of disorders range from correlations of .70 to .90.

Secondly, while problems in living may occur, Axis I diagnoses according to DSM-III are in fact syndrome diagnoses. A syndrome is a collection of signs and symptoms that is recurrently seen in the clinic. A syndrome may have multiple causes. For some types of depression, it is possible that a combination of stresses in association with psychological or biological vulnerability may operate as causes. However, syndromes are far more than simple problems in living. Many syndromes appear without any specifically associated life stresses.

Finally, descriptive diagnosis of affective disorders has already been shown to be extremely useful with regard to selection of biological treatments; more recently, evidence has been accrued that such descriptive classifications may be helpful in identifying patients who are, as a group, more or less responsive to psychosocial interventions (Prusoff, Weissman, Klerman, & Rounsaville, 1980).

DESCRIPTIVE DIAGNOSIS

Descriptive diagnosis now rests upon descriptive criteria of signs and symptoms. With regard to the diagnosis of major depressive disorder, the clinican asks the patient about his or her internal mood state, feelings of guilt and self-criticism, specific patterns of sleep, and specific history of weight loss, energy level, ability to experience pleasure, diurnal variation in mood, and so on. The examiner then works backward in time to determine when this complex group of signs and symptoms has most recently begun, and thereby develops a picture of this most recent episode of depressive syndrome. By moving backward in time, the examiner can identify multiple episodes of depressive syndrome.

In a similar manner, the examiner will evaluate the patient with regard to other types of affective and nonaffective psychopathological episodes. For example, has the patient met criteria for hypomania or mania in the past?

Once the episodes have been characterized over time, a descriptive diagnosis based on signs and symptoms and on the history of the present illness can be made. Symptom rating scales allow the examiner to measure the severity of the syndrome under question more specifically; however, these rating scales are not grounds for making a descriptive diagnosis.

DSM-III specifies the signs and symptoms of, as well as the clinical course of and related information about, the various descriptive depressive subtypes. For a detailed review of these criteria, the reader is referred to DSM-III. However, it is worth highlighting some of the criteria currently used for identifying certain common forms of depression.

A patient suffering from a major depressive episode will experience dysphoria, which is usually expressed as feelings of sadness. However, some patients may be dysphoric and express feelings of being anxious, irritable, tense, or upset. Thus, some patients will not state that they are sad. In addition to dysphoria, four or more of the following eight symptoms must be present to meet criteria for a major depression: poor appetite or a significant weight loss, or increased weight or significant weight gain; insomnia or hypersomnia; psychomotor agitation or retardation; loss of interest (withdrawal) or of pleasure (anhedonia) in usual activities or decrease in sexual drive; loss of energy or easy fatiguability; feelings of worthlessness, self-reproach, or excessive or inappropriate guilt; poor concentration, slow thinking, or indecisiveness not associated with incoherence or loosening of associations; and recurrent thoughts of death, suicidal ideation, wishes to be dead, or suicidal attempts.

DSM-III lists several criteria for exclusion of this diagnosis as well: The above symptoms should not be superimposed on schizophrenia, schizophreniform disorder, or paranoid disorder; the symptoms should not be due to any organic mental disorder or uncomplicated bereavement; and the symptoms must be present when bizarre behavior is present or when there is a preoccupation with mood-incongruent delusions or hallucinations. "Mood-incongruent" psychotic features are defined as follows: delusions or hallucinations, the content of which does not involve themes of personal inadequacy, guilt, death, disease, deserved punishment, or nihilism; thought insertion; thought broadcasting; and delusions of control.

Both major and minor depressive episodes, syndromes defined by specific criteria in DSM-III, may be caused by a variety of underlying medical disorders than can be difficult to recognize and that may pass through a general medical evaluation undetected. Several studies have shown that a significant proportion (10% to 50%) of psychiatric inpatients or outpatients have medical or physical disorders that are not diagnosed at the time of referral. (For a review, see Rush & Beck, 1978.) Specific medical disorders that are associated with depressive syndromes (and, indeed, with other types of psychopathology) included but are not limited to thyroid, adrenal, and parathyroid disorders; pernicious anemia; various cancers; viral infections; epilepsy; selected vitamin deficiencies; rheumatoid arthritis; so-called autoimmune diseases; and others.

In addition, a variety of medications are known to be associated with both minor and major depressive syndromes (Lipowski, 1975). Drugs such as reserpine, alpha-methyldopa (an antihypertensive), birth control pills, propandol (an antiarrhythmic drug), and steroids can cause various depressions. Treatment in these cases is obviously the discontinuation of these medications, if medically safe.

Conversely, patients with medical disorders may have a depression secondary to the impact of the disability on the patient (Schwab, Bialou, Holzer, Brown, & Stevenson, 1967; Schwab, Brown, & Holzer, 1967). That is, a physical illness may precipitate a psychiatric disorder, particularly depression. Studies of events precipitating or relating to the onset of severe depressions have shown that physical illnesses are the fifth most common antecedents of depressions (Leff, Roatch, & Bunney, 1970; Paykel, Myers, Dienelt, Klerman, Lindenthal, & Pepper, 1969). Often, effective treatment of the physical illness will relieve the depression itself. It should be recalled, however, that physical illnesses may not be recognized prior to a patient's seeking psychological or psychiatric assistance.

Finally, a minor or major depressive episode may coexist with and perhaps be etiologically related to another psychiatric disorder. For example, schizoaffective disorders or borderline syndromes appear to be entities that do *not* respond well to those psychosocial interventions that are routinely used for the treatment of straightforward minor or major depressions. Again, a careful descriptive diagnostic evaluation will identify such disorders and will, it is hoped, prevent these patients from entering into what may well be ineffective short-term psychotherapeutic treatment.

DIFFICULTIES IN DESCRIPTIVE DIAGNOSES

While interrater reliability has been dramatically improved by the use of criterion-based systems such as that found in DSM-III, other issues with regard to descriptive diagnoses have not been entirely resolved to date. One of the most common problems is the tendency of clinicians to use these criteria in an impressionistic, as opposed to a scientific, manner. That is, clinicians may well be familiar with the criteria in DSM-III, but they will not ask specific questions in a careful, explicit manner that allows for the identification of signs and symptoms. They may falsely assume, on the other hand, that patients will somehow know what are psychopathologic symptoms and what are not. This practice is particularly troublesome in the identification of patients with prior manic or hypomanic episodes.

A manic episode is defined as a distinct period lasting at least 1 week and characterized by feelings of euphoria and/or irritability, in association with hyperactivity, pressure of speech, flight of ideas, inflated self-esteem, distractability, decreased need for sleep, and excessive involvement in activities that have a high potential (unrecognized by the patient) for painful consequences. Associated symptoms often include an infectious quality to the elevated mood and/or a lability of mood, with rapid shifts between anger, euphoria, and depression. Speech may be disorganized and incoherent; flight of ideas may be severe; and loosening of associations and incoherence may occur even when there is no flight of ideas. Exclusion criteria are also used in the diagnosis of a manic episode.

In a so-called mixed episode, both depressive and manic symptoms may intermingle, occurring at the same time, or they may alternate rapidly within days. Hallucinations and delusions may well be present, although their content is usually but not always consistent with the predominant mood. Persecutory or grandiose delusions are not uncommon in severe episodes of mania. These patients may be misdiagnosed as schizophrenic during such episodes.

A bipolar disorder is diagnosed when the patient, by history, has evidence of major depressive and manic episodes. On the other hand, nonrecurrent or recurrent unipolar depression is diagnosed when there are one or more episodes of major depression without the presence of mania or hypomania.

If clinicians do not carefully and specifically inquire about each of the signs and symptoms of mania, hypomania, and major and minor depressions, they are *very* likely to miss essential information, and thus may fail to recognize schizoaffective disorder, bipolar illness, and other disorders that present as "depression." Many of these illnesses are not likely to respond to short-term psychotherapies.

Other factors also contribute to the difficulties in recognizing and diagnosing various subtypes of depression. The term "depression," as commonly used, may confuse our thinking in this regard. "Depression" commonly refers to an affect or a feeling state, usually labeled as "sadness," as well as a symptom, a syndrome, or a specific illness. Descriptive diagnostic approaches recognize syndromes and symptoms. "Sadness," the mood state, does not require treatment with any psychosocial or pharmacologic methods.

This terminological difficulty has an important impact on practice. In the Affective Disorders Clinic at the University of Texas in Dallas, over one-third of the patients who are referred for treatment for "depression" do *not* suffer from any form of depression whatsoever. Most of these patients are referred by psychiatrists or psychologists who are either unfamiliar with or are misapplying criterion-based diagnostic approaches.

Another difficulty affecting descriptive diagnosis is the "boundary" problem—that is, inability to recognize when a depression is not present and another disorder is present. This problem is exemplified by schizoaffective disorder, which is considered by some to include patients who have bipolar illness. Another example, "masked depression" (Lopez-Ibor, 1972), has added an even larger population of "depressions," while failing to clarify the concept of what a depression is.

Furthermore, the question of how premorbid personality affects the propensity to develop a depression, as well as its symptomatic manifestations, is far from resolved. Chodoff (1972) has stated that "the kind of person one is" may well affect "the kind of depression one has." In addition, particular kinds of personalities may be particularly vulnerable to the development of depression. Unipolar depressions have been said to occur in persons with a high degree of "neuroticism" (Perris, 1966). Involutional melancholias or severe endogenous depressions have been said to occur in patients with obsessional personalities (Chodoff, 1972). While these views represent summaries of clinical experience, further empirical investigations of the impact of depression on premorbid personality, and vice versa, are needed. The net result for the clinician, however, is that premorbid personality may confound and complicate the clinical picture of depression. Thus, depressions may be missed in certain personality disorders and overdiagnosed in others.

In addition, socioeconomic and ethnic characteristics appear to affect the clinical presentation of various depressions (Schwab, Bialou, Holzer, Brown, & Stevenson, 1967; Schwab, Brown, & Holzer, 1968). Studies by Hollingshead and Redlich (1958) have suggested that socioeconomic class affects the type of symptoms presented (e.g., lower socioeconomic class patients present with more somatic and fewer cognitive symptoms when depressed). The influence of gender on response to antidepressants and perhaps, by inference, on the nature of the symptoms presented, has also been reported (Blackwell, 1972; Mitchell, 1972; Raskin, 1972).

Another factor that can critically influence the nature of signs and symptoms elicited and reported is the context of the data collection itself (i.e., the clinical diagnostic interview). For example, the skilled interviewer can often precipitate an acute depression, with cognitive, behavioral, and affective manifestations, in some manic or hypomanic patients.

The timing of the interview in relationship to the onset or offset of the symptomatic episode is also critical. If the patient is evaluated early in an episode, a nonendogenous depression or mild nonpsychotic depression may be diagnosed. However, if the evaluation occurs later in the episode, some of these patients will have developed additonal symptoms that require a revision in diagnosis (e.g., psychotic or melancholic depression). Thus, the interviewer must be congnizant of the presenting signs and symptoms, the history of any previous episodes of depression, and the timing of the current evaluation in relation to the onset of recent symptoms.

SUBDIVIDING THE DEPRESSIONS

While most investigators now agree that the depressions are heterogenous with regard to etiology, biology, treatment response, genetics, and prognosis (Klerman, 1974; Mendels, 1974), clinically relevant and commonly agreed-upon descriptive distinctions between various subgroups of depressions are still controversial. Presently, no single scheme for subdividing the depressions on which all investigators can agree has been found.

While the unipolar–bipolar distinction mentioned above has gained the widest recognition and is perhaps best supported by genetic, treatment response, psychological, and descriptive historical differences, a number of other systems have been proposed for the subdivision of both unipolar depressions and all depressive disorders. Perhaps the most common methods for subdividing unipolar depressions include the endogenous–nonendogenous distinction, the neurotic–psychotic distinctions, the primary–secondary distinctions, and distinction based on family history (Winokur, Behar, Van Valkenburg, & Lowry, 1978).

The oldest distinction, that of the endogenous versus the reactive types of depression, was proposed by Gillespie (1929). This distinction between "reactive" depressions and "autonomous" or "endogenous" depressions was intended to differentiate depressions that arose in response to environmental events from those without an environmental precipitant. Such a distinction, however, no longer seems warranted. Rather, as a consequence of several studies (e.g., Leff *et al.*, 1970), it appears that even patients with such "autonomous" depressions as bipolar illness, if carefully and repeatedly interviewed, can be made to present one or more precipitants as explanations for the depressive episode. Thus, the diagnostic importance of the presence or absence of reportable life stress is minimal. It is for this reason that DSM-III assigns associated and environmental stress an axis separate from that used to diagnose the syndrome in question.

Currently, depressions are subdivided into those with and without melancholia by DSM-III. "Melancholia" refers to depressions that are associated with endogenous or endogenomorphic symptomatology. These episodes of depression would meet criteria for major depressive episodes. They are characterized, in addition, by the presence of loss of pleasure in all or almost all activities; lack of reactivity of mood to usual stimuli; and at least three of the following: distinct quality of depressed mood (distinctly different from the sorts of feelings experienced following the death of a loved one); regular worsening of the depressed mood in the morning; early morning awakening, at least 1 hour before the usual time of arising (terminal insomnia); marked psychomotor retardation or agitation; significant anorexia or weight loss; and excessive or inappropriate guilt. These so-called melancholic or endogenous depressions, it is presumed, are more likely to require and indeed to respond to medication treatment, with or without psychotherapy (Rush, in press).

The neurotic–psychotic distinction is drawn from a number of European studies (Rush, 1975). "Psychotic" refers to the presence of a break in reality testing, as manifested by hallucinations, delusions, or ideas of reference. According to this definition, about 15% of all depressions are "psychotic" depressions (Klerman & Paykel, 1970). It is no longer appropriate to use the term "psychotic" simply to refer to a more severe form of depression. "Psychotic" depressions, meaning those with hallucinations and delusions, appear to require significant amounts of medication and/or electroconvulsive therapy in virtually all cases.

A more recent dichotomy, the primary–secondary distinction, was proposed by investigators at Washington University, St. Louis, as a research strategy (Robins & Guze, 1972). This distinction is logically superordinate to the bipolar–unipolar dichotomy discussed above. "Primary affective disorder" refers to a disorder in a patient who has previously been well or whose only previous episodes of psychiatric disease have consisted of mania or depression. Thus, "secondary affective disorders" occur in patients who have previously had one or another psychiatric illness in the past. The presence or absence of an environmental stress and the issue of psychosis are irrelevant to this distinction. Given this methodology for subdividing depressions, it is apparent that secondary depressions must consist of various types of depression. The treatment implications of this subdivision are unclear at present.

Finally, there is the strategy proposed by Winokur *et al.* (1978), in which patients with primary depression are subdivided into those who have one or more first-degree relatives with a positive history of depression (Familial Pure Depressive Disease); those with first-degree relative(s) with a history of alcoholism and/or sociopathy without depressive disease (Depressive Spectrum Disorder); and those with first-degree relative(s) all of whom have no history of depression, sociopathy, or alcoholism (Sporadic Depressive Disorder). Again, any of these three family history subtypes may present with or without melancholic or psychotic symptomatology. Logic suggests that those with a positive genetic load for a depression would be more likely to require medication in addition to or instead of psychosocial interventions in order to obtain a full therapeutic response, whereas those with sporadic depressions would be more responsive to psychotherapy alone. However, the treatment implications of this subdivision strategy have yet to be empirically assessed.

In summary, several descriptive systems have been proposed for the subdivision of the depressions. However, as yet, no commonly agreed-upon system has evolved. The distinction of endogenous or melancholic depression versus nonendogenous or nonmelancholic depression is the only subdivision with specific treatment implications proposed so far. Melancholic patients are said to suffer from a primary deficiency in the pleasure center and a disinhibition in the pain center, whereas patients with nonendogenous depressions are reported to have generally negative outlooks and attitudes that, at least by inference, might be more treatable by psychosocial than by biomedical means (Klein, 1974). On the other hand, a number of studies have shown that antidepressant medications can be partially or fully effective in patients with nonendogenous or nonmelancholic depressions (Rush, 1981). It is unclear (1) whether one or another type of psychotherapy will improve what is only partial response to pharmacotherapy in some nonendogenous depressions, and/or (2) whether psychotherapy itself might produce prophylaxis once treatment is stopped that cannot be obtained with chemotherapy alone.

Recent data accrued by my colleagues and myself (Rush, Giles, Roffwarg, & Parker, in press) argue that the sleep electroencephalogram (Kupfer, 1976) and the dexamethasone suppression test (Carroll, Feinberg, Greden, Tarika, Aballa, Haskett, James, Krontrol, Lohr, Steiner, deVigne, & Young, 1981) offer independent validation of the endogenous–nonendogenous distinction, as opposed to the primary–secondary and family history subdivisions. These investigators found that the nonendogenous–endogenous dichotomy was best supported by these independent biological parameters. Further studies to replicate these preliminary findings and to evaluate their treatment implications are needed.

WHICH DEPRESSED PATIENTS ARE CANDIDATES FOR PSYCHOTHERAPY?

Various forms of psychotherapy appear to be directed at different objectives. Thus, in selecting patients for a particular therapeutic modality, it is wise to consider (1) what the objectives of the treatment are; (2) whether the patient, in fact, can participate in the treatment; and (3) whether the disorder will respond to the treatment selected. For example, some treatments are aimed directly at symptom reduction (e.g., behavioral therapy and cognitive therapy). On the other hand, certain psychotherapies (e.g., interpersonal therapy) aim at symptom reduction by more indirect methods. A second, although not less important, objective of some psychotherapies is prophylaxis. Behavioral therapy may also be used to induce prophylaxis, perhaps as exemplified by improvement of social skills. Cognitive therapists contend that they modify silent assumptions or schemas and thereby improve prophylaxis. Supportive therapeutic measures are aimed at reducing environmental stresses and increasing access to available resources. Again, prophylaxis might also be seen as an objective of these interventions. A third objective for psychosocial treatments is the reduction of the secondary consequences for the disorder itself. For example, marital therapy might be aimed at reducing marital tensions that have resulted from an illness, such as bipolar or manic–depressive illness. In this case, the psychotherapy is not aimed at symptom reduction, but may be said to attempt to reduce the secondary consequences of the disorder and/or to provide prophylaxis. Occupational therapy or training in social skills to increase employability among previously psychotic patients are also examples of attempts to reduce the secondary consequences of the disorder in question. Finally, psychosocial treatments may be aimed at increasing compliance with pharmacotherapy itself by providing information about the treatments and the disorders in question, by providing direct rewards for compliance, and/or by changing attitudes about medication and/or the disorder to be treated. Specific behavioral methods such as cueing or a reminder system for medication taking, as well as various cognitive-behavioral and interpersonal strategies, may help the patient to develop more compliant responses to pharmacotherapeutic prescriptions.

A second factor in selecting depressed patients for psychotherapy is the ability of the patient to participate in the treatment. A patient who is psychotic, meaning one who is hallucinating or delusional, will have difficulties in registering, storing, recalling, and appropriately utilizing instructions. These patients may be more amenable to psychotherapy once the psychotic symptomatology has been reduced with medication. Most psychotherapeutic studies have found that patients with greater "ego strength" do better in most psychotherapeutic endeavors (Luborsky, Chandler, Auerbach, Cohen, & Bachrach, 1971).

A third consideration in selecting depressed patients for psychotherapy is the question of whether the depression in question is responsive to psychotherapy at all. Few studies have carefully evaluated this question. However, recent reports (e.g., Prusoff *et al.*, 1980) have indicated that those patients diagnosed as endogenous by RDC (Spitzer *et al.*, 1978) did not respond well to interpersonal psychotherapy alone. However, they did respond to this psychotherapy when used in combination with antidepressant medications.

A further corroboration of the probability that endogenous (melancholic) depressions will respond best to medication with or without psychotherapy, is offered by Rush *et al.* (in press). Roughly 80% of patients with endogenous depression display biological abnormalities, as evidenced by the sleep electroencephalogram and/or the dexamethasone suppression test. While it is not entirely certain that such biological abnormalities make the patient *less* responsive to psychosocial treatments alone, it is not illogical to consider that the presence of such biological abnormalities does argue for the employment of medication. Indeed, Rush (in press) reports that 75% to 80% of those with one or both of these biological derangements do respond to medication alone.

On the other hand, a substantial proportion of depressed outpatients displays neither biological abnormality. However, from the viewpoint of symptoms, these patients also suffer from a major depressive disorder. In fact, in a study of 70 outpatients with non-psychotic, unipolar major depressive disorder, Rush *et al.* (in press) found that over one-third of the sample demonstrated neither biological abnormality. Most, but not all, of these patients were diagnosed as nonendogenous by RDC. Whether those patients without either biological derangement are preferentially responsive to one or another type of psychotherapy, or to psychotherapy as opposed to medication, remains to be determined. They have found that some two-thirds of patients with neither biological abnormality did evidence partial or complete response to medication (Rush, in press).

To summarize the available, although incomplete, evidence to date about whether a patient with depression should be subjected to therapy alone, the following guidelines may be recommended. Patients with psychotic depression (hallucinating or delusional) should be treated with biomedical interventions (anitdepressants and/or electroconvulsive therapy); psychotherapeutic techniques should be regarded as adjuncts rather than as primary treatments in these patients. Psychotherapeutic ventures might be best directed as assisting these patients in complying with medication treatments. Once the psychosis has cleared, however, patients may benefit from psychotherapeutic approaches, if particular objectives are identified and psychosocial treatments to obtain these objectives are applied. For example, reduction of the secondary consequences of the disorder, improvement in social skills, or change in dysfunctional attitudes might require psychosocial treatments in previously psychotically depressed patients. Patients with bipolar depression should be treated with medication and/or electroconvulsive therapy as primary treatments. Psychotherapeutic interventions should be reserved for the objectives noted above with psychotic depressions.

Patients with melancholic or endogenous depressions have a high probability of responding to antidepressant medication or electroconvulsive therapy alone in terms of symptom reduction. In these patients, these biomedical treatments would be considered first-line treatments, given our current knowledge of what types of patients respond to psychotherapy. However, it is possible with some outpatients who are diagnosed as endogenously depressed, without severe melancholia, that psychotherapy alone may be effective. In patients with nonendogenous or nonmelancholic depressions without psychosis (i.e., the majority of depressed patients), psychotherapeutic treatments may well have the most powerful effect; this is not to say that such depressions are medication-resistant, but, rather, that the case for psychosocial treatments alone or in combination with medication can most strongly be made for such depressions.

INDICATORS FOR A SPECIFIC TYPE OF PSYCHOTHERAPY

While descriptive diagnostic systems have been most fruitful in identifying patients for whom biological treatments are indicated, they have not yet been shown to be of use in identifying specific patients for whom a particular type of psychotherapy is indicated. In addition, no known biological markers for depression have been shown to have implications for selecting one type of psychotherapy over another. Even psychological measures do not yet indicate which types of depression will respond better to behavioral methods, as opposed to cognitive, interpersonal, or psychodynamic treatments.

In the chapters that follow, experienced practitioners of each form of psychotherapy have attempted to identify or describe those patients and/or depressions that seem to be most suited to a particular treatment in their clinical experience. However, empirical outcome studies to document these clinical impressions are largely lacking.

In addition, it has not yet been established that different forms of psychotherapy for depression (e.g., cognitive, interpersonal, psychodynamic, or behavioral) produce differential effects. It may well be that these four major forms of short-term psychotherapy for depression actually produce equivalent effects. Only additional comparative outcome studies will answer this question empirically.

CONCLUSIONS

At this point in time, the affective disorders appear to be a heterogeneous group. Given this heterogeneity with regard to genetics, biology, and treatment response, the would-be psychotherapist of depression must be sure that depressed patients assigned to psychotherapy, whether cognitive, behavioral, interpersonal, or psychodynamic, have undergone a thorough medical evaluation. Such an evaluation should identify underlying medical disorders that may present as or exacerbate depression; should screen out patients who are taking medications that produce depression; and should identify those sorts of depression (e.g., bipolar and endogenous unipolar depressions) that can and should be treated primarily with antidepressant medications or electroconvulsive therapy.

Once patients who appear to be suitable for psychotherapy are found, the therapist must continue to observe carefully, or must obtain repeated consultations to reevaluate, patients who do not respond to psychotherapy as anticipated. Misdiagnosis of the depressive disorders is not uncommon, even with the most careful initial evaluations. When possible, biological measures, such as the dexamethasone suppression test and the sleep electroencephalogram, should be used to validate the diagnosis. These tests are especially helpful in patients who are "resistant" to psychotherapeutic methods or for whom the diagnosis is unclear.

Once patients who are likely to respond to psychotherapy are identified, the therapist must rely on clinical judgment as to the sort of therapy to which the patient is best suited. It is still unclear whether patients who fail to respond to psychodynamic psychotherapy might respond to behavioral therapy, and so forth. Finally, the therapeutic methods chosen should be targeted toward specific objectives, whether the methods are cognitive, behavioral, interpersonal, or psychodynamic. The objective of therapy, whether symptom reduction, prophylaxis, reduction of the secondary consequences of the disorder, or improved compliance with medication treatment, should be determined at the outset. Which of these targets seems justifiable? It is usually wise to focus on one of these targets at a time.

Finally, whether psychotherapy can indeed produce prophylactic effects remains unclear, although some recent studies suggest that prophylaxis may ensue in some but not all depressions (Kovacs, Rush, Beck, & Hollon, 1981). Further studies of psychotherapy as a method of achieving prophylaxis and as a symptom reduction method are needed, as are studies to determine whether specific psychotherapies differ in their effectiveness and whether there are specific indications or contraindications for one or another form of therapy. In the following chapters, cognitive, behavioral, interpersonal, and pschyodynamic approaches will be described from the perspectives of both theoretical research and clinical experience.

REFERENCES

American Psychiatric Association. *Diagnostic and statistical manual of mental disorders* (3rd ed.). Washington, D.C.: Author, 1980.

Blackwell, B. Potential gender influences on outcome of antidepressant drug treatment. *Psychopharmacology Bulletin*, 1972, *8*, 27.

Carroll, B. F., Feinberg, M., Greden, J. F., Tarika, J., Aballa, A. A., Haskett, R. F., James, N. M. I., Krontrol, Z., Lohr, N., Steiner, M., deVigne, J. P., & Young, E. A specific laboratory test for the diagnosis of melancholia. *Archives of General Psychiatry*, 1981, *38*, 15–22.

Chodoff, P. The depressive personality: A critical review. *Archives of General Psychiatry*, 1972, *27*, 666–674.

Gillespie, R. D. Clinical differentiation of types of depression. *Guy Hospital Reprint*, 1929, *79*, 306–344.

Hollingshead, A. B., & Redlich, F. C. *Social class and mental illness*. New York: Wiley, 1958.

Klein, D. F. Endogenomorphic depression. *Archives of General Psychiatry*, 1974, *32*, 447–454.

Klerman, G. L. Unipolar and bipolar depression. In J. Angst (Chair), *Symposia Medica Hoechst 8: Classification and prediction of outcome of depression*. Stuttgart: F. K. Schaffauer Verlag, 1974.

Klerman, G. L., & Paykel, E. S. Depressive pattern, social background and hospitalization. *Journal of Nervous and Mental Disease*, 1970, *150*, 466–478.

Kovacs, M., Rush, A. J., Beck, A. T., & Hollon, S. D. Depressed outpatients treated with cognitive therapy or pharmacotherapy: A one-year followup. *Archives of General Psychiatry*, 1981, *31*, 33–39.

Kupfer, D. J. REM latency: A psychobiologic marker for primary depressive disease. *Biological Psychiatry*, 1976, *11*, 159–174.

Leff, M. J., Roatch, J. R., & Bunney, W. E. Environmental factors preceding the onset of severe depression. *Psychiatry*, 1970, *33*, 293–301.

Lehmann, H. Epidemiology of depressive disorders. In R. R. Fieve (Ed.), *Depression in the seventies*. Princeton: Exerpta Medica, 1971.

Lipowski, Z. J. Psychiatry of somatic diseases: Epidemiology, pathogenesis, classification. *Comprehensive Psychiatry*, 1975, *16*, 105–124.

Lopez-Ibor, J. J. Masked depressions. *British Journal of Psychiatry*, 1972, *120*, 245–258.

Luborsky, L., Chandler, M., Auerbach, A. H., Cohen, J., & Bachrach, H. M. Factors influencing the outcome of psychotherapy: A review of quantitative research. *Psychological Bulletin*, 1979, *75*, 145–185.

Mendels, J. Biological aspects of affective illness. In S. Arieti & E. B. Brady (Eds.), *American handbook of psychiatry*. New York: Basic Books, 1974.

Mitchell, J. R. Sex differences in drug metabolism. *Psychopharmacology Bulletin*, 1972, *8*, 28.

Paykel, E. S., Myers, J. K., Dienelt, M. N., Klerman, G. L., Lindenthal, J. J., & Pepper, M. P. Life events and depression: A controlled study. *Archives of General Psychiatry*, 1969, *21*, 753–760.

Perris, C. A study of bipolar (manic–depressive) and unipolar recurrent depressive psychoses. *Acta Psychiatrica Scandinavica*, 1966, *42* (Suppl.), 194.

Prusoff, B. A., Weissman, M. M., Klerman, G. L., & Rounsaville, B. J. Research diagnostic criteria subtypes of depression. *Archives of General Psychiatry*, 1980, *37*, 796–801.

Raskin, A. Sex differences in response to antidepressant drugs in hospitalized depressed patients. *Psychopharmacology Bulletin*, 1972, *8*, 26.

Robins, E., & Guze, S. Classification of affective disorders: The primary–secondary, the endogenous–reactive, and the neurotic–psychotic concepts. In T. A. Williams, M. M. Katz, & J. A. Shield, Jr. (Eds.), *Recent advances in the psychobiology of the depressive illnesses.* Washington, D.C.: U.S. Government Printing Office, 1972.

Rush, A. J. The why's and how's of diagnosing the depressions. *Biological Psychology Bulletin*, 1975, *4*, 47–61.

Rush, A. J. *New antidepressants.* Paper presented at the meeting of the American Psychopharmacological Association, New York City, February 1981.

Rush, A. J. Biological markers and treatment response in affective disorders. *McLean Hospital Bulletin*, in press.

Rush, A. J., & Beck, A. T. Adults with affective disorders. In M. Hersen & A. S. Bellack (Eds.), *Behavioral therapy in the psychiatric setting.* Baltimore: Williams & Wilkins, 1978.

Rush, A. J., Giles, D. E., Roffwarg, H. P., & Parker, C. R. Sleep EEG and dexamethasone suppression test findings in patients with unipolar major depressive disorders. *Journal of Biological Psychiatry*, in press.

Schwab, J. J., Bialou, M., Holzer, C. E., Brown, J. M., & Stevenson, B. E. Sociocultural aspects of depression in medical inpatients. *Archives of General Psychiatry*, 1967, *17*, 533–541.

Schwab, J. J., Brown, J. M., & Holzer, C. E. The Beck Depression Inventory with medical inpatients. *Acta Psychiatrica Scandinavica*, 1967, *43*, 255–266.

Schwab, J. J., Brown, J. M., & Holzer, C. E. Sex and age differences in depression. *Mental Hygiene*, 1968, *52*, 627–635.

Spitzer, R. L., Endicott, J., & Robins, E. Research diagnostic criteria: Rationale and reliability. *Archives of General Psychiatry*, 1978, *36*, 773–782.

Winokur, G., Behar, D., Van Valkenburg, C., & Lowry, M. Is familial definition of depression both feasible and valid? *Journal of Nervous and Mental Disease*, 1978, *166*, 764–768.

‡2‡

BEHAVIORAL THERAPY: THEORY AND RESEARCH

PETER MCLEAN

Historically, the field of behavior research and therapy has been slow to focus attention on what has been aptly described as "the common cold of mental health"—clinical depression. By definition, behavior research and therapy has been committed to behavior analysis (e.g., Skinner, 1970), and therefore to the understanding of behavior in terms of all of the carefully identified variables that influence its occurrence. Depression, considered to be a mood disturbance characterized by internal events and subjective bias, lends itself relatively less well to the objective description of behavior and its significant antecedent and consequential events than do other problems, such as phobias, interpersonal disorders, and the like, which can be more objectively measured. For example, a reduced activity rate is an insufficient indicator of depression, since the individual in question could merely have the flu, but then how do researchers operationally define and explain such concepts as "low self-esteem"? Since the inaugural article, from the behavioral viewpoint, on the topic of depression (Ferster, 1965), there has been a steady increase in interest within the behavior therapies in clinical depression, to the point that there are now a substantial number of theories and treatment-outcome studies available for critical review.

THE BEHAVIORAL APPROACH

If a sequential and repeating chain of events involving thoughts, feelings, and behaviors is considered, major psychological approaches to the treatment of depression can be identified by the choice of

Peter McLean. Department of Psychiatry, University of British Columbia, Vancouver, British Columbia.

modality in which they intervene: Psychotherapy works primarily in the area of feelings, cognitive therapy with cognitions, and behavior therapy with behavior. Clearly, each school considers the other two modalities, which are not focused on in a primary way, to be important as well. But changes in the modalities that are not focused on are assumed to follow, almost automatically, the therapeutic changes achieved in the target modality. Accordingly, the behavior therapies focus on the alteration of personal behavior in depressed individuals, in the belief that this is the most effective way to change thoughts and feelings as well as behavior.

There has been a recent popular trend to discuss cognitive and behavior therapies by the name of "cognitive-behavior therapy." This trend has followed an upsurge in interest in the role played by cognitions in the determination of behavior. Behavioristic theories maintain that cognitive events are subject to the same laws of learning as are behavioral events. However, many proponents of cognitive-behavior treatments assume that "thought *is* father to the deed" (Rosenthal, 1978; emphasis added), thus implying that cognitions have superincumbent and causal properties in relation to behavior. This is a curious development, inasmuch as there is no corresponding cognitive theory that has generated testable hypotheses vis-à-vis the determination of behavior (Allport, 1975; Eysenck, 1979). In the area of clinical depression, it is easy to see why a cognitive theory of causation has carried appeal. A feature characteristic of the depressed state is the preoccupation with high-frequency negative thoughts, the content of which (e.g., "I'm really a useless twit"), if believed, projects a desolate future indeed. But does depressive ideation mediate behavioral symptoms of depression? Teasdale and his colleagues (Teasdale & Bancroft, 1977; Teasdale & Rezin, 1978) have established a causal relationship between depressive ideation and depressed mood. Yet more recent evidence on depressed mood induction has shown that type of thought content (e.g., suggestions of somatic states, not self-devaluative statements) may be responsible for the effectiveness of the mood-induction manipulation (Frost, Graf, & Becker, 1979). From a behavioristic perspective, depressed thoughts, viewed as cognitive events that obey specific laws of learning, are accounted for in both theory and practice. In this case the "cognitive" side of cognitive-behavior therapy becomes redundant. It is worth nothing, however, that some advocates of cognitive-behavior therapy treat depressive cognitions as irrational belief systems to be exposed and discredited;

such treatment, therefore, more closely resembles a psychotherapeutic approach than it does a behavioral approach. The impulse to combine cognitive and behavior approaches seems to have confused the issue, while providing only superficial comprehensiveness in addressing both the overt and covert arenas of human experience. This issue is subject to much theoretical debate (e.g., Ledwidge, 1978, 1979; Mahoney & Kazdin, 1979) and may prove to be of little practical significance, since the treatment techniques of cognitive therapy for depression typically include a number of behavioral techniques.

A second feature that is descriptive of the behavioristic approach to the understanding and treatment of clinical depression is the role played by the law of effect. Specifically, there is a widespread belief that a change in the rate of reinforcement—whether self-delivered, socially delivered, or environmentally delivered—is central to the development, maintenance, and reversal of the psychological experience of depression. This is not to suggest that the law of effect or other behavioristic principles explain the occurrence of depression universally. Rather, the behavioristic approach should best be construed as a model for the investigation of the phenomenon of clinical depression in as scientific a manner as possible.

This chapter attempts neither a complete review of studies done in the behavioral vein nor a chronological review of this literature. For a systematic review of behavior theories of depression, readers are directed to Blaney (1977) or Eastman (1976); and, for a complete review of the behavioral treatment literature in depression, they are directed to Blaney (1981), Hollon (1981), Rehm and Kornblith (1979), or Whitehead (1979). The goal here is to review the major theories and treatment studies that have inspired developments within the behavioral approach to this disorder. In doing so, I tend to avoid theories that have not been experimentally tested (e.g., Costello, 1972), and I focus primarily on treatment studies and treatment-related theory. Finally, single-case studies will not be included in this review, due to the episodic, self-limiting nature of depression. Put differently, the baseline for clinical depression is not stable, but generally rises in severity to its peak and then declines toward the individual's nondepressed baseline, all over a period of 4 to 6 months—with or without treatment. Because no one would seriously consider the induction of clinical depression, comparison and control-group treatment designs are necessary in order to separate treatment from natural, or course-characteristic, effects. Indeed, this well-known recovery effect in clinical depression, which leads to the description of depression as being self-limited, cyclical, or episodic, is responsible for many false positive attributions in the bestowal of curative effects to nonsense treatments.

THE WAXING AND WANING OF THEORIES

Theory development usually progresses from the first conceptualizing of a theory through the development of hypotheses predicted from the theory, the testing of these hypotheses in situations analogous to the depressed state, and then the experimental evaluation of treatment strategies and procedures consistent with such theory. Given a variety of theories—which, in this instance, researchers and clinicians have—it is reasonable to expect that they would also have a number of distinct, theory-derived treatment procedures—which, with few exceptions, they do not have. A number of authors (e.g., Biglan & Dow, 1981) have pointed out that almost all behavioral treatments use a multicomponent approach to treatment despite emphasizing one or two theory-derived procedures, and Kazdin (1981) has suggested that there may be no treatment components specific to any one theory, but rather that the components are defined by the "theoretical interpretation of the technique." What researchers and clinicians presently have, then, is broad agreement on the characteristics of clinical depression (e.g., social withdrawal, procrastination, distortion of recall of feedback); divergent theory to account for the hypothesized mechanisms responsible for the etiology, maintenance, and reversal of depression; and strikingly similar treatment procedures deriving from these diverse theories.

This state of affairs is not peculiar to the behavior theories of depression. Theories, of necessity, are simplistic and become compromised in application. The tendency toward multicomponent (also called "broad-spectrum" and "package") treatments represents a recognition that there is no single theory of depression that enjoys universal validity; that treatments need multiple components in order to permit a greater match between treatment techniques and client characteristics; and that the appeal to the client of particular treatment rationales and techniques is no small factor in determining client adherence to, and progress in, treatment.

It would seem reasonable to speculate that the reason why divergent theories embrace similar treatment techniques, as well as the reason why standard single-component treatment techniques have given way to individually tailored single-component and multiple-component treatment programs, lies in the powerful role played by nonspecific factors in the treatment of clinical depression. These are the factors that compromise theories and represent the realities of the clinical task. They are nonspecific because present information about them is inconsistent. As any clinician knows, these factors—such as locale and structure of treatment delivery; age, culture, and sex differences between client and therapist; rationale provided to account for the development and treatment of depression; recruitment method; process variables such as the use of humor in treatment; and so forth—contribute greatly to the credibility and outcome of any treatment venture. To this extent, we have erred on the side of being too model-conscious in our testing of theories, to the relative neglect of both practical considerations in treatment delivery and the powerful role played by nonspecific effects. Accordingly, in reviewing the research literature, investigators should attend to these determinants of treatment outcome, as well as to the "theoretical interpretation of the technique," in order to achieve a balanced appraisal.

In the following review of the major research developments in behavioral approaches to clinical depression, treatment studies can be classified into a two-by-two format (see Figure 2.1). Standard treatments are those in which all clients are subjected to the same treatment; whereas in individually tailored treatments, either single or multiple components are selected as best serving the clinical needs of individual clients, based on pretreatment assessment information. In the case of single-component treatments, the single treatment component (e.g., increasing positive activities, changing adverse marital communication patterns, making use of cognitive self-control) is regarded as sufficient, when properly engaged, to reverse the clinical state. The multiple-component approach represents a broad-spectrum approach offering some variety in procedure to both client and therapist. In the early stages of development in the behavioral approach to depression, treatments tended to be standard and single-component in nature. As experience with the experimental application of behavioral techniques has increased, and as both the complexity of depression itself and the need to "market" treatment skillfully have become better understood, there has been a corresponding shift toward both multiple-component and individually tailored treatments.

	Single-component	Multiple-component
Standard treatment		
Individually tailored treatment		

FIGURE 2.1. Two-by-two classification of typical treatment delivery methods in the professional intervention of clinical depression.

PLEASANT ACTIVITIES AS REINFORCEMENT AGENTS

From the point of view of operant-learning theory, depression is considered to be the natural consequence of a sustained reduction in the amount of personal reinforcement an individual receives. Ferster (1965, 1966, 1973) first reported an explicitly operant interpretation of depression. He identified the reduction in adaptive behaviors that could be positively reinforced as the most salient feature of depression. Ferster speculated that the failure to produce behaviors that could then be positively reinforced may be due to one of several types of factors: sudden environmental changes, such as death of a spouse, residential relocation, or a career change, which would result in a disruption of the usual supply of reinforcement from familiar sources; engaging in aversive or punishable behavior, which preempts the possibility for positive reinforcement; and failure to attend to the interpersonal environment in sufficient detail to earn adequate levels of social reinforcement. Basically, the operant formulation specifies a contingency relationship between behavior and reinforcement. If there is no contingency between adaptive behavior and positive reinforcement, or if depressive behavior itself (e.g., inactivity, avoidance, crying, complaints) is inadvertently reinforced by a sympathetic interpersonal environment over an extended period of time, the primary conditions necessary for the experience of depression are present.

The concept of relative volume (i.e., major decrement of meaningful and valued recognition) of reinforcement and its responsive relationship to adaptive behavior represents the central theoretical theme in virtually all behavioral formulations of depression.

It is fair to say that Lewinsohn and his colleagues, over the last 10 years, have conducted the most systematic research program to develop a behavioral theory of depression. These efforts have been focused in two areas: determination of the relationships between pleasant and unpleasant mood-related events and depression; and the functional relationship between social competence and depression. Social competence is related to depression inasmuch as it represents a powerful means of influencing social reinforcement, and it is discussed later in this chapter.

Operant-learning theory defines positive reinforcers as events that increase the probability of the behavior they follow, and negative reinforcers as aversive events that reduce the probability of the behavior they follow. Accordingly, some "person × environment" interactions are strengthened, while others are weakened. In an attempt to identify standard events having reinforcing properties, MacPhillamy and Lewinsohn (1971) developed the Pleasant Events Schedule (PES), which consists of 320 questionnaire items relating to events that have been reported as sources of pleasure by a widespread population. The event described in each item is rated in terms of frequency of occurrence and subjective enjoyability, reflecting the recent rate of reinforcement and the potential reinforcement value of each event, respectively. Similarly, Lewinsohn (1975) and Lewinsohn and Talkington (1979) developed the Unpleasant Events Schedule (UES), a 320-item questionnaire designed to measure the occurrence of, and subjective value attached to, events considered aversive by many people. These questionnaires have been shown to have good psychometric properties, are correlated with mood (Lewinsohn & Amenson, 1978), and were designed to get around the practical problems of trying to determine which events have positive and negative reinforcing properties for depressed individuals by means of observation or interviews.

Lewinsohn (1974) identifies several prominent "assumptions" upon which his theory is based: (1) Depressed behaviors and dysphoric feelings result from a low rate of response-contingent positive reinforcement. (2) A low rate of response-contingent positive reinforcement is sufficient alone to account for the occurrence of other features of the depressed syndrome. (3) The total amount of response-contingent positive reinforcement received by people depends upon their reinforcement history (i.e., what is attractive to them), as well as upon the ability of their environment to engage in behaviors that elicit positive reinforcement.

Lewinsohn and his associates have systematically evolved and tested hypotheses important to their model of depression as a consequence of *a low rate of response-contingent positive reinforcement.* In doing so, they have discovered the following:

1. Depressed individuals elicit fewer behaviors than other people relative to normal controls (Shaffer & Lewinsohn, 1971; Libet & Lewinsohn, 1973).
2. The rate of response-contingent positive reinforcement is less in depressed than in nondepressed control groups (Lewinsohn, Youngren, & Grosscup, 1979).
3. There is a relationship between mood and both the number and kind of pleasant activities in which an individual is engaged (Lewinsohn & Amenson, 1978; Lewinsohn & Graf, 1973; Lewinsohn & Libet, 1972).
4. Depressed people receive less reinforcement, on average, than do nondepressed individuals (MacPhillamy & Lewinsohn, 1973).
5. Depressed individuals demonstrate a greater sensitivity to aversive stimuli than do nondepressed individuals (Lewinsohn, Lobitz, & Wilson, 1973).
6. The rate of positive reinforcement received by a depressed individual increases as a function of clinical improvement (Lewinsohn *et al.*, 1979).

Early clinical work that claimed theoretical commitment to the reinforcement model took the form of reports of two to six case studies. For example, Lewinsohn and Shaffer (1971) used home observations to determine the rates of positive and negative reinforcement exchanged in verbal communication between depressed and nondepressed spouses, primarily as an assessment tool and as a means of directing attention to the quality of interpersonal interaction as a therapeutic measure. Specifically, clients and their spouses were told how to be more positively reinforcing in their verbal interactions. No posttreatment verbal interaction data were collected, and while clients tended to improve, their improvement cannot be attributed to the intervention. Burgess (1969) introduced graded task assignment on small tasks, in a number of case studies, in order to encourage continuing opportunities for positive reinforcement and goal approximation. Although clinical improvement was noted, these case studies were uncontrolled experimentally.

To test the therapeutic merits of increasing pleasant activities as a means of overcoming depression, Hammen and Glass (1975) reported two studies in which depressed students were asked to increase their pleasant (reinforcing) activities, as a research exercise, for a 1-week period. The increased-activities group was contrasted with groups assigned two control conditions: self-monitoring and dietary change (protein increase). Although the experimental condition did indeed increase the students' rate of positive activities, there followed no corresponding improvement in their levels of depression. The authors point out that their data indicate that depressed subjects who increased their participation rate in pleasant activities tended to evaluate these activities more negatively than did other subjects; this would seem to suggest that mood, through the process of negative cognitive appraisal, may, in the normal course of affairs, affect activity rates. Clearly, in these experiments, increased engagement in pleasant activities did not elevate mood.

The question raised by Hammen and Glass, however, is a good one. Were these "pleasant activities" sufficiently valued to be reinforcing in the first place? Presumably, what is reinforcing to individuals when they are not depressed may be perceived as unreinforcing when they are depressed. The notion of variable appeal (reinforcement) as applied to the same activity at different times does support the view that the reinforcing value of events is determined, at least in part, by mood. But this does not detract in theory from the viability of Lewinsohn's position. It suggests simply that mood, reinforcement value, and rate of engagement in "pleasant" activities are interactive, and that in practice a therapist may have to look harder to find events that are still considered reinforcing, despite the client's veil of negative perception.

In a clinical study, Padfield (1976) compared the efficacy of a behavioral approach that focused on increasing the rate of pleasant activities with the efficacy of a nondirective counseling approach. It is of interest that the subjects in Padfield's study were not students, but 24 rural women of low socioeconomic status. These women received weekly treatment on an individual basis for 3 months. Taken together, the results did not favor one approach over the other. Further, the behavioral treatment was no more successful than the nondirective counseling treatment in increasing the clients' involvement in pleasant activities.

In another clinical study, Haeger (1977) applied a number of behavioral techniques (Premack Principle, verbal reinforcement, modeling, rehearsal, and instructions simply to increase target activities) in various treatment-group combinations. These treatments were contrasted with attention-placebo and no-treatment control conditions. Subjects in this study were all depressed at the moderate clinical level of severity and received eight treatment sessions. Results showed relatively uniform improvement across groups, with little relationship between increased frequency of completion of target behaviors and decreased depression scores.

Graf (1977), using mildly depressed students, conducted an interesting 2-week analogue study on the relationship between mood and rate of pleasant activity. There were three groups. The students in the first group were asked to increase their engagement in pleasant activities noted on a list of activities known to be mood-related, and to monitor their progress. The second group of students was asked to do the same, except that their list of activities was not mood-related. The students in the third group were asked to monitor how often they engaged in activities on the mood-related list, but were not instructed to increase their involvement with these activities. Unfortunately, the instruction to increase involvement in prelisted activities resulted in poor compliance, and therefore the hypothesis could not be tested. What this study does underscore are the difficulties that can be experienced in attempting to get individuals to engage in a set of normatively pleasant activities as the result of a behavioral prescription.

Turner, Ward, and Turner (1979) contrasted the effects of increased pleasant activities, a physical exercise program, and a client-centered therapy group in a three-group treatment study. Subjects were mildly to moderately depressed students and staff members, and treatment consisted of five individual sessions over a 1-month period. Results indicated that the subjects instructed to increase pleasant activities did, in fact, increase their rate of involvement in pleasant activities, and that this same group experienced a differential reduction in depressed mood, compared to the groups receiving the other two treatments.

Several further studies are relevant to the understanding of the relationship between mood and activity levels. Barrera (1977) assigned clinical subjects either to self-monitoring (simple recording of pleasant activities engaged in) or to 4 weeks of group therapy that focused on monitoring, graphing, and increasing the number of pleasant activities engaged in. Both of these treatment groups were compared to a no-contact control group. At the end of the 4-week period, all three groups had improved slightly on depression and activity measures, but not differentially so between groups. Barrera then exchanged the treatment each group received and ran a second 4-week treatment period with the same groups. The group that had previously been asked to increase pleasant activities failed to continue to do so now that the only requirement was to monitor pleasant-activity rates, and both the mood and activity levels in this group fell to near pretreatment baselines. The other group, which had previous practice in monitoring pleasant activity rates and was now asked to boost the rate of pleasant activity, did so and reported a corresponding improvement in mood. This time the increased-activity group maintained improved mood level over a 7-month follow-up period. These results suggest, but do not prove, that careful skill building may be necessary for clients to benefit from apparently straightforward treatment instigations. In this case, it is possible that the 4 weeks of self-monitoring provided the necessary level of task mastery to facilitate the increased engagement of pleasant activities.

Two more studies are worth noting here. The first study (Zeiss, Lewinsohn, & Muñoz, 1979) contrasted the efficacy of cognitive, social-skills, and increased-pleasant-activities treatments. In this study, particular attention was given to tailoring pleasant activities to the individual preferences of clinical subjects. The results showed that treatment modality was not differentially related to outcome. All groups improved on virtually every measure, and the authors attributed improvement to nonspecific effects vis-à-vis Bandura's self-efficacy model (1977).

Finally, Fuchs and Rehm (1977) contrasted a 6-week behavioral group treatment with a nonspecific group therapy and a waiting-list control condition. The subjects in the behavioral-treatment group split their focus during each of three treatment phases as follows: First they reviewed and discussed self-control principles relevant to depression, and then they monitored and increased their pleasant-activity rates as a homework task, using a 20-item summary of the PES (MacPhillamy & Lewinsohn, 1971) as a "guideline to suggest activities to log." The group receiving this treatment strategy succeeded in outperforming the two contrast groups on both self-report and behavioral measures of depression. The problem here, however, is that for the purposes of determining the nature of the relationship between mood and activity level, it is not clear what the "active ingredient" of treatment was—understanding of self-control principles, increased pleasant-activity rates, or both.

Status of the Pleasant-Events Model

Taken together, these studies show only mixed support for the theory that increased participation in pleasant (i.e., reinforcing) activities will result in rewarding experiences that are incompatible with, and therefore will alleviate, depression. The difficulties in attempting to draw conclusions here are symptomatic of those facing the field of depression research generally: namely, the difficulties of trying to attach value to the findings of studies that differ so markedly in quality and comparability of design. Most of the studies reported so far have such small numbers of subjects that significant group differences are unlikely. Much of the work has been done by graduate students in pursuit of thesis requirements, suggesting that therapist treatment inexperience is normative; furthermore, almost no study has been even closely replicated.

These general problems aside, it seems possible that the research to date has been overinvested in normative pleasant events. The essential component of Lewinsohn's theory is response-contingent positive reinforcement. It is not required that the reinforcement take the form of popular pleasant events. In fact, these events are, by definition, more "pleasant" to nondepressed individuals than to those who are depressed, since these items and their enjoyability ratings discriminate between depressed and nondepressed populations. The point here is that even if depressed clients increase their involvement in activities that are normally considered to be pleasant, these activities will lack their usual reinforcing qualities if they are not considered to be attractive by depressed individuals, and there would be no reason to expect an improvement in mood state as a function of increased involvement in these activities. Many depressed individuals may have a "ho-hum" attitude toward events in the PES; they may think, for example, that "These events would be fun if I were caught up on my commitments and deserved to enjoy them." If mood does determine the perception of reinforcement value, what would constitute a "pleasant event" for a depressed individual? This would have to be individually determined. It seems likely, however, that since many people are depressed because of chronic frustrations in a number of important life areas (e.g., job, marital realtionship, self-expression, interactions with children, substance abuse, financial affairs), any events that would serve to help solve these personal problems would be highly reinforcing. Put differently, it may be that standardized "pleasant events" lose their reinforcing properties because they are seen as not terribly relevant activities, if not outright unaffordable luxuries, in the context of a backlog of unresolved and nagging personal problems.

An individualized goal-attainment approach to treatment, in which clients' problems are resolved on a graduated basis, would potentially provide a source of reinforcement for depressed clients. Such an approach lacks methodological appeal in comparison with the PES, since reinforcement would not necessarily be scaled in terms of discrete events. What is lost in psychometric advantage, however, would probably be made up in reinforcement value as a result of the relevance of the activity (i.e., problem resolution). Both sources of reinforcement—catalogued pleasant activities and graduated personal problem resolution—are appropriate fare for Lewinsohn's theory, although the use of personal problem resolution may permit a more sensitive test of the theory.

Variability in reinforcer effectiveness indicates that in practice the therapist must make explicit the depressed clients' idiosyncratic criteria of what constitutes reinforcement. A man whose wife has left him may be nonreactive to the vast majority of his former "pleasant events," but he may consider any task, no matter how demeaning, to be rewarding if it earns him the opportunity to regain favor in the eye of his wife.

The application of the pleasant-events approach to the amelioration of depression is qualified in two ways by the value attached to a potential reinforcer on the part of the individual. First of all, perception of reinforcement value is colored by circumstance—a source of "state" variation. The prospect of a free dinner in an exclusive restaurant in the company of fascinating and enjoyable friends, for example, can elicit excitement, indifference, or terror, depending upon the mood of the prospective diner. But the value of a reinforcer can also be determined by an individual's standard of what is too much reinforcement. This is more likely to be a "trait" or personality determinant. An implicit assumption in the behavioral reinforcement model is that response-contingent positive reinforcement is curative and that more response-contingent positive reinforcement is more curative. Barron (1966) has provided experimental evidence to show that people alter both the rate and the direction of their activities in order to earn reinforcement at a rate to which they are accustomed. That is, people will manipulate, at least in experimental conditions, their behavior in unexpected ways in order to avoid reinforcement if the level of reinforcement exceeds their "social comfort zone." The therapeutic implications of these findings are that researchers and clinicians cannot assume the reinforcing effect of pleasant activities to be unidirectional. "Pleasant" may become "unpleasant," depending upon the amount of reinforcement already at hand. This "limelight" phenomenon presumably applies only to social reinforcement, in which people may avoid activities that would earn them attention when the level of attention exceeds that with which they are comfortable.

In conclusion, the pleasant-events model to date lacks consistent support from controlled clinical studies. Many of these studies have severe design limitations, and there seems to have been a rather simplistic approach taken to the identification of strong reinforcers in the case of depressed individuals. The positive value that depressed individuals attach to potential reinforcers seems likely to be determined by receptivity to the potential reinforcer and by mood, as well as by the intrinsic qualities of the reinforcer itself. And many depressed people are likely to find resolution of their depressing problems much more reinforcing than engagement of pleasant activities.

Lewinsohn's response-contingent positive reinforcement theory remains viable but not empirically established in controlled clinical studies. In large measure, the therapists in controlled clinical investigations must identify and behaviorally calibrate individual reinforcers more carefully, and must ensure that they are delivered in a response-contingent fashion before this theory can be considered adequately tested.

SOCIAL-INTERACTION MODEL OF DEPRESSION

Diverse sources of evidence suggest that social factors play an important, if not the most important, role in the causation, maintenance, and therapeutic resolution of clinical depression. Construed from the behavioral viewpoint, the mechanisms are entries and exits from individuals' social field, quantity and quality of social interaction, and rate of social reinforcement. Basically, the social-interaction model subscribes to the belief that individuals receive their sense of self-esteem from others, through our interactions with them, by means of social reinforcement (as broadly defined to include the concepts of approval, acceptance, recognition, support, etc.). In contrast to endogenous formulations of depression, the controlling variables that occasion the experience of depression in the social-interaction model are considered to reside outside the individual and within the context of the social environment.

This shift in focus from intrapsychic factors to the social environment as the cause of depression is supported by evidence from a variety of sources, including social isolation effects, the results of poor social skills, and the effects of chronic coercive marital-interaction patterns. Brown and Harris (1978), in a large epidemiological study, identify four main factors that render women vulnerable to depression: (1) low intimacy (low availability of husband or boyfriend as valued confidant); (2) unemployment; (3) having three or more children at home under the age of 14 years; and (4) loss of mother before 11 years of age. Of interest here is the fact that all four of these factors are social. Youngren and Lewinsohn (1977), investigating the functional relationship between depression and problematic interpersonal behavior, found that, in comparison with normal and psychiatric controls, people when they are depressed interact socially at lower rates; receive and offer less social reinforcement; report lower levels of enjoyment for those interactions in which they do engage; worry more about social interactions; are less comfortable in asserting themselves socially; and, by all accounts (self, peer, and observer ratings), display less skill in social interactions. An investigator might conclude from this that social-skills deficits only accompany depression episodes as a performance rather than a learning deficit. Bothwell and Weissman (1977), however, report social deficits in the functioning of their female sample well beyond the acute episode of depression, suggesting the presence of a learning deficit.

Depressed individuals are also known to be differentially reactive to success and failure in comparison with nondepressed populations, and Vaughn and Leff (1976) have found that family members and relatives of depressed patients are able to induce relapse by means of surprisingly little verbal criticism. Such criticism from family members and relatives may reflect the frustrations experienced by these people in attempting to motivate or simply to interact with a depressed person, since depressed subjects and normal subjects role-playing the part of depressed individuals have been shown to have an aversive effect on those with whom they interact (Coyne, 1976; Hammen & Peters, 1978). As a result, it seems that the interactions of depressed and nondepressed individuals are mutually coercive, and therefore probably avoided.

Stuart (1967) has described depression as an adaptation to maladaptive interpersonal encounters, characterized by the inability to communicate effectively; he advocates training to promote socially adaptive relationships that are incompatible with depression.

In an attempt to evaluate the utility of this treatment approach, McLean, Ogston, and Grauer (1973) assigned married depressed patients either to conventional group therapy or to a behavioral treatment, in which individual patients were seen together with their spouses. Behavioral treatment focused on (1) training in social learning principles; (2) immediate feedback as to the perception of verbal interactions between patient and spouse; and (3) training in the construction and use of reciprocal behavioral contracts. An objective recording procedure disclosed that the interpersonal feedback procedure (i.e., increase in the ratio of positive to negative verbal feedback) was successful, and a corresponding improvement was noted in both mood and in the resolution of problematic behaviors, beyond that of the group-therapy comparison group.

Taylor and Marshall (1977) employed behavioral techniques designed to "produce positive reinforcement in the client's social interactions." Depressed subjects in the behavioral-treatment group improved significantly but not differentially in comparison with a cognitive-treatment group. The combined treatment was additive in terms of therapeutic benefit. Similarly, Zeiss *et al.* (1979) found that social-skills training (assertion training, increased social activity, and improvement in style of interpersonal expressive behavior) produced clinical improvement, but no greater improvement than was achieved by two comparison groups (which received cognitive therapy and increased pleasant events). The results of attempts to remediate functional social interactions in the last two studies may be due to nonspecific treatment effects, as Zeiss *et al.* suggest.

There can be little question, however, that social interaction rates and the experience of depressed mood are related—at least in the case of individuals who have experienced a minimum of one episode of clinical depression. McLean (1978) selected clinical clients who had completed one of four treatments (McLean & Hakstian, 1979) and who were now within normal limits on the Beck Depression Inventory. Based on their rate of social activity alone, it was possible to predict subsequent levels of depression 3 months later; that is, subjects who were nondepressed and relatively socially inactive became depressed later, whereas subjects who were nondepressed and relatively active socially were significantly less prone to depression later on.

Status of the Social-Interaction Model

This model underscores the ability of an individual's social environment to "make or break" adaptive mood patterns. There is a critical mass of empirical data that establishes a relationship between depressed mood and social skills, and there is some indication that social deficits are the result of learning rather than of performance (i.e., desire or opportunity) factors, since many depression-prone individuals remain socially withdrawn and relatively unskilled in their social interactions even when they do not feel depressed (e.g., between episodes). Given the importance of clients' social network and their perception of this social network, its boundaries, and its expectancies, as well as their ability to interact with it in a skilled and adaptive manner, it is surprising that so many depressed individuals are seen alone for treatment when in fact they have an available spouse or living partner.

The potential for theory and treatment development within the social-interaction model from a behavioral viewpoint is tremendous. The challenge will be to identify further the antecedent and governing conditions for the promotion of normal social interactions, which serve a number of therapeutic purposes, including (1) the opportunity for social reinforcement; (2) the potential introduction of new and engaging people, interests, ideas, and so on; (3) competition, through the task demands of social interaction, with the tendency to lapse into a preoccupation with high-rate negative thoughts; (4) the opportunity for self-reinforcement for social interaction performance; and (5) the ability of others to act as a sounding board and to redirect irrational ideas and unrealistic standards or expectations before they become compelling enough to handicap the individual's social and personal functioning.

MULTICOMPONENT BEHAVIORAL-TREATMENT PROGRAMS

The recent growth in the number of multiple-component treatment studies in depression reflects an appreciation of the fact that no single treatment procedure can properly cope with all of the modalities through which depression is expressed. Also, individual clients react differentially to specific treatment components, either because of personal preference or because of the efficacy of treatment components. The multicomponent treatment approach combines a number of behavioral techniques designed to develop essential skills and to deploy specific countermeasures that help to motivate depressed clients systematically along a path of ever-increasing functional behavior. These programs are usually deployed in one of two formats. Either the selection and order of delivery is standard for all clients, or an attempt is made to tailor the component "package" to the needs of each client.

Every treatment program has multiple phases, requirements, or content areas. Multicomponent programs represent a modular approach to treatment and typically consist of core ingredients, considered to be essential, with a number of optional treatment modules (e.g., assertion training, relaxation, problem solving, and decision making) added as necessary. Mulitcomponent programs differ from traditional treatment programs in that the component treatment techniques are individually described and have their own rationale, their own set of behavioral prescriptions, and, in some cases, their own measures of treatment compliance. These "minitreatments" are typically offered in a natural sequence so that the skills learned in one component (e.g., self-monitoring) can be used to facilitate a subsequent component in the treatment program.

There are six controlled multicomponent studies available for review at this time. It is worth keeping in mind that the definition of "multicomponent" here is uncomfortably arbitrary and depends upon how well treatment components are individually described methodologically.

Shaw (1977) assigned clinically depressed clients to cognitive therapy, behavior therapy, nondirective therapy, or a waiting-list control condition. Behavior therapy consisted of increased involvement in pleasant activities, behavioral rehearsal, and verbal contracts for performance change. Treatment was delivered in group format during weekly meetings for 4 consecutive weeks. By the end of treatment, the cognitive-therapy group showed significantly better results than did groups receiving other treatments; the multicomponent treatment, although superior to the waiting-list condition, was indistinguishable from the nondirective therapy in terms of performance. Differences between the behavioral- and cognitive-treatment groups collapsed 1 month after treatment. A major drawback in the design of this study is that treatment in different treatment conditions was provided by the same therapist, thereby compromising the design principle, which calls for independent therapists.

Using chronically depressed clients who had been unresponsive to a variety of other treatment attempts, Harpin (1978) contrasted six clients in a waiting-list control condition with six subjects who received a variety of component behavioral treatments, including social-skills training, cognitive control training, anxiety management, self-monitoring of pleasant activities, role playing, and social support for adaptive interactions. All clients were on antidepressant medication at the time of the study. No significant differences emerged between the two treatment conditions.

McLean *et al.* (1973), in a study discussed earlier, found that the multicomponent behavioral program produced significant improvements on psychometric and functional measures of outcome, both at the end of treatment and at follow-up (3 months). In contrast, there was no significant improvement noted in the group-therapy contrast group. A precondition of admission to this study was spouse participation, which limits the generalization of these results.

Taylor and Marshall's study (1977), previously described, illustrates the potential utility of the multicomponent approach. They found that treatment group effects for cognitive and behavior therapy were similar, but that the combination, which was condensed to fit into the same time frame as the cognitive and behavioral groups (six 40-minute sessions), was more effective than was either behavior or cognitive treatment alone.

The Fuchs and Rehm study (1977) mentioned earlier falls within the classification of multicomponent behavioral treatment. This treatment program emphasized self-control training, which translates into daily recording of positive activities, goal identification and attainment, and a self-reinforcement procedure. Treatment was group-delivered over a 5-week period, and the results showed clear therapeutic advantages for the behavioral-training program, in contrast to a nonspecific treatment (group therapy) and a waiting-list control condition.

Finally, McLean and Hakstian (1979) assigned 154 clinical clients to one of four treatment conditions: behavior therapy, psychotherapy, antidepressant therapy, and relaxation training (control condition). Behavior therapy consisted of a goal-attainment approach to personal problem solving, increased positive social interactions, and increased behavioral production (task completion) as a core program, with optimal treatment components available subsequently as a function of apparent need. The behavioral condition proved to be the most effective treatment on the majority of outcome measures. Of particular interest here is the finding that treatment response was not modality-specific. That is, behavior therapy was effective in improving mood and somatic complaints, as well as in affecting change in behavioral domains. Similarly, antidepressant therapy was effective in behavioral as well as in somatic and mood domains. It seems, then, that a treatment either works or does not work, and when it does work, it does so rather uniformly across response domains.

Status of the Multicomponent Behavioral-Treatment Approach

Taken together, the above results show mixed support for a multicomponent approach to depression treatment. Ideally, an appropriate strategy for identifying critical components of a multicomponent program would be first to establish the efficacy of the entire treatment package and then to dismantle it by systematically removing components during a series of controlled clinical trials (Kazdin, 1981). This approach would be analogous to testing data sets for significance in a multivariate statistical test and then, if significance is reached, using pairwise multiple comparisons to identify those components or variables that contributed most to the overall significant difference.

A number of authors (e.g., Biglan & Dow, 1981; Liberman, 1979; McLean, 1976) recommend the use of a multicomponent approach to individualized treatment programs. Intuitively, the concept of matching treatment content to clients' individual needs carries much appeal. However, to date, there is no empirical basis by which client assessment information can be matched to treatment component selection to provide improved outcome. On the contrary, the only large-scale information available to date (McLean & Hakstian, 1979) indicates that treatment effects are surprisingly uniform across response domains within subjects. That is, different treatments tend not to be selective in the way the affect change within a given individual.

It may well be, however, that the most powerful reason for using a multicomponent approach is simply client preference. Most clients seem to come into treatment with preferences of one sort or another, and having options in the selection of treatment components may well serve to enhance the process of self-attribution and reduce noncompliance and dropout rates; this is in itself a strong argument for the multicomponent treatment approach.

A major weakness of many of the multicomponent behavioral programs is that there are insufficient process measures (or none at all) to monitor compliance with program instigations at the component level. As a result, it becomes a questionable act of faith to attribute outcome results to treatment procedure.

INTERPRETATION

FOUR COMMON DENOMINATORS OF TREATMENT

There is no question but that the concept and application of the principle of *reinforcement* is the primary common denominator of behavioral-treatment programs in the area of clinical depression.

From this point of view, the influence of Ferster, and particularly of Lewinsohn and his group, has been ubiquitous. The general acceptance of the law of effect by investigators in depression research is demonstrated by the widespread belief within the behavioral school that the most powerful antidepressant is successful performance, and that this is best arranged for through the systematic and discriminant use of reinforcers, both self-delivered and socially delivered. *Self-monitoring* of predetermined cognitive and behavioral events to permit an ongoing performance review and to keep clients task-oriented is another common feature of behavioral-intervention programs in the area of mood control, but is no longer unique to behavioral-treatment programs. Cognitive therapies, for example, typically include a self-monitoring procedure. The third common denominator in behavioral treatments is the focus on *goal attainment*. This procedural strategy is particularly important in order to "temporarily relocate" depressed individuals, since they tend to be passive observers of their present and past circumstances rather than active planners of their futures. Usually goals are pleasant activities (e.g., the PES) or are social in nature, but they can also be reflected problems restated in goal format in the form of graduated steps. Preparation for *adaptive coping* in the future is the fourth feature common to all behavioral-treatment programs, with the possible exception of those programs that attempt to accelerate pleasant activities. And even in this case, adaptive coping is the implicit goal of increased involvement with pleasant activities. Very often, training for adaptive coping involves preparation for dealing with those critical incidents that individual clients most frequently mismanage.

DEPRESSION DEFINITIONS

The unique requirement in any definition of depression is that of depressed mood. Perhaps because of this and the high visibility of dramatic verbal statements reflecting the experience of mood, other facets of the definition tend to be underrepresented in global assessments. For example, the Minnesota Multiphasic Personality Inventory (*D* scale) and the Beck Depression Inventory have relatively few questions related to nonoffice behavior. Mood, then, tends to be highlighted in questionnaires that define depression, but it is itself determined by thoughts and circumstances related to behavior. To define depression accurately, dimensions other than mood need to be evaluated and described within the context of both the disorder history and the individual's compensating assets. More than anything else, depressed mood appears to be a common side effect of a large variety of problems (e.g., marital discord, unemployment, physical illness), which, when severe enough, become functionally autonomous as the symptoms and their effects stimulate more depressed cognitions and behaviors.

MODEL EVALUATION

There are a number of competing theories to account for the etiology and maintenance of depression. The problem is that so many exceptions to the rule in the case of any one theory can be so easily considered. To be convincing, a theory must generate a clinical procedure that uniquely affects change in an operationally defined variable or construct that, in turn, has been demonstrated to be causally related to depression. To date, this challenge has not been met, and many highly developed theories are divorced from practical application. For example, the theory of learned helplessness has generated no unique treatment interventions. The great difficulty is that theories, when translated into therapeutic procedures and clinical practice, invariably become compromised by the effects of nonspecific factors, client expectations and foibles, and the task demands of the treatment process itself. And therapists tend not to think of themselves as artifacts in the lives of their clients; but when it is considered that most treatments are delivered on the basis of an hour a week, thereby leaving approximately 115 intervening waking hours during which clients are subjected to a variety of sources of social influence and personal advice, therapists most certainly must be artifacts.

It becomes difficult, and sometimes impossible, to meaningfully evaluate intervention models that claim theoretical distinctions from one another yet subscribe to common treatment procedures when delivering theory-derived treatment. It seems to me that researchers have overinvested in theory development to some degree. Atheoretical and empirically based field studies aimed at the identification of adaptive coping styles in normals offer considerable potential in the development of effective procedures and their social marketing in the form of treatments. Once established as effective, these treatments could then be subjected to the dismantling process. Theory construction would logically follow, being used to account for and to simulate in analogue environments the active ingredients of field-derived treatments. In any case, procedures without supporting theory and theories without supporting procedures are limited.

There are presently four to six models that are relatively complementary within the behavioral school of thought. These models have resulted in a variety of treatment procedures, many of which use common behavior-therapy techniques, and it is expected that large-scale dismantling studies will be necessary to evaluate the relative contribution of treatment techniques that are unique to any one model.

DESIGN CONCERNS

Evaluating behavioral-treatment programs in depression is much like trying to add apples and pineapples because of design differences. It is tempting to run a mental tally sheet counting the number of program outcomes for and against particular treatment approaches. To do so would be completely misleading, since the design characteristics are so divergent and often inadequate. To equate the treatment outcome of two studies, for example—one with 12 subjects and the other with 140, all else being equal—is folly. This state of affairs probably represents not so much a state of design illiteracy as it does one of research expediency; this should call attention to the substantial problems in mobilizing a well-designed clinical research program. An equivalent of the restaurant industry's five-star rating system should be applied to research designs to assist in establishing the value of findings.

At the very least, it would be of considerable help if fuller descriptions of research designs were available. These should include such factors as frequency and duration of treatment; client satisfaction; program costs; abrupt versus gradual termination; degree of program adherence; treatment costs to clients; disorder characteristics, such as severity and symptom variation over time course; client preference for specific treatment components; setting characteristics; therapists' qualifications and experience. This information, if made routinely available, would make it easier for researchers to engage in treatment-replication studies, the lack of which is a curious and glaring omission in this field of science.

Other design considerations are necessary as well. The discriminating reader will know that studies having subject cell sizes of fewer than 20 subjects are of little clinical significance, despite their potential statistical significance. Assessment must be standardized to a greater degree, and measures that functionally and reliably calibrate depressed and nondepressed behavior require much development. Such assessment tools would contribute nicely to a standardized multilevel assessment procedure. Depression assessment procedures, however, will remain incomplete until they account for depression-eliciting stimuli and for the coping, protective, normalizing, and other constructive skills that individuals possess. The assessment procedures traditionally used are largely pathology-oriented, with little rigor directed to the assessment of those client assets that could prove highly useful in treatment. Virtually all treatment-research programs have follow-up built in as a necessary component—a logical step, since depression is episodic in nature, and many (if not most) individuals with a history of at least one clinical episode of depression remain at high risk for relapse in between clinical episodes of depression. Extended and repeated follow-ups appear to be a good research investment as research interests gradually shift focus onto the question of long-term maintenance of treatment effects.

NONSPECIFIC EFFECTS

Traditionally considered part of the statistical error term in treatment studies, investigators are increasingly beginning to accord nonspecific effects the recognition and respect they deserve, even if their therapeutic benefits are not therapist-inspired. These effects are more than therapeutic by-products of the treatment process; they are active ingredients of the treatment environment and/or its perception on the part of clients. The task of researchers is to "decode" these influences to the point that they are well understood, and then to employ them where possible in treatment procedures and treatment context, in order to facilitate maximum treatment impact.

Therapist characteristics—independent of experience and formal qualifications—have powerful consequences in the determination of the therapist–client relationship (Wilson & Evans, 1976). Also, severity of depression has been shown to be a variable that affects the preparedness or ability of clients to participate and benefit from specific treatment instigations (Lick & Heffler, 1977; Williams,

Canale, & Edgerly, 1976). For example, self-management is most easily applied in the case of very mild depressions. Even the rationale given to clients by therapists to account for their disturbance influences their reaction to treatment in measurable ways (Farina, Fisher, Getter, & Fisher, 1978). Others have found that goal setting and monitoring is in itself a therapeutic measure (e.g., Hart, 1978).

We have found (McLean & Hakstian, 1979) that treatment structure facilitated treatment compliance and outcome. Clients responded well to specified procedures and mutually evolved treatment goals. Even clients in the attention control group (relaxation training), which was highly structured, remarked that they appreciated the concreteness of the program—knowing what was coming up in future sessions, receiving homework assignments, having rules or procedures to follow when anticipated events took place, and so on. Zeiss *et al.* (1979) found no treatment-specific effects in their comparison of treatments stressing interpersonal skills, cognitions, or pleasant events, although significant clinical improvement was noted across the board. These authors raise a good point in suggesting that research on treatment outcomes in depression should assess the specific impact of the identified treatment modality, as well as assessing the impact on depression. They attribute the treatment effects found in their study to nonspecific effects and suggest that "further research should explore the criteria hypothesized to be essential ingredients of any treatment for depression" (p. 438).

The relatively high degree of program structure associated with behavioral-treatment programs appears to produce nonspecific therapeutic effects that are clearly responsible for a significant portion of treatment outcome effects across response modalities. It is to be hoped that high priority will be given to identification of the source, scope, and effect of specific and nonspecific effects of treatment.

CONCLUSIONS

Given the status of the behavioral-treatment outcomes, both taken by themselves and compared generally with the other treatment modalities, several conclusions seem appropriate. First of all, there is no clear treatment of choice in the management of clinical depression. Several years ago, antidepressant medication, alone or in combination with psychotherapy, was considered to be the exclusive therapeutic choice. Outcome studies for behavioral and cognitive therapy in the meantime have plainly indicated therapeutic equivalence and, in some cases, superiority. Secondly, the contribution of nonspecific treatment factors to outcome appears to be more than minor. Nonspecific effects need to be better understood and exploited. Finally, much evidence indicates that the role of social relationships is central in the etiology, maintenance, and successful treatment of depression.

The obstinate search for a monolithic theory of depression has persisted. Researchers often attempt to construct theories around hypothesized general factors in depression from amongst a wide variety of causes (e.g., grief, social skill deficits, irrational expectations). In doing so, the ensuing treatment procedures become somewhat homogenized in clinical practice, with the result that theoretical distinctions do not often result in distinctions at the level of treatment presentation. The field of behavior therapy, however, has been responsible for the development of an impressive number of specific treatment procedures, which, judging from the controlled-outcome literature, are seldom second to any other form of treatment in terms of efficacy. There is a need, however, for behavior researchers and therapists to reassert the strength of the behavioral approach—namely, to provide careful attention to the operational definition and description of both evaluation and treatment tools, and to ensure that there is a solid empirical basis for program development and review. Change in this area could profitably take place in the area of improved research designs and independent replication.

The development of screening materials and prevention programs for people at high risk for clinical depression, the development of standardized assessment tools and self-help maintenance technologies, the study of normal coping strategies for dealing with the experience of depression, and the further investigation of the role that interpersonal factors play in the induction and treatment of depression are all highly relevant research areas with exciting potential.

REFERENCES

Allport, D. A. The state of cognitive psychology. *Quarterly Journal of Experimental Psychology*, 1975, *27*, 141–152.

Bandura, A. Self-efficacy: Toward a unifying theory of behavioral change. *Psychological Review*, 1977, *84*, 191–215.

Barrera, J., Jr. *An evaluation of a brief group therapy for depression.* Paper presented at a meeting of the Western Psychological Association, 1977.

Barron, R. M. Social reinforcement effects as a function of social reinforcement history. *Psychological Review*, 1966, *73*, 527–539.

Biglan, A., & Dow, M. G. Toward a second-generation model: A problem-specific approach. In L. P. Rehm (Ed.), *Behavior therapy for depression: Present status and future directions.* New York: Academic Press, 1981.

Blaney, P. Contemporary theories of depression: Critique and comparison. *Journal of Abnormal Psychology*, 1977, *86*, 203–223.

Blaney, P. The effectiveness of cognitive and behavioral therapies. In L. P. Rehm (Ed.), *Behavior therapy for depression: Present status and future directions.* New York: Academic Press, 1981.

Bothwell, S., & Weissman, M. Social impairment four years after an acute depressive episode. *American Journal of Orthopsychiatry*, 1977, *47*, 231–237.

Brown, G. W., & Harris, T. *Social origins of depression.* London: Tavistock, 1978.

Burgess, E. P. The modification of depressive behaviors. In R. D. Rubin & C. M. Franks (Eds.), *Advances in behavior therapy, 1968.* New York: Academic Press, 1969.

Costello, C. G. Depression: Loss of reinforcement or loss of reinforcer effectiveness? *Behavior Therapy*, 1972, *3*, 240–247.

Coyne, J. C. Depression and the response of others. *Journal of Abnormal Psychology*, 1976, *85*, 186–193.

Eastman, C. Behavioral formulations of depression. *Psychological Review*, 1976, *83* (4), 277–291.

Eysenck, H. J. Behavior therapy and the philosophers. *Behaviour Research and Therapy*, 1979, *17*, 511–514.

Farina, A., Fisher, J. D., Getter, H., & Fisher, E. H. Some consequences of changing people's views regarding the nature of mental illness. *Journal of Abnormal Psychology*, 1978, *87*, 272–279.

Ferster, C. B. Classification of behavioral pathology. In L. Krasner & L. P. Ullmann (Eds.), *Research in behavior modification.* New York: Holt, Rinehart & Winston, 1965.

Ferster, C. B. Animal behavior and mental illness. *Psychological Record*, 1966, *16*, 345–356.

Ferster, C. B. A functional analysis of depression. *American Psychologist*, 1973, *28*, 857–870.

Frost, R. O., Graf, M., & Becker, J. Self-devaluation and depressed mood. *Journal of Consulting and Clinical Psychology*, 1979, *47* (3), 958–962.

Fuchs, C. Z., & Rehm, L. P. A self-control behavior therapy program for depression. *Journal of Consulting and Clinical Psychology*, 1977, *45*, 206–215.

Graf, G. A mood-related activities schedule for the treatment of depression (Unpublished doctoral dissertation, Arizona State University, 1977). *Dissertation Abstracts International*, 1977, *38*, 1400B–1401B. (University Microfilms No. 77-17, 868)

Haeger, T. F. Application of the Premack differential probability hypothesis to the treatment of depression (Unpublished doctoral dissertation, American University, 1977). *Dissertation Abstracts International*, 1978, *38*, 3395B. (University Microfilms No. 77-29, 358)

Hammen, C. L., & Glass, D. R., Jr. Depression, activity, and evaluation of reinforcement. *Journal of Abnormal Psychology*, 1975, *84*, 718–721.

Hammen, C. L., & Peters, S. D. Interpersonal consequences of depression: Response to men and women enacting a depressed role. *Journal of Abnormal Psychology*, 1978, *87*, 322–332.

Harpin, R. E. A psychosocial treatment for some forms of depression? (Unpublished doctoral dissertation, State University of New York at Stony Brook, 1978). *Dissertation Abstracts International*, 1979, *39*, 2499B. (University Microfilms No. 78-20, 832)

Hart, R. R. Therapeutic effectiveness of setting and monitoring goals. *Journal of Consulting and Clinical Psychology*, 1978, *46*, 1242–1245.

Hollon, S. D. Comparisons and combinations with alternative approaches. In L. P. Rehm (Ed.), *Behavior therapy for depression: Present status and future directions*. New York: Academic Press, 1981.

Kazdin, A. E. Outcome evaluation strategies for the treatment of depression. In L. P. Rehm (Ed.), *Behavior therapy for depression: Present status and future directions*. New York: Academic Press, 1981.

Ledwidge, B. Cognitive behavior modification: A step in the wrong direction? *Psychological Bulletin*, 1978, *85*, 353–375.

Ledwidge, B. Cognitive behavior modification or new ways to change minds: Reply to Mahoney and Kazdin. *Psychological Bulletin*, 1979, *86*, 1050–1053.

Lewinsohn, P. M. *The Unpleasant Events Schedule: A scale for the measurement of aversive events*. Unpublished mimeograph, University of Oregon, 1975.

Lewinsohn, P. M. Clinical and theoretical aspects of depression. In K. S. Calhoun, H. E. Adams, & K. M. Mitchell (Eds.), *Innovative treatment methods in psychopathology*. New York: Wiley, 1974.

Lewinsohn, P. M., & Amenson, C. S. Some relations between pleasant and unpleasant mood-related events and depression. *Journal of Abnormal Psychology*, 1978, *87* (6), 644–654.

Lewinsohn, P. M., & Graf, M. Pleasant events and depression. *Journal of Consulting and Clinical Psychology*, 1973, *41*, 261–268.

Lewinsohn, P. M., & Libet, J. Pleasant events, activity schedules and depression. *Journal of Abnormal Psychology*, 1972, *79*, 291–295.

Lewinsohn, P. M., Lobitz, C., & Wilson, S. "Sensitivity" of depressed individuals to aversive stimuli. *Journal of Abnormal Psychology*, 1973, *81*, 259–263.

Lewinsohn, P. M., & Shaffer, M. Use of home observations as an integral part of the treatment of depression: Preliminary report and case studies. *Journal of Consulting and Clinical Psychology*, 1971, *37*, 87–94.

Lewinsohn, P. M., & Talkington, J. Studies on the measurement of unpleasant events and relations with depression. *Applied Psychological Measurement*, 1979, *3*, 83–101.

Lewinsohn, P. M., Youngren, M. A., & Grosscup, S. J. Reinforcement and depression. In R. A. Depue (Ed.), *The psychobiology of the depressive disorders: Implications for the effects of stress*. New York: Academic Press, 1979.

Liberman, R. P. *To each his own: Individualizing treatment strategies for depressed persons*. Paper presented at the Conference on Research Recommendations for the Behavioral Treatment of Depression, Pittsburgh, April 1979.

Libet, J., & Lewinsohn, P. M. The concept of social skill with special references to the behavior of depressed persons. *Journal of Consulting and Clinical Psycology*, 1973, *40*, 304–312.

Lick, J. R., & Heffler, D. Relaxation training and attention placebo in the treatment of severe insomnia. *Journal of Consulting and Clinical Psychology*, 1977, *45*, 153–161.

MacPhillamy, D. J., & Lewinsohn, P. M. *Pleasant Events Schedule.* Unpublished mimeograph, University of Oregon, 1971.

MacPhillamy, D. J., & Lewinsohn, P. M. *A scale for the measurement of positive reinforcement.* Unpublished mimeograph, University of Oregon, 1973.

Mahoney, M. J., & Kazdin, A. E. Cognitive behavior modification: Misconceptions and premature evacuation. *Psychological Bulletin*, 1979, *86*, 1044–1049.

McLean, P. D. Therapeutic decision-making in the behavioral management of depression. In P. O. Davidson (Ed.), *Behavioral management of anxiety, depression and pain.* New York: Brunner/Mazel, 1976.

McLean, P. D. *Social interactions and the treatment of depression: Clinical outcomes and implications.* Paper presented at a meeting of the Western Psychological Association, 1978.

McLean, P. D., & Hakstian, A. R. Clinical depression: Comparative efficacy of outpatient treatments. *Journal of Consulting and Clinical Psychology*, 1979, *47*, 818–836.

McLean, P. D., Ogston, K., & Grauer, L. A behavioral approach to the treatment of depression. *Journal of Behavior Therapy and Experimental Psychiatry*, 1973, *4*, 323–330.

Padfield, M. The comparative effects of two counseling approaches on the intensity of depression among rural women of low socio-economic status. *Journal of Consulting and Clinical Psychology*, 1976, *23*, 209–214.

Rosenthal, T. L. Bandura's self-efficacy theory: Thought is father to the deed. *Advances in Behavior Research and Therapy*, 1978, *1*, 203–209.

Rehm, L. P., & Kornblith, S. J. Behavior therapy for depression: A review of recent developments. In M. Hersen, R. M. Eisler, & P. M. Miller (Eds.), *Progress in behavior modification* (Vol. 7). New York: Academic Press, 1979.

Shaffer, M., & Lewinsohn, P. M. *Interpersonal behavior in the home of depressed versus non-depressed psychiatric and normal controls: A test of several hypotheses.* Paper presented at a meeting of the Western Psychological Association, 1971.

Shaw, B. F. Comparison of cognitive therapy and behavior therapy in the treatment of depression. *Journal of Consulting and Clinical Psychology*, 1977, *45*, 543–551.

Skinner, B. F. What is the experimental analysis of behavior? In R. Ullrich, T. Stachik, & J. Mabry (Eds.), *Control of human behavior* (Vol. 2). Glenview, Ill.: Scott, Foresman, 1970.

Stuart, R. B. Casework treatment of depression viewed as an interpersonal disturbance. *Social Work*, 1967, *12*, 27–36.

Taylor, F. G., & Marshall, W. L. Experimental analysis of a cognitive-behavioral therapy for depression. *Cognitive Therapy and Research*, 1977, *1*, 54–72.

Teasdale, J. D., & Bancroft, J. Manipulation of thought content as a determinant of mood and corrugator electromyographic activity in depressed patients. *Journal of Abnormal Psychology*, 1977, *86* (3), 235–241.

Teasdale, J. D., & Rezin, V. The effects of reducing frequency of negative thoughts on the mood of depressed patients: Tests of a cognitive model of depression. *British Journal of Social and Clinical Psychology*, 1978, *17* (1), 65–74.

Turner, R. W., Ward, M. F., & Turner, D. J. Behavioral treatment for depression: An evaluation of therapeutic components. *Journal of Clinical Psychology*, 1979, *35*, 166–175.

Vaughn, C. E., & Leff, J. R. The influence of family and social factors on the course of psychiatric illness. *British Journal of Psychiatry*, 1977, *129*, 125–137.

Whitehead, A. Psychological treatment of depression: A review. *Behaviour Research and Therapy*, 1979, *17* (5), 495–510.

Williams, R. L., Canale, J., & Edgerly, J. W. Affinity for self-management: A comparison between counseling clients and controls. *Journal of Behavior Therapy and Experimental Psychiatry*, 1976, *7*, 231–234.

Wilson, G. T., & Evans, I. M. Adult behavior therapy and the therapist–client relationship. In C. M. Franks & G. T. Wilson (Eds.), *Annual review of behavior therapy.* New York: Brunner/Mazel, 1976.

Youngren, M. A., & Lewinsohn, P. M. *The functional relationship between depression and problematic interpersonal behavior.* Unpublished manuscript, University of Oregon, 1977.

Zeiss, A. M., Lewinsohn, P. M., & Muñoz, R. F. Nonspecific improvement effects in depression using interpersonal, cognitive, and pleasant events focused treatments. *Journal of Consulting and Clinical Psychology*, 1979, *47*, 427–439.

3

BEHAVIORAL THERAPY: CLINICAL APPLICATIONS

PETER M. LEWINSOHN
J. MICHAEL SULLIVAN
SALLY J. GROSSCUP

This chapter describes social learning strategies and tactics for the treatment of primary unipolar depression. Although the overview is comprehensive, the emphasis is on the treatment approach developed over the past several years at the University of Oregon Depression Research Unit. We first make some general comments about the necessary components of any treatment approach for depression and the implications of social learning theories of depression for treatment. We then talk in more detail about the strategies and tactics that we, and other social learning therapists, have found useful in treating depressed persons. Finally, we present two cases to illustrate the treatment of depression within a social learning framework.

THEORY, STRATEGY, AND TACTICS

A comprehensive treatment approach for depression has three important components: (1) a theory; (2) a strategy; and (3) some tactics.

Some kind of *theory* of depression provides a useful guide for treatment efforts. In general terms, the theory specifies functional relationships between certain antecedent events and the occurrence of depression. These events presumably account for, or "explain," depression. For a given patient, the theory represents a *statement* about the likely reasons for his or her depression (i.e., Mrs. T. is

Peter M. Lewinsohn, J. Michael Sullivan, and Sally J. Grosscup. Department of Psychology, University of Oregon, Eugene, Oregon.

depressed because of "*x*"). To the extent that the theory is valid, accomplishing the intermediate goals (changing "*x*") should lead to a change in the level of depression. Because depression is a complex phenomenon, therapists without some systematic theoretical conceptualization are likely to have vague and confusing treatment goals and to have little success with patients.

But a theory is only a set of abstract statements suggesting general treatment goals for depressed persons (or at least for certain kinds of depressives). A comprehensive treatment approach must also have a *strategy.* A treatment strategy translates the theory into a set of specific operations and procedures that can be used to formulate treatment goals for the depressed person.

The first step of the strategy involves *differential diagnosis* of the patient. Diagnostic assessment must first determine whether or not depression is *the*, or at least *a*, problem for the individual. Differential diagnosis should also establish whether the depression is primary or secondary (Robins & Guze, 1969). As noted in Chapter 1, depression can be secondary to certain medical conditions and to other psychiatric disorders. A further complication is the fact that certain somatic symptoms (e.g., headaches and feelings of fatigue) are common among depressed persons.

Ruling out organic involvement is an important part of formulating an appropriate treatment plan. For example, a 50-year-old patient complained of depression during the intake interview. The intake worker correctly suggested a thorough medical evaluation after the patient also mentioned periods of hyperactivity along with substantial weight loss. Further examination and tests indicated that the patient had a hyperthyroid syndrome and needed medical treatment.

The differentiation between schizophrenia and depression can also be problematic. Thought disorders sometimes have affective components (e.g., the patient believes that parts of his or her body are shrinking), while some delusions occur in intense depressions (e.g., the patient believes that God is punishing him or her). Since the implications for treatment depend on which aspect is primary, resolving the issue is important. For example, a 21-year-old male came to our clinic with depression as the presenting symptom. During the first part of the intake interview, the patient appeared depressed and reported many of the typical depression symptoms. Gradually, however, the intake worker realized that the patient was experiencing delusions, ideas of reference, and hallucinations. After further questioning and testing, the proper diagnosis seemed to be paranoid schizophrenia. We referred the patient to a psychiatrist for adjunct drug therapy but continued to see him in psychotherapy. The patient showed improvement with medication and responded well to supportive therapy. Our usual "depression treatment package" was not particularly useful.

Furthermore, as detailed in Chapter 1, the distinction between unipolar and bipolar depression is an important one. While many depression subtypes have been suggested, the unipolar–bipolar distinction appears to have sufficient empirical support to be used routinely (Depue & Monroe, 1978). It should be recalled that lithium carbonate treatment is the treatment of choice for bipolar depression. For example, a 45-year-old patient came to the clinic seeking treatment for recurrent depression. He had sought treatment 4 years earlier and had received 6 months of insight-oriented therapy with minimal benefit. The history taken for the present intake indicated a family history of bipolar disorder and a personal history of manic and depressed episodes occurring with increasing severity over the past few years. The earlier assessment had apparently missed this bipolar component. In this case, lithium treatment proved to be effective.

The second step of the strategy is a *functional analysis*. Functional analysis involves pinpointing concrete events related to a particular person's depression. This part of the diagnostic process is needed to guide the formulation of a treatment plan designed to change the events accounting for the patient's depression.

The third step of a treatment strategy is *evaluation*. Evaluation involves periodic assessments throughout treatment, not only of changes in depression level, but also of concomitant changes in the events presumed to be related to the patient's depression. This two-pronged approach to evaluation permits the therapist to evaluate the effectiveness of the treatment in changing the targeted behavior patterns, as well as to test the original functional analysis by seeing whether or not there are concomitant changes in the depression level. For example, a therapist may hypothesize that the patient's difficulties with assertion are functionally related to the person's depression, and hence may recommend assertiveness training. Positive change in both the person's social interactions and the depression provides support for the original diagnosis. If neither the person's assertion nor the depression changes in the expected directions, a different therapy tactic is called for. On the other hand, if the client's assertion skills improve but there is no concomitant improvement in the depression level (or vice versa), the validity of the original functional diagnosis needs to be questioned. Unfortunately, therapists usually assess only changes in the depression level and not changes in the functionally related events.

The third element of a comprehensive treatment approach consists of treatment *tactics*. Tactics are the specific interventions used to accomplish the strategic goals of therapy. Useful tactics are those that dependably produce clinically desired changes in the events related to the depression. This is probably the part of therapy in which clinicians differ the most, in that therapists often use very different tactics to reach similar strategic goals. There are probably several reasons for this. Therapists must feel comfortable with a tactic and must be convinced that they can use it effectively. Also, the tactics must fit the patient. For example, directive interventions may not be appropriate for a client who is very sensitive to being controlled. Or intervention with a strong intellectual emphasis may not be suitable for action-oriented patients.

The treatment literature describes many potentially useful tactics. Although many of these are presented as all-purpose tactics (e.g., family therapy), they can often be adapted to very specific uses. In the final analysis, the clinician, in collaboration with the patient, must choose from among several potential tactics. For example, the clinician may suspect that a female patient's depression is related to constant conflict between her and her adolescent daughter. One possible tactic might be to help the patient become less sensitive to the conflict and to wait things out until the daughter leaves for college in 6 months. An alternative tactic might be to see the mother and daughter together to work at developing conflict-resolution skills. An advantage to the latter course of action is that this assists both persons to acquire skills for coping with similar situations in the future.

SOCIAL LEARNING THEORY

We assume depression and reinforcement to be related phenomena. The primary hypothesis states that a low rate of response-contingent reinforcement constitutes a critical antecedent for the occurrence of depression. Reinforcement is defined by the *quality* of the person's interactions with his or her environment. Those person–environment interactions with positive outcomes (i.e., outcomes making the person feel good) constitute positive reinforcement. Such interactions strengthen the person's behavior. The term "contingent" refers to the temporal relationship between a behavior and its consequences. The reinforcement must follow the behavior. We assume that the behavior of depressed persons does not lead to positive reinforcement to a degree sufficient to maintain their behavior. Hence, depressed persons find it difficult to initiate or to maintain their behavior, and they become increasingly passive. The low rate of positive reinforcement is also assumed to cause the dysphoric feelings that are so central to the phenomenology of depression. The experience of little or no rewarding interaction with the environment causes the person to feel sad and blue. The key notion is that being depressed results from few person–environment interactions having positive outcomes for the person.

A corollary hypothesis is that a high rate of punishing experience also causes depression. "Punishment" is defined as person–environment interaction with aversive (distressing, upsetting, unpleasant) outcomes. Punishing interactions with the environment may cause depression directly or indirectly by interfering with a person's engagement in and enjoyment of potentially rewarding activities.

There are three general reasons why a person may experience low rates of positive reinforcement and/or high rates of punishment: (1) the person's immediate environment may have few available positive reinforcers or have many punishing aspects (availability); (2) the person may lack the skills to obtain available positive reinforcers and/or cope effectively with aversive events (skill deficits); (3) the positive reinforcement potency of events may be reduced and/or the negative impact of punishing events may be heightened.

These notions, and research results consistent with them, are discussed elsewhere in more detail (Grosscup & Lewinsohn, 1980; Lewinsohn, 1976; Lewinsohn & Amenson, 1978; Lewinsohn, Biglan, & Zeiss, 1976; Lewinsohn & Talkington, 1979; Lewinsohn, Youngren, & Grosscup, 1979; MacPhillamy & Lewinsohn, 1974). In these studies, we have consistently found depressed persons to experience lower rates of positive reinforcement and higher rates of punishment than do members of relevant control groups. As depression level decreases, the rate of obtained positive reinforcement increases, and the rate of experienced punishment decreases. These changes are greatest for depressed persons who improve the most in therapy. Other studies have shown that depressed persons often are deficient in the social skills needed to interact effectively with others (Libet, Lewinsohn, & Javorek, 1973; Sanchez, 1976).

The absence of positively reinforcing events particularly relevant to the occurrence of depression fall into several clusters (Lewinsohn & Amenson, 1978): positive sexual experiences, rewarding social interactions, enjoyable outdoor activities, solitude, and competency experiences. Examples of these clusters include "being noticed as sexually attractive," "expressing my love to someone," "being with friends," "being relaxed," "seeing beautiful scenery," "doing a job well," and "doing a project my own way." Punishing events particularly important for depression fall into three clusters: marital discord, work-related difficulties, and negative reactions from others. Specific examples of these sorts of events include "arguments with a spouse, mate, or living partner," "working on something when I am tired," and "having someone evaluate or criticize me."

The relevance of these notions and findings for the treatment of depression are straightforward. To the extent that the theory is valid, treatment should aim to increase the person's rate (quantity and quality) of positively reinforcing interactions with the environment, and to decrease the person's rate (quantity and quality) of punishing interactions. We have found this framework useful in our clinical work.

SOCIAL LEARNING STRATEGIES

The following section details the strategies that we and other social learning therapists use for differential diagnosis, functional analysis, and outcome evaluation. Table 3.1 lists the steps we use in the Oregon Program as part of our treatment strategy.

DIFFERENTIAL DIAGNOSIS

We have found a multistage process useful in differential diagnosis. Persons seeking treatment at our clinic first complete a Health

TABLE 3.1. The Oregon Depression Unit Strategy

Differential diagnosis
1. Self-report questionnaires
   a. Minnesota Multiphasic Personality Inventory (MMPI)
   b. Health Questionnaire
2. Clinical interview using Schedule for Affective Disorders and Schizophrenia (SADS) outline
   a. Grinker Feelings and Concerns Checklist
   b. Research Diagnostic Criteria (RDC)

Functional analysis
1. Pleasant and Unpleasant Events Schedules (PES and UES)
2. Daily monitoring
   a. Personalized Activity Schedule
   b. Depression Adjective Checklists (DACL)
3. Behavioral interviewing
4. Behavioral observations

Outcome evaluation
1. Daily monitoring
   a. Personalized Activity Schedule
   b. DACL
2. Termination
   a. Measure of depression (e.g., Beck Depression Inventory; BDI)
   b. PES and UES
3. Follow-up (1 month)
   a. Measure of depression
   b. PES and UES

Questionnaire[1] and the Minnesota Multiphasic Personality Inventory (MMPI). In order to provide a detailed overview of the patient's current symptoms and history of previous disorders, he or she participates in a semistructured interview that generally follows the outline provided by the Schedule for Affective Disorders and Schizophrenia (SADS) (Endicott & Spitzer, 1978). The interviewer also asks questions about any medical problems checked by the patient on the Health Questionnaire. On the basis of this interview, the interviewer assigns a diagnosis using the categories of the Research Diagnostic Criteria (RDC) (Spitzer, Endicott, & Robins, 1978). The interviewer also rates the patient on the 26-item symptom checklist shown in Figure 3.1, which is a modification of the Feelings and

1. The Health Questionnaire, the Pleasant Events Schedule, the Unpleasant Events Schedule (see pp. 58–59), and other materials can be obtained by writing to Peter M. Lewinsohn, PhD, Psychology Department, University of Oregon, Eugene, Oregon 97403.

Date: ____________

Participant's name: ______________________________ Interviewer: ______________________________

0 = not present 1 = present to slight extent 2 = present to moderate extent 3 = present to marked extent

1. Feels hopeless	0 1 2 3	14. Feels envious of others	0 1 2 3
2. Feels that he or she is bearing troubles	0 1 2 3	15. Experiences free anxiety	0 1 2 3
3. Feels helpless and powerless	0 1 2 3	16. Feels a failure	0 1 2 3
4. Has feelings of tenseness	0 1 2 3	17. Concerned with making up for wrongs he or she has caused to others	0 1 2 3
5. Concerned with suffering that he or she has caused others	0 1 2 3	18. Uses depressive behavior for interpersonal gains	0 1 2 3
6. Feels problems would be relieved by the solving of certain "material" problems (e.g., money, job)	0 1 2 3	19. Feels guilt for not assuming family, job, and/or academic responsibilities	0 1 2 3
7. Feels sad and blue	0 1 2 3	20. Feels unable to make decisions	0 1 2 3
8. Feels self unworthy	0 1 2 3	21. Feels unloved	0 1 2 3
9. Considers self lazy	0 1 2 3	22. Feels burdened by the demands of others	0 1 2 3
10. Expresses concern for the welfare of family and friends	0 1 2 3	23. Feels "jittery"	0 1 2 3
11. Has ideas of committing suicide	0 1 2 3	24. Feels unable to act	0 1 2 3
12. Concerned with material loss (e.g., money, property)	0 1 2 3	25. Credits problems to excessive family and/or job responsibilities	0 1 2 3
13. Feels at "end of rope"	0 1 2 3		

26. Depression is the presenting syndrome. 5	Patient manifests other symptoms but depression is major. 4	Depression is about equal with other symptoms. 3	Depression is present but the major symptom is something else. 2
Depression is not among the presenting symptoms. 1	There are no significant presenting symptoms. 0		

Factor 1 score = Items 1 + 3 + 7 + 8 + 9 + 13 + 16 + 20 + 24 = ______ ÷ 9 = ______ Dysphoria
Factor 2 score = Items 6 + 12 + 22 + 25 = ______ ÷ 4 = ______ Material burden
Factor 3 score = Items 5 + 10 + 17 + 19 = ______ ÷ 4 = ______ Guilt
Factor 4 score = Items 4 + 15 + 23 = ______ ÷ 3 = ______ Anxiety
Factor 5 score = Items 2 + 14 + 18 + 21 = ______ ÷ 4 = ______ Social isolation
Grand total = ______
Overall mean = Grand total ÷ 21 = ______

FIGURE 3.1. Short version of the Feelings and Concerns Checklist.

Concerns Checklist (Grinker, Miller, Sabshin, Nunn, & Nunally, 1961). Items are summed and averaged to derive factor scores representing the major symptom clusters associated with depression (Dysphoria, Material Burden, Guilt, Social Isolation, and Anxiety).

Over the years, we have found that outpatients meeting the following criteria are likely to benefit from our treatment program:

1. No primary medical problems.
2. An MMPI *D* scale score ≥ 80 or ≥ 70 and < 80, with $D >$ other clinical scales.
3. Mean symptom ratings on all Feelings and Concerns Checklist factors $\geq .70$ and dysphoria score ≥ 1.0.
4. An RDC diagnosis of major, minor, or intermittent depressive disorder.

Because we see patients with bipolar depression, schizophrenia, or alcohol and substance abuse as requiring treatments different from those being offered by our program, we refer such patients to appropriate professionals or programs in the community. We do not encourage adjunct antidepressant medication for depressed patients. We feel that drug treatment encourages patients to adopt a passive attitude that interferes with the active participation our program requires.

FUNCTIONAL ANALYSIS

In order to pinpoint specific person-environment interactions related to the person's depression, we make extensive use of the Pleasant Events Schedule (PES) (MacPhillamy & Lewinsohn, 1971) and the Unpleasant Events Schedule (UES) (Lewinsohn, 1975).

The PES consists of 320 items assumed to represent an exhaustive sample of interactions with the environment that many people find pleasant. We assume that events experienced subjectively as pleasant have positive reinforcement value. The patient first rates the frequency of each event's occurrence during the past month on a three-point scale: 0—this has not happened in the past 30 days; 1—this has happened a few times (1-6) in the past 30 days; 2—this has happened often (7 or more times) in the past 30 days. The patient then rates the subjective enjoyability of the events on another three-point scale: 0—this was not or could not be very pleasant;

1—this was or could be somewhat pleasant; 2—this was or could be very pleasant. The frequency ratings are assumed to measure the individual's *rate* of engagement in the person–environment interactions on the list during the past month. The subjective enjoyability ratings are assumed to indicate the individual's *potential* for positive reinforcement. The sum of the cross-product scores of the frequency and enjoyability ratings is assumed to reflect the total amount of positive reinforcement obtained by the individual. In addition to the total scores based on all items, the PES also provides subscale scores for sexual interactions, solitude, outdoor activities, and social activities (MacPhillamy & Lewinsohn, 1975).

The UES consists of 320 items assumed to represent an exhaustive sample of interactions with the environment that many people find unpleasant. We assume that events experienced as subjectively unpleasant act as punishments; that is, that they are likely to leave the person feeling distressed. Using three-point rating scales analogous to those used with the PES, the client rates the items first for their frequency and then for their aversiveness. Again, the frequency scores are assumed to reflect the rate at which the events occurred; the aversiveness ratings are assumed to reflect the potential punishment value of the events; and the sum of the cross-product scores is assumed to reflect the amount of aversiveness experienced during the past month. Besides frequency, aversiveness, and cross-product scores, the UES provides subscale scores for "health and welfare"-related events, "material and financial" events, "sexual, marital, and friendship" events, "achievement–academic–job" events, "legal" events, and "social exits."

Normative data on both schedules allow evaluation of the patient's scores in relation to other persons of the same sex and age. PES scores below norms, and UES scores above the norms, on the various subscales suggest kinds of reinforcing and punishing events potentially related to the patient's depression. Patterns among scores are often important. For example, a patient may have a low score for pleasant sexual events and a high score for marital-distress events. This immediately suggests possible reasons for this patient's depression, and even some potential treatment tactics. We share these working hypotheses with the patient and use them to formulate some intermediate treatment goals.

In addition to generating hypotheses, the PES and UES ratings provide the basis for constructing a personalized Activity Schedule to be used for daily monitoring. Each patient's Activity Schedule consists of the 80 items that the client has rated as most pleasant and frequent on the PES and the 80 items that the client has rated as most unpleasant and frequent on the UES. The role played by the Activity Schedule in treatment is described below. In Figure 3.2, we present an "all-purpose" Activity Schedule consisting of 80 pleasant and 80 unpleasant items found to be related to mood in the general population (Lewinsohn & Amenson, 1978). The items on this list overlap very heavily with the individualized lists we have constructed for depressed individuals. Therapists for whom the clerical work needed to construct an individualized list poses a problem will find this list quite adequate.

DAILY MONITORING

As soon as possible after intake, patients begin rating their moods and monitoring the occurrence of the pleasant and unpleasant activities on their Activity Schedules on a daily basis. They continue this daily monitoring for the duration of treatment.

Daily mood ratings are made on the Depression Adjective Checklists (DACL) (Lubin, 1965). These are a series of seven alternate lists of adjectives designed to provide a measure of the individual's mood. Patients are asked to check each evening all those adjectives that describe how they felt that day. The number of *positive* adjectives *not* checked, plus the number of *negative* adjectives *checked*, constitutes the mood score. The higher the score, the *more* depressed the person has felt. The DACL score gives a measure of daily fluctuation in mood that often permits the therapist to spot particular days of the week when the patient becomes noticeably more or less depressed and to explore reasons for these changes. But the main function of the DACL scores is to enable the patient (and the therapist) to become aware of the covariation that typically prevails between mood and the rate of occurrence of pleasant and unpleasant activities.

To monitor the occurrence of events, patients use a three-point scale for each of the 80 pleasant events on their personalized schedule: 0—did not occur today; 1—occurred but was neutral; and 2—occurred and was pleasant. Patients mark a similar scale for the 80 unpleasant events on their schedule, except that they indicate whether or not the event was neutral or unpleasant if it occurred. This easily provides

Part A

Name: ______________________________ Date: __________

Please check within the parentheses to correspond to the activities of this day. *Only activities that were at least a little pleasant should be checked.*

Activity	Frequency (check)	Activity	Frequency (check)
1. Laughing	( )	32. Watching people	( )
2. Being relaxed	( )	33. Making a new friend	( )
3. Talking about other people	( )	34. Being complimented or told I have done well	( )
4. Thinking about something good in the future	( )	35. Expressing my love to someone	( )
5. Having people show interest in what I say	( )	36. Having sexual relations with a partner of the opposite sex	( )
6. Being with friends	( )	37. Having spare time	( )
7. Eating good meals	( )	38. Helping someone	( )
8. Breathing clean air	( )	39. Having friends come to visit	( )
9. Seeing beautiful scenery	( )	40. Listening to the sounds of nature	( )
10. Thinking about people I like	( )	41. Watching wild animals	( )
11. Having a frank and open conversation	( )	42. Driving skillfully	( )
12. Wearing clean clothes	( )	43. Talking about sports	( )
13. Having coffee, tea, a Coke, etc., with friends	( )	44. Meeting someone new of the same sex	( )
14. Wearing informal clothes	( )	45. Planning trips or vacations	( )
15. Being noticed as sexually attractive	( )	46. Having lunch with friends or associates	( )
16. Having peace and quiet	( )	47. Being with animals	( )
17. Smiling at people	( )	48. Going to a party	( )
18. Sleeping soundly at night	( )	49. Sitting in the sun	( )
19. Feeling the presence of the Lord in my life	( )	50. Being praised by people I admire	( )
20. Kissing	( )	51. Doing a project in my own way	( )
21. Doing a job well	( )	52. Being told I am needed	( )
22. Having a lively talk	( )	53. Watching attractive women or men	( )
23. Seeing good things happen to family or friends	( )	54. Being told I am loved	( )
24. Being popular at a gathering	( )	55. Seeing old friends	( )
25. Saying something clearly	( )	56. Staying up late	( )
26. Reading stories, novels, poems, or plays	( )	57. Beachcombing	( )
27. Planning or organizing something	( )	58. Snowmobiling or dune buggy riding	( )
28. Learning to do something new	( )	59. Petting; necking	( )
29. Complimenting or praising someone	( )	60. Listening to music	( )
30. Amusing people	( )	61. Visiting friends	( )
31. Being with someone I love	( )	62. Being invited out	( )
		63. Going to a restaurant	( )

FIGURE 3.2 Activity Schedule.

64. Talking about philosophy or religion ( )
65. Singing to myself ( )
66. Thinking about myself or my problems ( )
67. Solving a problem, puzzle, crossword, etc. ( )
68. Completing a difficult task ( )
69. Having an original idea ( )
70. Social drinking ( )
71. Getting massages or backrubs ( )
72. Meeting someone of the opposite sex ( )
73. Being in the country ( )
74. Seeing or smelling a flower or plant ( )
75. Being asked for my help or advice ( )
76. Doing housework or laundry; cleaning things ( )
77. Sleeping late ( )
78. Playing in sand, a stream, the grass, etc. ( )
79. Being with happy people ( )
80. Looking at the stars or moon ( )

Part B

Name: ______________________ Date: __________

Please check within the parentheses to correspond to the events of this day. *Only events and interactions that were at least somewhat unpleasant should be checked.*

Activity	Frequency (check)
1. Being dissatisfied with my spouse (living partner, mate)	( )
2. Working on something when I am tired	( )
3. Arguments with spouse (living partner, mate)	( )
4. Being disabled (unable to work, go to school, etc.)	( )
5. Having a minor illness or injury (toothache, allergy attack, cold, flu, hangover, acne breakout, etc.)	( )
6. Having my spouse (living partner, mate) dissatisfied with me	( )
7. Working on something I don't enjoy	( )
8. Getting grades or being evaluated	( )
9. Having too much to do	( )
10. Realizing that I can't do what I had thought I could	( )
11. Taking an exam (test, license examination, etc.)	( )
12. Looking for a job	( )
13. Leaving a task uncompleted; procrastinating	( )
14. Working at something I don't care about	( )
15. Being rushed	( )
16. Being near unpleasant people (drunk, bigoted, inconsiderate, etc.)	( )
17. Having someone disagree with me	( )
18. Being insulted	( )
19. Having a project or assignment overdue	( )
20. Having something break or run poorly (car, appliances, etc.)	( )
21. Living in a dirty or messy place	( )
22. Bad weather	( )
23. Not having enough money for extras	( )
24. Failing at something (a test, a class, etc.)	( )
25. Seeing animals misbehave (making a mess, chasing cars, etc.)	( )
26. Being without privacy	( )
27. Eating a disliked food	( )
28. Working under pressure	( )
29. Performing poorly in athletics	( )
30. Talking with an unpleasant person (stubborn, unreasonable, aggressive, conceited, etc.)	( )

FIGURE 3.2. *Continued.*

31. Realizing that someone I love and I are growing apart ( )
32. Doing something I don't want to do in order to please someone else ( )
33. Doing a job poorly ( )
34. Learning that a friend or relative has just become ill, is injured, is hospitalized, or is in need of an operation ( )
35. Being told what to do ( )
36. Driving under adverse conditions (heavy traffic, poor weather, night, etc.) ( )
37. Having a major unexpected expense (hospital bill, home repairs, etc.) ( )
38. Having family members or friends do something I disapprove (giving up religious training, dropping out of school, drinking, taking drugs, etc.) ( )
39. Learning that someone is angry with me or wants to hurt me ( )
40. Being misled, bluffed, or tricked ( )
41. Being nagged ( )
42. Being bothered with red tape, administrative hassles, paperwork, etc. ( )
43. Being away from someone I love ( )
44. Listening to people complain ( )
45. Having a relative or friend living in unsatisfactory surroundings ( )
46. Knowing a close friend or relative is working under adverse conditions ( )
47. Learning of local, national, or international news (corruption, government decisions, crime, etc.) ( )
48. Being alone ( )
49. Disciplining a child ( )
50. Saying something unclearly ( )
51. Lying to someone ( )
52. Breathing foul air ( )
53. Being asked something I could not or did not want to answer ( )
54. Being in very hot weather ( )
55. Being awakened when I am trying to sleep ( )
56. Doing something embarrassing in the presence of others ( )
57. Being clumsy (dropping, spilling, knocking something over, etc.) ( )
58. Receiving contradictory information ( )
59. Having family members or friends do something that makes me ashamed of them ( )
60. Being excluded or left out ( )
61. Losing or misplacing something (wallet, keys, golf ball, fish on a line, etc.) ( )
62. Learning that someone would stop at nothing to get ahead ( )
63. Being in a dirty or dusty place ( )
64. Not having enough time to be with people I care about (spouse, close friend, living partner, etc.) ( )
65. Making a mistake (in sports, my job, etc.) ( )
66. Running out of money ( )
67. Having a relative or friend with a mental health problem ( )
68. Losing a friend ( )
69. Doing housework or laundry; cleaning things ( )
70. Listening to someone who doesn't stop talking, can't keep to the point, or talks only about one subject ( )
71. Living with a relative or roommate who is in poor physical or mental health ( )
72. Being with sad people ( )
73. Having people ignore what I have said ( )
74. Being physically uncomfortable (being dizzy, being constipated, having a headache, being itchy, being cold, undergoing a rectal exam, having the hiccups, etc.) ( )
75. Having someone I care about fail at something (job, school,

FIGURE 3.2. *Continued.*

etc.) that is important to him or her ( )
76. Being with people who don't share my interests ( )
77. Having someone owe me money or something else that belongs to me ( )
78. Having someone I know drink, smoke, or take drugs ( )
79. Being misunderstood or misquoted ( )
80. Being forced to do something ( )

FIGURE 3.2. *Continued.*

scores for the pleasant and unpleasant events experienced that day. The mean pleasant-events score for daily monitoring in a normal population is 17.6, with a standard deviation of 10.35. The mean unpleasant-events score in a normal population is 5.1, with a standard deviation of 3.9. The daily frequency of various events provides immediate feedback on the impact of treatment in meeting the intermediate treatment goals of changing the overall rate of reinforcing and punishing events. This continuous feedback permits therapist and patient to adjust the treatment tactics continually, according to their success in meeting the strategic goals of therapy.

Finally, the covariation of certain pleasant and unpleasant events with changes in mood permits the evaluation of the functional diagnosis and further specification of person–environment interactions influencing the person's mood. Visual inspection of a graph of the daily mood and events scores gives an easy way of estimating concomitant changes in the levels of these three variables, and thereby of testing the overall diagnosis. Computer analysis provides a means of pinpointing precisely the specific events most highly correlated with mood fluctuations. The therapist and patient can use this information to fine-tune the diagnosis and the associated therapy goals.

TERMINATION AND FOLLOW-UP ASSESSMENTS

At the end of therapy, and 1 month later, patients repeat the various intake questionnaires, including the PES and the UES as well as some measure of depression level—for example, the Beck Depression Inventory (BDI) (Beck, Ward, Mendelson, Mock, & Erbaugh, 1961). Comparison of the pretherapy and posttherapy scores of the patient allows assessment of the direction and amount of change in person–environment interactions and depression level.

SOCIAL LEARNING TACTICS

The final major component of a comprehensive approach to the treatment of depression is a set of tactics with which to accomplish the goals that have been pinpointed during the diagnostic process. The most commonly used tactics are shown in Table 3.2. In general terms, the treatment tactics are aimed at increasing the person's pleasant interactions with the environment and at decreasing unpleasant ones. The tactics fall into three general categories: those that focus on changing environmental conditions; those that focus on teaching depressed individuals skills they can use to change problematic patterns of interaction with the environment; and those that focus on enhancing the pleasantness and decreasing the aversiveness of person–environment interactions.

TABLE 3.2. Social Learning Tactics

Environmental interventions
1. Environmental shifts
2. Contingency management

Skills training
1. Self-change methods
   a. Specifying the problem
   b. Self-observing and "baselining"
   c. Discovering antecedents
   d. Discovering consequences
   e. Setting a helpful goal
   f. Self-reinforcement
   g. Evaluating progress
   h. Time planning
2. Social skills
   a. Assertion
   b. Interpersonal style of expressive behavior
   c. Social activity
3. Relaxation
4. Stress management

Cognitive skills
1. Decreasing negative thinking by thought interruption, Premacking, worrying time, blow-up technique, self-talk procedures, identification, and disputing of irrational thoughts.
2. Increasing positive thinking by priming, noticing of accomplishments, positive self-rewarding thoughts, time projection.

Environmental interventions are especially useful when the patient's environment is highly impoverished and/or aversive, or when the individual has few personal resources. One kind of environmental intervention involves changing the physical and social setting of the patient by assisting the patient to move to a new environment. For example, we worked with an elderly depressed woman with a history of paranoid schizophrenia, in whom cognitive functioning was significantly reduced by arteriosclerosis. Our functional analysis suggested that social isolation was a major factor contributing to her depression. She accepted our recommendation that she move from a tiny studio apartment in an isolated house to a large retirement center with many ongoing recreational activities. Her depression improved substantially with the subsequent increase in social and recreational events in her life. Other examples of environmental shifts include moving to another city, separating from a spouse, and changing jobs. The literature is remarkably sparse in regard to the use of environmental shifts in the treatment of depression, perhaps because their therapeutic value is often so obvious.

Contingency management is another kind of environmental intervention. Contingency management involves changing the consequences of certain behaviors. With institutionalized patients, token economies, by means of which constructive (i.e., nondepressed) behaviors are positively reinforced and depressive behavior is negatively reinforced, have been instituted (Hanaway & Barlow, 1975; Hersen, Eisler, Alford, & Agras, 1973; Reisinger, 1972). With outpatients, the therapist may instruct family members to make attention, praise, and physical affection contingent on adaptive behaviors and to ignore depressed behaviors (Liberman & Raskin, 1971). The willingness of family members to become involved in this way may in itself constitute important prognostic information; for example, McLean and Hakstian (1979) found that, regardless of treatment modality, patients whose spouses were willing to become involved in the treatment were much more likely to improve.

Skills-training tactics focus on teaching depressed persons skills they can use to change problematic patterns of interaction with the environment, as well as skills they will need to maintain these changes after the termination of therapy. Specific skills-training interventions vary from case to case; they range from very structured and standardized programs to individually designed ad hoc procedures. Training typically involves didactic introduction to the skills involved; modeling and coaching by the therapist; role playing and rehearsal, and practice by the patient in and out of treatment sessions; and finally, application of the skills in the real world.

In our choice of self-management methods, we have made considerable use of procedures and techniques described by Goldfried and Merbaum (1973), by Mahoney and Thoresen (1974), by Thoresen and Mahoney (1974), and by Watson and Tharp (1972). Lakein's *How to Get Control of Your Time and Your Life* (1973) is also useful because it presents a systematic format for organizing time and activities so as to be able to meet responsibilities and still have time for pleasant activities.

Tactics aimed at allowing the patient to change the quantity and the quality of his or her interpersonal relationships typically cover three aspects of interpersonal behavior: assertion, interpersonal style of expressive behavior, and social activity. For assertion, a covert modeling procedure based on Kazdin's work (1974, 1975) has been used by us in a sequence involving instruction, modeling, rehearsal, and feedback. After the concept of assertion is presented, patients read *Your Perfect Right* (Alberti & Emmons, 1974), and a personalized list of problematic situations is developed by the patient and the therapist. The therapist may model some assertive possibilities for the patient; after that, the patient is encouraged to take over and to rehearse assertiveness using the covert modeling procedure. Transfer to *in vivo* practices is planned and monitored during later sessions.

Work on the interpersonal style of the patient follows the same format of instruction, modeling, rehearsal, and feedback. Patients and therapists together set goals, usually small and easily attained ones, based on preassessment problems and patients' preferences. Typical goals may include responding with more positive interest to others; reducing complaints or "whining"; increasing activity level in discussion; or changing other verbal aspects of behavior.

Finally, patients are encouraged to increase their social activity. Patients and therapists set goals for increase based on patients' preassessment frequency of social activity. Goals are gradually increased over several sessions. For this phase of treatment, a manual prepared by Gambrill and Richey (1976) is useful for specific help in areas such as initiating conversations or finding out about activities available in the local community.

Cognitive skills are intended to facilitate changes in the way patients think about reality. The locus of control over thoughts can clearly be identified as being in the patient, since only the patient can observe his or her thoughts. Patients may monitor their thoughts every day. They are taught to discriminate between positive and negative thoughts, necessary and unnecessary thoughts, and constructive and destructive thoughts.

A number of cognitive self-management techniques have been used by us, including thought stopping and "Premacking" of positive thoughts (described in Mahoney, 1974) and Meichenbaum's "self-taught procedure" (1975). Rational–emotive concepts may be covered, and a procedure for disputing irrational thoughts may be presented (Ellis & Harper, 1973; Krantzler, 1974). All techniques are presented as skills to be learned and practiced to become maximally useful.

Stress-management skills may include relaxation training (Benson 1975; Rosen, 1977). It begins by identifying three or four specific situations or interactions that are potentially stressful for the patient, and it makes heavy use of techniques and procedures described by Meichenbaum and Turk (1976) and by Novaco (1977). Stress-management training also involves teaching patients to recognize objective signs of dysphoria early in the provocative sequence. After the patients become aware of pending aversive situations and the effect that they are having on them, they may begin to pinpoint specific irrational beliefs, automatic thoughts, expectancies, and negative self-statements and self-appraisals. Other components of "cognitive preparation" involve teaching clients specific skills needed for dealing with aversive situations and preparing for aversive encounters; self-instruction; *in vivo* relaxation; other types of assertion; more effective communication skills; problem-solving skills; and other task-oriented skills.

TREATMENT MODULES

Each depressed person is unique, and hence treatment tactics must be flexible. Nevertheless, we have found it useful to develop several therapist manuals (treatment modules) to assist therapists with the implementation of specific tactics. One of the manuals we are currently using is called "Decrease Unpleasant Events and Increase Pleasant Events."[2] As the title implies, the first part of treatment is

2. Manuals and pamphlets named in this section without authorial citations can be obtained at cost by writing to Peter M. Lewinsohn, PhD, Psychology Department, University of Oregon, Eugene, Oregon 97403.

devoted to assisting the client in decreasing the frequency, and the subjective aversiveness, of unpleasant events in his or her life. The second phase concentrates on increasing pleasant ones. While the module is relatively specific in suggesting what should be done, it is meant to serve as a flexible guide and not as a rigid schedule.

Step 1: Daily Monitoring

We first teach patients to graph and to interpret their daily monitoring data. They seem to understand intuitively the relationship between unpleasant events and mood. But the covariation between pleasant events and mood is usually a revelation to patients. *Seeing* these relationships on a day-to-day basis impresses on patients in a powerful way the fact that the quantity and the quality of their daily interactions has an important impact on their depression. The depression is no longer a mysterious force but a reasonable experience. The graphing and interpretation provide clients with a framework for understanding their depression and suggest ways of dealing with it. Monitoring specific events helps clients focus on coping with particular unpleasant aspects of their daily life and, of equal importance, makes them aware of the range of pleasant experience potentially accessible to them. Patients, in a very real sense, learn to diagnose their own depression.

Step 2: Relaxation Training

The rationale for relaxation training is introduced at the end of the first session. Patients are told how tenseness can exacerbate the aversiveness of unpleasant situations and how it interferes with the enjoyment of pleasant activities. At the end of the first session, the patient is given the assignment of reading either a pamphlet (e.g., "Learning to Get Completely Relaxed") or a book (e.g., Benson, 1975; Rosen, 1977), and is instructed on how to become familiar with major muscle groups and how to tense and relax them. Much of the second session is used for progressive muscular relaxation intended to show patients how relaxed they can feel. The patient is then encouraged to practice relaxation two times per day and to keep a relaxation log. Later assignments involve patients' identifying specific situations in which they feel tense.

Step 3: Managing Aversive Events

The therapy then moves to teaching patients to manage aversive events. Patients often overreact to unpleasant events and allow them to interfere with their engagement in and enjoyment of pleasant activities. Relaxation training is, therefore, introduced early in treatment with the goal of teaching patients to be more relaxed generally, but especially in specific situations in which they feel tense.

The "decreasing unpleasant events" component then proceeds with pinpointing a small number of negative interactions or situations that trigger the patient's dysphoria. In order to reduce the aversiveness of these situations, the therapist has available a wide range of tactics, which might include teaching patients consciously to substitute more positive and constructive thoughts between the activating event and the feeling of dysphoria; to learn how not to take things personally; to prepare for aversive encounters; to learn how to use self-instructions; to prepare for failure; and to learn in other ways how to deal more adaptively with aversive situations. These tactics are described in greater detail by Beck (1976), Ellis and Murphy (1975), Krantzler (1974), Mahoney (1974), Meichenbaum and Turk (1976), and Novaco (1977).

Step 4: Time Management

Daily planning and time management training is another general tactic included in the module. In this phase, we have patients read and make considerable use of selected chapters from *How to Get Control of Your Time and Your Life* by Lakein (1973).

Depressed individuals typically make poor use of their time, do not plan ahead, and therefore have not made the preparations (e.g., getting a babysitter) needed in order to take advantage of opportunities for pleasant events. The training aims also to assist clients to achieve a better *balance* between activities that they want to do and activities that they feel they have to do. Using a daily time schedule, patients are asked to preplan each day and each week. Initially, this planning is done in the sessions with therapists' assistance; gradually, patients are expected to do the planning at home.

Step 5: Increasing Pleasant Activities

The daily planning is also useful in scheduling specific pleasant events, which becomes the focus of the next phase of the module. In helping patients to increase their rate of engagement in pleasant activities, the emphasis is on setting concrete goals for this increase and on developing specific plans for things the patients will do.

GENERAL CONSIDERATIONS

There are a number of general considerations that we feel are important in the treatment of depressed patients. We are always very concerned about providing patients with a rationale for what we are doing (i.e., daily monitoring, graphing, relaxation training, daily planning, etc.). The rationale must be acceptable to both patients and therapists. The treatment program is presented as being problem-solving, task-oriented, and educational in its goals. The specific procedures are necessary to accomplish those goals. We see it as important that the patient be clearly informed of all aspects of the program and participate actively in the selection of specific tactics and goals. The treatment is correctly perceived by the patient as highly structured. At the same time, provisions are always made for the patient to be able to take time to discuss problems that may be particularly pressing.

Contingency contracts of various kinds have proven useful. For example, using a sliding fee scale, we compute what the total cost of the treatment (typically, 12 sessions) will be. Patients are then informed that they can earn back as much as 40% of the total bill by keeping appointments, completing the daily monitoring, doing assignments, and so forth.

Throughout treatment, we make an ongoing effort to keep the intermediate treatment goals mutually meaningful and specific. It is our experience that unsuccessful cases have been those in which the therapist and the client were unable to pinpoint some relatively specific goals for change.

Finally, several sessions are devoted to planning for maintenance of any gains made during treatment. The therapist and the patient plan several tactics to help the patient resist the pressure of the old environment and to use any new skills. Often the last few sessions are spaced out over several weeks in order to fade out therapist support slowly and to make the transition easier for the patient.

The following case presentations illustrate social learning approaches in routine treatment.

CASE PRESENTATIONS

CASE 1

Alice was a 37-year-old White divorced female who lived in an apartment with her 9-year-old daughter and 14-year-old son and who worked as a secretary. She was self-referred and sought treatment for depression. Alice complained of feeling down; having difficulty with concentrating and with getting things done; withdrawing socially; losing interest in most activities; being irritable and tense; and having headaches.

Differential Diagnosis

Alice's intake data included the standard battery (MMPI and SADS interview) as well as the BDI. Her RDC diagnosis was Intermittent Depressive Disorder, and her depression scores are shown in Table 3.3.

Functional Analysis

Alice took home, completed, and returned the PES and the UES within 3 days after her intake. The PES scores (Table 3.4) indicated that Alice had a low overall rate of positive person–environment interactions and an especially low rate of positive social interactions. The PES scores suggested that Alice had a high potential for enjoyment. Examples of Alice's potentially most enjoyable interactions included "having lunch with friends and associates," "having a frank and open conversation," and "being with people I love."

The UES indicated that Alice had a high overall rate of unpleasant interactions (both in terms of frequency and experienced

TABLE 3.3. Case 1 Presentation: Depression Scores at Intake

MEASURE	SCORE
MMPI *D* scale	85
BDI	36
Grinker Feelings and Concerns Checklist	
a. Dysphoria factor mean	2.0
b. Total factor mean	1.8

aversiveness), particularly in the areas of "material–financial problems" and "domestic day-to-day inconveniences." Unpleasant events that Alice found especially aversive included "doing housework," "paying high prices," and "disciplining my children."

During the first therapy session, Alice and her therapist reviewed her UES and PES scores, using them as a starting point to identify specific problematic situations in Alice's life. Gradually, Alice and her therapist agreed that therapy would focus on increasing the

TABLE 3.4. Case 1 Presentation: Pleasant and Unpleasant Events Scores at Intake for Selected Scales

SCALE	PATIENT SCORES	NORMATIVE SCORES[a]
Total pleasant events		
Frequency of engagement	.60	.80
Potential enjoyability	1.07	1.09
Attained enjoyability	.81	1.12
Pleasant social events		
Frequency of engagement	.73	1.06
Potential enjoyability	1.13	1.15
Attained enjoyability	.92	1.40
Total unpleasant events		
Frequency of occurrence	.50	.58
Potential aversiveness	1.31	1.01
Attained aversiveness	.68	.47
Material–financial		
Frequency of occurrence	.54	.44
Potential aversiveness	1.35	1.14
Attained aversiveness	.77	.47
Domestic day-to-day		
Frequency of occurrence	.74	.76
Potential aversiveness	1.41	.86
Attained aversiveness	1.22	.57

[a]Average standard deviation for normative scores is approximately .1.

frequency of social activities and on decreasing the frequency and impact of financial problems, household chores, and parenting conflicts. Alice proved an accurate and articulate observer of her own behavior. Details of the functional analysis are reported below.

Tactics

The first half of treatment concentrated on Alice's coping more effectively with her unpleasant interactions. With financial matters, Alice did not know where her money went, and she felt as if her finances were "out of control." With the therapist's assistance, she began preparing a monthly budget and keeping a daily log of her expenditures. As a result, she reported money matters as less upsetting, and she worried less about finances.

Alice disliked household chores very much but did most of them herself. She also let her chores pile up and ended up trying to do them all on the weekend. The therapist encouraged her to organize her chores into smaller units, to schedule them throughout the week, to pair chores with pleasant events such as listening to the radio, and to reward herself for completing chores. Alice also assigned more chores for her children .to do.

Alice's parenting skills were poor. She disciplined her children inconsistently and relied on punishments to control them. However, being punitive made her feel guilty. Alice also felt totally responsible for any and all difficulties her children encountered. For example, her daughter would tell Alice about an argument with a school chum, and Alice would worry about the incident for hours. The therapist suggested that Alice ask herself whether it was "my problem, our problem, or their problem" when worrying about her children. This helped her locate the appropriate locus of responsibility for troublesome situations involving her children. Alice also role-played talking with her children in a calm and direct way about her reasons for certain parental decisions. Finally, Alice began to learn to pinpoint specific behaviors she desired from her children and to use money, praise, and physical affection to reward these behaviors.

Alice had withdrawn from social activities, especially heterosexual ones, for the past several years. Her various preoccupations and difficulties had absorbed her energy. She also believed that contacts with males *had* to lead to sex and marriage, and she felt very unassertive around men. The therapist and Alice discussed the difference between friendships and romantic relationships. Alice also role-played and practiced assertive responses to a number of heterosexual situations. Finally, Alice began planning social outings with friends.

During the last two sessions, the therapist talked to Alice about maintaining her gains. Together they reviewed key changes she had made. Alice also committed herself to an exercise group and several church activities for the next two months.

Outcome Evaluation

Ten days prior to her first session with her therapist, a staff member gave Alice her Activity Schedule and the DACL forms and instructed her as to how to monitor her events and moods on a daily basis. Alice was asked to bring to the first treatment session her 10 days of completed self-monitoring forms. She was told that the tracking of her mood and events would help her and her therapist to delineate which events she was or was not doing, how pleasant or unpleasant she experienced them to be, and how they might be related to her mood. Furthermore, the tracking would allow her and the therapist to assess treatment progress. Alice's attitude toward these assignments and explanations was positive.

After 21 days of self-monitoring, Alice's data were submitted to our computer program,[3] which, in addition to providing various kinds of means, also computes the correlation between the occurrence of each of the activities and events and the patient's fluctuations in daily mood. The 10 most highly correlated aversive events for Alice are shown in Table 3.5. They were also used to alert Alice to the potential importance of the events for her mood in the future.

The computer printout (and Alice's daily monitoring graph) also confirmed her low rate of engagement in pleasant activities. The computer program identified Alice's 10 most highly correlated mood-related pleasant activities. These are also shown in Table 3.5. As can be seen, they included a large number of social activities.

By the end of treatment (12 sessions), Alice reported feeling better. She reported being less worried about finances and felt more

3. This program is available at cost from Peter M. Lewinsohn, PhD, Psychology Department, University of Oregon, Eugene, Oregon 97403.

TABLE 3.5. Case 1 Presentation: 10 Pleasant and 10 Unpleasant Events Most Highly Correlated with Mood

KIND	SPECIFIC EVENT
Pleasant events	1. Buying things for myself.
	2. Buying things for my family.
	3. Learning to do something new.
	4. Planning trips or vacations.
	5. Going to a party.
	6. Making a new friend.
	7. Improving my health (having my teeth fixed, getting new glasses, changing my diet, etc.).
	8. Wearing expensive or formal clothes.
	9. Combing or brushing my hair.
	10. Playing party games.
Unpleasant events	1. Coming home to a messy house.
	2. Being bothered with red tape, administrative hassles, paperwork, etc.
	3. Being rushed.
	4. Having someone I know drink, smoke, or take drugs.
	5. Having something break or run poorly (car, appliances, etc.).
	6. Being unable to call or reach someone when it is important.
	7. Seeing natural resources wasted (trees left to rot, polluted streams, etc.).
	8. Seeing a dead animal.
	9. Riding in a car with a poor driver.
	10. Being socially rejected.

in control of money matters. She also said she felt more comfortable with her role as parent and with household chores. Alice had begun to attend social activities at her church and reported that she enjoyed them. Finally, she began to have successful friendships with two males.

Her daily monitoring data, shown in Figure 3.3, confirmed these trends. Early in treatment her rate of unpleasant interactions dropped and then stabilized at a low level. Her mood showed moderate improvement. Later, Alice's pleasant interactions increased dramatically, and her mood was considerably improved.

Alice's BDI scores at termination and 1-month follow-up were in the "no to minimal" depression range. Her PES scores showed an overall increase in pleasant activities as well as in social events. On the UES, Alice reported a marked decrease in material–financial and in domestic problems. At the follow-up Alice expressed her positive

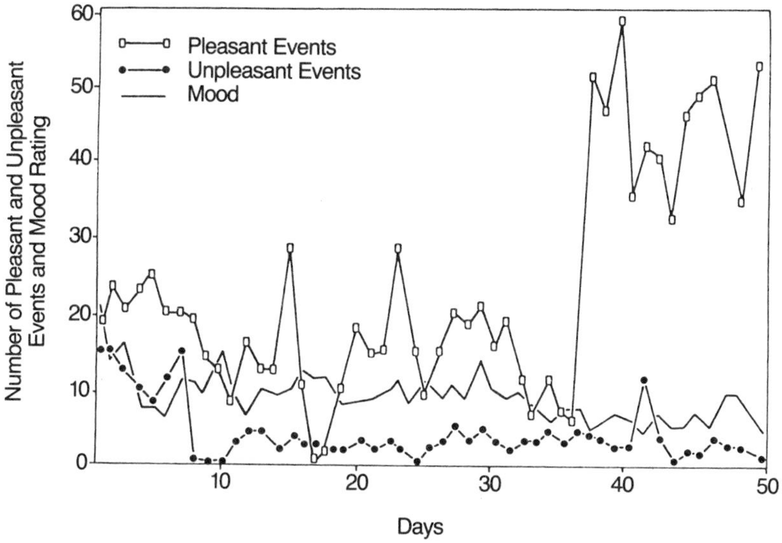

FIGURE 3.3. Case 1 presentation: Daily monitoring of pleasant and unpleasant events and mood.

feelings about her progress. She said that she felt more knowledgeable and skillful regarding what to do and what not to do to control her depressions.

CASE 2

Fred was a 29-year-old White divorced male who lived with a female partner and with his son (age 8) and daughter (age 4) from a previous marriage. Fred worked part-time as an assistant city administrator. He was self-referred. Fred complained of feeling seriously depressed for the past month; having a poor appetite; worrying constantly; having difficulty concentrating; feeling hopeless, fatigued, and tense; having lost interest in most activities; and having thoughts (but no plans) of suicide.

Differential Diagnosis

Fred's intake data included the standard battery (MMPI and SADS interview) as well as the BDI. His RDC diagnosis was Major Depressive Disorder, along with a history of Intermittent Depressive Disorder. His intake depression scores, shown in Table 3.6, indicate that Fred was seriously depressed.

Functional Analysis

Fred completed the PES and the UES at home and returned them a day later. His scores, shown in Table 3.7, suggest not only that Fred had a large number of potentially pleasant interactions with his environment, but that he also engaged in many of these activities. Examples of interactions Fred enjoyed and did frequently included "being with friends," "doing a job well," and "petting/necking." Fred also reported a high overall rate of aversive interactions on the UES, particularly in the areas of "health and welfare," "achievement–academic–job" events, and "sexual–marital–friendship" events. Examples of unpleasant events included "working at something I don't enjoy," "having too much to do," and "having arguments with my partner or spouse."

During the first few therapy sessions, Fred and his therapist, using the UES scores as a starting point, developed in greater detail his health-related, job-related, and interpersonal concerns. As part of the functional assessment, Fred tape-recorded several verbal exchanges with his partner, and he and the therapist listened to these interactions to enhance their understanding of the relationship problems. Fred and the therapist agreed that therapy would focus on decreasing the frequency and impact of his unpleasant interactions at home and at work.

TABLE 3.6. Case 2 Presentation: Depression Scores at Intake

MEASURE	SCORE
MMPI *D* scale	92
BDI	19
Grinker Feelings and Concerns Checklist	
a. Dysphoria factor mean	1.6
b. Total factor mean	1.6

TABLE 3.7. Case 2 Presentation: Pleasant and Unpleasant Events Scores at Intake for Selected Scales

SCALE	PATIENT SCORES	NORMATIVE SCORES[a]
Total pleasant events		
Frequency of engagement	.97	.82
Potential enjoyability	1.50	1.00
Attained enjoyability	1.61	.99
Total unpleasant events		
Frequency of occurrence	.84	.58
Potential aversiveness	1.39	.91
Attained aversiveness	1.05	.41
Health and welfare		
Frequency of occurrence	.65	.27
Potential aversiveness	1.73	1.30
Attained aversiveness	.95	.30
Achievement–academic–job		
Frequency of occurrence	.80	.52
Potential aversiveness	1.07	.69
Attained aversiveness	.67	.33
Sexual–marital–friendship		
Frequency of occurrence	.68	.57
Potential aversiveness	1.45	.96
Attained aversiveness	.86	.34

[a]Average standard deviation for normative scores is approximately .1.

Tactics

In discussing situations in the home, it became clear that Fred categorized them into those that were "controllable" and those that were "uncontrollable." He felt bad when the former occurred, because he felt he should have been able to prevent them. He felt bad when the latter occurred, because they were "uncontrollable." For example, he felt that he should be able to control the behavior of his children, and he would feel bad when they misbehaved. On the other hand, he felt that he had no control over the behavior of his partner toward his children and felt bad when she treated them in ways he did not approve of. The therapist had Fred keep a log of these types of situations labeling them as "controllable" or "uncontrollable." By working with the therapist on his use of these labels, Fred could see that some situations were more "controllable" than he had thought (e.g., open and tactful discussions with his partner revealed that she too was dissatisfied with her relationship with his children and interested in change). Others (e.g., the occasional misbehavior of his children), as it turned out, could be managed more effectively.

Fred was also very dissatisfied and tense about his job situation. The relaxation training enabled Fred to reduce his tension level while at work but did not increase his satisfaction with the work. With more detailed discussion of Fred's vocational interests and goals, it became clear that Fred disliked administrative work. Fred decided that he liked working with children and made plans to return to school for an advanced degree in child development.

Listening with the therapist to audiotapes of his interactions with his partner suggested to Fred that he was finding it difficult to communicate with her in a task-oriented way—for example, to discuss the place in which they wanted to settle and her role vis-à-vis his children. With therapist assistance, Fred role-played communication skills and then used these in discussing important issues with his partner.

Fred's self-monitoring data (presented in Figure 3.4) showed that

FIGURE 3.4. Case 2 presentation: Daily monitoring of pleasant and unpleasant events and mood.

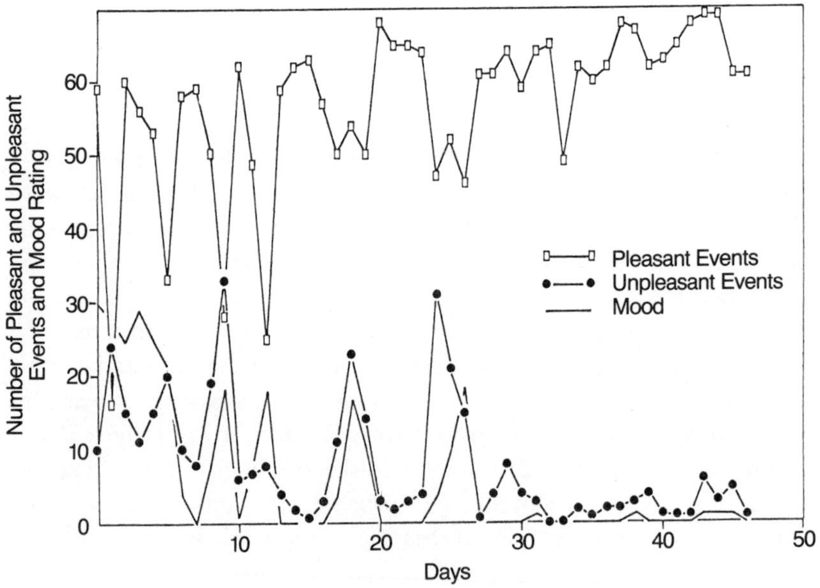

while his general rate of pleasant activities was high, the activities varied a great deal from day to day. After some discussion, the therapist and Fred could see that he did little or no planning of his time and consequently spent it haphazardly. Using his long-term goals (wanting to have a better family life, to feel more productive at work, and to make better use of his leisure time) as a general guide, Fred planned his days so as to include more pleasant activities with the family, as well as time for his hobbies. At work, Fred was able to move ahead with plans to organize a series of workshops on goal setting and achievement for city employees, which he enjoyed doing.

Fred and the therapist spent the final two sessions developing a plan for Fred to self-monitor his moods and activities for a few days every month as a preventive measure.

Outcome Evaluation

Fred's self-monitoring data (Figure 3.4) supported the functional diagnosis in showing that his mood fluctuated with the problematic interactions. The daily monitoring focused the large fluctuations in his rate of pleasant events, which was included as a target for intervention.

At the end of treatment, Fred reported that he felt good and that he no longer feared he had a "mental health" problem. He said that he felt in control of his life and that he was satisfied with his relationship and even with his job. Fred's daily monitoring reflects these changes (Figure 3.4). The reported overall occurrence of unpleasant events—particularly those relating to job, family, and health—decreased with a concomitant improvement in mood. Fred's pleasant-activities rate also became more stable.

At termination and at follow-up Fred's BDI scores showed no evidence of depression. His PES scores continued high, even a little higher than they were at intake. Fred showed greatest change in the unpleasant interactions targeted for intervention. He reported a substantial decrease in both the frequency and the impact of problems with health, relationship, and job.

Four months after treatment, Fred sent his therapist a letter stating, "I continue to feel well for the first time in literally years. I am no longer riding that crazy roller coaster I was on and I feel like I'm back in control of my life, feelings, and everything."

CONCLUDING COMMENTS

In this chapter, we have tried to present a rationale, a strategy, and some tactics for the treatment of depressed individuals within a social learning framework. Our aim has been to present the approach in a manner that facilitates its use by therapists working with depressed individuals. The relationship between depression and reinforcement is central to our approach. Depressed individuals are assumed to be on a low rate of response-contingent positive reinforcement. Diagnostic procedures are used in order to pinpoint specific person–environment interactions related to a given individual's depression. Finally, specific tactics aimed at enhancing the quantity and quality of the person's reinforcement-related interactions are introduced. The main virtue of this approach is that it provides a structured setting in which a few clear-cut and functional goals can be pinpointed and defined as targets for intervention.

There are several practical concerns that need to be addressed. Patient compliance with procedures is critical. The approach used by us requires considerable effort on the part of the patient and is dependent upon the patient's keeping accurate records, being willing to learn how to chart the daily monitoring data on a graph, and agreeing to carry out other assignments from time to time. Reservations regarding the ability of depressed individuals to carry out such assignments are frequently expressed. We have not found this to be a problem. Patients typically are quite cooperative, as long as they are convinced that the procedures are an integral part of a treatment program designed to benefit them. The crucial factor in a patient's cooperation is the therapist's ability to present a convincing rationale for the procedures. This is vital. The therapist must be able to convince the patient that the self-monitoring and other assignments are an integral part of treatment that will help him or her pinpoint specific goals, learn self-management of depression techniques, and evaluate progress. In order to be able to present a convincing rationale, the therapist must accept the rationale and believe that it is a potentially sound way of working with a particular individual. In helping student therapists to use this approach, we have found that role-playing "rationale presentation" to patients is helpful. In addition, self-monitoring their own daily activities and moods helps therapists gain a good understanding of the data and their potential usefulness.

Adaptations and simplifications are sometimes necessary. For example, we treated a depressed individual who had suffered from a stroke that made it difficult for her to write. Consequently, her husband was asked to assist her in completing the daily monitoring forms. A fringe benefit of involving him in this way was that he became very actively involved in other aspects of his wife's treatment program.

The veracity of daily monitoring of data, although typically not a problem, is of occasional concern. When the therapist suspects that a client is not careful in his or her self-monitoring, it is important to explore this with the patient. Often the problem is the result of misunderstanding of the instructions or doubts on the part of the client as to the value of self-monitoring in the treatment process.

Perhaps the most formidable obstacle to the implementation of the treatment by clinicians centers around the scoring of some of the instruments (PES, UES) and the statistical operations we perform on the daily monitoring data. The frequency and the potential enjoyability (aversiveness) scores can easily be computed with a pocket calculator. However, computing the cross-product scores (which we see as providing important diagnostic information about the total amount of positive reinforcement and of punishment obtained by the patient) represents more of a challenge. Similarly, computing the daily monitoring totals (number of pleasant activities engaged in, number of unpleasant events that occurred, daily mood score) is straightforward. However, computing the 160 correlations between the events on the patient's Activity Schedule and daily mood ratings requires access to a computer. We have developed computer programs that will generate the above mentioned scores very efficiently, and we are prepared to make these available to interested users at cost.[4]

However, we also feel that, with certain improvisations, much of the module can be utilized without the statistical trimmings. For example, by having the patient engage in self-monitoring on the standard Activity Schedule shown in Figure 3.2, it is possible to generate baseline data for the patient's rate of engagement in pleasant activities and for the rate of occurrence of unpleasant events. The patient's rates can then be compared with means of approximately 18 pleasant activities and 5 unpleasant events, obtained with lists of

4. They can be obtained from Peter M. Lewinsohn, PhD, Psychology Department, University of Oregon, Eugene, Oregon 97403.

similar length with nondepressed individuals (Lewinsohn & Graf, 1973; Lewinsohn & Talkington, 1978). Another possible shortcut is to have the patient monitor daily mood on a 10-point scale instead of on the DACL, as illustrated in Figure 3.5.

Last but not least, the question of the therapeutic efficacy of the treatment approach needs to be addressed. As is well known, ques-

FIGURE 3.5. A visual analogue depression scale.

Daily Mood Rating Form

Please rate your mood for this day (how good or bad you felt), using the 9-point scale shown. If you felt really great (the best you have ever felt or can imagine yourself feeling), mark 9. If you felt really bad (the worst you have ever felt or can imagine yourself feeling), mark 1. If it was a "so-so" (or mixed) day, mark 5.

If you felt worse than "so-so," mark a number between 2 and 4. If you felt better than "so-so," mark a number between 6 and 9. Remember, a low number signifies that you felt bad and a high number means that you felt good.

Very depressed ______________________________ Very happy
1 2 3 4 5 6 7 8 9

Enter the date on which you begin your mood ratings in Column 2 and your mood score in Column 3.

Monitoring day	Date	Mood score	Monitoring day	Date	Mood score
1			16		
2			17		
3			18		
4			19		
5			20		
6			21		
7			22		
8			23		
9			24		
10			25		
11			26		
12			27		
13			28		
14			29		
15			30		

TABLE 3.8. Intake, Termination, and Follow-Up Depression Scores for Three Cohorts Treated at the Oregon Depression Unit

COHORT	MEASURE	INTAKE	TERMINATION	FOLLOW-UP
Group I ($n=14$)	MMPI *D* scale	90	68	65
Group II ($n=21$)	MMPI *D* scale	93	71	77
	BDI	25	8	6
Group III ($n=12$)	BDI	26	12	10

Note. Scores represent group means.

tions about whether psychological treatment "*x*" is superior to psychological treatment "*y*" have been difficult to answer. Studies, including our own (Zeiss, Lewinsohn, & Muñoz, 1979) indicate that the null hypothesis of no differences between treatments is difficult to reject. Perhaps more important to the clinician is to have some idea about how much clinical improvement, on the average, to expect. Information relevant to this question is provided in Table 3.8, which gives the changes in depression level for three cohorts of patients using treatment modules similar to the one described in this chapter. As can be seen, the amount of clinical improvement was very substantial and is in all instances highly statistically significant. Finally, the treatment we have described is probably most suitable for unipolar, nonpsychotic depressives, and other treatments (e.g., lithium and other medication) should be considered for bipolar and/or psychotic patients.

REFERENCES

Alberti, R. E., & Emmons, M. L. *Your perfect right.* San Luis Obispo, Calif.: Impact, 1974.

Beck, A. T. *Cognitive therapy and the emotional disorders.* New York: International Universities Press, 1976.

Beck, A. T., Ward, C. H., Mendelson, M., Mock, J., & Erbaugh, J. An inventory of measuring depression. *Archives of General Psychiatry*, 1963, *4*, 561–571.

Benson, H. *The relaxation response.* New York: William Morrow, 1975.

Depue, R. A., & Monroe, S. M. The unipolar–bipolar distinction in the depressive disorders. *Psychological Bulletin*, 1978, *85*, 1001–1029.

Ellis, A., & Harper, R. A. *A guide to rational living.* Hollywood, Calif.: Wilshire, 1973.

Ellis, A., & Murphy, R. *A bibliography of articles and books on rational-emotive therapy and cognitive behavior therapy.* New York: Institute for Rational Living, 1975.

Endicott, J., & Spitzer, R. L. A diagnostic interview for affective disorders and schizophrenia. *Archives of General Psychiatry*, 1978, *35*, 837–844.

Gambrill, E., & Richey, C. A. *It's up to you: The development of assertive social skills.* Millbrae, Calif.: Les Femmes, 1976.

Goldfried, M. R., & Merbaum, M. (Eds.). *Behavior change through self-control.* New York: Holt, Rinehart & Winston, 1973.

Grinker, R. R., Miller, J., Sabshin, M., Nunn, R., & Nunally, J. C. *The phenomena of depressions.* New York: Paul B. Hoeber, 1961.

Grosscup, S. J., & Lewinsohn, P. M. Unpleasant and pleasant events and mood. *Journal of Clinical Psychology*, 1980, *36*, 252–259.

Hanaway, T. P., & Barlow, D. H. Prolonged depressive behaviors in a recently blinded deaf-mute: A behavioral treatment. *Journal of Behavior Therapy and Experimental Psychiatry*, 1975, *6*, 43–48.

Hersen, M., Eisler, D., Alford, G., & Agras, W. S. Effects of token economy on neurotic depression: An experimental analysis. *Behavior Therapy*, 1973, *4*, 392–397.

Kazdin, A. E. Effects of covert modeling and model reinforcement on assertive behavior. *Journal of Abnormal Psychology*, 1974, *83*, 240–252.

Kazdin, A. E. Covert modeling, imagery assessment, and assertive behavior. *Journal of Consulting and Clinical Psychology*, 1975, *43*, 716–724.

Krantzler, G. *You can change how you feel.* Eugene: University of Oregon Press, 1974.

Lakein, A. *How to get control of your time and your life.* New York: New American Library, 1973.

Lewinsohn, P. M. Activity schedules in the treatment of depression. In J. D. Krumboltz & C. E. Thoresen (Eds.), *Counseling methods.* New York: Holt, Rinehart & Winston, 1976.

Lewinsohn, P. M. *The Unpleasant Events Schedule: A scale for the measurement of aversive events.* Unpublished mimeograph, University of Oregon, 1975.

Lewinsohn, P. M., & Amenson, C. Some relations between pleasant and unpleasant mood-related activities and depression. *Journal of Abnormal Psychology*, 1978, *87*, 644–654.

Lewinsohn, P. M., Biglan, T., & Zeiss, A. Behavioral treatment of depression. In P. O. Davidson (Ed.), *The behavioral management of anxiety, depression, and pain.* New York: Brunner/Mazel, 1976.

Lewinsohn, P. M., & Graf, M. Pleasant activities and depression. *Journal of Consulting and Clinical Psychology*, 1973, *41*, 261–268.

Lewinsohn, P. M., & Talkington, J. The measurement of aversive events and relations to depression. *Applied Psychological Measurement*, 1979, *3*, 83–101.

Lewinsohn, P. M., Youngren, M. A., & Grosscup, S. J. Reinforcement and depression. In R. A. Depue (Ed.), *The psychobiology of the depressive disorders: Implications for the effects of stress.* New York: Academic Press, 1979.

Liberman, R. P., & Raskin, D. E. Depression: A behavioral formulation. *Archives of General Psychiatry*, 1971, *24*, 515–523.

Libet, J., Lewinsohn, P. M., & Javorek, F. *The construct of social skill: An empirical study of several measures on temporal stability, internal structure, validity, and situational generalizability.* Unpublished mimeograph, University of Oregon, 1973.

Lubin, B. Adjective checklists for the measurement of depression. *Archives of General Psychiatry*, 1965, *12*, 57–62.

MacPhillamy, D., & Lewinsohn, P. M. *Manual for the Pleasant Events Schedule.* Unpublished mimeograph, University of Oregon, 1975.

MacPhillamy, D. J., & Lewinsohn, P. M. *Pleasant Events Schedule.* Unpublished mimeograph, University of Oregon, 1971.

MacPhillamy, D. J., & Lewinsohn, P. M. Depression as a function of desired and obtained pleasure. *Journal of Abnormal Psychology*, 1974, *83*, 651–657.

Mahoney, M. J. *Cognition and behavior modification.* Cambridge, Mass.: Ballinger, 1974.

Mahoney, M. J., & Thoresen, C. E. *Self-control: Power to the person.* Monterey, Calif.: Brooks/Cole, 1974.

McLean, P. D., & Hakstian, A. R. Clinical depression: Comparative efficacy of outpatient treatments. *Journal of Consulting and Clinical Psychology*, 1979, *47*, 818–836.

Meichenbaum, D. Self-instructional methods. In F. H. Kanfer & A. P. Goldstein (Eds.), *Helping people change.* New York: Pergamon, 1975.

Meichenbaum, D., & Turk, D. The cognitive-behavioral management of anxiety, anger, and pain. In P. O. Davidson (Ed.), *The behavioral management of anxiety, depression, and pain.* New York: Brunner/Mazel, 1976.

Novaco, R. W. Stress innoculation: A cognitive therapy for anger and its application to a case of depression. *Journal of Consulting and Clinical Psychology*, 1977, *45*, 600–608.

Reisinger, J. J. The treatment of "anxiety-depression" via positive reinforcement and response cost. *Journal of Applied Behavior Analysis*, 1972, *5*, 125–130.

Robins, J. N., & Guze, S. B. Classification of affective disorders: The primary-secondary, the endogenous-reactive and the neurotic-psychotic concepts. In T. A. Williams (Ed.), *Recent advances in the psychobiology of the depressive illnesses.* Chevy Chase, Md.: Department of Health, Education, and Welfare, 1969, *10*, 283–295.

Rosen, G. M. *The relaxation response.* Englewood Cliffs, N.J.: Prentice-Hall, 1977.

Sanchez, V. C. *A comparison of depressed, psychiatric control and normal control subjects on two measures of assertiveness.* Unpublished master's thesis, University of Oregon, 1976.

Spitzer, R. L., Endicott, J., & Robins, E. Research Diagnostic Criteria: Rationale and reliability. *Archives of General Psychiatry*, 1978, *35*, 773–782.

Thoresen, C. E., & Mahoney, M. J. *Behavioral self-control.* New York: Holt, Rinehart & Winston, 1974.

Watson, D. L., & Tharp, R. G. *Self-directed behavior: Self-modification for personal adjustment.* Belmont, Calif.: Wadsworth, 1972.

Zeiss, A. M., Lewinsohn, P. M., & Muñoz, R. F. Nonspecific improvement effects in depression using interpersonal, cognitive, and pleasant events focused treatments. *Journal of Consulting and Clinical Psychology*, 1979, *47*, 427–439.

4

INTERPERSONAL PSYCHOTHERAPY: THEORY AND RESEARCH

GERALD L. KLERMAN
MYRNA M. WEISSMAN

INTRODUCTION

Interpersonal psychotherapy (IPT) is based on the premise that depression—regardless of symptom patterns, severity, the presumed biological vulnerability, or personality traits—occurs in a psychosocial and interpersonal context, and that understanding and renegotiating the interpersonal context associated with the onset of symptoms is important to the depressed person's recovery and possibly to the prevention of further episodes. IPT is a brief (12–16 weeks) weekly psychological treatment for the ambulatory, nonbipolar, nonpsychotic depressed patient, which focuses on improving the quality of the depressed patient's current interpersonal functioning. It is suitable for use, following a period of training, by experienced psychiatrists, psychologists, or social workes; it can be used alone or in conjunction with pharmacologic approaches.

IPT has evolved over 10 years' experiences by the New Haven–Boston Collaborative Depression Project in the treatment and research of ambulatory, nonpsychotic, nonbipolar depressed patients. Variants of IPT have been tested, as it has evolved, in three clinical trials of depressed patients (to be described later). Two studies have been completed, one of maintenance (Klerman, DiMascio, Weiss-

Gerald L. Klerman. Psychiatric Service, Massachusetts General Hospital, Boston, Massachusetts.

Myrna M. Weissman. Department of Psychiatry, Yale University School of Medicine, New Haven, Connecticut; Connecticut Mental Health Center, New Haven, Connecticut.

man, Prusoff, & Paykel, 1974; Weissman, Klerman, Paykel, Prusoff, & Hanson, 1974), and one of acute treatment (DiMascio, Weissman, Prusoff, Neu, Zwilling, & Klerman, 1979; Weissman, Prusoff, Di-Mascio, Neu, Goklaney, & Klerman, 1979). One study of depressed methadone-maintained patients is still under way (Kleber, Weissman, & Rounsaville, 1977).

The concept, techniques, and strategies of IPT have been specified in a procedural manual that has undergone a number of revisions (Klerman, Rounsaville, Chevron, Neu, & Weissman, 1979). This manual was developed to assist training in the techniques so that further refinement of the procedures and replication of the efficacy studies may be undertaken. A program is currently under way at Yale University to develop methods for the training of experienced therapists of different disciplines—psychiatrists, psychologists, and social workers (Klerman *et al.*, 1979).

It is our belief that a variety of treatments may be suitable for depression and that the depressed patient's interests are best served by availability and scientific testing of different psychological as well as pharmacological treatments, to be used alone or in combination; ultimately, such testing will determine which is the best treatment for the particular patient.

This chapter describes the theoretical and empirical basis for IPT, outlines our concept of depression, and summarizes data demonstrating its efficacy with ambulatory depressed patients. Chapter 5 of this volume describes the strategies used in IPT.

THEORETICAL FRAMEWORK FOR IPT

IPT is derived from a number of theoretical sources. The earliest source is Adolph Meyer, whose psychobiological approach to understanding psychiatric disorders placed great emphasis on the patient's current psychosocial and interpersonal experiences (Meyer, 1957). In contrast to Kraepelin and the biomedical model of illness, derived from continental European psychiatry, Meyer saw psychiatric disorders as part of the patient's attempt to adapt to the environment, usually the psychosocial environment. He viewed the patient's response to environmental change and stress as determined by early developmental experiences in the family and by the patient's membership in various social groups. Meyer attempted to apply the concepts of role adaptation to understanding psychiatric illness. In this respect, he was strongly influenced by the pragmatist school and also by the views of Darwin.

Among Meyer's associates, Harry Stack Sullivan stands out for his theory on interpersonal relations and also for his writing linking clinical psychiatry to the emerging social sciences, particularly anthropology, sociology, and social psychology (Sullivan, 1953a, 1953b). The theoretical foundation of IPT has been best summarized by Sullivan, who noted that psychiatry is the scientific study of people and the processes that involve or go on between people, in contrast to the study of only the mind, society, or the brain. Hence, the unit of study is the interpersonal situation at any one time.

The IPT emphasis on interpersonal and social factors in the understanding and treatment of depressive disorders follows the work of others. An interpersonal approach to the treatment of depression, as distinguished from an exclusively intrapsychic or biological approach, has a long tradition, starting with the writings of Sullivan and Fromm-Reichmann. More recently, these ideas have been explicated by Mabel Blake Cohen and her coworkers at the Washington School of Pyschiatry, in a comprehensive study of the disrupted interpersonal relations in the childhood experiences of 12 manic–depressives (Cohen, Baker, Cohen, Fromm-Reichmann, & Weigert, 1954)..Results indicated that the early experiences of these manic–depressives were reflected in adult personality structures that were consistently associated with particular kinds of interpersonal problems. Moreover, these interpersonal problems were manifest in the way these patients functioned in psychotherapy.

The interpersonal conceptualization was applied to therapeutic strategies in the writings of Frank (1973), who stressed mastery of current interpersonal situations as an important social-psychological component in psychotherapy. Among others, Becker (1974) and Chodoff (1970) have also emphasized the social roots of depression and the need to attend to the interpersonal aspects of the disorder.

EMPIRICAL BASIS FOR UNDERSTANDING DEPRESSION IN AN INTERPERSONAL CONTEXT

The empirical basis for understanding and treating depression in an interpersonal context derives from several divergent sources, including developmental theory based on ethological work and the study of children, as well as on clinical and epidemiologic studies of adults. This review of empirical studies is meant to be illustrative rather than exhaustive.

ATTACHMENT BONDS AND DEPRESSION

Attachment theory emphasizes that the most intense human emotions are associated with the formation, disruption, and renewal of affectional bonds. The studies of Bowlby, based on earlier investigations of the animal ethologists and later applied to studying the mother–child relationship, demonstrated the importance of attachment and social bonds to human functioning; the vulnerability of individuals to impaired interpersonal relations if strong attachment bonds did not develop early; and the vulnerability of individuals to depression or despair during disruption of attachment bonds (Bowlby, 1969). Many types of psychiatric disorders result from a person's inability to make and keep affectional bonds. The way in which affectional bonds are made is determined largely by events within the family, especially but not exclusively during early childhood.

Based on these observations, Bowlby (1977) has proposed a system of psychotherapy. This psychotherapy was designed to assist the patient in examining current interpersonal relationships in order to understand how they may be construed on the basis of the patient's experiences with attachment figures in childhood, adolescence, and adulthood.

The work of Bowlby has been expanded by Rutter (1972) to show that relationships other than that of the mother and child have an impact on the formation of attachment bonds, and to relate disruption and deprivation of bonds to the onset of depression. Closely derived from these theories has been the work of Henderson and his colleagues (Henderson, Byrne, Duncan-Jones, Adcock, Scott, & Steele, 1978; Henderson, Duncan-Jones, Byrne, Scott, & Adcock, 1978; Henderson, Duncan-Jones, McAuley, & Richie, 1978). In a series of studies, this group has found that deficiency in social bonds in the current environment is associated with neurosis. "Social bonds," for this work, have been defined as provisions of social relationships in the person's primary group or immediate social environment. These provisions include availablility of adequate attachments and social integration; opportunity for nurturing others; reassurance of worth; and a sense of reliable alliance and guidance. Henderson and his colleagues have shown that deficiency in social bonds is associated with neurosis, whether or not the stress associated with adverse experiences is present. A longitudinal study under way will relate the time sequence of deficiencies in primary group ties to the development of neurosis. While the current publication of this work is based on a general health questionnaire, the Present State Examination has also been included and, it is hoped, will provide more direct information on depression.

In related work with patients, Henderson's group (Henderson, Duncan-Jones, McAuley, & Richie, 1978) found that patients with neurotic disorders (primarily depression), as compared to matched normal controls, had affectively unpleasant interaction in their primary group; had fewer friends and fewer attachment figures; and felt that their attachment figures gave them insufficient support.

INTIMACY AS A PROTECTION AGAINST DEPRESSION

The most sophisticated empirical work defining an aspect of attachment bonding (intimacy—a confiding relationship) and examining its relationship to the development of depression has been completed by Brown, Harris, and Copeland (1977). In a community survey of women living in the Camberwell section of London, this group found that the presence of an intimate, confiding relationship with a man, usually the spouse, was the most important protection against developing a depression in the face of life stress.

In a similar work with medical patients, Miller and Ingham (1976) found that women who reported the lack of an intimate confidant to general physicians had more severe psychological symptoms.

RECENT SOCIAL STRESS AND THE ONSET OF DEPRESSION

Stemming from the demonstration in 1950 by Holmes, Goodell, and Wolf that the rate of upper respiratory illness increases with the number of life events, a considerable body of research demonstrating the relationship between "stress" (defined as recent life events), and the onset of psychiatric illness, particularly depression, has emerged (Paykel, Myers, Dienelt, Klerman, Lindenthal, & Pepper, 1969; Rabkin & Struening, 1976; Schless & Mendels, 1977; Uhlenhuth & Paykel, 1973).

The Paykel *et al.* work (1969) is most relevant to the study of stressful life events and depression. This group studied depressed patients and found that exits of persons from the social field occurred more frequently with depressed patients than such exits occurred with normals in the 6 months prior to the onset of depression. This group also found that marital friction was the most common event reported by depressed patients prior to the onset of depression.

Comparable observations were made by Ilfeld (1977) in a survey of about 3000 adults in Chicago. Depressive symptoms were closely related to stress, particularly to stresses in marriage but less frequently to those of parenting. In a closer look at the data, Pearlin and Lieberman (1979) found that chronically persisting problems within intact marriages were as likely to produce distress and depressive symptoms as was the total disruption of the marriage by divorce or separation.

Bloom, Asher, and White (1978), in a critical analysis of several studies related to the consequences of marital disputes and divorce, linked these events (marital disruption) with a wide variety of emotional disorders, including depression.

IMPAIRMENT OF INTERPERSONAL RELATIONS ASSOCIATED WITH DEPRESSION

The impairment in close interpersonal relations of depressed women has been studied in considerable detail by Weissman and Paykel (1974). In a comparison study of depressed women and their normal neighbors, they found that the depressed women were considerably more impaired in all aspects of social functioning—as workers, wives, mothers, family members, and friends. This impairment was greatest with close family, particularly spouses and children, with whom considerable hostility, disaffection, and poor communication were evident. With symptomatic recovery, most but not all of the impairments diminished. Marital relationships often remained chronically unhappy and explosive. There has been some debate as to whether the marital difficulties associated with depression are the cause or the consequence of the disorder (Briscoe & Smith, 1973; Kreitman, Collins, Nelson, & Troop, 1970). Studying the interactions of depressed patients and normal subjects, Coyne (1976) has demonstrated that depressives elicit characteristic, unhelpful responses from others.

This brief review is meant to illustrate some of the key empirical findings that provide a rationale for understanding depression in an interpersonal context and for developing a treatment strategy for depression based on interpersonal concepts. In general, studies show the importance of close and satisfactory attachments to others in the prevention of depression, and, alternatively, the role of disruption of attachments in the development of depression. The studies are varied; they include both community samples and patients under treatment, and they examine both depressive symptoms and depression as a clinical syndrome.

ROLE IMPAIRMENTS

IPT is concerned with problems in social roles and interpersonal relations associated with the onset of depression. This section defines these relationships and describes pathways to their disruption that possibly lead to depression.

DESCRIPTION OF ROLES

All persons hold multiple hierarchical positions in the social system and play specific roles appropriate to these positions. The roles occur within the nuclear family (e.g., parent, child, sibling, spouse); within the extended family; within the work situation (supervisor, supervisee, or peer); within the neighborhood or community; and within friendship groups.

Interpersonal roles can be assessed within the following components:

1. The patient in relationship to one or more significant others.
2. The *interaction* between or among these persons, which, if extended over time, becomes the history of these relationships.
3. The *cognitions* that the parties hold about their roles, including their beliefs about the meaning, norms, and expecta-

tions of role performance, and also terminology and labeling employed to describe behavior within roles.

4. *Affects* (variously called emotions, moods, and feelings) related to the transactions within roles, including sadness, anger, anxiety, trust, surprise, fear, guilt, and shame.

PATHWAYS TO IMPAIRMENTS

Impairments in roles may occur by a number of pathways, such as the following:

Biological abnormalities: The patient may have a neurological defect or a psychiatric illness that is associated with certain drugs, genetically determined, or cerebrovascular. These conditions may produce cognitive impairment, psychomotor retardation, or other dysfunctions that have a consequent impact upon the patient's social functioning. Whereas the pathways listed below are amenable to treatment by IPT, there is little likelihood of biological impairment being helped by our treatment program.

Aging: Physical impairment or death of significant others may produce role changes that are experienced negatively.

Developmental lags: The patient may not have learned skills of social competence, and this may be reflected in his or her poor adult functioning.

Psychodynamic conflicts: The patient may have a conflict between wishes and conscience (as, for example, between sexual wishes and restrictive social codes), or between different definitions of masculinity and femininity.

Changes in sex-role definitions: The feminist movement has created pressures on changes in sex-role definition. Sexual role mastery depends on the individual's ability to tolerate rapid changes, while incorporating those changes that he or she finds acceptable or purposeful. (It might be noted that homosexuals and heterosexuals face adjustments similar to those caused by the Women's Liberation Movement. Homosexuals often struggle with being accepted as normal members of society; heterosexuals, particularly parents, struggle to understand and accept the homosexuals. Depression may develop when the homosexual person finds it impossible to find a stable identity.)

Regression: The patient may have achieved one level of role functioning, but may have regressed under stress and now may be functioning at a level lower than that of the previous attainment.

Personality patterns: The patient may have developed various maladaptive patterns that result in chronic poor functioning. These enduring personality patterns are less likely to be affected by IPT.

Cross-cultural difficulties: Patients may have been raised in one cultural group and have difficulty in acculturation (as in the case of migration). Or the patient may encounter members of other ethnic subgroups in American society through intermarriage or at work.

Interpersonal role dispute: Differences in the definition of role expectations between the patient and significant others may result in disputes and impairment in functioning.

Loss of employment and occupational role impairment: Losing a job frequently, but not always, causes financial hardship and thus impairs the individual's coping mechanisms. In other instances, in addition to this or instead of it, the loss of a job causes loss of status or disadvantageous changes in the professional or occupational "power ladder."

Change in family status: For multiple reasons—loss of job, physical illness, and the increased consciousness of women—roles within the family may change. This is particularly a source of tension in those families in which extensive role reversals take place.

Downward social mobility: In American society, the expected social movement is upward. Downward social movement generally causes a threat to the self-esteem of the individual and/or his or her family. Downward social movements may precipitate a depressive episode by loss of a more secure and prestigious social level and by the inferred or real reaction of those being joined "further down."

OVERALL DESCRIPTION OF IPT

The conceptualization of depression that forms the foundation of IPT has been derived from the important work of the interpersonal and cultural schools, although the therapeutic goals are somewhat different. While we acknowledge the influence of early developmental experiences on adult patterns of interpersonal relationships, we do not believe that reconstruction of the patient's early experiences is essential to change. The focus of IPT on *current* interpersonal relationships is based on the assumption that interpersonal experiences in the patient's family of origin will be reflected in current interpersonal attitudes and behavior. Because IPT was developed as a short-term psychotherapy, it is aimed primarily at symptom reduction and improved interpersonal functioning; it does not attempt to restructure the patient's character.

As noted previously, IPT is based on the premise that depression, regardless of biological vulnerability or personality, occurs in a psychosocial and interpersonal context. There are at least two general ways in which IPT facilitates recovery: (1) by relieving the depressive symptoms, and (2) by helping the patient develop more productive strategies for dealing with current social and interpersonal problems associated with the onset of symptoms.

The first goal is achieved by helping the patient understand that the vague and uncomfortable symptoms of depression are part of a known syndrome that is well described, well understood, and relatively common; that responds to a variety of treatments; and that has a good prognosis. Psychopharmacologic approaches may be used in conjunction with IPT to alleviate symptoms more rapidly.

The second goal is achieved by determining with the patient which of four common problems (grief, role disputes, role transitions, and interpersonal deficits) associated with the onset of depression is related to the patient's depression, and by focusing the therapy around the strategies of the particular problem. These problem areas and the therapeutic strategies for each are described in Chapter 5.

Within this framework, depression is viewed as having three component processes:

1. *Symptom formation*, which involves the development of depressive affect and the negative signs and symptoms, and may derive from psychobiological and/or psychodynamic mechanisms.
2. *Social and interpersonal relations*, which involve interactions in social roles with other persons and which derive from learning based on childhood experiences, concurrent social reinforcement, and/or personal mastery and competence.
3. *Personality*, which involves the enduring traits such as inhibited expression of anger, guilt, poor psychological communication with significant others, and/or difficulty with self-

esteem. These traits determine the person's unique reactions to interpersonal experience. Personality patterns may provide part of the person's predisposition to manifest symptom episodes.

IPT attempts to intervene in the first two processes—symptom formation and social and interpersonal relations. Because of the relatively brief time of treatment and the low level of psychotherapeutic intensity, there are few claims that this treatment will have marked impact upon enduring aspects of personality structure, although personality functioning will be assessed. Interpretation and personality reconstruction are not attempted; rather, reliance is upon familiar techniques such as reassurance, clarification of internal emotional states, improvement of interpersonal communication, and reality testing of perceptions and performance.

These techniques conventionally are grouped under the rubric of "supportive" psychotherapy. However, in our view, the term "supportive" psychotherapy is a misnomer. Most of what is called "supportive" psychotherapy attempts to assist the patient to modify his or her interpersonal relations, to change perceptions and cognitions, and to reward behavior contingencies.

The main thrust of IPT is to intervene in symptom formation and in social adjustment and interpersonal relations, working predominantly on *current* issues at conscious and preconscious levels. Although unconscious factors are recognized implicitly, they are not given explicit expression. The emphasis is upon current problems, conflicts, frustrations, anxieties, and wishes defined in an interpersonal context. The influence of early childhood experiences is recognized as significant to the presenting problems, but this component is not emphasized in therapy. Rather, an effort is made to define problems in "here-and-now" terms.

In agreement with Jerome Frank (1974), we believe that the procedures and techniques described by many of the different schools have much in common. Important common elements include developing in the patient a sense of mastery; combating social isolation; restoring a sense of group belonging; and providing meaning to life. One major difference among the psychotherapies is that of whether they conceptualize the causes of the patient's problems as lying in the far past, the immediate past, or the present.

We acknowledge that there are alternative approaches and that debate exists about the relative therapeutic importance of social reorganization (as represented by women's consciousness groups) or of intrapsychic reorganization (as used in psychoanalysis and other intensive psychotherapies). However, our past research with the use of interpersonal, present-oriented mastery techniques in similar patient groups has supported the techniques' efficacy and appropriateness, as is described later.

In summary, the focus of IPT is mainly on the patient in current life situations, with the psychotherapist engaging the patient in an evaluation of himself or herself and the current situation. IPT differs from other therapies in that it is time-limited, focused primarily on the patient's current symptoms of depression and on the interpersonal context associated with the depression. It includes a systematic analysis of relations with "significant others" in the patient's current situation. It has been developed for the treatment of a single disorder—depression. There is an *acknowledged* amalgam of therapeutic styles. Clearly, the brevity of the therapy (12–16 sessions) precludes major reconstruction of personality, and no assumptions are made about unique personality styles in persons who become depressed.

THE CONCEPT OF DEPRESSION

"Depression" covers a broad spectrum of moods and behaviors that range from the disappointment and sadness of normal life to bizarre suicidal acts of severe melancholia. There are at least three meanings to the term: a mood, a symptom, and a syndrome.

Depression as a normal mood is a universal and transient phenomenon that no one escapes. As a symptom or abnormal mood, depression is also common, and the differentiation between the normal and pathological can be indistinct. Depression of mood that is unduly persistent and pervasive is generally considered pathological. Depressive symptoms are common. They occur in many persons who do not have psychiatric disorders, as well as in those with medical disorders and with psychiatric disorders other than depression.

DEPRESSION AS A CLINICAL SYNDROME

IPT has been designed for patients who meet the criteria of depression as a clinical syndrome, not just a mood or a symptom. A clinical syndrome includes a number of specific symptoms of certain severity and persistence, producing impairment and/or disability and occurring in the absence of other symptoms or disorders that may better explain the condition.

As noted in Chapter 1, the syndrome of major depression (Spitzer, Endicott, & Robins, 1978) includes a dysphoric mood, as well as at least five other symptoms; persistence of at least 2 weeks; functional impairment or necessity of treatment; and exclusionary symptoms to eliminate other disorders, such as schizophrenia.

Current efficacy data on IPT in depressed patients are for ambulatory, nonpsychotic, and nonbipolar patients of either sex and of all races and educational levels. Mentally retarded and chronic alcoholic patients have been exlcuded from these studies. Persons with personality disorders as defined by the DSM-III or the Research Diagnostic Criteria (RDC) have not been excluded from efficacy studies, and the value of IPT or the required modification of it (if any) with certain personality disorders requires further testing. IPT is currently being tested (Kleber *et al.*, 1977) in drug-addicted individuals. Spiegel (1957, 1971) has applied similar concepts of IPT to disturbed children and families. However, the efficacy of IPT in these other populations is unknown.

EFFICACY DATA ON IPT

Two trials of IPT have been conducted by the New Haven–Boston Collaborative Depression Project and have become increasingly specified. A third study of IPT with depressed methadone-maintenance patients is under way.

IPT AS MAINTENANCE TREATMENT

The first study began in 1967 and was an 8-month maintenance trial of 150 women recovering from an acute depressive episode who were treated for 6 to 8 weeks with a tricyclic antidepressant (amitriptyline). Criteria for entrance into the study of acute treatment were definite depression of at least 2 weeks' duration and of sufficient intensity to reach a total score of 7 or more on the Raskin Depression Scale (range 3–15). The majority of patients (88%) were diagnosed as having a neurotic depression according to DSM-II. The RDC and the DSM-III criteria were not available in 1967.

This study tested the efficacy of IPT (administered weekly by experienced psychiatric social workers) as compared with that of a low-contact control (brief monthly visits for assessments), with either amitriptyline, placebo, or no pill, using random assignment in a 2 × 3 factorial design. The full design, methodology, and results have been reported elsewhere (Klerman *et al.*, 1974; Weissman *et al.*, 1974). For this discussion, we focus on the results of IPT as compared to low contact.

The findings showed that maintenance IPT as compared with low contact had no significant differential impact on prevention of relapse or symptom return, but enhanced social and interpersonal functioning for patients who did not relapse. The effects of IPT on social functioning, assessed by the Social Adjustment Scale (Weissman & Paykel, 1974), took 6 to 8 months to become statistically apparent. Patients receiving IPT were significantly less impaired in work performance, in the extended family, and in marriage than were those receiving low contact. The overall mean of social adjustment items assessed reflected these differences between groups, as did the rated overall global evaluation of the patients. The percentage score of improvement in social adjustment was substantially greater in IPT (44%) than it was in low contact (28%).

There were several problems in this maintenance study, however. First, the sample of depressed patients, while all women, was not diagnostically homogenous. In 1967, the new research diagnostic approaches, which included operationalized diagnostic criteria and systematic methods for collecting information on signs and symptoms to make these diagnoses, were not available. The main diagnostic criteria used for depression were those of the DSM-II, accompanied by a symptom severity measure. Secondly, although the psychotherapy was as described, in terms of conceptual framework, goals, frequency of contact, and criteria for therapist suitability, the techniques and strategies had not yet been operationalized in a procedural manual. Finally, the maintenance study was not the best design for testing the efficacy of a psychological treatment. Patients who entered into maintenance treatment were all drug responders. The IPT did not begin until the patients had had at least 4 weeks of drug treatment. Thus, the patients had already established a therapeutic relationship with their psychiatrists (who were not administering IPT) and were not acutely depressed at the point of randomization to the social workers (who were administering IPT).

IPT AS ACUTE TREATMENT

In 1973, we initiated a study of the acute treatment of ambulatory depressed men and women, using IPT alone, amitriptyline alone, and the two in combination against a nonscheduled treatment group for 16 weeks (Weissman *et al.*, 1979). IPT was administered weekly by experienced psychiatrists. A total of 81 patients entered the study and accepted the randomized treatment assignment.

Based on the experience in the maintenance study, changes were incorporated into this acute treatment study that resulted in a better design for a clinical-trial, testing-out psychotherapy. By 1973, the Schedule for Affective Disorders and Schizophrenia (SADS)–RDC (Spitzer *et al.*, 1978) were available for making more precise diagnostic judgments, therefore allowing the inclusion of a more homogenous sample of depressed patients. Based on the SADS–RDC approach, the inclusion criteria were nonbipolar, nonpsychotic, ambulatory pateints who were experiencing an acute, primary, major depression of sufficient intensity to reach a score of at least 7 on the Raskin Depression Scale.

A procedural manual for IPT was developed. Patients were randomized into IPT at the beginning of treatment. The treatment was limited to 16 weeks, since this was an acute and not a maintenance treatment trial. There was a follow-up 1 year after treatment had ended to determine any long-term effects of treatment. The assessment of outcome was made by a clinical evaluator who was independent of and blind to the treatment the patient was receiving. The full details of this study have been described elsewhere (DiMascio, Weissman, Prusoff, Neu, Zwilling, & Klerman, 1979; Weissman *et al.*, 1979). The control for IPT was nonscheduled treatment.

For this discussion, we focus on IPT as compared to nonscheduled treatment. In nonscheduled treatment, patients were assigned a psychiatrist whom they were told to contact whenever they felt a need for treatment. No active treatment was scheduled, but the patient could telephone, and if his or her needs were of sufficient intensity, a 50-minute session (maximum of one a month) was scheduled. Patients requiring further treatment—that is, those who were still symptomatic (Raskin 9 or more) after 8 weeks, or whose clinical condition had worsened sufficiently to require other treatment—were considered failures of this treatment and were withdrawn from the study. This procedure served as an ethically feasible control for psychotherapy in that it allowed a patient to receive periodic supportive help "on demand" (DiMascio, Klerman, Weissman, Prusoff, Neu, & Moore, 1979).

The probability of symptomatic failure over 16 weeks, as assessed by the Hamilton–Raskin scale, was significantly lower in IPT than it was in nonscheduled treatment. These results were upheld by other measures of symptom outcome, both self-reports and clinical ratings. As noted earlier, there were no differential effects of IPT on the patients' social functioning at the end of four months of maintenance treatment; they took 6 to 8 months to develop. Similarly, in the acute treatment study, which ended at 4 months, no differential effects of IPT on social functioning were found. However, at the 1-year follow-up, patients who had received IPT were functioning at a less impaired level in social activities, as parents, and in the family unit than were the patients who had not; this difference was reflected in the rater's global assessment.

CONCLUSION

The field of psychotherapy outcome research is rapidly developing. In addition to the use of randomized treatment assignment and independent and blind clinical assessment of outcome, the work presented here has attempted to incorporate two important methodologic advances for psychotherapy clinical trials. These are operationalized and defined diagnostic criteria to allow for relatively homogenous patient groups, and operationalized and defined psychotherapeutic procedures to facilitate comparability of goals and focus between therapies and to allow for replication. This work has been evolving as we gain experience and as new methodology becomes available. IPT has been refined further since the studies were completed and is now ready for replication studies outside of the New Haven–Boston centers.

Substantively, we have demonstrated the efficacy of (1) maintenance IPT as compared to low contact in helping depressives recover enhanced social functioning; and (2) IPT as compared to nonscheduled treatment of acute depressives in achieving symptom reduction and later in enhancing social functioning. The effects of social functioning take at least 6 to 8 months to become apparent. These findings are consistent with the general concept of IPT.

ACKNOWLEDGMENTS

The development and testing of IPT has been supported over the years by grant numbers MH13738, MH15650, MH26466, and MH26467 from the Psychopharmacology Research Branch, Clinical Research Branch of the National Institute of Mental Health, Alcohol, Drug Abuse and Mental Health Administration.

This work has involved the efforts of many people over the years, particularly the late Alberto DiMascio, PhD, who led the Boston portion of this project; Brigitte Prusoff, PhD, who was in charge of the data analysis for the two clinics; and Carlos Neu, MD, who assisted in the earlier versions of the IPT manual and supervised clinical work in the Boston acute treatment study.

REFERENCES

Becker, J. *Depression: Theory and research.* New York: Wiley, 1974.

Bloom, B. L., Asher, S. J., & White, S. W. Marital disruption as a stressor: A review and analysis. *Psychological Bulletin*, 1978, *85*, 867–894.

Bowlby, J. *Attachment and loss.* London: Hogarth, 1969.

Bowlby, J. The making and breaking of affectional bonds: II. Some principles of psychotherapy. *British Journal of Psychiatry*, 1977, *130*, 421–431.

Briscoe, C. W., & Smith, J. B. Depression and marital turmoil. *Archives of General Psychiatry*, 1973, *28*, 811–817.

Brown, G. W., Harris, T., & Copeland, J. R. Depression and loss. *British Journal of Psychiatry*, 1977, *130*, 1–18.

Chodoff, P. The core problem in depression. In J. Masserman (Ed.), *Science and psychoanalysis* (Vol. 17). New York: Grune & Stratton, 1970.

Cohen, M. B., Baker, G., Cohen, R. A., Fromm-Reichmann, F., & Weigert, E. A. An intensive study of twelve cases of manic-depressive psychoses. *Psychiatry*, 1954, *17*, 103–137.

Coyne, J. C. Depression and the response of others. *Journal of Abnormal Psychology*, 1976, *85*, 186–193.

DiMascio, A., Klerman, G. L., Weissman, M. M., Prusoff, B. A., Neu, C., & Moore, P. A control group for psychotherapy research in acute depression: One solution to ethical and methodologic issues. *Journal of Psychiatric Research*, 1979, *15*, 189–197.

DiMascio, A., Weissman, M. M., Prusoff, B. A., Neu, C., Zwilling, M., & Klerman, G. L. Differential symptom reduction by drugs and psychotherapy in acute depression. *Archives of General Psychiatry*, 1979, *36*, 1450–1456.

Frank, J. D. *Persuasion and healing: A comparative study of psychotherapy.* Baltimore: Johns Hopkins University Press, 1973.

Frank, J. D. Psychotherapy: The restoration of morale. *American Journal of Psychiatry*, 1974, *131*, 271–274.

Henderson, S., Byrne, D. G., Duncan-Jones, P., Adcock, S., Scott, R., & Steele, G. P. Social bonds in the epidemiology of neurosis. *British Journal of Psychiatry*, 1978, *132*, 463–466.

Henderson, S., Duncan-Jones, P., Byrne, D. G., Scott, R., & Adcock, S. *Social bonds, adversity, and neurosis.* Paper presented at W.P.A. Section on Epidemiology and Community Psychiatry, St. Louis, October 1978.

Henderson, S., Duncan-Jones, P., McAuley, H., & Richie, K. The patient's primary group. *British Journal of Psychiatry*, 1978, *132*, 74–86.

Holmes, T. H., Goodell, H., & Wolf, S. *The nose: An experimental study of reactions within the nose in human subjects during varying life experiences.* Springfield, Ill.: Charles C Thomas, 1950.

Ilfeld, F. W. Current social stressors and symptoms of depression. *American Journal of Psychiatry*, 1977, *134*, 161–166.

Kleber, H., Weissman, M. M., & Rounsaville, B. *Psychotherapy of opiate dependent individuals.* Protocol for United States Public Health Service contract, National Institute of Alcohol Abuse and Alcoholism, Alcohol, Drug Abuse and Mental Health Administration, Rockville, Md., 1977.

Klerman, G. L., DiMascio, A., Weissman, M. M., Prusoff, B. A., & Paykel, E. S. Treatment of depression by drugs and psychotherapy. *American Journal of Psychiatry*, 1974, *131*, 186–191.

Klerman, G. L., Rounsaville, B., Chevron, E., Neu, C., & Weissman, M. M. *Manual for short-term interpersonal psychotherapy (IPT) of depression.* Unpublished manuscript, 1979.

Kreitman, N., Collins, J., Nelson, B., & Troop, J. Neurosis and marital interaction: I. Personality and symptoms. *British Journal of Psychiatry*, 1970, *117*, 33–46.

Meyer, A. *Psychobiology: A science of man.* Springfield, Ill.: Charles C Thomas, 1957.

Miller, P., & Ingham, J. G. Friends, confidants and symptoms. *Social Psychiatry*, 1976, *11*, 51–58.

Paykel, E. S., Myers, J. K., Dienelt, M. N., Klerman, G. L., Lindenthal, J. J., & Pepper, M. P. Life events and depression: A controlled study. *Archives of General Psychiatry*, 1969, *21*, 753–760.

Pearlin, L. I., & Lieberman, M. A. Social sources of emotional distress. In R. Simmons (Ed.), *Research in community and mental health.* Greenwich, Conn.: JAI, 1979.

Rabkin, J. G., & Streuning, E. L. Life events and illness. *Science*, 1976, *194*, 1013–1020.

Rutter, M. *Maternal deprivation reassessed.* London: Penguin, 1972.

Schless, A. P., & Mendels, J. Life events and psychopathology. *Psychiatry Digest*, 1977, *28*, 25–35.

Spiegel, J. P. The resolution of role conflict within families. *Psychiatry*, 1957, *20*, 1–16.

Spiegel, J. P. *Transactions: The interplay between individual, family, and society.* New York: Science House, 1971.

Spitzer, R. L., Endicott, J., & Robins, E. Research Diagnostic Criteria: Rationale and reliability. *Archives of General Psychiatry*, 1978, *35*, 773–782.

Sullivan, H. S. *Conceptions of modern psychiatry.* New York: Norton, 1953. (a)

Sullivan, H. S. *The interpersonal theory of psychiatry.* New York: Norton, 1953. (b)

Uhlenhuth, E. S., & Paykel, E. S. Symptom intensity and life events. *Archives of General Psychiatry*, 1973, *28*, 473–477.

Weissman, M. M., Klerman, G. L., Paykel, E. S., Prusoff, B. A., & Hanson, B. Treatment effects on the social adjustment of depressed patients. *Archives of General Psychiatry*, 1974, *30*, 771–778.

Weissman, M. M., & Paykel, E. S. *The depressed woman: A study of social relationships*. Chicago: University of Chicago Press, 1974.

Weissman, M. M., Prusoff, B. A., DiMascio, A., Neu, C., Goklaney, M., & Klerman, G. L. The efficacy of drugs and psychotherapy in the treatment of acute depressive episodes. *American Journal of Psychiatry*, 1979, *136*, 555–558.

5

INTERPERSONAL PSYCHOTHERAPY: CLINICAL APPLICATIONS

BRUCE J. ROUNSAVILLE
EVE CHEVRON

INTRODUCTION

Interpersonal psychotherapy (IPT) is a brief, individual, weekly outpatient treatment for nonbipolar, nonpsychotic depressed patients. The therapeutic goals and focus have been described by Klerman and Weissman in Chapter 4 of this volume, and detailed descriptions of the techniques are available in a manual (Klerman, Rounsaville, Chevron, Neu, & Weissman, 1979). What is probably most definitive of short-term IPT is the concentration on bringing about improvement in defined problem areas of the depressed patient's current interpersonal functioning.

It is a fundamental assumption of IPT that depressive symptomatology and interpersonal problems are interrelated. Depression can predispose the patient to interpersonal problems, and interpersonal problems can precipitate depression. It is further assumed that dealing with interpersonal problems is essential for alleviating the depression and possibly for preventing further episodes.

Depressed patients, when they present to treatment, usually see symptom relief as their primary goal. To form a working alliance, the therapist must address the patient's symptoms. For severely symptomatic patients, it is very difficult to work on interpersonal issues before some symptom relief is experienced. Thus, short-term inter-

Bruce J. Rounsaville and Eve Chevron. Department of Psychiatry, Yale University School of Medicine, New Haven, Connecticut; Connecticut Mental Health Center, New Haven, Connecticut.

personal psychotherapy has two goals: (1) alleviating depressive symptoms, and (2) helping the patient devise more effective strategies for dealing with social and interpersonal problems. This chapter emphasizes approaches for attaining these goals.

MANAGING THE DEPRESSIVE STATE

Depression as a clinical state or syndrome involves many symptoms, such as appetite loss, sleep disturbances, anhedonia, agitation, or retardation, that are not directly dealt with by psychotherapeutic techniques of IPT. In helping the patient manage the depressed state, what IPT does attempt to do is to combat demoralization and to instill hope (Frank, 1974). When depressive symptoms such as uncontrollable sad moods begin, depressed patients frequently feel that they are "falling apart" and that they are helpless to change things. Thus, in addition to other symptoms of depression, these patients develop a characteristic hopelessness. In IPT, this hopelessness is dealt with by educating patients about their depression and engaging them in a problem-solving therapeutic alliance.

EDUCATING THE PATIENT ABOUT DEPRESSION

A careful history of the depressive symptoms is obtained as the first step in educating patients about depression. This history taking is both reassuring for the patients and essential for therapists' understanding of patients and planning of treatment; it should be done even if the therapy takes place in the context of a research project in which patients have been thoroughly screened and diagnosed. By eliciting a history of depressive symptoms in a systematic fashion, therapists convey both their interest in the patient and their familiarity with depression, and thus imply that they are competent to deal with the patient's problems. When a therapist reviews a patient's symptoms, the patient often feels that the therapist has "guessed" all of his or her problems. What has been seen by the patient previously as disparate, vague, and unconnected problems is understood as part of a single clinical syndrome.

Following this review of symptoms, the therapist attempts to instill in the patient a sense of hope by explicitly educating the patient about the diagnosis. Depressed patients characteristically feel that their symptoms will never lift, or that a permanent disability will result even if some improvements are made. They should be informed that this pessimism, along with other symptoms such as sleep loss, appetite disturbances, and so on, are all part of this depressive episode. In addition, the patient can be told that depression is a common disorder affecting 3% to 4% of the adult population at any time, and that it is relatively benign even though he is suffering now.

To enlist patients' involvement in therapy, the following information about treatment can be given to them: Depressions do respond to treatment; there are a variety of treatments that are effective; and the treatment that the patient will be undergoing has been shown to be effective in several clinical studies. Most depressives recover promptly with treatment, and the prognosis is quite good. Patients can be further reassured that they will feel better and will return to their ordinary levels of functioning when the symptoms improve. The psychotherapy will help them to understand the problems that have led to this depression.

SYMPTOM MANAGEMENT

In early phases of treatment, the patient may be counseled regarding ways of managing or mitigating depressive symptoms. In taking the history, the therapist should take special notice of circumstances that occurred at the onset of, or are associated with the exacerbation of, depressive symptoms. For instance, if a patient becomes more depressed when left alone, the therapist and the patient may explore both emergency measures and long-term strategies for reducing social isolation. Similarly, if it is learned that a patient's condition worsens in the presence of specific other people who are hostile or unhelpful in other ways, the patient can be helped to find ways to avoid contact with these individuals, in both the short and the long term. Some depressed patients are overwhelmed by the work that has been left undone as a result of their depressive symptoms. They may respond well to an approach that emphasizes reducing expectations and working around symptoms. For instance, if a patient's symptoms are worse in the morning and improve throughout the day, the patient may be helped to arrange his or her schedule so that a few essential tasks are planned for later in the day.

The fear of loss of control is especially important in suicidal patients or in patients disturbed by hostile fantasies. For these patients, the therapist's extended availability may be particularly useful as treatment begins. Several meetings with the therapist per week, daily phone calls, or provision of 24-hour availability by phone may reassure severely disturbed patients. However, these measures should be reserved only for those patients who really seem to need that much support; the offer of extraordinary measures may be perceived with alarm by less disturbed patients, who may get the message that the therapist considers them "really sick."

EVALUATING THE NEED FOR MEDICATION

As described in Chapter 4, clinical trials of tricyclic antidepressants and psychotherapy have demonstrated the differential effectiveness of psychotherapy on social functioning and of pharmacotherapy on symptom reduction, as well as the greater overall efficacy of both treatments in combination. IPT can be used in combination with pharmacotherapy (tricyclic antidepressants for depressed patients). Whether or not a drug is used, and which drug is used, will depend on such factors as the patient's preference, severity of symptoms, medical contraindications, and previous drug response. A detailed discussion of the choice of drug and technique for administering medication as treatment for depression is beyond the scope of this chapter and is available elsewhere (Hollister, 1978).

INTERVENTION IN INTERPERSONAL PROBLEM AREAS

Because IPT is short-term, it is usually concentrated on one or two current interpersonal problems. A definition of problem areas is needed as a first step in formulating a treatment strategy with the patient. In this section, we describe four major interpersonal problem areas commonly presented by depressed patients. Each problem area will be defined and related to the therapeutic goals and treatment strategies of IPT. The problem areas are (1) grief; (2) interpersonal disputes; (3) role transitions; and (4) interpersonal deficits.

These problem areas are not necessarily mutually exclusive. Patients may present with a combination of problems in several areas, or there may be no clear-cut significant difficulty in any one area. For a patient with wide-ranging problems, the therapist may be guided in the choice of focus by the precipitating events of the current depressive episode and by the identification of areas in which change can take place.

The area of focus may change as therapy progresses. Occasionally, the patient and the therapist will not agree about the most appropriate focus. Patients are often unwilling or unable to recognize the degree to which a particular problem is bothering them. For instance, patients with marital role disputes may be reluctant to complain of problems, because they feel threatened by the possibility of endangering the marital relationship; or patients with pathological grief reactions may be totally unaware of the source of their annual episodes of depression. In cases in which the therapist and the patient do not agree about the preferred focus of treatment, the therapist can take one of three tacks. The therapist may (1) delay setting treatment goals until the patient realizes the importance of the issue; (2) set very general goals in the hope of being able to focus the treatment more specifically as therapy progresses; or (3) accept the patient's priorities in the hope that, after these issues are looked into, the focus can shift to more central issues. For example, F.A., a middle-aged woman, came in with a complaint that "My children are driving me crazy." Several sessions later, she brought up her more pressing distress over her husband's extramarital affairs.

GRIEF

DEFINITION AND DESCRIPTION

Grief in association with the death of a loved one can be either normal or abnormal. IPT deals with the depression associated with abnormal grief reactions, which result from the failure to go through normal mourning following the death of a person important to the patient.

Normal Grief

The experience of normal grief following the death of a loved one has much in common with depression, but these conditions are not equivalent, and IPT is not used to treat normal grief reactions.

Grieving normally occurs when a person sustains an important loss of a significant other and, during the bereavement period, experiences symptoms such as sadness, disturbed sleep, agitation, and decreased ability to carry out day-to-day tasks. These symptoms are considered normal and tend to resolve themselves without treatment in 2 to 4 months. In normal grief, the bereaved characteristically goes through a process of gradual weaning from remembered experiences with the loved one. A detailed account of the normal grieving process has been provided elsewhere (Lindemann, 1944; Siggins, 1966).

Abnormal Grief

The principal assumption behind the therapeutic strategy described in this section is that inadequate normal grieving can lead to depression, either immediately after the loss or at some delayed time when the patient is somehow reminded of the loss. Abnormal grief processes of two general kinds are commonly noted in depressed persons: delayed grief and distorted grief.

Delayed Grief Reaction. Grief can be postponed and experienced long after the loss. When grieving is delayed, it may not be recognized as a reaction to the original loss. However, the symptoms are those of normal grieving. A delayed or unresolved grief reaction may be precipitated by a more recent, less important loss. In some cases, delayed reactions are precipitated when the patient achieves the age at which the unmourned loved one died. Questioning the grieving person about earlier losses may reveal these dynamics.

Distorted Grief Reaction. Distorted grief reactions do not resemble normal grieving and may occur immediately following the loss or years afterwards. There may be no sadness or dysphoric mood; instead, nonaffective symptoms may be present. These manifestations may involve different medical specialists before a psychiatrist is called to the task of deciphering the nature of such reactions.

DIAGNOSIS OF ABNORMAL GRIEF REACTIONS

Frequently, it is clear that the patient's depression began with a significant loss, but in other cases there may be only an indirect relationship between the current depression and a previous loss. In reviewing the patient's interpersonal relationships, it is essential to obtain a history of significant relationships with those who are now dead or otherwise absent. This should include the circumstances of the death and the patient's behavioral and emotional reaction to the death in each case. Evidence of one or more of the following factors suggests a pathological mourning process:

1. Psychological factors such as overwhelming multiple losses.
2. Inadequate or absent grief in the bereavement period, such as lack of crying, absence from the funeral, or failure to reminisce about the deceased.
3. Avoidant behavioral patterns, such as failing to visit the grave site or to participate in activities that were shared prior to the death of the loved one.
4. Physical symptoms similar to those of the lost object, either shortly after the death or at a symbolically relevant date.
5. Negative social factors, such as death in an intensive care unit.
6. Evidence of prolonged symptoms, such as incessant guilt or a continued sense of loss, which at the time of the death would have been considered part of the normal grief reaction.
7. Evidence of grief symptomatology occurring in response to mild nonspecific stress.
8. Phobia about the illness that caused the death of the loved one.
9. History of preserving the environment as it was when the loved one died, and/or
10. Radical change in life style after the occurrence of the death.
11. Absence of family, friendship, and religious support during the bereavement period.

GOALS AND STRATEGIES OF TREATMENT

The two general goals of the treatment of depression that centers around grief are (1) to facilitate the mourning process, and (2) to help patients to re-establish interests and relationships that can substitute for the ones they have lost. The therapist's major task is to help the bereaved patient to assess the significance of the loss realistically and to emancipate himself or herself from a crippling attachment to the dead person, thus facilitating the cultivation of new interests and the formation of satisfying new relationships. The therapist adopts and utilizes strategies and techniques that help the patient bring memories of the lost person, as well as the emotions related to the patient's experiences with the lost person, into focus.

Nonjudgmental Exploration and Elicitation of Feelings

Abnormal grief reactions are often associated with the lack of a supportive social network that, when present, tends to help the bereaved with the normal process of mourning. Consequently, the major psychotherapeutic strategy is to encourage the patient (1) to think about the loss; (2) to present the sequence and consequence of events prior, during, and after the death; and (3) to explore associated feelings, with the psychotherapist substituting for the missing social network.

Reassurance

Often the patient expresses the fear of bringing up that which "has been buried." The patient may express fears of "cracking up," of not being able to stop crying, or of otherwise losing control. In such instances, the psychotherapist may let the patient know that these fears are not uncommon and that mourning in psychotherapy rarely leads to decompensation.

Horowitz (1976) has identified some common themes that are typical of the dysphoric thoughts of those who have experienced stressful events such as a painful loss:

1. Fear of repetition of the event even in thought.
2. Shame over helplessness at being unable to prevent or stop the event.
3. Rage at the person who is the source of the event (in this case, the deceased).
4. Guilt or shame over aggressive impulses such as destructive fantasies.
5. Survivor guilt (i.e., guilt that the loved has died and that the survivor is relieved to remain alive).

6. Fear of identification or merging with the victim.
7. Sadness in relationship to the loss.

It is helpful for the therapist to be alert to the patient's expression of these themes and to help the patient articulate them. In fact, it is frequently reassuring if the therapist can "anticipate" the patient's complaints by inquiring about throughts and feelings along these lines.

Reconstruction of the Patient's Relationship with the Deceased

Patients with abnormal grief reactions are frequently fixated on the death itself, thus avoiding the complexities of their relationship with the deceased. The therapist should lead a thorough and, if possible, exhaustive factual and affective exploration of the patient's relationship to the deceased, both during the period when the deceased was alive and in the present context. The patient may not wish to acknowledge angry or hostile feelings toward the deceased, which may arise as a result of the patient's feeling abandoned by the loved one. When the mourning process is blocked by strongly negative feelings toward the deceased, the psychotherapist should encourage the patient to express these feelings. The feelings should not be encouraged to emerge in confrontation, because this may provoke a shift in the hostility from the deceased to the psychotherapist. If negative feelings emerge too rapidly, the patient may not return to psychotherapy because of the guilt that will have developed. However, if the psychotherapist reassures the patient that these negative feelings will be followed by positive and comforting feelings, as well as by a positive attitude toward the deceased, the patient will be much better prepared to acknowledge mixed feelings.

Development of Awareness

Following the above steps, the patient may formulate a new and healthier way of understanding memories of the deceased. For instance, a particular patient may no longer regard his father as a villain but instead may come to realize that he was a sick person; the patient may thus be able to accept the father's behavior and his own reaction to it. To help patients achieve a new understanding, the psychotherapist may attempt to elicit both affective and factual responses that lead the patients to a better understanding of the elements contributing to their difficulties in mourning loved ones. The therapist may need to confront patients in regard to their felt need to maintain a pathologically strong bond to the deceased.

Behavioral Change

As patients lose their investment in maintaining continued, abnormal grieving, they may be more open to developing new relationships to "fill the empty space" left by lost loved ones. At this point, the therapist may be very active in leading patients to consider various alternative ways (e.g., dating, church, organizations, work) to become more involved with others again.

CASE EXAMPLE OF THE TREATMENT OF ABNORMAL GRIEF

Initial Assessment (Sessions 1–2)

R.F. was a 68-year-old White woman who presented for treatment of depression, which she "became aware of" following her husband's death after a progressively debilitating course of illness. Her symptoms included unshakable sadness and preoccupation with guilty feelings of hopelessness and futility in ever trying to improve her situation. She had restricted her social contacts to seeing her two children, and she felt that she was a burden on them.

Mrs. F. associated her depression with the death and protracted illness of her husband, who had been progressively debilitated from the time he and she had retired 4 years earlier. Although they had planned to travel during their retirement and had postponed taking vacations in anticipation of this, she had accepted a restricted, isolated life style that revolved largely around caring for her husband. She had seldom left home without him and had cut off contacts with friends and acquaintances outside the family. Most disturbing about her husband's illness had been his mental deterioration; shortly before his death, he had had to be hospitalized at a state psychiatric hospital. There his physical condition had deteriorated, and this had then necessitated a transfer to another hospital and mutilating surgery. From that point until his death, Mrs. F.'s husband had been completely mentally incoherent.

The review of the past family life led to Mrs. F.'s assertion that the relationship had been fine and completely satisfying before her husband's illness. They had been married for 45 years. Her relationship with the two children had been characterized by her difficulty in giving up control over them.

However, the patient reported a highly disorganized or disrupted childhood. Her mother had died when she was 5, and the state had split up the family when she was 7, taking the children away from her alocholic father. From that time until the age of 18, she had lived for relatively brief periods at a series of foster homes. She described this experience as painful and frustrating, because the foster parents had tended to treat the foster children as unpaid household help. At age 18, she had moved in with an older sister. Five years later, after a lengthy courtship, she had married her husband, who had been her only serious suitor.

Although Mrs. F. acknowledged that she needed to develop new activities and social contacts, she felt pessimistic about ever being able to do so. She described having a "dual personality" about this issue, because there was a marked contrast between what she experienced with other people and what she tended to anticipate. As a secretary, she had performed well at her job and had had a number of friends from work. She felt that she had no difficulty making friends or meeting them, although she had tended to center her activities around her family. Her husband's illness had led her to cut off contact with friends more or less completely, especially during the last year of his life. Mrs. F. felt that she would not be welcomed by her old friends, because they would be offended that she had not kept up her relationship with them. Thus, she anticipated rejection when she attempted to get involved with people.

This anticipation of rejection was in marked contrast with what actually occurred on the occasions when others asked her to join them in social activities. In fact, she reported that she did enjoy herself and that others seemed to appreciate her company. She realized that she would probably be able to perform adequately in social relations if only she could only refrain from anticipating a bad time and could free herself to plan activities. She also brought out her long-standing fears of being taken over and exploited by others if she allowed friendships to reach more than a superficial level of interaction.

Plans for Treatment

The two general aims of treatment with this patient were (1) to facilitate the mourning process, and (2) to help the patient to re-establish interests and relationships that could substitute for the ones she had lost. After the first session, many features of her husband's death could be hypothesized as being important in preventing Mrs. F. from mourning his loss successfully. She had responded to his long illness and gradual deterioration with denial, which had led her to expect him to act more responsibly than he was capable of doing. Thus, his mental deterioration and helplessness had led her to become angry at him (and probably to wish his death). These feelings were the source of severe guilt after his death. She felt especially bad about participating in his final hospitalization. Although his illness had been out of his control, Mrs. F. also felt angry about the fact that her husband's debility had caused them both to give up their plans for a happy retirement.

From Mrs. F.'s description of her current and past social life, it was clear that she was capable of considerable improvement, if she received encouragement and if her guilt could be relieved. An important aspect of her current apathy was her lifelong sense that her own happiness was less important than that of others, to which she should devote herself. This feature could, on the one hand, be considered a liability that might necessitate attempting to help her devise ways of living for herself. However, another possibility for the focus of therapy was to help her use this tendency to get involved in new activities, such as volunteer work. From her description of her past activities and even of her current ones, she appeared to have many social assets. She had even been liked by her husband's roommates in the hospital, had several friends from the past, and had made some effort to start a college course. Her difficulties seemed to ensue largely from anticipatory anxiety, which, once involved in an activity, she was able to forget. In that she recognized her tendency to exaggerate the negative possibilities in attempts at new behavior, she could probably respond to encouragement and gentle prodding in this area, once she experienced some relief from depressive symptoms and reduced guilt. To speed the reduction of depressive symptoms, the patient was placed on amitriptyline (100 mg per day) after the second session.

Intermediate Phase of Therapy (Sessions 3–9)

The patient's course in therapy was one of continuing improvement and recovery from the depressive episode. With the therapist helping to focus her progress, the patient discussed material relevant to the two principal treatment goals in each session.

Mourning the Husband. In nearly every session, the patient discussed aspects of the loss of her husband. In several sessions, she reviewed the last 2 years of his life, adding significant new details each time. As treatment progressed, it became very clear how painful and infuriating the husband's behavior had been to Mrs. F. He had had jealous delusions, and he had had to be watched lest he get into trouble. Moreover, his physician had tried to minimize his problems, making Mrs. F. feel that she was crazy to be so upset. These discussions culminated in the eighth session, when she revealed that she had physically attacked her husband once in a moment of desperation. After sharing this "secret," she seemed to feel relieved.

Another way in which the husband's death was mourned was through repeated discussions of the many small ways in which she was continually reminded of him. Topics such as details of her life alone in the house they had shared, her handling of his medical bills, and her feelings on being unable to find his grave in the cemetery were discussed in an effort to help make it very clear to the patient that her husband was, indeed, dead.

Developing New Relationships. From the beginning of treatment, this patient made impressive efforts at filling the space that the loss of her husband had created in her life. She renewed old friendships and made new friends by becoming involved in the local senior citizens' center. She began going out with others several times each week and successfully completed her first college course. In addition, she began to make changes in her home that she had refrained from making in the past because she feared her husband's disapproval. As these new activities were discussed, the patient revealed guilty feelings at allowing herself to be happy when he was dead. She began to realize that her husband had been very restrictive of her, and that many of the ways in which she had limited her life were in reaction to him. She fruitfully realized that, now that he was dead, she not only had lost many things but had gained more freedom than she had had in years. She was then able to decide how she wanted to manage her life, setting her own individual priorities.

Termination (Sessions 10–12)

In termination sessions, reviewing the depression and the therapy and discussing the termination of therapy were focused upon. The husband's decline and the patient's reaction to it were again briefly reviewed—as was the progress she had made during treatment, which included an improved mood, increased comfort and freedom in her new independence, improved relationships with her children, a wider range of activities and interests, and many new friends.

She also discussed her reactions to the therapy. Although she was initially rather apprehensive, she had become increasingly positive about it during the treatment. She expressed concern that she had gotten better too quickly; she could not understand how things could change so much. The therapist explained that he felt that the therapy had not really made her different, but had allowed her to use the strengths and resources that she already possessed. Her depression, it was explained, was largely a result of her becoming socially isolated because of her husband's long illness and because of the difficulty she had had in accepting her feelings about his illness and death. What therapy had done was to help her put this loss and her feelings about him in perspective. Doing only this had been sufficient to allow her to grow according to her own interests and abilities.

INTERPERSONAL ROLE DISPUTES

DEFINITION AND DESCRIPTION

An "interpersonal role dispute" refers to a situation in which the patient and at least one significant other have nonreciprocal expectations about their relationship. This definition would probably pertain to every relationship at least part of the time, because role disputes are an inevitable part of life. However, IPT therapists choose to focus on role disputes only if, in their judgment, these are important in the genesis and perpetuation of a depression. Typically, these sorts of disputes are stalled or repetitious, with little hope for improvement. In such circumstances, patients lose self-esteem because they feel that they can no longer control the disputes. There is a threatened loss of what others provide for them, or of their feeling of competence in managing their lives. Typical features that perpetuate role disputes are patients' demoralized sense that nothing can be done, poor habits of communication, and/or truly irreconcilable differences.

DIAGNOSIS OF INTERPERSONAL ROLE DISPUTES

In order for a therapist to choose role disputes as the focus of IPT, a patient must give strong evidence that he or she is currently having overt or covert conflicts with a rather significant person. Role disputes are usually revealed in the patient's initial complaints or in the course of the interpersonal inventory. In previous trials of IPT, role disputes with the spouse were the most frequent problem area presented (Rounsaville, Weissman, Prusoff, & Herceg-Baron, 1979). In practice, however, recognition of important interpersonal disputes in the lives of depressed patients may be difficult. Typically, patients when depressed are preoccupied with their hopeless feelings and feel that they alone are responsible for their condition. When there is no clear precipitant for a depressive episode, and when the patient does not identify problems in current interpersonal relationships, it is important for the therapist performing an assessment of past and present relationships to listen as much for what is omitted as for what is said. Failure to elaborate on a current or recent relationship that seems to be important, or the presentation of a relationship in overly idealized terms, may be clues to difficulties that the patient is unwilling to recognize and/or explore in treatment. To understand the interpersonal impact of the patient's depression, it is important to question the patient carefully about ways in which relationships may have changed prior to the onset of depressive symptoms. An understanding of ways in which interpersonal problems may have precipitated the depression, or of ways in which they are involved in preventing recovery, may suggest a strategy for therapy.

GOALS AND STRATEGIES OF TREATMENT

The general goals for treatment of an interpersonal role dispute are, first, to help the patient identify the dispute; then, to guide him or her in making choices about a plan of action; and, finally, to encourage the patient to modify maladaptive communication patterns (if present) or to reassess expectations in order to bring about a satisfactory resolution of the dispute. Improvements in role disputes may result from behavioral changes by the patient and/or the significant other, from attitude changes by the patient (with or without attempts to satisfy needs outside the relationship), or from a satisfactory dissolution of the relationship. IPT therapists have no particular commitment to guiding patients to any particular resolution of difficulties, and they make no attempt to preserve unworkable relationships.

In developing a treatment plan, the therapist first determines the stage of the role dispute as follows: "Renegotiation" implies that the patient and the significant other are openly aware of difficulties and are actively attempting, even if unsuccessfully, to bring about changes. "Impasse" implies that discussion between the patient and the significant other has stopped and that the smoldering, low-level resentment typical of "cold marriages" exists. "Dissolution" implies that the relationship is irretrievably disrupted. The therapist's tasks and expectations at these three stages differ. For example, intervening in an impasse situation may involve increasing apparent disharmony in order to reopen negotiations, while the task of treating a dispute at the stage of unsatisfactory negotiations may be to calm down the participants in order to facilitate conflict resolution. As with treatment of grief described above, the therapist attempts to help the patient to put the relationship in perspective, and even to become free to form new attachments if the role dispute is at the stage of dissolution.

The IPT therapist's general treatment strategy with interpersonal disputes is to help patients understand how nonreciprocal role expectations relate to the disputes and to help them to begin steps that will bring about resolution of disputes and role negotiations. This movement from exploration to action may take place over the entire course of therapy, with early sessions devoted to exploration and communication analysis, and later sessions to systematic review of options for change. In dealing with particular, circumscribed problems, however, the movement from exploration to decision making may take place in a single session.

In exploring a role dispute, the therapist seeks information on different levels. At a practical level, the following questions should be answered: What are the ostensible issues in the dispute? What are the differences in expectations and values between the patient and the significant other? What are the patient's wishes in the relationship? What are the patient's options? What is the likelihood of alternatives coming about? What resources does the patient have at his or her command to bring about change in the relationship?

In understanding the emotional importance of the particular dispute, the therapist attempts to discover parallels in previous relationships. The parallels may be obvious (as in a female patient who repeatedly becomes involved with alcoholic men), or subtle (as in a man who, with apparently disparate individuals and relationships, manipulates others to reject him). When parallels are discovered, the key questions to explore are these: What does the patient gain by this behavior? What are the central unspoken assumptions that lie behind the patient's behavior?

In understanding how disputes are perpetuated, special attention to the interpersonal strategies of the disputants frequently reveals problems in communication patterns. For instance, repetitious, painful disputes are frequently perpetuated when participants are overly afraid of confrontation and expression of negative feelings; they may prefer to ignore solvable problems by simply waiting for things to "blow over."

Finally, helping the patient become aware of his or her personality style (as well as of the style of the significant other) may result in greater acceptance of conflicts, even if disputes recur in truncated form. In brief therapy, a patient may not discover and resolve any unconscious conflicts underlying a tendency toward a pathological personality trait or pattern, such as pathological jealousy of a spouse. However, short of this, the treatment can be helpful if, for example, the patient can come to recognize the irrational nature of these suspicions and to devise strategies for managing these feelings, such as avoiding situations in which they arise or reducing impulsive behavior based on irrational suspicions.

When the patient has developed a sufficiently clear understanding of role disputes, including the part he or she plays in them, the process of decision analysis can be fruitfully taken up. In this process, the therapist's role is not to suggest any particular plan of action, but to assist the patient in considering the consequences of a number of alternatives thoroughly before proceeding.

CASE EXAMPLE OF THE TREATMENT OF ROLE DISPUTES

Initial Assessment (Sessions 1–2)

A.R. was a 28-year-old married Black woman, currently working in her husband's business. Mrs. R., a high school graduate, had been married for 10 years. Her chief complaints were a lack of interest in everything around her, increasing irritability, and marital problems. She stated that her relationship with her husband, M., had deteriorated markedly over the previous 4 or 5 months. She believed that he "took her for granted" and that he was only interested in her insofar as she fulfilled his needs as a sex partner and as an employee. The patient vacillated between self-blame and feelings of helplessness on the one hand, and angry accusations about her husband's inattentiveness and lack of concern for her wishes on the other. Her symptoms included sadness of mood, difficulty in falling asleep, loss of interest, and a profound sense of inadequacy "as a woman." She related her depression to her husband's all-consuming interest in his business and to what she perceived as the resulting change in their relationship.

As Mrs. R. reviewed the history of their marriage, she expressed nostalgia for the "good old days" when they were poor but happy, struggling *together* to make ends meet. She reported feeling increasingly left out since he purchased a business 5 years ago. Exploration of her interpersonal relationships revealed a paucity of social supports. She acknowledged lifelong feelings of loneliness associated with her inability to establish and/or maintain intimate relationships. The family history revealed that she was one of nine children, fathered by six or seven different men. The family was somewhat fragmented. Although they all resided in the same city, she had only minimal contact with her brothers and sisters. She described having felt fairly close to her mother, but this relationship had been somewhat strained by the patient's belief that her mother never really approved of her marriage to M.

The therapist's stance with this patient was unusually active and explicitly supportive. She needed frequent reassurance that psychotherapy was the appropriate treatment for her problems (or, alternatively, that she deserved it), and that her complaints were more than a reflection of her demandingness.

At the end of the first session, the therapist was uncertain as to how to conceptualize the patient in terms of the IPT problem types. Although the social history made it clear that this patient had chronic interpersonal deficits, she presented with the specific problem of an interpersonal role dispute. It seemed advisable to delay the setting of goals until the marital situation was better understood.

A.R. arrived three-quarters of an hour early for her second appointment. In this session, she focused on her ambivalence about her marriage. Although she was only 28, she expressed vague, uneasy feelings that life was passing her by and that she had never accomplished anything on her own. Exploration focused on a comparison of her expectations and the day-to-day reality of being married. A.R. described the gradual process by which she had become more and more dependent upon and controlled by her husband. She related to him as if he were a disapproving father; she was fearful of offending him, yet angry because she seemed unable to please him. She had a severely restricted view of the options available to her—either denying her own wishes in order to please M., or getting out of the marriage. A review of her past relationships revealed a lifelong pattern of withdrawal, denial, and/or indirect communication of her wishes. She seemed to expect others to "know" what she needed, and she felt rejected if her needs were not magically anticipated and met. Her husband had been spending more and more time away from home, supposedly working; A. rather obliquely suggested that she had her doubts about his actual whereabouts, although she was unwilling to articulate her suspicions. In terms of the relationship with her mother, A. spoke sadly of feeling as if she were the least favored child in her family. She tearfully described her brother's large wedding, in sharp contrast to her own, which no one in the family had bothered to attend.

Goal Setting

Much of the work in these sessions focused on communication analysis and on attempts to sort out with Mrs. R. how she thought things would have to change in order for her to be more comfortable in her marriage. Since she voiced a commitment to the marriage, goals were set in terms of working on improving communications between A. and her husband, and of developing some independent interests so she would be less dependent on him to fulfill all of her needs. The treatment strategy followed logically from the identification of the problem type as an interpersonal role dispute (somewhere between the active negotiation phase and the impasse phase).

Initial Phase of Therapy (Sessions 3–4)

Initially, the focus was on the patient's communication problems with her husband. For instance, she described a fight they had had the previous night. Analysis of the communication revealed the manner in which her indirect expression of anger and resentment tended to sabotage any real sharing of feelings. For the first time, she was able to acknowledge that perhaps her customary way of avoiding confrontation on the real issues was contributing to the increased estrangement between them. A. stated that the only time she was able to express what she really wants was when she was angry, but the depth of her rage frightened her and made her feel guilty. She then withdrew into silence but continued to seethe. During these sessions, A.R. started to talk, albeit indirectly, about her suspicions that M. was "fooling around" with a young girl (K.) who worked in the store with them. As if she could not trust her own judgment, she said, "Everybody says it's so but I just can't see it . . . I don't know." She finally acknowledged that M. had had a series of girlfriends over the past few years, but that she felt certain that he would not leave her. The fourth session ended with her assertion that she was going to try to begin to talk to M. about what she expected of him without waiting until she blew up. Typically, however, she said, "But, you'll see . . . it won't work."

Intermediate Phase of Therapy (Sessions 5–8)

A. began the fifth session by giving the therapist a letter her husband had written to her the previous night. In it he talked about his love for A., his sadness about their deteriorating marriage, and his frustration about his seeming inability to "turn things around." The therapist was quite moved by the letter, but, when this feeling was shared with the patient, A. expressed doubts about her husband's sincerity in writing the letter: "I just can't get myself to believe it—it seems he just wants to get me where he wants me, and then it just starts all over again." When it was suggested that M. participate in one session, the patient became quite restless and said, "I don't want to talk about him any more. I just want to talk about my probems." When the therapist commented that the two were somewhat related, she countered with, "He won't come anyway—I know him." Most of this session was spent in exploring her seeming unwillingness to ask M. to come in, but she finally agreed to do so.

Mr. and Mrs. R. were then seen conjointly. The communication problems that A. had reported in previous sessions were played out in this hour. She remained silent for most of the hour, allowing her husband to do most of the talking. When the therapist tried to involve her, she reluctantly began to talk about her complaints, but with great hesitancy. With great difficulty, she finally confronted him about his involvement with the salesgirl, K., which he unconvincingly denied. By the end of the hour, they had begun to talk to each other more directly.

Following the conjoint session, there was a marked change in A.R.'s appearance. She had, until this time, appeared rather shabby and sullen and had usually been dressed in black. She started wearing bright colors, and her overall attitude took on a bright, confident quality. She described their social activities and their improved life as a couple. They had gone out to dinner a couple of times, and had visited with relatives with whom they had not socialized for a long time. Although she acknowledged feeling some satisfaction with this broadening of their activities, she nevertheless continued to express doubt about her husband's motives. She described several occasions in which she felt rebuffed when she had begun to tell him about her wishes. What was most impressive, however, was her determination to "let him know what's on my mind whether he wants to hear it or not." A. also spoke about her fear that people (especially her family) might think that she was "uppity" since she and M. had become financially secure. She described her humble background and her own discomfort with M.'s new "classy" ways. Whereas M. enjoyed his success and the respect it afforded him in the community, A. felt somewhat embarrassed by it because it seemed to represent yet another barrier separating her from her family and former friends.

At the eighth session, A. reported having been "depressed and confused" the previous week. Initially she could offer no explanation for the worsening of her depression, but she implied that she had "something" on her mind. She stated that, although she believed therapy was helping her, she wondered if perhaps she was "trying to progress too fast." After talking rather disjointedly about her "ups and downs" and her feelings of confusion, she finally commented that what she really wanted to talk about was "the girl" (K.). She wanted desperately to believe her husband when he assured her that there was nothing more than friendship between K. and him. However, M.'s mother had been needling A. and telling her to "keep an eye on those two," and this had aroused her suspicions again. A. was finally able to relate these events to her feelings of depression during the previous week. It was also in this hour that A., for the first time, was able to recognize and explore her maladaptive patterns of communication on her own. Her relatively introspective stance in regard to her tendency to cut off communication was impressive, considering her previous tendency to blame her difficulties on external factors.

Much of the discussion in these middle sessions was directed at exploring A. and M.'s efforts to reestablish some contact with each other and with their families. Toward the end of the eighth hour, she asked how many therapy sessions remained, and she acknowledged her anxiety about termination. Her husband called in the following week to cancel A.'s appointment because "A. is sick and she didn't want to call you herself."

Termination (Sessions 9–12)

At the next scheduled session, A. once again started to talk about difficulties with her husband. Both the content and the quality of her comments were reminiscent of the first sessions. She catalogued her complaints about M. and the way in which he took her for granted. The relatively introspective stance of the previous sessions had all but disappeared. Midway into the hour, however, A. became quiet and appeared somewhat thoughtful. She finally said, "I'm scared to show M. my love, that's all it is." In discussing these feelings, she commented almost casually that M. had been talking about getting a divorce. Despite her insistence that she really did not take it seriously, it appeared to have a disorganizing effect on her functioning. Toward the end of the hour, A. again raised the issue of termination and voiced her concern about not yet feeling strong enough to go it on her own. In addition to her very real concerns about the marriage, her fragmented presentation in this hour seemed to be her way of saying, "I'm not ready."

In the following session, A. described an incident at the store in which a male customer came in and complimented her on her appearance. She responded with sarcasm. In trying to explain her response, she acknowledged that she tended to "put herself down" and therefore to assume that others who praised her were merely teasing her. "I don't feel nice-looking or glamorous." This led to a discussion of her sense of inadequacy as a woman: "It's like I told M. the other day, I feel like I'm less a woman. You know, I try to observe women, you know, how the other women carry theirself . . . like nothing bothers them—you know; I don't carry myself that way." What emerged from this discussion was that, even though the friction between A. and her husband appeared to have diminished, she was once again feeling somewhat depressed.

These feelings were related to termination, but she had a tendency to avoid the issue or to deny that she had any special feelings about it. She brought in a box of cookies and commented that Christmas shopping had not turned out to be as unpleasant as she had anticipated. A. then commented that she and M. had been arguing more frequently. Part of the conflict seemed to focus on his desire to have a baby and A.'s ambivalence about being tied down further. She also voiced her fear that he might leave her if she had a baby. This was not unjustified, since both M.'s father and A.'s had, in fact, abandoned their families. It was interesting that, despite the increase in overt arguments between them, A. reported feeling less depressed than she had been previously. She acknowledged that "letting it out is better than keeping the stuff inside." At the final session, A. appeared extremely agitated, and attempts to explore her feelings about the termination were responded to with denial and thinly disguised anger. Three days after this stormy termination session, however, A. telephoned to "apologize" and to inform the therapist that she was, in fact, feeling better after all. A referral was offered for further treatment, but A. said, "I think I'd like to try it on my own."

Summary and Conclusion

For A.R., role disputes with her husband arose out of conflicting interests and role definitions that resulted from his business success. Mrs. R. perceived her husband's involvement in the business as an attempt to get away from her, and she felt inadequate to fill the role of a financially successful man's wife. The changes that had taken place in her marriage exacerbated but did not create her long-standing feelings of low self-esteem, her lack of assertiveness, her paucity of social skills, and her excessive dependency needs.

During evaluation, it was discovered that, regardless of the issues involved, Mrs. R. failed to communicate adequately demands, anger, or affection to her husband. She had withdrawn from him and had cut off meaningful discussions. Whenever possible, IPT therapists attempt to focus on specific areas of behavior in current interpersonal relationships in which change can take place in a short time. Thus, it seemed most logical to concentrate treatment efforts on opening up negotiations between Mrs. R. and her husband. No attempt was made to explore the origins of her chronic low self-esteem directly or to understand *why* she communicated as she did. Rather, the focus was on *how* she failed to communicate and how she could change this.

In the course of treatment, the patient made considerable progress in dealing with her husband more directly and in understanding her own part in maintaining the distance between them. Her depressive symptoms had abated somewhat, and she took a more active role in solving her own problems in other areas of her life. Her difficulty in acknowledging feelings at the time of termination is representative of long-standing problems in forming and giving up intimate relationships—personality issues that remained unresolved at the end of the treatment. However, this therapy did bring about changes in a number of behaviors under her conscious control, such as communication, and these changes may have been sufficient to enable her to mitigate the effect of self-destructive tendencies on her interpersonal interactions.

ROLE TRANSITIONS

DEFINITION AND DESCRIPTION

Depressions associated with role transitions occur when patients experience great difficulty in trying to cope with life changes. Role-transition problems are most commonly associated with changes that are perceived by the patient as losses. The transition may be immediately apparent, as in the case of divorce, or it may be more symbolic, as with the sense of loss of freedom following the birth of a child or a change in social or professional status. In either case, patients feel unable to cope with these role changes, possibly because the situations are experienced as threatening to their self-esteem and senses of identity. In general, patients' difficulties in coping with role transitions are associated with the following issues: (1) loss of familiar social supports; (2) management of accompanying affect (e.g., anger or fear); (3) demands for a new repertoire of social skills; and (4) cognitive factors (e.g., diminished self-esteem or a sense of anomie).

Individuals hold multiple roles in the social system, and these roles become indelibly interwoven with the sense of self. The roles held by individuals, as well as the status attached to these roles, have an important influence on the individual's social behavior and patterns of interpersonal relationships. Impairment in social functioning frequently occurs in response to demands on the individual for rapid adaptation to new and initially strange roles, especially to roles that are perceived by the individual as representing diminished status.

Individuals undoubtedly differ in their overall vulnerability to the stress associated with role transitions. In addition, individuals differ in regard to the particular *kinds* of changes that are likely to produce stress, depending on the "meaning" of the event to the individual's self-esteem. For example, a lawyer whose sense of fulfillment and self-esteem is derived largely from his professional affiliations may not be as likely to be affected by a divorce as his wife may be, particularly if her status in the community and sense of identity are derived in large part from being "Attorney _____'s wife." In general, women tend to be more vulnerable to role transitions involving separations. Because of the way in which women are socialized, their sense of identity is more frequently derived from their connections to other people (e.g., as wife, mother). By the same token, role changes resulting from retirement are likely to place greater stresses on men than on women, since the socialization of men in our society places great emphasis on achievement and instrumentality.

DIAGNOSIS OF ROLE-TRANSITION PROBLEMS

In order for the therapist to choose role-transition problems as the focus of treatment, there must be evidence that recent events in the life of the patient have produced major changes in the patient's constellation of roles. Evidence of change per se is not necessarily predictive of problems in the area of role transition. It is the significance of the change to the individual, as reflected in impaired interpersonal relationships and reduced self-esteem, that is associated with depression. It is essential, therefore, that the therapist carefully investigate both the factual nature of the changes in the patient's life style and, even more importantly, the impact these changes have had on the patient in terms of social supports, role definition, and the affects associated with the transition.

For IPT, two components of role-transition problems are distinguished: (1) the patient's feelings about the actual person or thing that has been lost (e.g., spouse, job), and (2) the patient's reaction to the concomitant role changes occasioned by the loss. The former is similar to a grief reaction in that the patient is unable to deal with the loss as such and tends to remain fixated around the lost *object*. It is the second component of the role-transition problem, involving the inability to cope with the *change* itself, that distinguishes this problem from a traditional grief reaction. For example, a patient presenting for treatment following the dissolution of her marriage may report that her marriage was intolerable for many years, and that it was in fact she who initiated the divorce proceedings, with the expectation that her life would markedly improve if only she could extricate herself from an essentially "impossible relationship." Following the divorce, however, she may find that her married female friends, who have hitherto been an important source of support, begin to withdraw from her because they perceive her as a threat to their own marriages. In addition, the patient may experience feelings of inadequacy as a mother because her children seem to blame her for "sending Daddy away." She begins to feel increasingly unable to discipline her teenage children now that her husband is no longer providing "backup." Feeling lonely, abandoned, inadequate, and deprived of her usual social supports, she seeks treatment. What distinguishes this patient's problem from a grief reaction is that she is not mourning her husband so much as her former *role* of "married woman"; her depression is not related to the separation from her husband as such, but to her difficulty in coping with the transition from the role of wife and mother to the role of single parent.

Ordinarily, patients with role-transition problems will spontaneously relate their depression to the recent change in their life situation. However, they may not be aware of the connection between the psychological significance of the change and their diminished self-esteem. As the therapist explores such a patient's perception of the old and new role requirements and the feelings associated with each, he or she will be better able to formulate a realistic treatment plan.

GOALS AND STRATEGIES OF TREATMENT

The two general goals in the treatment of depression associated with role transitions are (1) to enable the patient to regard the new role in a more positive, less restrictive manner, perhaps as an opportunity for growth; and (2) to restore self-esteem by developing in the patient a sense of mastery vis-à-vis the demands of the new role-related attitudes and behaviors.

Abnormal grief and role-transition problems have much in common, in that both involve a reaction to a life change, frequently associated with a loss of some kind. Thus, the IPT strategies and techniques for dealing with problems associated with giving up old roles are similar to those recommended for grief (see pp. 111–120). The therapeutic tasks are to facilitate the patient's realistic evaluation of what has been lost; to encourage the appropriate expression of affect; and, finally, to help the patient develop a social support system and the repertoire of social skills that are called for in the new role.

The therapist will help the patient in a systematic review of the positive and negative aspects of both the old role and possible new roles. Patients will frequently feel frightened by the change itself, and, as a result, will tend to romanticize the positive aspects of what has been lost. For this reason, they need to be encouraged to explore the opportunities offered in the new role. As a rule, patients' resistances to change make it difficult for them to imagine themselves functioning efficiently in different ways. The therapist must actively support these patients as they gradually disengage themselves from the familiar old roles and begin to venture out into new, and as yet unexplored, ways of feeling and behaving.

CASE EXAMPLE OF THE TREATMENT OF ROLE TRANSITIONS

Initial Assessment (Sessions 1–3)

E.F. was a 27-year-old married working mother of a 6-year-old son, who presented for treatment 3 weeks after a suicide attempt with a combination of nonprescription medications. The precipitant of this had been the end of her first extramarital affair. She had been chronically dissatisfied with her marriage of 10 years to an ungiving alcoholic husband who provided her with steady financial support but little affection or interest. Moreover, when the husband was drinking, which occurred several times weekly, he was verbally and sometimes physically abusive. The patient's extramarital affair "made me realize what I had been missing." The affair had lasted only a few months when the boyfriend returned to another woman. The patient felt abandoned and hopeless, making an impulsive suicide attempt immediately after getting the news. She was treated in an emergency room and sent home. Following this, she developed a moderate level of depressive symptoms, which persisted 3 weeks before she sought professional psychiatric help. This was her first depressive episode.

Mrs. F. saw her depression as clearly related to her conflict over ending the marriage. She had left her husband for a 2-month period several years previously, but had taken him back, as his treatment of her improved when they were apart. However, old patterns were quickly resumed, and Mrs. F. felt trapped again in her marriage. She stated that she hoped treatment might "help me to leave him." She stated that she deserved better treatment than she received from her husband, but felt unsure that she could actually make the break. She was currently feeling apathetic, anhedonic, and pessimistic that any positive changes could take place.

Mrs. F. and a sister 5 years younger had been raised by a domineering, passive–aggressive mother, her father having left the family for another woman when the patient was 6 years old. Her mother had not become reinvolved with other men, and she recalled feeling that the entire family seemed to her to be unattractive, outcast women who could not gain the attention of a supportive man. This was in contrast, at least, to her own actual personal attractiveness and social abilities; she herself had been a popular and good student throughout her high school years. Her mother's relationship with her, however, had been overwhelming and excessively close, and marriage to her current husband at the age of 17 had been seen as a welcome opportunity to leave home. However, this had not completely interrupted her mother's intrusiveness into her affairs. She still had qualms about contradicting her mother, and she felt that this was also something that she would like to work on in treatment.

By the second session, the patient had asked her husband to leave the house; he had willingly agreed, expressing his own discontentment with the marriage. The patient felt an initial elation at this and reported an improvement in depressive symptoms. She also described being surprisingly free of conflict about breaking up with her husband, in that she had been thinking of doing this for several years. She also described starting to become more forthright and direct with her mother in disagreements about such things as when she would take a vacation. These two sessions were largely taken up by reviewing in detail her relationship to both her husband and her mother. From this discussion, it emerged that E. avoided taking responsibility for her decisions and got others, such as her mother or her husband, to make them for her. She tended to mistrust her own judgment and was hesitant to think through issues clearly. Related to her discomfort with taking responsibility for herself was her conviction that losing her man (or getting him to leave) would mean being unattractive, unwomanly, and devalued, as she felt her mother and she had been after her father had left. Her pattern of becoming involved with a man was to get involved and to stay with the man at all costs, overlooking the man's faults. She also expressed fears of being alone, however, having never lived on her own as the head of a household.

Therapeutic Strategy

From the information gathered in the first three sessions, it was decided that the focus of therapy would be on helping E.F. to manage the role transitions involved in separating from her husband. It was anticipated that this would involve the following steps: (1) helping her to identify new sources of support outside of her husband and her husband's family; (2) exploring and correcting her irrational fears of being alone and her tendency to mistrust her own judgments; (3) assisting her as she developed a new repertoire of social skills, such as managing the discipline of her child; and (4) helping her to recognize the distinction between her own value and the value of having a man, any man. It was decided to treat her case as one of role transitions, rather than one of role disputes, because of the patient's conviction that the differences between her and her husband were irreconcilable and her professed certainty that she wanted out of the marriage.

Intermediate Phase of Therapy (Sessions 4–9)

The patient at first felt very good about her separation from her husband. In search of alternative sources of support, she initially turned to her extended family, including her in-laws and her mother, who directly or indirectly encouraged her to get back together with her husband (by describing, for instance, how "pathetic" he seemed to be without her). She realized that seeking help from these people had contributed to her getting back together with her husband previously, and she began to deepen her friendships with women friends with whom she had previously been less involved. Before the fifth session, the husband had called on her, asking her to take him back; she had flatly refused, particularly as she noted that he had been drinking at the time of the request. The therapist then engaged her in a clear consideration of her alternatives in regard to a reconciliation—in particular, discussing the circumstances under which she would find reconciling an acceptable thing to do. From this, it emerged that she felt that under no circumstances would she be willing to take him back.

About 4 weeks after separating from her husband, she began to date again and found this a positive experience, although she felt strange at having to reconsider what she wanted and expected from men that she dated, not having gone out casually with men for over 10 years. Coincident with the dating, she began to have troubles with her 6-year-old son, who was beginning to act up at school and at home. She revealed that she had tended to leave the disciplinary activities up to her husband and that she had been uncomfortable about discussing the separation with her son. Parts of several sessions were spent discussing in detail ways in which she related to her son, ways in which she could talk to her son about the separation, and alternative approaches to discipline. The result was that the son displayed improved behavior both at home and at school, and she began to feel a greater closeness to him. From the fifth to the ninth sessions, the patient's symptoms were somewhat abated. She still had good and bad days, but she stated that the anhedonic, lethargic, hopeless feelings had passed.

As the patient continued to date new men and started to become interested in one of them, she examined in therapy her original attraction to her husband. He was "safe" because he had become so dependent on her early and because he was so "pathetic" without her. She realized that she seemed attracted to men who were quickly and unconditionally interested in her, because she felt so fearful of being rejected by men. As a result, she was not very discriminating about the men she became involved with, and had previously been quite hesitant to become clear with herself about what she wanted from a relationship with a man. She also began to discuss with the therapist early signs she might use to help her detect similar nonproductive patterns in her future relationships with men.

Termination (Sessions 11-13)

As the end of treatment approached, the patient began to experience feelings of emptiness and boredom and a sense that her life was going nowhere. She did not relate this to the end of treatment, but spoke principally of her reemerging sense of worthlessness in living without a man, even if this was recognized as not necessarily a permanent situation. More material about her adolescent feelings of self-condemnation and worthlessness at growing up without a father was discussed at this time, and the patient also began to talk about such dismaying things as growing older and becoming more ugly. The therapist related these feelings to the termination and the patient's fears of being on her own, and tried to contrast the patient's fears with her actual level of competence and indicators of her attractiveness. At this time, the husband made a renewed attempt to induce the patient to take him back. Although tempted, she again reminded herself of the old patterns and decided that, even though she felt lonely and unhappy now, she would be condemning herself to a more enduring unhappiness if she resumed the marriage. In the final session, she reviewed the changes she had made, including her improved relationship with her child, her growing circle of friends (both male and female), her dating, her greater ability to communicate her needs and her disagreements with others, and her improved sense of independence and competence. On the basis of this, she concluded that she did not want to resume her old life, even if she had to put up with a certain amount of loneliness that separation brought her.

INTERPERSONAL DEFICITS

DEFINITION AND DESCRIPTION

Interpersonal deficits are chosen as the focus of treatment when a patient presents with a history of social impoverishment involving inadequate or unsustaining interpersonal relationships. These patients may never have established lasting or intimate relationships as adults and have frequently experienced severe disruptions of important relationships as children. In general, patients who present with a history of severe social isolation tend to be more severely disturbed than do those with other presenting problems.

DIAGNOSIS OF INTERPERSONAL DEFICITS

Optimal social functioning would include close relationships with intimates or family members, less intense but satisfying relationships with friends and acquaintances, and adequate performance and relationships in some sort of work role. It may be useful to distinguish three types of patients with interpersonal deficits:

1. Those who are *socially isolated* and lack relationships with either intimates, friends, or a work role. These patients may have long-standing or temporary deficiencies in social skills.
2. Those who have an adequate number and range of relationships but who are *socially unfulfilled*. Such individuals may have chronic low self-esteem, despite apparent interpersonal or occupational success, or they may complain angrily about chronic exhaustion that results from repeatedly taking on more than they can manage.
3. Those who are *chronically depressed* from a lingering depressive episode that was untreated or inadequately treated in the past. Although some of such patients' acute symptoms may have resolved, persistent multiple symptoms of low intensity continue to cause distress. For these patients, interpersonal functioning may have become impaired only after the onset of an apparently unprecipitated depressive episode. In such individuals, role impairment may take place in one or a number of

roles, but this difficulty has not led to disputes with the significant other.

Persons with interpersonal deficits may become depressed during periods of change or transition, when the absence of satisfying social relations becomes more critical.

GOALS AND STRATEGIES OF TREATMENT

The goal of treatment of interpersonal deficits is to reduce the patients' social isolation. Because many of these patients have no current meaningful relationships, the focus of treatment is on past relationships, the relationship with the therapist, and the tentative formation of new relationships.

Review of past significant relationships, particularly childhood relationships with family members, assumes a greater importance with these patients. As each relationship is reviewed, it is important to determine about each both the best and the worst part of the relationship discussed. Discussion of past relationships at their best may provide a model for helping the patient to develop satisfying new relationships. For example:

B.A., a highly withdrawn 28-year-old man, although having broken off contact with his parents in his late teens, remembered with satisfaction the task-oriented work that he and his father were able to perform together. Although he was unable to enjoy socializing with others in unstructured situations, he was able to reduce his isolation by taking a volunteer job at a local hospital.

Detailed evaluation of failed relationships or of past interpersonal difficulties may alert the therapist to predictable problem areas that may arise in new relationships. The therapist should look for regularities in the kinds of situations that lead to difficulty for the patient and should help the patient identify these situations, with the hope either of avoiding them in the future or of working on gradual resolution of these difficulties. For example:

F.E., a 30-year-old woman, had closed herself off from social contacts with others and had lost a job, largely because of her extreme anxiety at interacting socially with more than two to three people at a time. In these circumstances, she felt excluded, disliked, and anxious—feelings related to her early family situation. She developed psychophysiological symptoms in group situations and absented herself in an embarrassing manner on many occasions. On identifying the specific nature of her problem, the patient was able to find more acceptable employment in a small business in which she had frequent interactions with only one boss, and was able to reduce her isolation somewhat by entertaining friends at home one at a time.

For socially isolated patients, the attention paid to the patient–therapist relationship is more important than for patients with other types of problems. This relationship provides the therapist with the most direct data about such a patient's style of relating to others. In addition, solving problems that arise in the patient–therapist relationship may provide a model for the patient to follow in developing intimacy in other relationships. Of particular importance is the open discussion of the patient's distorted or unrealistic negative feelings about the therapist or the therapy. Typically, such patients prefer severing relationships to openly confronting other persons and resolving issues. For example:

K.A., a 24-year-old man, was particularly silent at the beginning of the seventh session and began to discuss quitting. He stated that he did not think that he could be helped. When the therapist asked whether he had been upset about something the therapist had done or not done, he replied that the therapist was just acting as others had previously done by rejecting him. When asked to explain what he meant, it turned out that the patient had completely misheard an encouraging statement the therapist had made. The patient was then relieved both that he had discovered his mistake and that he had communicated his complaint to the therapist. This interchange also provided the basis for more extended discussion of the patient's generally inhibited communication with others.

For a patient with interpersonal impoverishment, dealing with negative feelings toward the therapist not only provides a model of interpersonal learning, but also acts as a safety valve to prevent the patient from terminating therapy prematurely because of some imagined slight.

In helping these patients apply the learning taking place in treatment to outside situations, therapists may make extensive use of *communication analysis* and *role playing*. When patients have attempted, successfully or unsuccessfully, to increase their interactions with others, a detailed review of these attempts may reveal easily correctable deficits in the patients' communication skills. In helping the patients overcome their hesitations in approaching others, therapists may invite the patients to role-play difficult situations with them.

In conclusion, it should be emphasized that the brief treatment of interpersonal deficits is a most difficult task, and, therefore, goal setting should be limited to "starting" to work on these issues, not necessarily extended to solving them.

CONCLUSION

We have described common problem areas presented by depressed patients and the methods for handling them in short-term IPT. This approach is currently being developed further in two ways. First, although originally used as treatment of primary unipolar depressives, it is being adapted for use with depressed drug abusers maintained on methodone, for whom issues of role transitions and interpersonal deficits assume greater importance. A controlled clinical trial of IPT with this population is currently under way. Second, the use of IPT with primary depressives will be further tested in a multicenter collaborative psychotherapy study sponsored by the National Institute of Mental Health. In this clinical trial, IPT alone and in combination with antidepressants will be compared with cognitive therapy (Beck, 1976) and antidepressant medication in an attempt to replicate and expand on previous work by ascertaining whether the treatments are differentially applicable and effective with specific subtypes of depressed patients.

ACKNOWLEDGMENTS

This research was supported by grants MH26466 and MH26467 from the Clinical Research Branch, National Institute of Mental Health, Alcohol, Drug Abuse and Mental Health Administration.

This work has involved the efforts of many people over the years, particularly Gerald L. Klerman, MD, who developed the original IPT manual; Myrna M. Weissman, PhD, who led the New Haven portion of the New Haven–Boston Collaborative Project; the late Alberto DiMascio, PhD, who led the Boston portion of this project; Brigitte Prusoff, PhD, who was in charge of the data analysis for the two clinics; and Carlos Neu, MD, who assisted in the earlier versions of the IPT manual.

REFERENCES

Beck, A. *Cognitive therapy and the emotional disorders*. New York: International Universities Press, 1976.

Frank, J. D. Psychotherapy: The restoration of morale. *American Journal of Psychiatry*, 1974, *131*, 271–274.

Hollister, L. E. Tricyclic antidepressants. I. *New England Journal of Medicine*, 1978, *299*, 1106–1109.

Horowitz, M. J. *Stress response syndrome*. New York: Jason Aronson, 1976.

Klerman, G. L., Rounsaville, B., Chevron, E. S., Neu, C., & Weissman, M. M. *Manual for short-term interpersonal psychotherapy (IPT) of depression*. Unpublished manuscript, 1979.

Lindemann, E. Symptomatology and management of acute grief. *American Journal of Psychiatry*, 1944, *101*, 141–148.

Rounsaville, B. J., Weissman, M. M., Prusoff, B. A., & Herceg-Baron, R. Marital disputes and treatment outcome in depressed women. *Comprehensive Psychiatry*, 1979, *20*, 483–490.

Siggins, L. Mourning: A critical survey of the literature. *International Journal of Psychoanalysis*, 1966, *47*, 14–25.

‡6‡

COGNITIVE THERAPY: THEORY AND RESEARCH

A. JOHN RUSH
DONNA E. GILES

INTRODUCTION

The cognitive theory (Beck 1967, 1976) has provided a more heuristic approach to depression. Three elements of psychological function are viewed as critical in the development and maintenance of depression: concepts of self, world, and future (the cognitive triad); logical errors; and schemas. Views of self, world, and future are systematically and negatively distorted in such a way that external events are construed to represent loss and/or deprivation. The logic of depressed persons is characterized by errors in drawing inferences about the self, future, and world from daily observations. "Schemas"—rules or silent assumptions—represent organizing principles for screening and encoding information. These rules are based largely on early learning experiences, and are said to account for an ongoing vulnerability to relapse (Beck & Rush, 1978; Rush & Beck, 1977).

DEFINING DEPRESSION

As detailed in Chapter 1 of this volume, "depression" may represent a mood (sadness), a symptom (e.g., as seen in endocrinopathies), a syndrome, or a disease. The mood "depression" can be a normal

A. John Rush and Donna E. Giles. Department of Psychiatry, University of Texas Health Science Center at Dallas, Dallas, Texas.

response to stress or loss and occurs in almost everyone. As a symptom, depression is associated with a number of medical and psychiatric disorders, and as a syndrome, depression has been associated with a large number of symptoms by at least one theoretician or clinician in each case. Watts (1966) recorded 71 different symptoms in a survey of 590 office-treated depressed patients. A review of 16 depression measurement instruments (Levitt & Lubin, 1975) generated a list of 54 symptoms deemed depression-related, including such items as anger, lack of anger, readiness to cry, stoicism, guilty concern for others, lack of interest in others, agitation, and retardation.

Kraepelin (1913) formulated two types of depression: manic–depression and exogenous depression. While exogenous depression has been assigned a psychosocial etiology by some in recent time, Kraepelin held that *both* types of depression were primarily organic in origin. Manic–depression developed from organic degeneration or genetic determinants, while exogenous depression presupposed bacterial, chemical, or other toxins. His system was revised to include involutional melancholia—depression in which agitation and age range were dominant diagnostic features. In the last two decades, manic depression has been thought by some to include two distinct subtypes: unipolar recurrent and bipolar depressions. In addition, controversy persists as to whether exogenous depressions are psychosocially or biologically determined.

The issue of whether depressions are indeed meaningfully heterogeneous or are simply different manifestions of a single disease entity continues as a point of academic debate with serious clinical implications. One group of theoreticians espouses a unitary conceptualization (e.g., Lewis, 1934, 1938; Kendell, 1968; Paskind, 1930), and another group argues for a binary viewpoint (e.g., Kiloh & Garside, 1963; Kraepelin, 1913; Sandifer, Wilson, & Green, 1966). Several systems for subdividing the depressions have been proposed (see Chapter 1). The endogenous versus exogenous distinction was noted as long ago as 1586 by Timothy Bright. Autonomous versus reactive depression (Gillespie, 1929); agitated versus retarded depression; bipolar plus severity axes (Eysenck, 1970); primary versus secondary depression (Robins & Guze, 1972); and treatment-response-based systems (Klein, 1974) all represent examples of systems to classify depression into meaningful subdivisions. No commonly agreed-upon system has yet been derived.

Beck and other cognitive theorists have aligned themselves with the unitary position. Depression is seen as a continuum in which severity is a quantitative accumulation of symptoms generated primarily by negative cognitive distortions (Beck, 1976). With "depression" so defined—that is, depression as an affective disturbance primarily accounted for by cognitive factors—theoretical and practical research and development become focused.

COGNITION AND BEHAVIOR

In the 20th century, theoretical formulations for understanding the process of depression have been diverse. The century began with Freudian theory, prompting some to view psychopathology from other than a model of medical disease. Childhood development as it affected the adult personality was emphasized, as were social and cultural factors. Early psychoanalytic writers viewed depression as an attempt at reparation; the loss of a loved object and the attending psychic injury led to self-punishment. Depression was understood as intense narcissistic cravings, ambivalence, introjection, self-accusation, and subconscious oral and anal symbolism in dreams and fantasies (Mendelson, 1974). Freud (1917/1959) wrote that the melancholic depressive senses personal loss and humiliation from a significant other, but cannot tolerate his or her own aggressive impulses at being wounded. By psychologically incorporating the other within the self, the melancholic symbolically punishes the other by the ego's own suffering.

In radical opposition to the inferential nature of psychoanalytic thought, the stimulus–response position proposed to account for all forms of behavior (e.g., Watson, 1913). The unconscious was considered a reified hypothetical construct and was abandoned. All dysfunction was referenced to external contingencies. Skinner (1938) updated this fundamental notion. He contended that the contents of the "black box" or mind cannot be known at this time because of human inability to measure subjective experience reliably. Research should be directed at ascertaining salient features of an observable stimulus event and at recording and characterizing emitted responses. Thus, altering the stimulus and/or response conditions becomes the method of clinical change. This position generated both controversy and promise for theoreticians and clinicians. Because of its exclusive reliance on objectively observable events, many important questions remained unanswered.

Existential psychology developed in reaction to the ontological inadequacies of both behavioral and Freudian theories. According to this school, it is essential that the study of humanity be contextually relevant to the subject. That is, humanness has meaning; hence, the study of humanness has meaning, but only if it is allowed to remain intact. Science can only enhance understanding when it is maintained within the context of the holistic development of the self and subjective reality. Depression represents an individual reaction to attack on the essence of the self, to the subjective experience of threat, or to nonacceptance of the self by another through external judgment.

Although behavioral, psychoanalytic, and existential schools have historically differed with regard to the relative weight assigned different psychological determinants, recent writings suggest that these theories may share a common emphasis on the importance of subjective perceptions of reality. Early psychoanalytic thinkers emphasized unconscious drives as essential determinants of affective and behavioral responses, and they focused particularly on the *affective* unconscious. More contemporary ego psychoanalytic thinkers have forsaken the emphasis on sexual and aggressive drives and have turned toward the *cognitive* unconscious (Weiner, 1975) as an important source of motivation (Klein, 1970).

Within the behavioral camp, the cognitive-behaviorists are now contending that subjective events, such as thoughts and images, should now be included as data sources. For example, Bowers (1973) argues for an interactionist approach to subjective and environmental events, while others (e.g., Lazarus, 1971; Mahoney, 1974) have become increasingly militant in directing research efforts toward subjective conceptualizations of ongoing experiences. Behavior-therapy research has begun to show that environmental events, although important, are not sufficient to explain behavioral patterns. These events must be considered within the context of subjective interpretation (Meichenbaum, 1974). Furthermore, recent evidence suggests that conditioning does not occur automatically and appears to be cognitively mediated, at least in humans (Bandura, 1974; Brewer, 1974).

Existential psychology epitomizes a subjectivisitic approach to understanding behavior. It has long insisted that an individual's *interpretation* of the internal and external environment are primary. Development of generalizable and testable hypotheses has not followed, however. Although the existentialists argue that a component analysis of human behavior denies organism wholeness, such an analysis, while it may oversimplify certain aspects of human behavior, does not ipso facto destroy humanness.

Thus, recent trends in the psychoanalytic, behavioral, and existential schools would appear to have to share a common focus on the individual's representational reality as a critical element in understanding human behavior and conducting psychotherapy.

Cognitive theory places heavy emphasis on subjective reality, and it provides a descriptive, testable model of psychological dysfunction. This idea is not entirely new. At the turn of the century, Adler (in Ansbacher & Ansbacher, 1956) coined the term "phenomenal field" to refer to the ongoing conscious experience of an individual from a personal perspective. This construct assumes that behavior derives from a subjective representation of reality, the "phenomenal field," which itself derives from early developmental experiences. Subsequently, Kelly (1955) gave further theoretical impetus to a cognitive formulation of human experience. In emphasizing "personal constructs" (specific psychological dimensions that define a person's view of internal and external events), he pioneered a testable account of human behavior and laid the groundwork for the cognitive theory and therapy that followed.

EMOTION

Emotion represents a complex response made up of three components: perception, physiological changes, and cognition. Perception involves sensory feedback indicating a change in the environment. Physiological changes include neuronal activation and/or inhibition of respiration, heartbeat, muscle tone, and circulation. Cognition entails the process of interpreting and labeling the experience as threatening, surprising, fearful, joyous, and so on. Theorists generally agree that emotion is an interaction of all three components, but the specific sequence to these processes remains an area of controversy.

The James–Lange theory of emotion (1884; cited in Cannon, 1927; Goldstein, 1968) stimulated a dramatic reconceptualization of emotional responding. Independently, both James (1884) and Lange proposed that physiological responses occur concurrently with perception, and that cognitions follow to account for these responses.

Based on observations of the physiological effects of cortical and thalamic lesions, Cannon (1927) proposed an alternative model.

Within his framework, afferent messages prepare the thalamus for activation and stimulate the cortex, where, on the basis of past learning (defined as sensitized neural pathways), the thalamus may be released from inhibition. The thalamus then sends messages downward to activate skeletal muscles and viscera, and upward to the cortex, providing the conscious experience of emotion. Although current thought suggests that limbic-system activation rather than thalamic activation is related to emotion (Brady, 1958), the form and sequencing of Cannon's theoretical structure continues to be generally accepted.

Marston (1928) emphasized greater cortical involvement in emotion. Marston contended that emotions were not experienced as sensations, but, rather, that emotions were centrally mediated. In contrast to the notion that emotions result from complex sensations derived from peripheral afferent feedback, Marston suggested that emotions were direct awareness of central reactions.

Recent research provides support for this emphasis on the central as opposed to the peripheral nervous system. Visceral organs are relatively insensitive to stimulation, and, when responses are identified, they are almost instantaneous. Recent experiments suggest that anger is associated with increased epinephrine secretion, whereas fear coincides with increased epinephrine secretion (Goldstein, 1968). While this finding might point toward explicit, definable biological mechanisms that relate to particular emotional and cognitive processes, its relevance to psychopathological conditions is unknown.

The precise relationship between emotion and cognition remains unclear at present. Schachter and Singer (1962) and Singer (1973) focused on the interaction between emotion and cognition. Emotions and cognitions are said to be initiated in the infant's response to a novel and changing environment (Singer, 1973). "Interest" is stimulated by novelty, which serendipitously maintains exploration and accommodation. Successful accommodation of novelty reduces excitement, whereas failure to accommodate novelty activates distress, startles, or creates fear. Thus, affective processing and cognitive processing interact from the beginning. As biological development ensues, cognitive functions are heuristically elaborated to provide greater assimilation and control over both internal and external stimuli, including emotional stimulation. Increasing ability to appraise, interpret, and evaluate emotion contributes to the meaning and purpose of control over human function.

Thus, a greater emphasis on cognition has evolved over the 20th century, although the role of cognition in emotional responses continues to be controversial. Against this background, Beck (1967) proposed a cognitive theoretical framework of depression, which was to revolutionize both theoretical and practical approaches to these psychopathological conditions.

THE COGNITIVE THEORY OF DEPRESSION

Beck's congnitive theory of depression (1967, 1974, 1976) evolved from his initial attempts to test psychoanalytic theory empirically by study of depressed patients' dreams. He found that these dreams included themes of disappointment, injury, punishment, incompetence, or ugliness. As interpreted by Freud, these dream themes reflected wish fulfillment (i.e., a "wish to suffer"). Beck hypothesized that a need to suffer was central to the experience of depression, and he tested this notion by examining dreams for evidence of masochistic tendencies. Freud (1917/1959) conceived of masochism as either an indirect manifestation of retroflected hostility or a direct manifestation of self-punishment. Thus, dreams of depressed subjects should show greater rage or guilt than those of controls. Contrary to these hypotheses, Beck found *less* retroflected rage and no more symbols of guilt or unacceptable wishes in the manifest dream content of depressed patients than he did in that of controls (Beck & Rush, 1978). Further testing of the fundamental assumption of wish fulfillment seemed contraindicated. A major reconceptualization was required.

Beck itemized two critical requirements for research into the psychology of depression: (1) A specific psychological constellation or construct must be isolated to meaningfully differentiate depression from other syndromes. (2) Referents of this constellation must be empirically testable in clinical populations. He reconceptualized depressives' dreams as reflections of their view of the world when awake. Thus, a dream of being thwarted was interpreted to indicate that the dreamer viewed important others as rejecting or frustrating. Beck and Hurvich (1959) tested this reformulation. They found that, indeed, reports of rejection and frustration were significantly more prevalent with depressed subjects.

A series of case studies and clinical investigations led Beck to the notion that depressed persons interpret a wide variety of events in terms of failure, deprivation, or rejection, independent of objectively based disconfirmatory information. Thus, the preliminary step for a cognitive theory of depression had been taken.

In 1967, Beck published his cognitive theory of depression. Depression was viewed as a disturbance in cognition. The cognitive triad was identified: Depression was seen not as a primary disturbance of mood, but rather as a result of distorted, negatively biased views of self, future, and world. Although recognizing involvement of multiple psychological and physiological systems, Beck focused attention on cognitive disturbances that influenced these affective, motivational, behavioral, and vegetative manifestations. Cognition was considered primary. A continuous interaction of cognition and emotion was posited to account for the interactive processes of dysphoria and distorted thinking. "Feelings" become part of the stimulus field and influence cognitions, as do external stimuli (Beck, Brady, & Quen, 1977). This model accounts for the characteristic downward spiral of depression.

The first component of the cognitive disturbance, view of self, centers around the depressed person's view of self as inadequate, unworthy, deficient, and/or defective in mental, moral, or physical character. There is a causal relationship between perceived defects and judgment of personal unworthiness. Operationally, this takes the form of personal criticism and underestimates of oneself.

The second component—view of experiences, world, or domain—focuses on the individual's perception that interactions with the environment are inordinately demanding or obstructive. Experiences are construed as evidence for defeat and loss. This evidence is then taken as support for notions of personal rejection, deprivation, and increased dependence. In comparison to others, depressed persons think of themselves as particularly inadequate; success experiences are minimized and failures are emphasized.

The third component, view of the future, leads to negative future anticipations. The depressive views the future as holding nothing of value. Motivational changes (escape, avoidance, suicidal ideas and/or attempts, increased dependency, paralysis of will) are viewed by Beck as responses to perceptions of the future in which any undertaking appears doomed. Increased dependency follows from a belief system that both overestimates the difficulty of normal tasks and underestimates personal performance and competency. Thus, the depressed person expects failure or other negative consequences.

Indecision follows from an overwhelming conviction of the likelihood of errors in judgment. Consequently, many depressed people seek assistance and reassurance from those close to them whom they consider competent. Suicidal ideas and attempts represent the ultimate statement of the futility of attempting change.

According to the theory, these negative cognitive patterns also account for the physical or somatic correlates of depression. Psychomotor inhibition, apathy, fatigue, and low energy are posited to proceed from a cognitive set predisposed to view all activity as leading to failure.

Although it is not formally stated in Beck's theory, a review of the theory suggests that a negative view of self logically precedes and is fundamental to negative views of the world and the future. Distortions of both world and future follow directly from a negative self-view. Given that the individual perceives the self as inadequate or deficient, it follows that the personal domain becomes demanding or obstructive. "Routine" problems in living are particularly difficult if a person assumes insufficient resources are available for responding in a meaningful and constructive manner. A negative view of the future logically follows from the assumption that stable characterological defects preclude effective problem-solving behavior. The perception of unremitting pain is consistent with the perception that suffering is due to shortcomings that are integral parts of the self.

The theory makes a clear causal relationship between cognition and behavioral, affective, and physiological disturbances. The theory goes beyond descriptive detailing of the experience of depression and asserts that cognitions cause and maintain the depressive syndrome.

The following sections present data that are relevant to the cognitive theory. Methodological and interpretive strengths and problems will be noted. The review is not exhaustive, but provides a representative picture of directions taken to examine the theory.

VIEW OF THE SELF

Observations on psychiatric patients' "view of the self" are based largely on data from measures of self-concept. Beck (1967, 1974) found a significant inverse relationship ($r = -.66$) between the severity of depressive symptomatology as measured by the Beck Depression Inventory (BDI) (Beck, Ward, Mendelson, Mock, & Erbaugh, 1961) and self-concept as measured by an unpublished self-concept test (Beck & Stein, 1960). Depressed subjects also tended to rate themselves high on socially undesirable traits and low on socially desirable traits (Beck, 1967). Laxer (1964) compared depressed inpatients with paranoid and "other" psychiatric inpatients using a real–ideal self-concept semantic differential scale; he found that depressives had significantly lower self-concepts than did the other inpatients. Moreover, low self-concept on hospital admisson was elevated at discharge, presumably a function of lessened depressive affect (Beck, 1967).

Loeb, Feshbach, Beck, and Wolf (1964) examined the effect of social manipulation on self-concept ratings of depressed psychiatric patients. Subjects given failure feedback indicated greater depressed mood and were unlikely to volunteer for another task. Subjects given success feedback, however, indicated higher levels of confidence and saw themselves and others as happier. These findings were interpreted to suggest that depressed subjects are more sensitive to actual performance. Beck (1974) reported similar findings when he showed that inpatients who had successfully completed a hierarchy of tasks significantly increased their global ratings of optimism and self-concept.

Studies of college students have investigated self-ratings and performance dimensions to examine their views of self. Steiner (1975) found that depressed female college students who rated themselves interpersonally incompetent were, in fact, less interpersonally competent than were controls. Hammen and Krantz (1976) found that depressed students selected a greater number of depressed distorted responses and fewer nondepressed nondistorted choices in a story-completion task. The task was subsequently administered to a series of populations (Krantz & Hammen, 1979), including male and female undergraduates, psychiatric outpatients and inpatients, and role players instructed to act as though depressed. In all samples, there was a consistent relationship between level of depression as assessed by the BDI and choice of depressed distorted response. Moreover, subjects with highest depressed distorted scores at initial testing had highest levels of depression of retesting.

Rizley (1978) developed a chance task to examine attributions made by depressed subjects. Subjects were instructed that results of their performances on a number-guessing task were due to chance or task difficulty (external attributions) or to effort or ability (internal attributions). Although depressed subjects were similar to nondepressed subjects in the success condition, depressed subjects in the failure condition made significantly more *internal* attributions. In the second phase of the experiment, subjects were required to instruct other subjects in the task. Depressed subjects were more likely to evoke internal factors (i.e., personal effort or ability) to account for performances of their instructees.

In a similar paradigm, Klein, Fencil-Morse, and Seligman (1976) found that depressed subjects were more likely to attribute failure to ability than were nondepressed subjects. Depressed subjects also showed greater performance decrement on a subsequent task.

Another research direction has involved experimental induction of depressed mood through cognitive procedures. Velten (1968) required subjects to read self-referent statements biased to relate either to depression or to elation. Changes were found in both self-report and behavior measures in the biased direction. Strickland, Hale, and Anderson (1975) and Hale and Strickland (1976) confirmed the finding that statements induced mood changes. Coleman (1975) found that statements of self-evaluation, positive or negative, without mention of mood, induced significant changes in elation or depression. Moreover, subjects who judged themselves to be characteristically depressed or elated showed changes in the manipulated direction, independent of their self-descriptions. Teasdale and Bancroft (1977) provided further evidence when they found that *thinking* rather than *reading* happy or sad thoughts affected mood.

Another procedure to evaluate the effect of cognitions on mood has involved giving specific types of personal feedback and measuring mood or mood changes. Flippo and Lewinsohn (1971) manipulated the rate of positive reinforcement delivered to depressed subjects. As predicted, a lower rate of reinforcement was followed by lower self-esteem scores. Ludwig (1975) presented bogus feedback to female college students. Subjects who were told that psychological testing indicated that they were immature and uncreative showed significantly greater depressed mood. Wortman, Panciera, Shusterman, and Hibscher (1976) led their subjects to attribute failure in a laboratory task either to personal incompetence or to external factors. Subjects who believed that their performance resulted from personal incompetence reported significantly greater depressed mood.

In general, the studies of view of self indicate that self-perception discriminates between depressed and nondepressed subjects. These studies also suggest that negative views of self attend depressed mood and follow procedures designed to devalue one's concept of oneself. Blaney (1977) summarized these experimental procedures in terms of their relationship to focus of attention (e.g., Velten, 1968) and theoretically central beliefs (e.g., Ludwig, 1975). In summary, these data are consistent with the notion that a negative view of self is associated with a depressed mood and the clinical syndrome of depression. Whether such negative views are distinctly and exlusively characteristic of the depressive syndrome, as opposed to other types of psychopathology or medical illnesses, deserves further investigation.

VIEW OF THE WORLD

In early work, Beck and his associates used projective tests and dream-content analyses. Using the Focused Fantasy Test, Beck (1961) found that depressed subjects more often identified with a protagonist who was hurt than did the nondepressed. Similarly, Beck and Ward (1961) found that depressed inpatients and depressed outpatients had similar dream content in terms of themes of loss and deprivation. This was interpreted to mean that environmental factors were independent of the subjective process of depression. Consistent with these findings, Hauri (1976) found that depressed subjects, even when remitted, continued to report dreams of frustration, desertion, injury, and deprivation.

Another research strategy has focused upon information-process disturbances in depressed individuals. Consistent results have been obtained in paradigms to assess negative versus positive recall. Lishman (1972) found that depressed subjects tended to recall a greater amount of negative material than did their nondepressed counterparts. In a subsequent study, Lloyd and Lishman (1975) noted that increasing levels of depression were associated with a lower ratio of pleasant to unpleasant memories. That is, the bias of positive recall diminished as depression increased. In their follow-up, Lloyd and Lishman were able to rule out idiosyncratic characteristics, since these same subjects recalled positive memories more quickly when the depressed mood had abated. DeMonbreun and Craighead (1977) gave a predetermined rate of positive reinforcement to depressed and nondepressed subjects. In the low-reward condition, both groups recalled reinforcement accurately. In the high-reward condition, however, both groups were inaccurate. The nondepressed subjects *over-*

estimated the amount of reinforcement, whereas the depressed subjects significantly *underestimated* the amount.

Wener and Rehm (1975) used a common word-association task and found that a lower rate of reinforcement was followed by increased depressed mood. In addition, they noted that some depressed subjects misperceived the high rate of reinforcement. Nelson and Craighead (1977) followed up this finding and showed that depressed subjects recalled less positive and more negative reinforcement in general than did nondepressed subjects. The effect was greater in their high-positive and low-negative combination condition. This condition was assumed to be least consistent with depressed subjects' expectations and therefore most likely to elicit the greatest distortion. Buchwald (1977) also found that underestimating of positive reinforcement was directly related to depressed mood.

Hammen and Glass (1975) found that instructing subjects to increase participation in presumably pleasurable activities over a 2-week period resulted in subjects reporting *greater* depression and *fewer* enjoyable activities. Another equally depressed group who engaged in similar activities without explicit instructions to do so did not show these changes. One interpretation of these results is that actual performance is not as powerful a mediator of mood as are cognitive processes. Teasdale (1978), however, presented evidence that contradicts the primacy of cognitions. He found that subjects who were told to *recall* successful performances on a letter-substitution task did not improve their performance on anagrams after unsolvable problems. *Actual* success in the letter-substitution task was necessary to eliminate deficits on the anagram test.

In a study by Forrest and Hokanson (1975), depressed and normal subjects were assessed within a response-avoidance contingency paradigm. Depressed subjects were superior to normal ones in learning the response contingency when the required response was self-punishment. In a situation in which they were attacked interpersonally, depressed subjects showed greater self-punishment. Contrary to findings for normal subjects, autonomic arousal decreased more quickly when depressed subjects were involved in self-harming behavior. This rapid learning and accommodation may result from the notion of an "easy match" between a depressed view of the world (e.g., "I will be punished") and the negative contingency.

Studies have also been conducted to examine effects of feedback on the actual appearance of depression. Laird (1974) requested normals to contort their faces to mimic frowns and found that these subjects reported less elation than did subjects induced to assume smiles. Batsel (1976) controlled for confounding facial-musculature feedback and simply informed subjects of their apparent expressions. He obtained results consistent with those of Laird.

In an investigation of interpersonal perception, Lunghi (1977) found that depressed subjects reported more negative relationships. He inferred that negative perception may elicit negative relationships and that the actual number of negative relationships may increase. Other studies show that interpersonal relationships in depression are objectively more problematic and subjectively viewed as more negative. Stockton (1975) found that depressed outpatients displayed and reported impairments in their expression of feelings, and that they were more dependent and rigid than were nondepressed outpatients. When normal subjects conversed by telephone with depressed and nondepressed subjects, they reported increased depressed mood, anxiety, hostility, and feelings of rejection after speaking with depressed subjects (Coyne, 1976). Normal subjects instructed to play roles of depressed persons were rejected more often in telephone conversations than they were when instructed to be "normal" (Hammen & Peters, 1978). These results were taken as support for the interactive process of depressive affect, reduced social skill, and the lowered likelihood of social involvement and reward.

In a study comparing interpersonal problem-solving performance to impersonal problem solving (anagram task), Gotlib and Asarnow (1979) found that depressed subjects performed significantly more poorly on the interpersonal task. However, all groups performed comparably on the anagram task. Gotlib and Asarnow interpreted this as evidence for the specificity of an interpersonal problem-solving deficit with depressed individuals.

Findings related to interpersonal issues and depression are not straightforward, however. Rehm and Plakosh (1975) found that, contrary to expectation, depression was not associated with a preference for social reinforcement. In addition, Tanner, Weissman, and Prusoff (1975) found that remitted depressed subjects showed no improvement in social adjustment (defined as role function, interpersonal relationships, and satisfaction in various role areas) when compared to acutely depressed subjects.

In research concerning locus of control, an association between externality and depression has been found by a number of studies (e.g., Calhoun, Cheney, & Dawes, 1974; Naditch, Gargan, & Michael, 1975). This finding is problematic for Beck's theory. Logical errors and the centrality of the negative concept of self suggest that depressives *internalize* negative events or failures, though they externalize positive experiences or successes. Consistent with Beck's prediction, however, Lamont (1973) found that, when depressed subjects listened to a tape of "We don't have that much control over other people's feelings and we don't have to feel responsible for how other people feel," their mood improved significantly. That is, when depressives are explicitly instructed to externalize the locus of control, their mood improves. Rizley (1978) also found that depressed subjects internalized failure. Beck is not explicit about locus of control. These studies taken together, however, suggest that locus of control is not clear in depressives.

Depressed psychiatric patients may differ from depressed college students. McNitt and Thornton (1978) found that depressed college students showed greater reactivity to success experiences than did nondepressed subjects. That is, they showed greater change in success expectation after exposure to a high-reinforcement condition. On the other hand, depressed psychiatric subjects tend to show greater reactivity to failure than to success (cf. DeMonbreun & Craighead, 1977).

In summary, research into the depressives' world view largely suggests that depression is associated with a negative view of the world. Depressives tend to recall more negative material and to perceive and engender more negative social interactions. While an external locus of control is suggested by some studies, greater internality is noted in failure situations, whereas success experiences yield equivocal results.

CONCEPT OF FUTURE

Perhaps the most striking feature of studies that relate future perception to depression is the consistency of the findings. Depression is clearly associated with a negative view of the future. Loeb, Beck, Diggory, and Tuthill (1967) found that depressed subjects had increased pessimism after failure. In research to follow up this finding, Vatz, Winig, and Beck (1969) developed a Generalized Expectancy Scale, later revised as the Hopelessness Scale (Beck, Weissman, Lester, & Trexler, 1974). They found severity of depression in inpatients was directly correlated with negative views of the future and a constricted sense of future time. These results were consistent at both admission and discharge.

The concept of constricted time perspective or narrow view of the future in depression has been found by several investigators (Dilling & Rabin, 1967; Melges & Bowlby, 1969; Melges & Weisz, 1971; Wohlford, 1966). More detailed studies of this finding have focused on the relationship between hopelessness or a pessimistic view of the future and suicidal ideation and attempts. Minkoff, Bergman, Beck, and Beck (1973) found a direct relationship between hopelessness as assessed by the Hopelessness Scale and severity of depression as assessed by the BDI. A series of studies have indicated that hopelessness is a better correlate of suicidal intent than is severity of depression in patients who have attempted suicide (Beck, Weissman, Lester, & Trexler, 1974; Beck, Kovacs, & Weissman, 1975; Minkoff, Bergman, Beck, & Beck, 1973; Wetzel, 1976).

Another group of investigations has studied suicide as it relates to other components of depression. Pichot and Lemperiere (1964) and Cropley and Weckowicz (1966) independently conducted factor-analytic studies of BDI items and found a major factor of pessimism among subjects with suicidal wishes. Among suicide notes analyzed, Bjerg (1967) found that 81% contained the theme of a desire which could not or would not be fulfilled. A secondary theme was the expectation of continued deprivation and suffering. These results provide support for a pronounced difference between depressed subjects' perceptions of the future and those of normals.

Little research has been conducted on depressed college students' view of the future. Hammen and Krantz (1976) gave subjects bogus feedback concerning their therapeutic potential. Those depressed subjects who were informed that their test results indicated failure were lowest in their predictions of future success.

Depressives' view of the future as discrepant from that of normals is singularly well supported in the literature to date. It is clear that, at least in terms of constricted time sense and negative or pessimistic expectations, depressed subjects have a relatively uniform outlook.

CRITIQUE OF EMPIRICAL SUPPORT FOR COGNITIVE THEORY

An empirical evaluation of the cognitive triad requires that measures of the views of self, world, and future be taken in the same sample. In this way, the interrelationships between these views can be directly evaluated. While research to date generally supports the notion that depressed patients are characterized by negative views, only Hammen and Krantz (1976) have attempted to consolidate the triad into a single experimental procedure. There have been no attempts to discriminate among each of the three components to assess their interrelationships.

A more central flaw in many studies to date is the use of the BDI as the criterion instrument. The BDI correlates significantly with both a negative view of the future (Loeb, Beck, Diggory, & Tuthill, 1967) and with a negative self-concept (Vatz, Winig, & Beck, 1969). By selecting subjects on the basis of an instrument that relates highly to the constructs under investigation, researchers are artificially enhancing the probability of significant outcome. Subjects who score high on a measure directly correlated with low self-esteem can be expected to indicate more negative self-reference. Clearly, the use of this instrument as a sample selection device biases the experiment in favor of hypothesis confirmation.

Another methodological difficulty is that much of the experimental research to date, particularly as it relates to view of self, has been conducted with populations of college students. Of the 15 studies cited in support of the notion that a negative self-view typifies depression, only four examined clinically depressed populations. Thus, the majority of data is derived from groups of mildly dysphoric people aged 19 to 25. It is not clear that college students' responses are indicative of the general population. This is not to say that continued investigation with college students is unjustified. Exciting and promising directions have been developed with this group. The point is that statements concerning the phenomenon of depression in this population are necessarily and deservedly limited. Comparability of a college population with a clinical population can only be determined empirically.

Third, while both clinical experience and much of the literature support the notion that depressed people think depressed thoughts and see things negatively, it is not clear that they *distort* information concerning self, world, and future as compared to normal subjects. In order to test this assumption, a paradigm must be set up so that objective measures of actual performance interface with subjective perceptions. Most studies using success–failure strategies have not used methods in which actual performance could be meaningfully ascertained. Rizley (1978) used a chance-generated list of numbers; Ludwig (1975) gave subjects failure or success reports on personality measures; Klein, Fencil-Morse, and Seligman (1976) utilized solvable or unsolvable anagrams. Loeb, Feshbach, Beck, and Wolf (1964) required subjects in the failure condition to complete a longer word list. In addition, their sample of 40 subjects was comprised of 31 who had been diagnosed schizophrenic. Disordered thinking is the sine qua non of a diagnosis of schizophrenia.

Only one investigation (Loeb, Beck, & Diggory, 1971) has used a success–failure procedure that allows the objective measure of performance. The Loeb, Beck, and Diggory study proposed specifically to examine the negative-distortion assumption. This study has been challenged (Miller, 1975) on both methodological and interpretive grounds. Two groups, depressed and nondepressed male outpatients, were developed on the basis of BDI scores and psychiatrists' ratings. Subjects were given two card-sorting tasks. They were asked to estimate their level of aspiration and probability of success for each of seven trials per task. All subjects were given experimenter-controlled success or failure feedback on the first task (50% were led to believe they succeeded, 50% believed they failed); all subjects received failure feedback on the second task. Actual performance was measured throughout by counting the number of cards in each trial.

Loeb, Beck, and Diggory interpreted their findings to indicate that depressed subjects tried as hard and performed as well as did nondepressed subjects, but that they believed they had less chance of achieving the goal. They concluded that success experience generated higher success estimates, greater aspiration, and better actual performance in the depressed group. However, the data presented do not support this conclusion. Miller (1975) noted that success, relative to failure, resulted in "better actual performance" for depressives only in the sense that "their performance deteriorated less after success than after failure" (p. 248). In addition, the data across tasks depicts different findings. The mean performance of each group in each condition (nondepressed–success, nondepressed–failure, depressed–success, depressed–failure) indicates that subject estimates of the probability of success declined for both groups after failure; contrary to the authors' interpretation, depressed subjects estimated a lower probability of success after success feedback, although the decline was less than that of the depressed-failure group. Only the nondepressed-success group *increased* their probability of success estimates from the first task to the second. Interestingly, the finding that depressed subjects appeared to adjust their expectations downward with failure but did not react to success experiences is *more* consistent with Beck's theory of devalued positive feedback.

Thus, there are insufficient data to answer the question: Do depressives exhibit negatively distorted perceptions of themselves, their experiences, and their future, in comparison with other groups? In view of the clearly stated specificity of these distortions to depressed individuals, future research must compare perceptions of clinically depressed subjects with those of nondepressed clinically disturbed subjects, as well as with those of "normals."

In addition, cognitive theory implies that cognitive dysfunctions are to be found in, or account for, all types of depression. Little investigation of this question has been reported. Krantz and Hammen (1979) noted great variability in the results of depressives' Story Completion Test, suggesting that negative cognitions are not unidimensional, as previously implied. Furthermore, it is not clear whether cognitive dysfunctions are etiological, descriptive, or, perhaps, epiphenomenal in nature. Is it true that negative distortions *lead* to depression? Does the primacy of negative cognitive biases differ when individuals are depressed or remitted? What is the influence of environmental stressors, developmental histories, and/or interpersonal styles on these cognitive biases? Many unanswered questions provide fertile grounds for further investigation.

SCHEMAS

According to cognitive theory, depression results from the stimulation of major constructs, or "schemas," in the sensitized person's repertoire. A developmental model is proposed to account for the formation and maintenance of these schemas. The child learns to evaluate self and environment through interaction with significant others, and to construct reality through personal experience. The attitudes and beliefs developed by the child may be adaptive and thus may facilitate healthy adjustment, or they may provide grounds for vulnerability to psychological dysfunction. These attitudes are the basis for lifelong silent assumptions that remain unquestioned and largely outside of awareness. Cognitions and/or views of day-to-day experiences proceed from these assumptions and tend to reinforce or support these beliefs.

Cognitions are premised upon a hierarchy of assumptions or "schemas." Schemas are enduring cognitive patterns that have developed through interactions with the environment. While reinforced by interpretations of ongoing experience, these notions are intially derived from childhood experiences. Through a matrix of schemas, the individual categorizes, selects, and encodes incoming data. In this way, current experiences are concretized into the cognitions discussed above.

While schemas appear to play a core role in cognitive theory and are specifically implicated in vulnerability to relapse, studies to define the actual role of schemas are few. It may be intuitively obvious that some organizing principles must give structure to our world; yet operationalization of these principles is difficult.

Consider the concept of gravity. A person maintains a grip on a plate throughout its journey from sink to cupboard because of an implicit belief in the concept of gravity. When the person is challenged about maintaining this hold on the plate, the answer is, "If I don't, it'll drop." When pressed, the person might elaborate that past experiences have shown that whenever the plate is released, it falls, and that there is no reason to believe that it will do otherwise in this case. Thus, this person acts as though he or she believes that this event will occur in the present because it has occurred in the past. The person acts as though he or she believes that the plate will fall *down*. That is, the person supports the plate from underneath. These sorts of consistent assumptions are hypothesized to operate in emotional and behavior responses. However, measurement of such psychological schemas is problematic. One of many schemas may be active in a particular situation at a particular time. Because they are typically *implicit* in behavior and are not articulated by the subject, measuring such assumptions objectively can be difficult.

Evidence for inferring schemas can be derived from behavior, given knowledge of specific stimulus events and the history those stimuli have for the individual. Thus, inferences about more idiosyncratic schemas, such as those hypothesized in depression, can be made from consistent behavioral patterns. Schemas are useful heuristic and theoretical tools to the extent that behavior can be understood, explained, predicted, and possibly changed as a consequence of their invocation.

Does invoking this construct of "schemas" allow investigators to explain or predict behavior? Do all individuals have similar types of schemas but apply them differently, or do schemas meaningfully differentiate types of people or particular psychopathological conditions? That is, are there qualitative *and* quantitative differences in these organizing principles? What are the necessary and sufficient conditions that schemas must satisfy? "Schemas" are defined here as abstract and generalizable rules regarding regularities in relationships among internal representation of events. They are relatively stable across time and situations of similarly perceived stimulus content. They guide behavior and direct the assimilation of incoming information. They are based on developmental events (i.e., the interaction of perceptions, events, and responses to those events), coupled with contingent reward–nonreward–punishment. They can be idiosyncratic, but all are nomothetic.

The current research challenge is to develop procedures to measure schemas. Methods of assessment can be conceived to fall along empirical lines of unstructured, semistructured, and structured techniques. Examples of unstructured data sources include the clinical and therapeutic interviews. Although rich in material, these methods are highly individualized, subject to interactions between therapist and patient, and virtually impossible to replicate. Alternatively, these data sources can provide very fertile ground for the generation of categories, dichotomies, and dimensions that may be operationalized.

Semistructured techniques include such possibilities as standardized presentation of selected Thematic Apperception Test (TAT) cards, construct repertory grid tests with predefined comparisons, and open-ended sentence completion tests.

Structured techniques may vary among tachistoscopic methods, Q-sorts along various dimensions, psycholinguistic methods such as internal analysis of speech structure, rank ordering of events, self-concept measures, and rating scales. Optimal use of these techniques would involve serial assessment, in which hypotheses are flexibly structured to respond to each successive finding or direction.

In essence, various methodologies might be developed to provide a technology with which to decipher the value of the notion of schemas.

In a recent study (Rush, Giles, Dougherty, & Sullivan, submitted), schemas were operationalized in the form of a self-report inventory, the Dysfunctional Attitude Scale (DAS) (Weissman, 1979). In this study, more severe depressive symptomatology was associated with a greater endorsement of dysfunctional attitudes in both bipolar and unipolar depressed subjects, as compared to attitudes indicated by those less symptomatic or remitted. However, the relationships between cognitions and schemas was not as clearcut as predicted by cognitive theory. In addition, nearly half of the symptomatic subjects did *not* endorse any more dysfunctional attitudes than did normal college students without measured psychopathology. Either the DAS is an inadequate instrument to measure schemas, or schemas play a key role in only a subgroup of depressed patients. Further research into the role and relevance of schemas is needed.

COGNITIVE THERAPY

Cognitive therapy (Beck, Rush, Shaw, & Emery, 1979) consists of a specific treatment package derived from cognitive theory. Treatment focuses on specific cognitive elements in depression. Both behavioral and verbal procedures are used to (1) define and detect cognitions or automatic thoughts; (2) examine and test these cognitions; (3) develop alternative constructions of day-to-day events; (4) record dysfunctional thoughts; (5) develop alternative, more flexible schemas; and (6) rehearse both cognitive and behavioral responses based on these new assumptions.

Tables 6.1–6.4 summarize the comparative outcome studies on cognitive therapy. Many of these studies have been done as dissertations or master's theses. Most studies have relied on inadequate selector measures such as the BDI (Beck *et al.*, 1961) or another measure, usually the MMPI or MMPI *D* scales or the Hamilton Rating Scale for Depression (HRSD) (Hamilton, 1960, 1967). It is suggested that criterion-based descriptive diagnostic systems (e.g., Feighner, Robins, Guze, Woodruff, Winokur, & Muñoz, 1972; Spitzer, Endicott, & Robins, 1975) represent better systems for defining depression, since they are not allied with a specific theoretical position.

Populations included clinic patients ($n = 10$), college students ($n = 6$), and community volunteers ($n = 4$). Group cognitive therapy was employed in 11 studies, whereas individual therapy was used in 10 studies (individual and group formats were compared in one study).

Of the 20 studies reviewed, 17 indicated that cognitive therapy or a variation on it (e.g., cognitive modification) was more effective than no treatment or waiting list, and that it equaled or exceeded the contrasting active treatment. Cognitive therapy or cognitive modification was effective independent of time (Schmickley, 1976), and was found superior to imipramine hydrochloride (Rush, Beck, Kovacs, & Hollon, 1977), behavior therapy and nondirective therapy (Shaw, 1977), insight therapy (Morris, 1975), and supportive psychotherapy (Shipley & Fazio, 1973). Cognitive therapy alone was as effective as were cognitive therapy and amitriptyline combined in two studies (Beck *et al.*, 1979; Blackburn & Bishop, 1980).

While many studies have been conducted on "depressed college-student volunteers," three recent trials have been carried out on psychiatric patients (Tables 6.1 and 6.2). In one study (Rush *et al.*, 1977), the effects of cognitive therapy exceeded the effects of imipramine. Two more recent studies also contrasted behavioral–cognitive therapy with antidepressant medication. McLean and Hakstian (1979) reported that the behavioral–cognitive approach exceeded the effects of amitriptyline. In addition, it was superior to relaxation training and short-term psychotherapy. Blackburn and Bishop (1979, 1980) found that with depressed outpatients in a general practice, cognitive therapy was superior to antidepressants, while cognitive therapy was equivalent to antidepressant medication in psychiatric-clinic outpatients. By nearly all dependent measures, the combination treatment exceeded either treatment alone.

Tables 6.3 and 6.4 summarize studies of cognitive therapy in a group format. Cognitive therapy was more effective than was behavioral, insight, or client-centered therapy (Magers, 1978; Morris, 1975; Shaw, 1977). One study (Rush & Watkins, 1981b) has evaluated the question of whether the format (e.g., group vs. individual) affects the efficacy of cognitive therapy. The group format appeared to be *less* effective than individual therapy was. A couples format has not been formally studied, although cognitive therapy is easily adapted to such a format. One clinical report (Rush, Shaw, & Khatami, 1980) has suggested specific indications and techniques for involving couples

TABLE 6.1. Individual Therapy: Clinic Patients

STUDY	MEASURES	TREATMENT	SESSIONS NO.	SESSIONS WKS.	RESULTS[c]
Schmickley (1976)	BDI, MMPI ($n = 11$)	1. Cognitive modification	4	2	Within-subject improvement
Rush, Beck, Kovacs, & Hollon (1977)	BDI, HRSD ($n = 41$)	1. Cognitive therapy 2. Imipramine	20	11	Cognitive therapy > imipramine
Beck, Rush, Shaw, & Emery (1979)	BDI, HRSD ($n = 26$)	1. Cognitive therapy 2. Cognitive therapy + amitriptyline	20	12	Cognitive therapy = cognitive therapy + amitriptyline
McLean & Hakstian (1979)[a]	BDI, DACL[b] ($n = 154$)	1. Amitriptyline 2. Relaxation training 3. Behavioral–cognitive therapy 4. Insight therapy	10	10	Behavioral–cognitive therapy > amitriptyline = relaxation training > insight therapy
Blackburn & Bishop (1980)	BDI, HRSD ($n = 64$)	1. Cognitive therapy 2. Antidepressant medications 3. Combination	13–16	12	Hospital clinic outpatients: Combination > cognitive therapy = antidepressant medications General practice outpatients: Cognitive therapy = combination > antidepressant medications

[a]Included community volunteers and clinic patients.
[b]Depression Adjective Checklist.
[c]Explanation of symbols: = denotes "equaled in overall efficacy"; > denotes "more effective than."

TABLE 6.2. Individual Therapy: College-Student Volunteers and Community Volunteers

STUDY	MEASURES	TREATMENT	SESSIONS NO.	SESSIONS WKS.	RESULTS[b]
COLLEGE-STUDENT VOLUNTEERS					
Taylor & Marshall (1977)	BDI, D-30 ($n = 28$)	1. Cognitive modification 2. Behavioral modification 3. Cognitive modification and behavioral modification 4. Waiting list	6	3	Cognitive modification and behavioral modification > cognitive modification Cognitive modification and behavioral modification > behavioral modification Cognitive modification = behavioral modification Each > waiting list
COMMUNITY VOLUNTEERS					
Muñoz (1977)	MMPI *D*	1. Cognitive modification 2. Waiting list 3. Normal control 4. High MMPI (nondepressed) control	12	4	All improved, but cognitive modification = waiting list
Besyner (1979)	BDI ($n = 41$)	1. Cognitive modification 2. Behavioral therapy 3. Nonspecific therapy 4. Waiting list	4[a]	4	Behavioral therapy > cognitive modification Cognitive modification = waiting list Behavioral therapy, cognitive modification, waiting list > nonspecific therapy
Zeiss, Lewinsohn, & Muñoz (1979)	MMPI *D* ($n = 44$)	1. Cognitive modification 2. Social skills 3. Pleasant activities 4. Waiting list	12	4	Cognitive modification = social skills = pleasant activities > waiting list

[a]2-hour sessions.
[b]Explanation of symbols: = denotes "equaled in overall efficacy"; > denotes "more effective than."

TABLE 6.3. Group Therapy: Clinic Patients

STUDY	MEASURES	TREATMENT	SESSIONS NO.	SESSIONS WKS.	RESULTS[e]
Rush & Watkins (1981b)	BDI, HRSD ($n = 38$)	1. Group cognitive therapy 2. Individual cognitive therapy 3. Individual cognitive therapy + antidepressants	10	10–12	Group cognitive therapy < individual cognitive therapy = individual cognitive therapy + antidepressants
McDonald (1978)	BDI, DACL[b] ($n = 28$)	1. Cognitive modification + day care 2. Day care	12	4	Improved, but cognitive modification + day care = day care
Magers (1978)	BDI, MMPI, TSCS[c] ($n = 18$)	1. Cognitive–behavioral therapy 2. Waiting list	6	6	Cognitive–behavioral therapy > waiting list
Shaw (1977)[a]	BDI, HRSD ($n = 32$)	1. Cognitive modification 2. Behavioral modification 3. Nondirective therapy 4. Waiting list	6	3	Cognitive modification > behavioral modification Cognitive modification > nondirective therapy Behavioral modification = non-directive therapy Each > waiting list
Morris (1975)	BDI, SRSD[d] ($n = 51$)	1. Cognitive modification 2. Insight group therapy 3. Waiting list	6	3	Cognitive modification > insight group therapy > waiting list

[a]Student health clinic patients.
[b]Depression Adjective Checklist.
[c]Tennessee Self-Concept Scale.
[d]Self-Rating Scale for Depression.
[e]Explanation of symbols: = denotes "equaled in overall efficacy"; > denotes "more effective than"; < denotes "less effective than."

in cognitive therapy for depression. More studies are needed to evaluate the effect of format on outcome.

The question of when and whether to combine antidepressant medication with psychotherapy remains unanswered. Three reports have evaluated the combination treatment. Rush and Watkins (1981a) found no difference between individual cognitive therapy alone and the combination in outpatients. However, the sample size may have precluded detection of significant differences. Recently, Beck *et al.* (1979) found that adding amitriptyline did not add to the efficacy of cognitive therapy alone. No advantage accrued to the combination treatment over cognitive therapy alone in general-practice depressed outpatients (Blackburn & Bishop, 1980), whereas the effects of combination treatment exceeded those of cognitive therapy alone in psychiatric-clinic outpatients. Apparently some, but clearly not all, patients are uniquely benefited by the combination treatment. Other patients may benefit from cognitive therapy without medication.

As yet, there are no predictors for patients best suited to cognitive therapy alone, medication alone, or the combination. Further studies are needed to identify the specific indications for cognitive therapy or the combined approach.

DOSAGE

There are few data available that evaluate the relationship between the frequency of treatment sessions (dosage) and outcome. Only one pilot study has assessed this question (Rush, Beck, Kovacs, Khatami, & Wolman, 1975). For moderately to severely depressed outpatients, twice-a-week treatment was associated with a lower dropout rate and better symptom reduction than was once-a-week treatment. However, treatment assignment was not randomized. This preliminary report and clinical experience suggest that once-a-week treatment may be sufficient for mildly to moderately depressed patients, whereas twice-weekly sessions are indicated for moderately to severely depressed outpatients. Hospitalized or severely depressed patients may require treatment three times a week or more. Behavioral techniques may be indicated for the more severely depressed, whereas techniques designed to elucidate and change cognitions and silent assumptions are used in mildly to moderately depressed patients (Beck *et al.*, 1979; Rush, 1980).

TABLE 6.4. Group Therapy: College Students and Community Volunteers

STUDY	MEASURES	TREATMENT	SESSIONS NO.	SESSIONS WKS.	RESULTS[d]
		COLLEGE STUDENTS			
Kirkpatrick (1977)	Self-report of depression/ anxiety ($n = 46$)	1. Cognitive modification 2. Relaxation training 3. Attention placebo 4. No treatment	4	2	Cognitive modification = relaxation training = attention placebo = no treatment
Head (1978)	BDI, POMS[a]	1. Cognitive modification 2. Assessment only	11	11	Improved, but cognitive modification = assessment only
Hodgson & Urban (1976)	Lubin,[b] Zung[c] ($n = 38$)	1. Cognitive modification 2. Behavioral modification 3. Waiting list	8	4	Behavioral modification > cognitive modification Each > waiting list

Gioe (1975)	BDI ($n = 40$)	1. Cognitive modification 2. Positive group experience 3. Cognitive modification and positive group experience 4. Waiting list	5	1	Cognitive modification and positive group experience > cognitive modification Cognitive modification and positive group experience > positive group experience Cognitive modification = positive group experience Each > waiting list
Shipley & Fazio (1973)	Zung,[c] MMPI ($n = 38$)	1. Functional problem solving (cognition) 2. Supportive therapy 3. Waiting list	3	3	Functional problem solving > supportive therapy > waiting list
		COMMUNITY VOLUNTEERS			
Fuchs & Rehm (1977)	BDI, MMPI *D* ($n = 28$)	1. Self-control 2. Nonspecific therapy 3. Waiting list	6	6	Self-control > nonspecific therapy > waiting list

[a]Profile of Mood States.
[b]Lubin Multiple Adjective Checklist.
[c]Zung Depression Scale.
[d]Explanation of symbols: = denotes "equaled in overall efficacy"; > denotes "more effective than."

Maintenance treatment may consist of once- or twice-monthly "booster" sessions for 6 to 12 months after treatment is completed. The effect of maintenance treatment has not yet been empirically evaluated, however.

UNIQUE EFFECTS

If unique effects could be found with a particular psychotherapy, clinicians might infer specific indications for employing the intervention. Rush, Beck, Kovacs, Weissenberger, and Hollon (in press) found that cognitive therapy had a more pervasive and significant impact on self-concept than did amitriptyline by the end of treatment. In addition, cognitive therapy resulted in a quicker reduction in hopelessness than did medication. While these findings require replication, they suggest that cognitive therapy improves patients' views of themselves and their future more profoundly than chemotherapy does.

It might be speculated that depressions characterized by negative cognitive distortions are particulary likely to benefit from cognitive therapy. This contention is supported by Shaw's report on cognitive therapy with a group of drug-free depressed inpatients (1980). Those inpatients who evidenced greater cognitive distortions, as assessed by a card-sorting task, responded better to cognitive therapy than did patients with less negative thinking. Further studies to identify unique effects, as well as predictions of response and nonresponse, are needed.

PROPHYLACTIC EFFECTS

Even if psychotherapeutic methods can be shown to be effective, the cost of such treatment must be weighed against the effect obtained. Most therapists hope that psychotherapy teaches new, more adaptive behaviors and attitudes. Thus, future symptomatic episodes should be reduced. Only one study (Kovacs, Rush, Beck, & Hollon, 1981) has examined this question in cognitive therapy. Subjects treated with cognitive therapy alone ($n = 28$) or with imipramine and brief supportive therapy ($n = 17$) were followed up monthly for 1 year after active treatment was terminated. The imipramine-treated group had twice the "risk of relapse" during follow-up, although this between-group difference did not reach statistical significance. Those who had received cognitive therapy continued to report lower levels of depression as assessed by the BDI. A total of 56% of the cognitive therapy group and 35% of the drug-treated patients remained in remission (no BDI $\geq$ 16). These findings were not confirmed with a smaller sample on which the HRSD was completed, however. This study suggests that some prophylaxis does result for cognitive therapy, at least for a group of depressed outpatients. Obviously, further studies are needed.

CONTRAINDICATIONS

While Beck *et al.* (1979) caution that many depressed patients may require medication or may not respond to cognitive therapy, specific contraindications to this treatment are yet to be identified. Clinical experience suggests that patients with impaired reality testing (e.g., hallucinations or delusions), reasoning abilities, or memory function (e.g., organic brain syndromes); those with borderline personality structures; and those with schizoaffective disorders will not respond to this treatment. Three patients with severe endogenous depressions and evidence of biological dysregulation recently treated by Rush failed to respond to cognitive therapy alone. Perhaps, in the future, specific biological measures will help investigators to identify responders and nonresponders to cognitive or other psychotherapies.

ADVERSE REACTIONS

There are as yet no reports of adverse reactions to cognitive therapy, but adverse reactions may be difficult to differentiate from lack of efficacy. For instance, suicide attempts, premature terminations, and increased depression may be evidence of either adverse reactions or lack of efficacy. Two studies (McLean & Hakstian, 1979; Rush *et al.*, 1977) found that cognitive–behavioral methods were associated with a significantly lower dropout rate than was antidepressant pharmacotherapy alone, although another study (Blackburn & Bishop, 1979, 1980) did not replicate these findings. It might be that the structured, directive nature of this approach helps retain depressed outpatients. If so, cognitive therapy might be particularly useful in lower socioeconomic class outpatients, in whom dropout from psychotherapy is particularly high.

Lacking research evidence for adverse reactions, investigators must rely on clinical experience. An example of an adverse reaction might be the patient who misuses therapy to justify inappropriate behavior. One patient came to believe that her need for approval was excessive and decided to disregard completely her previous overconcern for the feelings and opinions of others, particularly her husband. She began a series of affairs, which she readily disclosed to her husband. Research into adverse reactions to cognitive therapy might shed light on either the specific active ingredients or the contraindications.

SUMMARY

Research to date provides support for the salience and persistence of negative biases in the depressed individual's repertoire, as elaborated in concepts of self, of world, and of future. Whether these negative views are equally present in different types of depression is unclear. The role of schemas posited by cognitive theory has received little confirmatory empirical support. On the other hand, psychotherapeutic techniques derived from cognitive theory do appear to be effective in many depressed patients. It remains to be determined for which patients these approaches are of most utility. Further research into the generalizability of cognitive theory to various types of depression, into the role of schemas, and into the selection of patients that are most responsive to cognitive therapy is needed.,

REFERENCES

Ansbacher, H. L., & Ansbacher, R. R. (Eds.). *The individual psychology of Alfred Adler: A systematic presentation in selections from his writings.* New York: Basic Books, 1956.

Bandura, A. Behavior theory and the models of man. *American Psychologist*, 1974, *29*, 859–869.

Batsel, W. M. *Cognitive alteration of depressive affect: A false feedback experiment.* Unpublished doctoral dissertation, University of Texas at Austin, 1976.

Beck, A. T. A systematic investigation of depression. *Comprehensive Psychiatry*, 1961, *2*, 163–170.

Beck, A. T. *Depression: Clinical, experimental, and theoretical aspects.* New York: Hoeber, 1967. (Republished as *Depression: Causes and treatment.* Philadelphia: University of Pennsylvania Press, 1972.)

Beck, A. T. The development of depression: A cognitive model. In R. Friedman & M. Katz (Eds.), *Psychology of depression: Contemporary theory and research.* Washington, D.C.: Winston-Wiley, 1974.

Beck, A. T. *Cognitive therapy and the emotional disorders.* New York: International Universities Press, 1976.

Beck, A. T., & Beamesderfer, A. Assessment of depression: The depression inventory. In P. Pichot (Ed.), *Modern problems in pharmacopsychiatry* (Vol. 7). Basel, Switzerland: S. Karger, 1974.

Beck, A. T., Brady, J. P., & Quen, J. M. *The history of depression.* New York: Insight Communications, 1977.

Beck, A. T., & Hurvich, M. S. Psychological correlates of depression: I. Frequency of "masochistic" dream content in a private practice sample. *Psychosomatic Medicine*, 1959, *21*, 50–55.

Beck, A. T., & Rush, A. J. Cognitive approaches to depression and suicide. In G. Serban (Ed.), *Cognitive defects in development of mental illness.* New York: Brunner/Mazel, 1978.

Beck, A. T., Rush, A. J., Shaw, B. F., & Emery, G. *Cognitive therapy of depression.* New York: Guilford, 1979.

Beck, A. T., & Stein, D. *The self-concept in depression.* Unpublished manuscript, 1960.

Beck, A. T., & Ward, C. H. Dreams of depressed patients. *Archives of General Psychiatry*, 1961, *5*, 66–71.

Beck, A. T., Ward, C. H., Mendelson, M., Mock, J. E., & Erbaugh, J. K. An inventory for measuring depression. *Archives of General Psychiatry*, 1961, *4*, 561–571.

Beck, A. T., Weissman, A., Lester, D., & Trexler, L. The measurement of pessimism: The Hopelessness Scale. *Journal of Consulting and Clinical Psychology*, 1974, *42*, 861–865.

Besyner, J. K. The comparative efficacy of cognitive and behavioral treatments of depression: A multiassessment approach (Doctoral dissertation, Texas Tech. University, 1978). *Dissertation Abstracts International*, 1979, *39*(9), 4568B. (University Microfilms No. 79-04956)

Bjerg, K. The suicidal life space. In E. S. Schneidman (Ed.), *Essays in self-destruction.* New York: Science House, 1967.

Blackburn, I., & Bishop, S. *A comparison of cognitive therapy, pharmacotherapy, and their combination in depressed outpatients.* Paper presented at the annual meeting of the Society for Psychotherapy Research, Oxford, England, July 1979.

Blackburn, I., & Bishop, S. *Pharmacotherapy and cognitive therapy in the treatment of depression: Competitors or allies?* Paper presented at the First World Congress on Behavior Therapy, Jerusalem, Israel, July 1980.

Blaney, P. H. Contemporary theories of depression: Critique and comparison. *Journal of Abnormal Psychology*, 1977, *86*, 203–223.

Bowers, K. S. Situationism in psychology: An analysis and critique. *Psychological Review*, 1973, *80*, 307–336.

Brady, J. V. The paleocortex and behavioral motivation. In H. F. Harlow & C. N. Woolsey (Eds.), *Biological and biochemical bases of behavior*. Madison: University of Wisconsin Press, 1958.

Brewer, W. F. There is no convincing evidence for operant or classical conditioning in adult humans. In W. B. Weiner & S. W. Palermo (Eds.), *Cognition and the symbolic process*. New York: Halsted Press, 1974.

Buchwald, A. M. Depressive mood and estimates of reinforcement frequency. *Journal of Abnormal Psychology*. 1977, *86*, 443–446.

Calhoun, L. G., Cheney, T., & Dawes, A. S. Locus of control, self-reported depression and perceived causes of depression. *Journal of Consulting and Clinical Psychology*, 1974, *42*, 736.

Cannon, W. B. The James–Lange theory of emotions: A critical examination and an alternative theory. *American Journal of Psychology*, 1927, *39*, 106–124.

Coleman, R. E. Manipulation of self-esteem as a determinant of mood in elated and depressed women. *Journal of Abnormal Psychology*, 1975, *84*, 695–700.

Coyne, J. C. Depression and the response of others. *Journal of Abnormal Psychology*, 1976, *85*, 186–193.

Cropley, A. J., & Weckowicz, T. E. The dimensionability of clinical depression. *Australian Journal of Psychology*, 1966, *18*, 18–25.

DeMonbreun, B. G., & Craighead, W. E. Distortion of perception and recall of positive and neutral feedback in depression. *Cognitive Therapy and Research*, 1977, *1*, 311–329.

Dilling, C. A., & Rabin, A. I. Temporal experience in depressed states and schizophrenia. *Journal of Consulting Psychology*, 1967, *31*, 604–608.

Eysenck, H. J. The classification of depressive illnesses. *British Journal of Psychiatry*, 1970, *112*, 241–250.

Eysenck, H. J. *The manual of the Maudsley Personality Inventory*. London: University of London Press, 1959.

Eysenck, H. J., & Eysenck, S. B. G. *The manual of the Eysenck Personality Inventory*. London: University of London Press, 1964.

Feighner, J. P., Robins, E., Guze, S. B., Woodruff, R. W., Winokur, G., & Muñoz, R. Diagnostic criteria for use in psychiatric research. *Archives of General Psychiatry*, 1972, *26*, 57–63.

Flippo, J. R., & Lewinsohn, P. M. Effects of failure on the self-esteem of depressed and nondepressed subjects. *Journal of Consulting and Clinical Psychology*, 1971, *36*, 151.

Forrest, M. S., & Hokanson, J. E. Depression and autonomic arousal reduction accompanying self-punitive behavior. *Journal of Abnormal Psychology*, 1975, *84*, 346–357.

Freud, S. Mourning and melancholia. In *Collected Papers* (Vol. 4). New York: Basic Books, 1959. (Originally published, 1917.)

Fuchs, C., & Rehm, L. P. A self-control behavior therapy program for depression. *Journal of Consulting and Clinical Psychology*, 1977, *45*, 206–215.

Gillespie, R. D. Clinical differentiation of types of depression. *Guy Hospital Reprint*, 1929, *79*, 306–344.

Gioe, V. J. Cognitive modification and positive group experience as a treatment for depression (Doctoral dissertation, Temple University, 1975). *Dissertation*

Abstracts International, 1975, *36*, 3039–3040B. (University Microfilms No. 75-28219)

Goldstein, M. Physiological theories of emotion: A critical historical review from the standpoint of behavior therapy. *Psychological Bulletin*, 1968, *69*, 23–40.

Gotlib, I. H., & Asarnow, R. F. Interpersonal and impersonal problem-solving skills in mildly and clinically depressed university students. *Journal of Consulting and Clinical Psychology*, 1979, *47*, 86–95.

Hale, W. D., & Strickland, B. R. Induction of mood states and their effect on cognition and social behaviors. *Journal of Consulting and Clinical Psychology*, 1976, *44*, 155.

Hamilton, M. A rating scale for depression. *Journal of Neurology, Neurosurgery and Psychiatry*, 1960, *12*, 6–62.

Hamilton, M. Development of a rating scale for primary depressive illness. *British Journal of Social and Clinical Psychology*, 1967, *6*, 278–296.

Hammen, C. L., & Glass, D. R., Jr. Depression, activity and evaluation of reinforcement. *Journal of Abnormal Psychology*, 1975, *84*, 718–721.

Hammen, C. L., & Krantz, S. Effects of success and failure on depressive cognitions. *Journal of Abnormal Psychology*, 1976, *85*, 577–586.

Hammen, C. L., & Peters, S. D. Interpersonal consequences of depression: Responses to men and women enacting a depressed role. *Journal of Abnormal Psychology*, 1978, *87*, 322–332.

Hauri, P. Dreams in patients remitted from reactive depression. *Journal of Abnormal Psychology*, 1976, *85*, 1–10.

Head, R. *Cognitive therapy with depressed college students*. Unpublished master's thesis, University of Miami, 1978.

Hodgson, J. W., & Urban, H. B. *A comparison of interpersonal training programs in the treatment of depressive states*. Unpublished manuscript, Pennsylvania State University, 1975.

James, W. What is emotion? *Mind*, 1884, *9*, 188–204.

Kelly, G. A. *The psychology of personal constructs*. New York: Norton, 1955.

Kendell, R. E. *The classification of depressive illnesses*. London: Oxford University Press, 1968.

Kiloh, L. G., & Garside, R. F. The independence of neurotic and endogenous depression. *British Journal of Psychiatry*, 1963, *109*, 451–463.

Kirkpatrick, P. W. The efficacy of cognitive behavior modification in the treatment of depression (Doctoral dissertation, University of Texas at Austin, 1977). *Dissertation Abstracts International*, 1977, *38*(5), 2370B. (University Microfilms No. 77-22661)

Klein, D. C., Fencil-Morse, E., & Seligman, M. E. P. Learned helplessness, depression and the attribution of failure. *Journal of Personality and Social Psychology*, 1976, *33*, 508–516.

Klein, D. F. Endogenomorphic depression. *Archives of General Psychiatry*, 1974, *31*, 447–454.

Klein, G. S. *Perception, motives and personality*. New York: Knopf, 1970.

Kovacs, M., Rush, A. J., Beck, A. T., & Hollon, S. D. Depressed outpatients treated with cognitive therapy or pharmacotherapy. A one-year followup. *Archives of General Psychiatry*, 1981, *38*, 33–39.

Kraepelin, E. [Manic–depressive insanity and paranoia.] In R. M. Barclay (Ed. and trans.), *Textbook of psychiatry*. Edinburgh: Livingstone, 1913.

Krantz, S., & Hammen, C. Assessment of cognitive bias in depression. *Journal of Abnormal Psychology,* 1979, *88*, 611–619.

Laird, J. D. Self-attribution of emotion: The effects of expressive behavior on the quality of emotional experience. *Journal of Personality and Social Psychology*, 1974, *29*, 475–486.

Lamont, J. Depressive mood and power over the feelings of other persons. *Journal of Clinical Psychology,* 1973, *29*, 319–321.

Laxer, R. M. Self-concept changes of depressive patients in general hospital treatment. *Journal of Consulting Psychology*, 1964, *28*, 214–219.

Lazarus, A. A. *Behavior therapy and beyond*. New York: McGraw-Hill, 1971.

Levitt, E. E., & Lubin, B. *Depression: Concepts, controversies and some new facts*. New York: Springer, 1975.

Lewis, A. Melancholia: A clinical survey of depressive states. *Journal of Mental Science*, 1934, *80*, 277–378.

Lewis, A. States of depression: Their clinical and aetiological differentiation. *British Medical Journal*, 1938, *2*, 875–883.

Lishman, W. A. Selective factors in memory. II: Affective disorder. *Psychological Medicine*, 1972, *2*, 248–253.

Lloyd, G. G., & Lishman, W. Effect of depression on the speed of recall of pleasant and unpleasant experiences. *Psychological Medicine*, 1975, *5*, 173–180.

Loeb, A., Beck, A. T., & Diggory, J. Differential effects of success and failure on depressed and nondepressed patients. *Journal of Nervous and Mental Disease*, 1971, *152*, 106–114.

Loeb, A., Beck, A. T., Diggory, J. C., & Tuthill, R. Expectancy, level of aspiration, performance and self-evaluation in depression. *Proceedings of the 75th Annual Convention of the American Psychological Association*, 1967, 193–194.

Loeb, A., Feshbach, S., Beck, A. T., & Wolf, A. Some effects of reward upon the social perception and motivation of psychiatric patients varying in depression. *Journal of Abnormal and Social Psychology*, 1964, *68*, 609–616.

Ludwig, L. D. Elation–depression and skill as determinants of desire for excitement. *Journal of Personality*, 1975, *43*, 1–22.

Lunghi, M. E. The stability of mood and social perception measures in a sample of depressive inpatients. *British Journal of Psychiatry*, 1977, *130*, 598–604.

Magers, B. D. Cognitive–behavioral short-term group therapy with depressed women (Doctoral dissertation, California School of Professional Psychology, 1977). *Dissertation Abstracts International*, 1978, *38*(9), 4468B. (University Microfilms No. 78-01687)

Mahoney, M. J. *Cognition and behavior modification*. Cambridge, Mass.: Ballinger, 1974.

Marston, W. M. *Emotions of normal people*. New York: Harcourt, Brace, 1928.

McDonald, A. C. A cognitive/behavioral treatment for depression with veterans administration outpatients (Doctoral dissertation, University of Utah, 1978). *Dissertation Abstracts International*, 1978, *39*(6), 2994B. (University Microfilms No. 78-22829)

McLean, P. D., & Hakstian, A. R. Clinical depression: Comparative efficacy of outpatient treatments. *Journal of Consulting and Clinical Psychology*, 1979, *47*, 818–836.

McNitt, P. C., & Thornton, D. W. Depression and perceived reinforcement: A reconsideration. *Journal of Abnormal Psychology*, 1978, *87*, 137–140.

Meichenbaum, D. *Cognitive-behavior modification*. Morristown, N.J.: General Learning Press, 1974.

Melges, F. T., & Bowlby, J. Types of hopelessness in psychopathological process. *Archives of General Psychiatry*, 1969, *20*, 690–699.

Melges, F. T., & Weisz, A. E. The personal future and suicidal ideation. *Journal of Nervous and Mental Disease*, 1971, *153*, 244–250.

Mendelson, M. *Psychoanalytic concepts of depression*. New York: Spectrum, 1974.

Miller, W. R. Psychological deficit in depression. *Psychological Bulletin*, 1975, *82*, 238–260.

Minkoff, K., Bergman, E., Beck, A. T., & Beck, R. Hopelessness, depression, and attempted suicide. *American Journal of Psychiatry*, 1973, *130*, 455–459.

Morris, N. E. *A group self-instruction method for the treatment of depressed outpatients*. National Library of Canada, Canadian Theses Division, No. 35272, 1975.

Muñoz, R. F. *A cognitive approach to the assessment and treatment of depression*. Unpublished doctoral dissertation, University of Oregon, 1977.

Naditch, M. P., Gargan, M. A., & Michael, L. B. Denial, anxiety, locus of control and the discrepancy between aspirations and achievements as components of depression. *Journal of Abnormal Psychology*, 1975, *14*, 1–9.

Nelson, R. E., & Craighead, W. E. Selective recall of positive and negative feedback, self-control behaviors and depression. *Journal of Abnormal Psychology*, 1977, *86*, 379–388.

Paskind, H. A. Manic–depressive psychosis in private practice: Length of attack and length of interval. *Archives of Neurology and Psychiatry*, 1930, *23*, 789–794.

Pichot, P., & Lemperiere, T. Analyse factorielle d'un questionnaire d'auto-évaluation des symptômes dépressifs. *Revue de Psychologie Appliqué*, 1964, *14*, 15–29.

Rehm, L. P., & Plakosh, P. Preference for immediate reinforcement in depression. *Journal of Behavior Therapy and Experimental Psychiatry*, 1975, *6*, 101–103.

Rizley, R. C. Depression and distortion in the attribution of casuality. *Journal of Abnormal Psychology*, 1978, *87*, 32–48.

Robins, E., & Guze, S. Classification of affective disorders: The primary–secondary, the endogenous–reactive, and the neurotic–psychotic concepts. In T. A. Williams, M. M. Katz, & J. A. Shield, Jr. (Eds.), *Recent advances in the psychobiology of the depressive illnesses*. Washington, D.C.: U.S. Government Printing Office, 1972.

Rush, A. J. Psychotherapy of the affective psychoses. *American Journal of Psychoanalysis*, 1980, *40*, 99–123.

Rush, A. J., & Beck, A. T. Cognitive therapy of depression and suicide. *American Journal of Psychotherapy*, 1977, *32*, 201–219.

Rush, A. J., Beck, A. T., Kovacs, M., & Hollon, S. Comparative efficacy of cognitive therapy and imipramine in the treatment of depressed outpatients. *Cognitive Therapy and Research*, 1977, *1*, 17–37.

Rush, A. J., Beck, A. T., Kovacs, M., Khatami, M., & Wolman, T. *A comparison of cognitive and pharmacotherapy in depressed outpatients: A preliminary report.* Paper presented at Society for Psychotherapy Research, Boston, June 1975.

Rush, A. J., Beck, A. T., Kovacs, M., Weissenburger, J., & Hollon, S. Differential effects of cognitive therapy and pharmacotherapy on hopelessness and self-concept. *American Journal of Psychiatry*, in press.

Rush, A. J., Giles, D., Dougherty, R., & Sullivan, D. *Cognitive distortions, schemas and depressive symptomatology.* Manuscript submitted for publication to *British Journal of Social and Clinical Psychology.*

Rush, A. J., Shaw, B., & Khatami, M. Cognitive therapy of depression: Utilizing the couples system. *Cognitive Therapy and Research*, 1980, *4*, 103–113.

Rush, A. J., & Watkins, J. T. Cognitive therapy with psychologically naive depressed outpatients. In G. Emery, S. D. Hollon, & R. C. Bedrosian (Eds.), *New directions in cognitive therapy: A casebook.* New York: Guilford, 1981. (a)

Rush, A. J., & Watkins, J. T. Group versus individual cognitive therapy: A pilot study. *Cognitive Therapy and Research*, 1981, *5*, 95–103. (b)

Sandifer, M. G., Wilson, I. C., & Green, L. The two type thesis of depressive disorders. *American Journal of Psychiatry*, 1966, *123*, 93–97.

Schachter, S., & Singer, J. E. Cognitive, social and physiological determinants of emotional state. *Psychological Review*, 1962, *69*, 379–399.

Schmickley, V. G. *The effects of cognitive behavior modification upon depressed outpatients.* Unpublished doctoral dissertation, Michigan State University, 1976.

Shaw, B. F. Comparison of cognitive therapy and behavior therapy in the treatment of depression. *Journal of Consulting and Clinical Psychology*, 1977, *45*, 543–551.

Shaw, B. *Predictors of successful outcome in cognitive therapy: A pilot study.* Paper presented at the First World Congress on Behavior Therapy, Jerusalem, Israel, July 1980.

Shipley, C. R., & Fazio, A. F. Pilot study of a treatment for psychological depression. *Journal of Abnormal Psychology*, 1973, *82*, 372–376.

Singer, J. L. *The child's world of make-believe: Experimental studies of imaginative play.* New York: Academic Press, 1973.

Skinner, B. F. *The behavior of organisms.* New York: Appleton-Century-Crofts, 1938.

Spitzer, R. L., Endicott, J., & Robins, E. Clinical criteria for psychiatric diagnosis and DSM-III. *American Journal of Psychiatry*, 1975, *132*, 1187–1192.

Steiner, R. E. A cognitive–developmental analysis of depression: Interpersonal problem solving and event interpretation among depressed and nondepressed women (Doctoral dissertation, Clark University, 1974). *Dissertation Abstracts International*, 1975, *35*(8), 4197B. (University Microfilms No. 75-3939)

Stockton, C. T. The depressive style of life (Doctoral dissertation, United States International University, 1975). *Dissertation Abstracts International*, 1975, *36*(3-B), 1420–1421. (University Microfilms No. 75-19123)

Strickland, B. R., Hale, W. D., & Anderson, L. Effect of induced mood states on activity and self-reported affect. *Journal of Consulting and Clinical Psychology*, 1975, *43*, 587.

Tanner, J., Weissman, M., & Prusoff, B. Social adjustment and clinical relapse in depressed outpatients. *Comprehensive Psychiatry*, 1975, *16*, 547–556.

Taylor, F. G., & Marshall, W. L. Experimental analysis of a cognitive-behavioral therapy for depression. *Cognitive Therapy and Research*, 1977, *1*, 59–72.

Teasdale, J. D. Effects of real and recalled success on learned helplessness and depression. *Journal of Abnormal Psychology*, 1978, *87*, 155–164.

Teasdale, J. D., & Bancroft, J. Manipulation of thought content as a determinant of mood and corrigator electromyographic activity in depressed patients. *Journal of Abnormal Psychology*, 1977, *86*, 235–241.

Vatz, K. A., Winig, H. R., & Beck, A. T. *Pessimism and a sense of future time constriction as cognitive distortions in depression*. Unpublished mimeograph, University of Pennsylvania, 1969.

Velten, E. A laboratory task for induction of mood state. *Behaviour Research and Therapy*, 1968, *6*, 473–482.

Watson, J. B. Psychology as the behaviorist views it. *Psychological Review*, 1913, *20*, 158–177.

Watts, C. A. H. *Depressive disorders in the community*. Bristol, England: J. Wright, 1966.

Weiner, B., Frieze, I., Kukla, A., Reed, L., Rest, S., & Rosenbaum, R. M. *Perceiving the causes of success and failure*. New York: General Learning Press, 1971.

Weiner, M. L. *The cognitive unconscious: A Piagetian approach to psychotherapy*. New York: International Psychological Press, 1975.

Weissman, A. N. The Dysfunctional Attitude Scale: A validation study (Doctoral dissertation, University of Pennsylvania, 1979). *Dissertation Abstracts International*, 1979, *40*, 1389B–1390B. (University Microfilms No. 79-19533)

Wener, A. E., & Rehm, L. P. Depressive affect: A test of behavioral hypotheses. *Journal of Abnormal Psychology*, 1975, *84*, 221–227.

Wohlford, P. Extension of personal time, affective states and expectation of personal death. *Journal of Personality and Social Psychology*, 1966, *3*, 559–566.

Wortman, C. B., Panciera, L., Shusterman, L., & Hibscher, J. Attributions of causality and reactions to uncontrollable outcomes. *Journal of Experimental Social Psychology*, 1976, *12*, 301–316.

Zeiss, A. M., Lewinsohn, P. M., & Muñoz, R. F. Nonspecific improvement effects in depression using interpersonal skills training, pleasant activities schedules, or cognitive training. *Journal of Consulting and Clinical Psychology*, 1979, *47*, 427–439.

‡ 7 ‡

COGNITIVE THERAPY: CLINICAL APPLICATIONS

JEFFREY E. YOUNG
AARON T. BECK

DEFINITION

Cognitive therapy is a relatively short-term form of psychotherapy in which the patient and the therapist work in collaboration to relieve symptoms. Cognitive therapy helps patients to learn more effective methods for dealing with those difficulties that contribute to their suffering.

The thrust of cognitive therapy is problem-oriented. Patients generally have a combination of *internal* problems, which are psychological in nature, and *external* problems, which are situational or interpersonal. The therapist and patient work together to break down or reduce the patient's distress into a set of specific problems that can be corrected.

The term "cognitive therapy" is used because we have found that psychological disturbances frequently stem from specific, habitual errors or deficits in thinking. For example, patients may reason on the basis of self-defeating assumptions; may incorrectly interpret life stresses; may judge themselves too harshly; may jump to inaccurate conclusions; or may fail to generate adequate plans or strategies to deal with external problems. The cognitive therapist works with patients to test the validity of their thoughts by applying reason and logic. These tools enable patients to overcome their present problems and to help prevent recurrences.

Jeffrey E. Young and Aaron T. Beck. Center for Cognitive Therapy, University of Pennsylvania, Philadelphia, Pennsylvania.

MISCONCEPTIONS

Many mental health professionals with whom we have spoken share certain misconceptions about cognitive therapy. First, many believe that cognitive therapy is merely a collection of techniques. They assume that cognitive therapy consists of whatever they are already doing with patients *plus*, for example, exposing and correcting the patient's incorrect assumptions about life. On the contrary, cognitive therapy is a comprehensive approach to therapy. It is based on a theory of psychological distress that requires a significant "paradigm shift" for therapists already steeped in another approach, such as behaviorism, psychoanalysis, or client-centered therapy. Cognitive therapy involves, therefore, a new way of viewing patients and their problems. This new conceptual paradigm requires the therapist to take a particular stance vis-à-vis the patient. This stance, which we call "collaborative empiricism," sets guidelines for the manner in which the therapist applies cognitive techniques. Cognitive therapy thus consists of a particular therapeutic *style*, as well as of a set of techniques.

A second misconception about cognitive therapy is that it is purely rational and does not allow for the expression of emotion. Quite the opposite is true. As we make clear, patients are encouraged to express their feelings (although this expression is rarely the end goal of therapy). One of the objectives in cognitive therapy is to identify maladaptive emotions—those that interfere with patients' functioning—and to help alter self-defeating thoughts and assumptions so that patients can bring their undesired emotions under control. Patients will then be freer to feel and express adaptive positive and negative emotions, without this expression interfering with their ability to live happily.

Third, many therapists mistakenly include cognitive therapy with other behaviorally oriented therapies that downplay the importance of the relationship between the patient and the clinician. This chapter stresses the importance of such qualities as empathy, genuineness, concern, and rapport in applying the therapy. Cognitive therapy elaborates (more so than many so-called "relationship" therapies) the specific behaviors that therapists can adopt to promote a spirit of collaboration—for example, providing rationales for each technique; asking inductive questions instead of debating with patients; asking regularly for feedback about the treatment; and inviting patients to participate in the decision-making process of therapy.

Cognitive therapy is constantly evolving in response to clinical evidence about the effectiveness of various therapeutic styles and techniques with particular types of problems and patients. In this chapter, therefore, we describe cognitive therapy for depression at its present stage of evolution. We discuss the therapeutic relationship and collaborative empiricism; we outline the structure and process of therapy sessions; we review specific cognitive and behavioral strategies and techniques with depressed patients; we highlight the uses of questioning in therapy; and, finally, we suggest self-help homework assignments and explain their role in cognitive therapy.

COLLABORATION

RATIONALE

One of the fundamental precepts of cognitive therapy is that there must be a collaborative relationship between the patient and the therapist. This collaboration takes the form of a therapeutic alliance in which therapist and patient work together to fight a common enemy: the patient's distress.

This collaborative approach has at least three goals. First, collaboration helps insure that the patient and the therapist have compatible goals at each point in the course of treatment. Thus, they will not be working at cross-purposes. Second, the process minimizes the patient resistance that often arises when the therapist is viewed as a competitor or an aggressor, or is seen as trying to control or dominate the patient. Third, the alliance helps prevent misunderstandings between patient and therapist. Such misunderstandings can lead the therapist to go down blind alleys or can lead the patient to misinterpret what the therapist has been trying to convey.

INTERPERSONAL QUALITIES

This collaboration demands, first, that the patient trust the therapist. In order to develop this trust, we place a great deal of emphasis on the interpersonal skills of the therapist. A variety of research studies support the importance of these "nonspecific" variables in favorable outcomes of psychotherapy (e.g., Truax & Mitchell, 1971).

Cognitive therapists should be able to communicate that they are genuine, sincere, and open. They should not act in a manner that seems patronizing or condescending, nor should they seem to be holding back impressions or information, or evading patients' questions. Thus, the experienced cognitive therapist does not seem to be playing the *role* of a therapist, but comes across as straightforward and direct.

Coupled with this openness, cognitive therapists should convey warmth and concern through the content of what they say and through such nonverbal behaviors as tone of voice and eye contact. To maintain rapport, therapists must be careful that, in the course of questioning patients' point of view, they do not seem to be criticizing, disapproving, or ridiculing the patients' perspective. The therapist can often use and encourage humor in establishing a positive relationship.

Although it may at first appear contrary to the notion of collaboration, it is also vital for therapists to display a professional manner. Without seeming distant or cold, cognitive therapists must convey a relaxed confidence about their ability to help depressed patients. This confidence can serve as a partial antidote to a patient's initial hopelessness about the future. A professional manner may also make it easier for the therapist to take a directive role, impose structure, and be convincing in expressing alternative points of view. Although patients and therapists share responsibility for the therapy, effective therapists must be able to use the leverage accorded them as professionals when necessary.

JOINT SELECTION OF A TARGET PROBLEM

The cognitive therapist attempts to get the patient involved as an active participant in a variety of ways. Initially, the patient and the therapist together develop a set of problems to address during the course of therapy. These might include specific depressive symptoms, such as apathy, lack of motivation, crying, or difficulty concentrating; or external problems in the patient's life, such as marital problems, career issues, child-rearing concerns, or financial difficulties. Once the patient and the therapist agree on the main problems, they then set priorities on the basis of which problems are most distressing to the patient and which are most quickly amenable to therapeutic change. Some of the most common mistakes we observe in novice cognitive therapists are (1) failure to agree on specific problems to focus on; (2) selection of a peripheral problem to attack, rather than a central concern; and (3) a tendency to skip from problem to problem across sessions, instead of persistently seeking a satisfactory solution to one problem at a time.

At the beginning of each session, the patient and the therapist set an agenda of items to cover during the interview. It is through this process of agenda setting, explained in greater detail (pp. 189–190), that the selection of target problems is implemented on a week-by-week basis.

CONTINUAL FEEDBACK

The cognitive therapist strives throughout each session to be certain that the patient is responding positively to the therapeutic process. Beginning with the first session, the therapist carefully elicits the patient's thoughts and feelings about all aspects of therapy. He or she routinely asks for the patient's evaluation of each session and encourages the patient to express any negative reactions to the therapist, to the way a particular problem was handled, to homework assignments, and so forth. The therapist must also be sensitive to any negative, covert reactions (both verbal and nonverbal) to the interview, and should ask for the patient's thoughts when such clues are noticed. Whenever possible, the therapist should ask the patient to make suggestions about how to proceed, or to make decisions between alternative courses of action.

Another element of the feedback process is for the therapist to explain the rationale for each intervention he or she makes. This rationale demystifies the process of therapy and thus makes it easier for the patient to question the validity of a particular approach. Furthermore, when the patient can see the relationship between a particular homework assignment or technique and the solution to a problem, it is more likely that the patient will participate conscientiously.

A final feature of the feedback process is for the therapist to check continually to be certain that the patient understands the therapist's formulations. Depressed patients often indicate that they understand something when they do not, simply out of a desire to show compliance. Thus, the therapist should regularly provide capsule summaries of what has happened during the session and should ask the patient to abstract the main points from the therapy session. In fact, it is often helpful to have the patient write down these conclusions to review during the week. Similarly, it is important for the therapist to summarize regularly what he or she believes the patient is saying and to ask the patient to modify, correct, or "fine-tune" the therapist's summary.

COLLABORATIVE EMPIRICISM

Once their collaboration has been successfully established, the patient and the therapist can act as an investigative team. Although we elaborate on this investigative process later, a brief overview is appropriate at this point. Each of the patient's maladaptive thoughts or underlying assumptions is approached in the same way that a scientist would approach a question. The thought or assumption is posed as a hypothesis to be tested. The patient and the therapist collect all evidence that either supports or refutes the hypothesis. These data may consist of events in the past, circumstances in the present, or possibilities for the future. The evidence is subjected to logical analysis, and the patient and the therapist reach a conclusion about whether to accept or reject the hypothesis. They may also devise experiments to test the validity of the patient's cognitions. As a result, the therapist does not have to *persuade* patients that their views are illogical or inconsistent with reality; the patients "discover" the inconsistencies instead of having them pointed out. This process of guided discovery is a widely accepted educational method and is a vital component of cognitive therapy.

PROCESS OF COGNITIVE THERAPY: AN OVERVIEW

In this section, we attempt to convey a sense of how a particular cognitive-therapy session is structured, as well as a sense of the course of treatment over several sessions. A detailed discussion of specific techniques follows later.

THE INITIAL SESSIONS

In the early stages of treatment, the therapist has six major goals. The first of these is to work with the patient to define specific problems to focus on. The therapist does this by obtaining a comprehensive picture of the patient's life situation and specific psychological problems, including material about the depth of depression, the presence of suicidal wishes, and particular symptomatology. In order to understand patients' problems as fully as possible, cognitive therapists are especially concerned with delineating exactly what patients are feeling and how the patients view their problems.

A second goal in the early stages is to set priorities regarding the order in which to attack the problems already defined. In order to make a wise decision about these priorities, the cognitive therapist must be able to see the relationship between particular thoughts, particular life situations, and particular distressing emotions. This understanding will permit the therapist to help the patient decide which problem is most suitable to begin working on. Normally, as noted, this decision is made on the basis of which life problems or cognitions are most central to the patient's emotional distress and which are most amenable to change.

A third goal in the early phases, and an important consideration in selecting a target problem, is to show the patient that he or she need not feel hopeless. The most effective way to do this is for the therapist to select an initial problem that can be resolved or alleviated rapidly, and whose alleviation will have a noticeable effect on the patient's emotional state. If this goal can be accomplished, patients inclined to hopelessness will have empirical evidence to refute the thought that their problems are insoluble and that they cannot feel better.

A fourth objective early in therapy is to illustrate for the patient the relationship between cognition and emotion. The therapist can often accomplish this most effectively by observing the patient undergo a mood shift during a session (such as crying); pointing out the change in affect; asking the patient what he or she was thinking just before the shift; labeling the negative thought for the patient; and pointing out its relationship to the mood shift. The therapist can also assign homework to help the patient see the link between specific thoughts and specific feelings.

Fifth, the therapist begins in the first session to socialize the patient into the therapeutic milieu of cognitive therapy. Unlike other forms of therapy, cognitive therapy is active and structured, and all but "therapy virgins" may expect a more unfocused, abstract, insight-oriented, nondirective approach—an approach characteristic of analytically oriented and Rogerian therapies. The cognitive therapist can help the patient to make this transition by maintaining a problem-oriented stance. This stance often involves gently interrupting patients who wander off-track or who continually make abstract, untestable interpretations about the sources of their problems. The therapist can model appropriate behaviors by focusing on concrete thoughts, behaviors, and feelings, as well as by staying with one problem at a time.

A sixth function early in therapy is for the therapist to stress the importance of self-help homework assignments. The therapist can facilitate establishing a permanent pattern of completion of homework assignments by explaining that the homework is, in fact, more important than the time spent during the session, and that patients who do these assignments are generally the ones who improve most rapidly. From the very first session, therefore, the cognitive therapist assigns homework. The process of implementing self-help homework assignments is treated separately later in this chapter.

SETTING AN AGENDA

Because cognitive therapy is a relatively short-term, problem-solving therapy, the limited time available for each interview must be used judiciously. At the beginning of each session, the therapist and the patient together establish an agenda, so that the most pertinent issues can be addressed in an efficient manner.

The agenda usually begins with a brief review of the patient's experiences since the last session. This includes discussion and feedback regarding homework from the past week. The therapist may then ask the patient what problems he or she would like to work on during the session. The therapist will often then suggest topics that he or she feels should be included in the agenda.

After the list of possible topics has been completed, the patient and the therapist discuss and reach conclusions about the topics to be included, the order in which to cover them, and, if necessary, the amount of time that should be allotted to each topic. Some of the considerations in setting priorities include the stage of therapy; the severity of the depression; the presence of suicidal wishes; the degree of distress associated with each problem area; the likelihood of making progress in solving the problem; and the number of different life areas affected by a particular theme or topic. The therapist must be sensitive to patients' occasional desires to discuss or "ventilate" regarding issues that are important at the particular moment, even though such discussions may not seem to offer much relief in the long run. Such flexibility epitomizes the collaborative relationship in cognitive therapy.

THE PROGRESS OF A TYPICAL THERAPY SESSION

After the agenda has been set, and the events and homework of the previous week have been discussed, the therapist and the patient proceed to discuss the other issues on the agenda in order of importance. Generally, it is only possible to make progress on one or two problems in a particular session.

In attacking a typical problem, the therapist usually begins by asking the patient a series of questions to clarify why the patient is experiencing difficulty: Is the patient misinterpreting events? Are the patient's expectations realistic? Is the patient's view based on maladaptive assumptions? Is the patient's behavior appropriate? If the problem is "real," has the patient considered all of the possible solutions? The therapist thus asks a series of questions, the answers to which should suggest a cognitive–behavioral conceptualization of why the patient is experiencing difficulty in this area. As the end product of this conceptualizing process, the therapist usually selects one or two key thoughts, assumptions, images, or behaviors to modify. Once this target has been selected, the therapist chooses the most appropriate cognitive or behavioral techniques to apply and explains the rationale to the patient. These techniques (explained in detail later) may include hypothesis testing, setting up an experiment, behavior rehearsal, cognitive rehearsal, generating alternatives, diversion, weighing advantages and disadvantages, mastery and pleasure ratings, activity scheduling, and so forth.

In the last few minutes of the session, the therapist asks the patient to summarize (often in writing) the major conclusions from the session. He or she also asks for the patient's reactions to the session and ascertains whether the therapist said anything that annoyed or disturbed the patient. Finally, the therapist suggests a self-help homework assignment. Usually, the assignment is designed to help the patient apply the concepts or skills learned during the session to solving the target problem during the week that follows.

MIDDLE AND LATER SESSIONS

The structure of cognitive-therapy sessions does not change as treatment progresses; however, the content often does. The initial sessions are generally aimed at identifying problems, overcoming hopelessness, setting priorities, establishing empathy and rapport, demonstrating the relationship between cognition and emotion, labeling errors in thinking, making rapid progress on a readily solvable problem, and socializing the patient into the cognitive-therapy system.

The middle and later sessions are more likely to focus on problems that require more intensive cognitive probing to understand and modify. For example, the therapist in an early session might use behavioral techniques to help the patient become more active, whereas in a middle session he or she might deal with the patient's automatic thought that "No one can ever love me." In general, the middle sessions are more likely to focus on more complex problems, often those involving several dysfunctional thoughts and behaviors. The middle sessions are also more likely than are the earlier ones to be spent in helping the patient to integrate concepts already learned. This is accomplished through homework assignments requiring the continual repetition and application of specific rational responses to combat specific dysfunctional thoughts.

By the later sessions, the patient is generally feeling less depressed, and the focus often shifts from specific thoughts about specific problems to more general assumptions about life. These "silent" assumptions may underlie many of the patient's problems. Assumptions in therapy can be compared to themes in novels—they can be abstracted from the behavior of the "characters" in a wide range of situations. An example in therapy is the belief that "Unless I perform perfectly, I am a failure." If these maladaptive assumptions can be altered, the patient will become less predisposed to future episodes of depression.

During the later sessions, the patient generally takes an increasing amount of responsibility for identifying problems, generating solutions, and implementing them through homework. The therapist serves more as an advisor or consultant as the patient learns to apply the techniques of cognitive therapy without constant support. The frequency of sessions can be reduced, and eventually discontinued, as the patient becomes a more effective problem solver.

COGNITIVE TECHNIQUES

Four major processes comprise the cognitive approach: (1) eliciting automatic thoughts; (2) testing automatic thoughts; (3) identifying maladaptive underlying assumptions; and (4) analyzing the validity of maladaptive assumptions. Each process is discussed separately.

ELICITING AUTOMATIC THOUGHTS

Conscious thoughts often intervene between external events and an individual's emotional reactions to these events. Patients are often unaware of these automatic thoughts because they occur so often and so quickly, as if by reflex. The cognitive therapist trains patients to focus on their automatic thoughts. These automatic thoughts tend to be repetitive, plausible to the patient, and idiosyncratic. If the patient does not learn to recognize these thoughts, therapy cannot proceed effectively.

Ideally, the therapist and the patient work together as collaborators to discover the specific thoughts that precede such emotions as anger, sadness, and anxiety. To accomplish this goal, the therapist can employ one or more of the following possible strategies.

Inductive Questioning

The therapist can ask the patient a series of questions designed to explore some of the possible reasons for the patient's emotional reactions. Skillful questioning can provide patients with a strategy for introspective exploration that they can later employ by themselves when the therapist is not nearby.

Imagery

If patients can identify events or situations that seem to trigger the emotional response, the therapist may urge such patients to picture the distressing situations in detail. If the images are realistic and clear, patients are often able to identify the automatic thoughts they were having at the time. The following excerpt illustrates this technique:

PATIENT: I can't go bowling. Every time I go in there, I want to run away.

THERAPIST: Do you remember any of the thoughts you had when you went there?

PATIENT: Not really. Maybe it just brings back bad memories, I don't know.

THERAPIST: Let's try an experiment to see if we can discover what you were thinking. Okay?

PATIENT: I guess so.

THERAPIST: I'd like you to relax and close your eyes. Now imagine you are entering the bowling alley. Describe for me what's happening.

PATIENT: (*Describes entering the alley, getting a score sheet, etc.*) I feel like I want to get out, just get away.

THERAPIST: What are you thinking now?

PATIENT: I'm thinking, "Everyone is going to laugh at me when they see how bad I play."

THERAPIST: Do you think that thought might have led to your wish to run away?

PATIENT: I know it did.

Role Playing

When the trigger event is interpersonal in nature, role playing is often more effective than imagery. With this strategy, the therapist plays the role of the other person involved in the upsetting situation, while patients "play" themselves. If patients can involve themselves in the role play, the automatic thoughts can often be elicited with the assistance of the therapist.

Mood Shifts during the Session

The therapist can take advantage of any changes in mood that take place during the session by pointing them out to the patient as soon as possible. The therapist then asks the patient what he or she was thinking just prior to the increase in dysphoria, tears, anger, or other reactions.

Daily Record of Dysfunctional Thoughts

This is the simplest method of pinpointing automatic thoughts, once the patient is familiar with the technique. The patient lists automatic thoughts at home in the appropriate column on the Daily Record of Dysfunctional Thoughts (Figure 7.1). The therapist and patient review these thoughts during the session.

It is important to distinguish this process of eliciting automatic thoughts from the "interpretations" made in other psychotherapies. The cognitive therapist does not tell the patient an automatic thought that he or she (the patient) has not already mentioned. This "clairvoyance" undermines the patient's role as collaborator and makes it difficult for the patient to identify these thoughts at home when the therapist is not nearby. Even more important, the therapist's "intuition" may be wrong, and the patient will be going down a blind alley. On occasion, it will be necessary for the therapist to suggest several plausible automatic thoughts (a multiple-choice technique) when the nondirective strategies have failed.

The example of "clairvoyance" that follows provides a contrast to the imagery technique illustrated previously:

PATIENT: I can't go bowling. Every time I go in there, I want to run away.

THERAPIST: Why?

PATIENT: I don't know. I just want to leave.

DATE	**SITUATION** Describe: 1. Actual event leading to unpleasant emotion, or 2. Stream of thoughts, daydream, or recollection, leading to unpleasant emotion.	**EMOTION(S)** 1. Specify sad/ anxious/ angry, etc. 2. Rate degree of emotion, 1-100.	**AUTOMATIC THOUGHT(S)** 1. Write automatic thought(s) that preceded emotion(s). 2. Rate belief in automatic thought(s), 0-100%.	**RATIONAL RESPONSE** 1. Write rational response to automatic thought(s). 2. Rate belief in rational response, 0-100%.	**OUTCOME** 1. Rerate belief in automatic thought(s), 0-100%. 2. Specify and rate subsequent emotions, 0–100.

Explanation: When you experience an unpleasant emotion, note the situation that seemed to stimulate the emotion. (If the emotion occurred while you were thinking, daydreaming, etc., please note this.) Then note the automatic thought associated with the emotion. Record the degree to which you believe this thought: 0% = not at all; 100% = completely. In rating degree of emotion: 1 = a trace; 100 = the most intense possible.

FIGURE 7.1. Daily Record of Dysfunctional Thoughts.

THERAPIST: Do you tell yourself, "I wish I didn't have to bowl by myself"?

PATIENT: Maybe. I'm not sure.

THERAPIST: Well, maybe you keep thinking that bowling isn't going to solve the problems in your life. You're right, but it's a beginning.

Ascertaining the Meaning of an Event

Sometimes, skillful attempts by the therapist to elicit automatic thoughts are not successful. The therapist should then attempt to discern, through questioning, the specific meaning for the patient of the event that preceded the emotional response. For example, one patient began to cry whenever he had an argument with his girlfriend. It was not possible to identify a specific automatic thought. However, after the therapist asked a series of questions to probe the meaning of the event, it became obvious that the patient had always associated any type of argument or fight with the end of a relationship. It was this meaning, embedded in his view of the event, that preceded his crying.

TESTING AUTOMATIC THOUGHTS

Once the therapist and the patient have identified a key automatic thought, the therapist asks the patient to suspend temporarily any conviction that the thought is undeniably true, and, instead, to view the thought as a hypothesis to be tested. The therapist and the patient collaborate in gathering data, evaluating evidence, and drawing conclusions.

This experimental method is basic to the application of cognitive therapy. The therapist helps patients learn a *process* of thinking that resembles scientific investigation. The therapist demonstrates to the patient that the *perception* of reality is not the same as reality itself. Patients learn to design experiments that will test the validity of their own automatic thoughts. As a result, they thus learn how to modify their maladaptive thinking so that they can maintain their gains after treatment ends.

There are several procedures for testing the validity of automatic thoughts:

Examining Available Evidence

The therapist asks the patient to draw on previous experiences to list the evidence supporting and contradicting the hypothesis. After weighing *all* available evidence, patients frequently reject their automatic thoughts as false, inaccurate, or exaggerated.

Setting Up an Experiment

The therapist asks the patient to design an experiment to test the hypothesis. Once the experiment has been planned, the patient predicts what the outcome will be, then gathers data. Frequently, the data contradict the patient's prediction, and the patient can then reject the automatic thought. In the example below, the therapist sets up an experiment to test the automatic thought, "I can't concentrate on anything anymore."

PATIENT: I can't concentrate on anything anymore.

THERAPIST: How could you test that out?

PATIENT: I guess I could try reading something.

THERAPIST: Here's a newspaper. What section do you usually read?

PATIENT: I used to enjoy the sports section.

THERAPIST: Here's an article on the Penn basketball game last night. How long do you think you'll be able to concentrate on it?

PATIENT: I doubt I could get past the first paragraph.

THERAPIST: Let's write down the prediction. (*Patient writes "one paragraph."*) Now let's test it out. Keep reading until you can't concentrate anymore. This will give us valuable information.

PATIENT: (*Reads the entire article.*) I'm finished.

THERAPIST: How far did you get?

PATIENT: I finished it.

THERAPIST: Let's write down the results of the experiment. (*Patient writes "eight paragraphs."*) You said before that you couldn't concentrate on anything. Do you still believe that?

PATIENT: Well, my concentration's not as good as it used to be.

THERAPIST: That's right. However, you have retained some ability. The next step is to improve your concentration.

It is important that the therapist remain neutral regarding the patient's initial prediction and not assume automatically that the patient's belief is inaccurate or distorted. In some instances, the patient's prediction will be correct.

Inductive Questioning

When the previous two approaches are not appropriate or applicable, the therapist may produce evidence from his or her own experience that contradicts the patient's hypothesis. This evidence is presented in the form of a question that poses a logical dilemma for the patient (e.g., "90% of my patients say they won't get better, yet most of them do improve. Why do you think you are different from them?"). Alternatively, the therapist, through questioning, may point out logical flaws within the patient's own belief system (e.g., "You say you have always been a weak person. Yet you also tell me that before you were depressed, you got along fine. Do you see any inconsistency in your thinking?").

Operationalizing a Negative Construct

Sometimes, as a step in testing an automatic thought, the therapist and the patient have to define in more concrete terms what the patient means by using a particular word or expression. For example, one patient at our clinic kept telling himself, "I'm a coward." To test the thought, the therapist and patient first had to define and give referents of the construct. In this instance, they operationalized "cowardice" as not defending oneself when being attacked. After this criterion had been agreed upon, the therapist and patient examined past evidence to assess whether the label of "coward" was a valid one. This procedure can help patients recognize the arbitrary nature of their self-appraisals and bring them more in line with common-sense definitions of these negative terms.

Reattribution

One of the most powerful techniques for testing automatic thoughts is "reattribution." When patients unrealistically blame themselves for unpleasant events, the therapist and the patients can review the situation to find other factors that may explain what happened other than, or in addition to, the patients' behavior. This technique may also be used to show patients that some of the problems they are having are symptoms of depression (e.g., loss of concentration) and not indications of permanent physiological deterioration.

Generating Alternatives

When patients view particular problems as insoluble, the therapist can work with the patients to generate solutions to the problems that have not been considered. Sometimes a patient has already considered a viable solution, but has prematurely rejected it as unworkable or unlikely to be effective.

These six desirable techniques can be contrasted with one of the most common stylistic errors we observe in trainees. The therapist's behavior sometimes inappropriately resembles that of a high-pressure salesman, persuading patients that they should adopt the therapist's point of view. We have found that therapists can guide patients to adjust their thinking to reality more effectively through questioning than they can through direct exhortation or debate. We have observed that, when patients are encouraged to think through issues and reach their own conclusions, they are more likely to integrate the new concepts and retain them. In a debate, the "weaker" party often feels defensive and under attack, and is unlikely to absorb the "opponent's" reasoning. Here is a brief example of this "high-pressure" approach:

> *PATIENT:* I just can't do anything right in school anymore.
>
> *THERAPIST:* That's easy to understand. You're depressed. And when people are depressed, they have a hard time studying.
>
> *PATIENT:* I think I'm stupid.
>
> *THERAPIST:* But you did very well up until a year ago, when your father died and you got depressed.

PATIENT: That's because the work was easier then.

THERAPIST: Surely there must be *something* you are doing right in school. You're probably exaggerating.

PATIENT: Not really.

IDENTIFYING MALADAPTIVE ASSUMPTIONS

We often observe general patterns that seem to underlie patients' automatic thoughts. These patterns or regularities act as a set of rules that guide the way a patient reacts to many different situations. We refer to these rules as "assumptions." These assumptions may determine, for example, what patients consider "right" or "wrong" in judging themselves and other people.

Although patients can often readily identify their automatic thoughts, their underlying assumptions are far less accessible. Most people are unaware of their "rule books." "In order to be happy, I have to be successful in whatever I undertake," or "I can't live without love," are typical unarticulated assumptions. When these rules are framed in absolute terms, are unrealistic, or are used inappropriately or excessively, they often lead to such disturbances as depression, anxiety, and paranoia. We label rules that lead to such problems as "maladaptive."

One of the major goals of cognitive therapy, especially in the later stages of treatment, is to help patients identify and challenge those maladaptive assumptions that affect their ability to avoid future depressions.

In order to identify these maladaptive assumptions, the therapist can listen closely for themes that seem to cut across several different situations or problem areas. The therapist can then list several related automatic thoughts that the patient has already expressed on different occasions, and ask the patient to *abstract the general "rule" that connects the automatic thoughts.* If the patient cannot do this, the therapist can suggest a plausible assumption, list the thoughts that seem to follow from it, and then ask the patient whether the assumption "rings true." The therapist should be open to the possibility that the assumption does not fit that patient, and should then work with the patient to pinpoint a more accurate statement of the underlying "rule."

ANALYZING THE VALIDITY OF MALADAPTIVE ASSUMPTIONS

The cognitive therapist emphasizes questioning in the modification of underlying assumptions. We find that the most effective approach is one in which the patient develops evidence against the assumption, either alone or in collaboration with the therapist.

It should be noted that there is often a fine line between *guiding* a patient and trying to *persuade* a patient. In some instances, the cognitive therapist may need to reiterate forcefully a point that the therapist and the patient have already established. The main distinction, then, in deciding whether a therapist is acting in a desirable manner is not whether the therapist is forceful or tenacious, but whether the therapist generally seems to be *collaborating* with the patient rather than *arguing* with the patient.

After an assumption has been identified, one strategy for modifying it is for the therapist to ask the patient if it seems reasonable to him or her. If it does, the therapist can ask the patient a series of questions to demonstrate the contradictions or problems inherent in the assumption. In the excerpt that follows, the therapist uses questioning to demonstrate to the patient the maladaptive consequences of holding the assumption that one should *always* work up to one's potential.

PATIENT: I guess I believe that I should always work up to my potential.

THERAPIST: Why is that?

PATIENT: Otherwise I'd be wasting time.

THERAPIST: But what is the *long-range* goal in working up to your potential?

PATIENT: (*Long pause.*) I've never really thought about that. I've just assumed that I should.

THERAPIST: Are there any positive things you give up by always having to work up to your potential?

PATIENT: I suppose it makes it hard to relax or take a vacation.

THERAPIST: What about "living up to your potential" to enjoy yourself and relax? Is that important at all?

PATIENT: I've never really thought of it that way.

THERAPIST: Maybe we can work on giving yourself permission *not* to work up to your potential at all times.

Another strategy for testing assumptions is for the therapist and patient to generate *lists of the advantages and disadvantages* of changing an assumption. Once the lists have been completed, the therapist and patient can discuss and weigh the competing considerations. A related approach is for the patient to weigh the long-term and short-term utility of assumptions.

Many assumptions take the form of "shoulds"—rules about what patients should ideally do in given situations. A behavioral strategy, "response prevention," has been adapted as a technique for overcoming these "shoulds." Once the "should" has been identified, the therapist and patient devise an experiment to test what would happen if the patient did *not* obey the rule. The patient makes a prediction about what the result will be; the experiment is carried out; and the results are discussed. Generally, it is desirable to generate a series of graded tasks that violate the "should," so that the patient attempts less threatening changes first.

BEHAVIORAL TECHNIQUES

The cognitive therapist also uses a variety of behavioral techniques to help the patient cope better with situational or interpersonal problems. These behavioral techniques are "action-oriented" in the sense that patients practice specific procedures for dealing with concrete situations or for using time more adaptively. In contrast to strictly cognitive techniques, therefore, behavioral techniques focus more on how to act or cope than they do on how to view or interpret events.

One of the principal goals of each behavioral technique is to modify dysfunctional cognitions. For example, patients who believe that "I can't enjoy anything any more" often modify this automatic thought after completing a series of behavioral assignments designed to increase the number and variety of pleasurable activities they engage in. Thus, behavioral change is often used as evidence to bring about cognitive change.

Behavioral techniques are incorporated throughout the course of treatment, but are usually concentrated in the early stages of therapy. This is especially true with more severely depressed patients who are immobilized, passive, anhedonic, socially withdrawn, and having trouble concentrating. The most commonly used behavioral techniques are briefly described here.

SCHEDULING ACTIVITIES

The therapist uses an activity schedule to help the patient plan activities hour by hour during the day. The patient then keeps a record of the activities that were actually engaged in, hour by hour. Scheduling activities is usually one of the first techniques used with a depressed patient. It often seems to counteract loss of motivation, hopelessness, and excessive rumination.

MASTERY AND PLEASURE

One of the goals in activity scheduling is for patients to derive more pleasure and a greater sense of accomplishment on a day-to-day basis. To do this, the patient rates each completed activity for both mastery and pleasure on a scale from 0 to 10. These ratings generally serve to contradict directly patients' beliefs that they cannot enjoy anything and cannot obtain a sense of accomplishment anymore.

GRADED TASK AND ASSIGNMENT

In order to help some patients initiate activities for mastery and pleasure, the therapist will have to break down an activity into subtasks, ranging from the simplest part of the task to the most complex and taxing. This step-by-step approach permits depressed patients eventually to tackle tasks that originally seemed impossible or overwhelming to them. These graded tasks provide immediate and unambiguous proof to patients that they can succeed.

COGNITIVE REHEARSAL

Some patients have difficulty carrying out tasks requiring successive steps for completion. Frequently, this is a result of problems in concentration. "Cognitive rehearsal" refers to the technique of asking the patient to imagine each step leading to completion of the task. Rehearsal imagery helps patients focus their attention on specific tasks, and it permits the therapist to identify potential obstacles that may make the assignment difficult for a particular patient.

SELF-RELIANCE TRAINING

The therapist may have to teach some patients to take increasing responsibility for their day-to-day activities, instead of relying on other people to take care of all their needs. For example, patients may begin by showering, then may go on to making their own beds, cleaning the house, cooking their own meals, shopping, and so forth. This responsibility also includes gaining control over their emotional reactions. Graded task assignments, assertiveness training, and running experiments may all be used as part of self-reliance training.

ROLE PLAYING

In the context of cognitive therapy, role playing may be used (1) to elicit automatic thoughts in specific interpersonal situations; (2) to practice new cognitive responses in social encounters that had previously been problematic for a patient; and (3) to rehearse new behaviors in order for the patient to function more effectively with other people. A variation, role reversal, is often effective in guiding patients to "reality-test" how other people would probably view their behavior, and thus to allow patients to view themselves more sympathetically. Role playing can also be used as part of assertiveness training. Role playing frequently is accompanied by modeling and coaching procedures.

DIVERSION TECHNIQUES

Patients can use various forms of diversion of attention to reduce temporarily most forms of painful affect, including dysphoria, anxiety, and anger. Diversion may be accomplished through physical activity, social contact, work, play, or visual imagery.

QUESTIONING

Throughout this chapter, we have repeatedly emphasized the importance of questioning in cognitive therapy. In fact, the majority of verbalizations by the therapist in each session should be in the form of questions.

Questions can be used to serve a wide variety of purposes. For example, a single question can simultaneously make the patient aware of a particular problem area; help the therapist evaluate the patient's reactions to this new area of inquiry; provide specific data about the problem; generate possible solutions to problems that the patient had viewed as insoluble; and raise serious doubt in the patient's mind about previously distorted conclusions.

We have developed a list of at least 15 purposes for which questioning can be employed:

1. To obtain significant biographical, diagnostic, and background data.
2. To obtain an overview of the general nature of patients' presenting problems.
3. To generate information about specific external situations, stressors, and patients' interpersonal networks.
4. To assess patients' current coping styles, tolerance for stress, level of functioning, and ability to observe themselves objectively.
5. To recast vague complaints as specific problems that can be attacked. For example, a patient entered therapy reporting that her depression had been diagnosed as "existential" because she did not know who she was or what her role should be. The therapist posed the question, "What specific problem have you been grappling with?" The patient answered that she could not decide whether to return to school to initiate a law career or to remain a housewife. The patient and therapist could then proceed to discuss the advantages and disadvantages of these discrete options.
6. To encourage patients to begin the decision-making process by developing alternative approaches.
7. To assist patients in resolving decisions by weighing the pros and cons of alternatives that have already been generated, thus narrowing the range of desirable possibilities.
8. To prompt patients to consider the consequences of continuing to engage in dysfunctional behaviors.
9. To examine the potential advantages of behaving in more adaptive ways.
10. To elicit specific automatic thoughts preceding unpleasant emotions or maladaptive behavior.

11. To determine the *meaning* that patients attach to a particular event or set of circumstances.

12. To help patients define criteria for applying certain maladaptive self-appraisals (see the discussion of the technique of operationalizing a negative construct, p. 198).

13. To demonstrate to patients how they are selectively focusing on only negative information in drawing conclusions. In the excerpt that follows (from Beck, Rush, Shaw, & Emery, 1979), a depressed patient was disgusted with herself for eating candy when she was on a diet.

PATIENT: I don't have any self-control at all.

THERAPIST: On what basis do you say that?

PATIENT: Somebody offered me candy and I couldn't refuse it.

THERAPIST: Were you eating candy every day?

PATIENT: No, I just ate it this once.

THERAPIST: Did you do anything constructive during the past week to adhere to your diet?

PATIENT: Well, I didn't give in to the temptation to buy candy every time I saw it at the store. . . . Also, I did not eat any candy except that one time when it was offered to me and I felt I couldn't refuse it.

THERAPIST: If you counted up the number of times you controlled yourself versus the number of times you gave in, what ratio would you get?

PATIENT: About 100 to 1.

THERAPIST: So if you controlled yourself 100 times and did not control yourself just once, would that be a sign that you are weak through and through?

PATIENT: I guess not—not *through* and *through*. (*Smiles*.)

14. To illustrate to patients the way in which they disqualify positive evidence. In the example below (from Beck *et al.*, 1979), the patient recognizes that he has ignored clearcut evidence of improvement.

PATIENT: I really haven't made any progress in therapy.

THERAPIST: Didn't you have to improve in order to leave the hospital and go back to college?

PATIENT: What's the big deal about going to college every day?

THERAPIST: Why do you say that?

PATIENT: It's easy to attend these classes because all the people are healthy.

THERAPIST: How about when you were in group therapy in the hospital: What did you feel then?

PATIENT: I guess I thought then that it was easy to be with the other people because they were all as crazy as I was.

THERAPIST: Is it possible that whatever you accomplish you tend to discredit?

15. To open for discussion certain problem areas that patients have prematurely reached closure on and that continue to influence maladaptive patterns.

SELF-HELP ASSIGNMENTS AT HOME

The systematic completion of homework is of crucial importance in cognitive therapy. Unless patients can apply the concepts learned in the therapy sessions to their lives outside the clinic, there will be little progress. Homework, therefore, promotes transfer of learning. It also provides a structure for helping patients gather data and test hypotheses, and thereby for modifying maladaptive cognitions so that they are more consistent with reality. Homework thus encourages patients to *concretize* the abstract concepts and insights that have traditionally been the province of psychotherapy, making psychotherapy a more active, involving process. Finally, homework encourages self-control rather than reliance on the therapist, and therefore is important in assuring that the improvement is maintained after termination of treatment.

PROVIDING RATIONALE

The therapist must stress the importance of homework in treatment. This can be accomplished by explaining the benefits to be derived from each assignment in detail, as well as by periodically reminding patients how vital these benefits will be in helping them improve.

ASSIGNING HOMEWORK

The therapist tailors the assignment to the individual patient. Ideally, it should follow logically from the problems discussed during the session. The assignment should be clear and very specific, and should be written down in duplicate (one copy for the therapist and one for the patient), usually near the end of the session. Some typical assignments include asking patients to do the following:

1. Keep a Daily Record of Dysfunctional Thoughts (Figure 7.1) with rational responses.
2. Schedule activities.
3. Rate mastery and pleasure.
4. Review a list of the main points made during the session.
5. Read a book or article relevant to a particular problem.
6. Count automatic thoughts, using a wrist counter.
7. Listen to or view a tape of the therapy session.
8. Write an autobiographical sketch.
9. Fill our questionnaires like the Dysfunctional Attitude Scale (DAS) or the Beck Depression Inventory (BDI).
10. Graph or chart hour-by-hour mood changes, such as increases in anxiety, sadness, or anger.
11. Practice coping techniques, such as diversion or relaxation.
12. Try out new behaviors that patients may have difficulty with (e.g., assertiveness, meeting strangers).

ELICITING REACTIONS AND POSSIBLE DIFFICULTIES

It is absolutely essential that the therapist ask patients for their reactions to assignments ("Does it sound useful?" "Does it seem manageable?" "Is the assignment clear?"). It is often helpful for the therapist to suggest that the patient visualize carrying out the assignment in order to identify any obstacles that might arise. Finally, as therapy progresses, the patient should play an increasing role in suggesting and designing homework assignments.

REVIEWING PREVIOUS HOMEWORK

Unless the therapist routinely reviews homework assigned from the previous week, the patient may come to believe that there is no need to complete the assignments carefully. Near the beginning of each session, the therapist and the patient should discuss each assignment, and the therapist should summarize the conclusions derived or progress made.

DIFFICULTIES IN COMPLETING HOMEWORK

Many patients fail to complete homework assignments or do them halfheartedly. It is vital that the therapist not assume that the patient is being "resistant" or "passive-aggressive." The cognitive therapist assumes a problem-solving stance by trying to identify automatic thoughts, assumptions, or behavioral deficits that explain why a particular patient is not completing homework. Once the problems have been identified, the therapist and the patient work together to overcome the obstacles. Some common problems and possible solutions include the following:

(1) A patient does not fully understand the assignment. In this case, the therapist should review the assignment in much greater detail, being as specific as possible about what is expected. Cognitive rehearsal or beginning the assignment in the office with the therapist's assistance may be helpful.

(2) A patient believes that he or she is "by nature" a disorganized person who lacks self-control and cannot keep records or follow through on assignments. With such patients, the therapist can challenge this notion by asking whether there were times in the past when the patients kept lists (for example, while planning a party or a trip). The therapist can also ask these patients whether they would be able to complete the assignment if the therapist paid them a million dollars to do so. This approach helps patients recognize that they would probably be able to exert self-control if they believed that the payoff from doing the assignment were great enough. At this point, the therapist and the patients can generate a list of the advantages to completing the assignment. The patients can then review the advantages each day before attempting the self-help assignment.

Some patients need help in structuring their time to include homework as a daily activity. This can be accomplished by setting a specific time each day to work on the assignment. In unusual cases, the patient can establish a self-administered reward or punishment procedure to insure homework completion. For example, the patient can set up a specific reward for doing the assignment each day (such as purchasing a "luxury" item), or a penalty for not doing the assignment (such as not watching a favorite sports event on television until the homework is completed).

(3) A patient believes that his or her problem is too deep-seated and complex to be solved by simple assignments. The therapist can explain to such patients that even the most complex endeavors can be achieved by taking small steps. Patients can also be asked to experiment for a period of time before concluding that the assignments will not help. In some instances, patients feel that they have not made enough progress and therefore that the homework is not helping. Such patients can be helped to set more realistic expectations about the length of time it may take to see significant results. Alternatively, the therapist can highlight any improvements that have, in fact, been made, but that the patient may be ignoring or minimizing.

(4) A patient seems to resent being given assignments. In such instances, patients can be encouraged to develop their own self-help assignments with the therapist's guidance. Or the therapist can offer the patients several alternative assignments to choose from. As a last resort, the therapist can concede that these patients are free not to do the assignments, and can label such noncompliance as one of the options the patients may choose. The therapist can then work with the patients to evaluate the consequences of selecting this option.

(5) A patient is afraid of failing or of doing the assignment imperfectly. The therapist can explain to such patients that self-help assignments cannot be "failed" and that the patients are not being evaluated on their performance. Doing an assignment with 50% success is certainly more helpful than not attempting it at all. Furthermore, the therapist can explain that any "mistakes" in the assignment provide valuable data about problems that still have not been resolved, and that the patients and the therapist can then work together to solve these problems. In summary, homework is a "no-lose" activity when viewed adaptively.

(6) A patient believes that he or she can improve as quickly without doing written assignments. One strategy for handling this

assumption is for the therapist to provide evidence that most patients who have believed this were wrong and that therapy progressed more slowly with these patients. Another alternative with such patients is for the therapist to set up an experiment for a predetermined period of time during which the patients do not do written assignments. At the end of this trial period, the patients and the therapist together can evaluate the degree of improvement. In some cases, patients do, in fact, seem to be able to integrate cognitive and behavioral changes rapidly without written assignments.

SPECIAL PROBLEMS

With a significant proportion of patients, it is not possible for the therapist to follow the "standard" format for therapy outlined above. The therapist must be flexible enough to adapt to the special problems presented by many patients. The novice trainee often makes the error of rigidly persisting in following the standard format, even when it is not working.

One set of special problems concerns difficulties in the relationship between patient and therapist. When the therapist senses that the patient is dissatisfied, angry, or "resistant," it is essential for the therapist to express these observations to the patient in a direct fashion. The therapist can ask the patient whether these observations are accurate, what the patient has been feeling, and what thoughts the patient might be having about the therapist. Some common thoughts are these:

1. The therapist is impersonal and does not treat me as an individual.
2. The therapist does not really understand my problems.
3. The therapist said or did a particular thing that proves that he or she does not really care about me.

In all such cases, it is essential for the therapist to remain open to the possibility that he or she has said or done something that can easily be misinterpreted. For example, a trainee reduced the number of sessions from two a week to one a week because the patient had been making such good progress. The patient interpreted this as rejection, because the therapist had not explained the rationale for the reduction. The therapist can approach such thoughts in the same way that he or she helps patients test other thoughts—by gathering evidence and considering alternative explanations for the evidence. If the therapist does not appear defensive, the patient and the therapist can almost always resolve the problem through discussion. At times, it may be desirable for the therapist to modify his or her behavior to meet the specific needs of a given patient better. For example, with a patient who complains that the therapist is impersonal, it may be helpful for the therapist to engage in more self-disclosure and share more personal reactions. With a patient who feels that the therapist does not understand, the therapist can check more carefully with the patient to be sure that his or her formulations of the patient's cognitions are accurate.

The important point in situations like these is for the therapist not to assume that the patient is being stubbornly resistant or totally irrational. Therapists must ally themselves with patients to get help in understanding the patients' reactions. In many instances, these reactions provide evidence about the types of distorted judgments patients make in other relationships, and therefore they provide an opportunity within therapy to work out maladaptive interpretations that have far-reaching consequences for other relationships.

A second major set of problems arises when therapy does not seem to be working, even though the patient is assiduously completing homework assignments and cooperating with the therapist. There are many possible explanations for such apparent failure. First, the patient's or the therapist's expectations about the speed or consistency of change may be inappropriate. Either the patient or the therapist may be minimizing small changes that have already taken place. One of them may feel that therapy is not progressing as rapidly as it "should." In such instances, it is essential for both patient and therapist to expect ups and downs during the course of treatment, and for therapists to accept the reality that progress may be much slower with some patients than with others. It is important to focus on the "small steps" that may have been made.

In other cases, the techniques of cognitive therapy may have been misapplied. For example, the therapist may not recognize that the patient does not really find many of the rational responses convincing. Therefore, in such a case, they are ineffective. Another patient may be having difficulty remembering rational responses at times of emotional upset. It is essential, therefore, for the therapist to ascertain the amount of belief that this patient has in each of the rational responses. The therapist must also help the patient incorporate the responses as soon as possible at the time that each automatic thought occurs.

In many instances, there is little progress because the therapist has selected a peripheral problem to focus on. When there seems to be minimal change in depression level, even though the patient seems to have made progress in a particular problem area, the therapist should investigate the possibility that the most distressing problem has been postponed or is still hidden. A typical case of this type is a patient who complains of difficulty at work as the major problem when, in fact, a marital problem is leading to this difficulty; the real issue may seem too frightening for the patient to deal with.

Another possible problem is that the therapist is too rigidly applying one technique. For example, it is often necessary to experiment with several behavioral or cognitive techniques before finding an approach that the patient responds to. The therapist must persist for a while before giving up on a particular technique, but he or she still must be willing to try alternative ones when it is apparent that the patient is not responding. For example, behavioral assignments are sometimes more helpful with particular patients, even though cognitive homework might appear more appropriate.

Sometimes the patient's basic hopelessness leads to a disqualification of successes. In these instances, the therapist must elicit the specific thoughts that lead to this hopelessness. Here are some examples:

1. These changes are superficial. My problems are too deep-seated.
2. Even though my behavior may change, I am basically a worthless person.
3. My problem does not really lie in the way I view things; it is the result of an impossible situation.
4. Even though my mood can change, the depression will come back again. I'll always be a depressed person.

In all of these cases, the therapist will have to correct basic misconceptions about the process of change and the nature of depression before therapy can proceed.

Finally, the therapist may have to accept the fact that cognitive therapy does not work for everyone. It is not a panacea for psychological problems of all sorts. If, after the therapist has tried all available approaches and consulted with other cognitive therapists, the patient still is not improving, it may be appropriate to refer the patient to another therapist with the same or a different therapeutic orientation.

Regardless of why therapy does not seem to be working, therapists must be attentive to their own dysfunctional cognitions. They must maintain a problem-solving approach instead of succumbing to patients' own hopelessness or viewing themselves as incompetent. Some of these dysfunctional cognitions are as follows:

1. Cognitive therapy won't work with this patient—the problems are too deep-seated.
2. I don't know what I'm doing. I'm screwing up.
3. The patient wants to feel bad, so there's nothing I can do to help.
4. The patient is still depressed. I haven't accomplished anything.
5. Progress is too slow. I must be doing something wrong.

If therapists can resist such cognitions, they will be better able to focus on finding solutions to patients' problems.

REFERENCES

Beck, A. T., Rush, A. J., Shaw, B. F., & Emery, G. *Cognitive therapy of depression.* New York: Guilford, 1979.

Truax, C. B., & Mitchell, K. M. Research on certain therapist interpersonal skills in relation to process and outcome. In A. E. Bergin & S. L. Garfield (Eds.), *Handbook of psychotherapy and behavior change: An empirical analysis.* New York: Wiley, 1971.

‡ 8 ‡

PSYCHODYNAMIC THERAPY: THEORY AND RESEARCH

HANS H. STRUPP
JANET A. SANDELL
GLORIA JENNINGS WATERHOUSE
STEPHANIE SAMPLES O'MALLEY
JANIS L. ANDERSON

INTRODUCTION

This volume reflects the intensified search for better understanding of depression as a major mental health problem and for the development of treatment methods that are maximally effective, efficient, and humane. Since psychoanalytic thinking continues to have a profound influence on the theories and practices of many clinicians throughout the country, it might be expected that major contributions to the treatment of depression would have come from this perspective. Despite a sizable and growing clinical literature, such has not been the case. To understand the reasons for this relative lack of progress, it is necessary to consider the manner in which the problem of depression has been viewed in the psychoanalytic literature, as well as to examine the evolution of principles and techniques of time-limited forms of psychodynamic psychotherapy in general. Another part of this task will be to evaluate the empirical evidence of treatment outcomes in an effort to determine the value of these findings for the clinician and researcher. Throughout these critical analyses, investigators must confront the basic question: Can there be a time-limited form of psychotherapy for depression from the psychoanalytic viewpoint?

Hans H. Strupp, Janet A. Sandell, Gloria Jennings Waterhouse, Stephanie Samples O'Malley, and Janis L. Anderson. Department of Psychology, Vanderbilt University, Nashville, Tennessee.

From a research perspective, progress in psychotherapy has been predicated on the "specificity principle," a formulation that links relatively specific therapeutic interventions to a relatively specific "problem" or "condition" in need of modification or remediation. Once a reasonable alignment of these two basic conditions has been achieved, it may become possible to examine the effectiveness of a particular treatment. Conversely, in the absence of such an articulation, assessments of treatment outcomes must necessarily remain indeterminate. The evaluation of treatment outcomes in all forms of psychotherapy, including those dealing with depression, has been greatly hampered by vaguely defined patient populations and clinical problems, insufficient descriptions of treatment methods, and lack of rigorous outcome criteria. The complexities of these issues have become increasingly appreciated, and steps are gradually being taken to address them.

The foregoing difficulties apply not only to research designed to assess the effectiveness of particular forms of psychotherapy; they are (or ought to be) equally relevant to clinical practice. Psychotherapists must ask themselves: What is the nature of the problem for which this particular patient is seeking help? How can I as a psychotherapist effect therapeutic change? What might be optimal interventions (treatment techniques)? What goals are to be pursued in the treatment of this particular person? How can I determine whether a particular goal has been achieved? In short, the problem of tailoring treatment interventions to the nature of a particular clinical disorder should loom large in every therapist's mind. Indeed, this problem is inescapable, whether or not it is explicitly recognized.

It may be seen, however, that the "specificity principle," as delineated in the foregoing discussion, is not especially congenial with the psychoanalytic tradition. To be sure, it may be recalled that Freud in his early work viewed psychoanalytic psychotherapy as uniquely applicable to the "transference neuroses"; that is, he took credit for having devised a method of treatment claimed to be uniquely effective in treating a relatively specific set of conditions. This early thrust, however, was eventually lost in the course of the "broadening scope" of psychoanalysis, although it has regained a certain viability in the writings of those authors who have concerned themselves with short-term dynamic psychotherapy (see pp. 221–225). It might also be mentioned that over the years certain adaptations of psychoanalytic technique have been recommended (e.g., adaptations for use with borderline patients and in crisis intervention). This, however, does not negate the fact that the objective of developing relatively specific treatments for relatively specific clinical conditions has been basically alien to psychoanalytic psychotherapy. Consequently, it is hardly surprising that no *specific* psychoanalytic treatment for depression has emerged, despite the resurgence of theoretical and clinical interest in this disorder. Because of its diffuse, complicated, and multifaceted character, depression may also serve as a particularly telling illustration of the enormous difficulties besetting the seemingly simple goal of developing specific forms of treatment for specific conditions. Depression, as everyone recognizes, is clearly not a "specific condition."

In keeping with the aforementioned objectives, we begin with a discussion of depression from the psychoanalytic perspective. Next, we review the principles, techniques, and aims of short-term dynamic psychotherapy; this is followed by an examination of the empirical evidence. Finally, we attempt to integrate the foregoing topics, with a view toward refining both clinical practice and research. An important part of this concluding section is the delineation of the limitations inherent in short-term dynamic treatments of depression—impediments that may apply to other treatment approaches as well.

CLASSIFICATIONS AND MAJOR CONCEPTS

A review of the extensive literature on depression from the psychoanalytic perspective is clearly beyond the scope of this chapter; furthermore, it is a task that has been very capably performed by a number of authors (e.g., Arieti & Bemporad, 1978; Mendelson, 1974). Instead, we attempt a highly selective review of concepts and clinical phenomena bearing on psychotherapeutic approaches to depression, particularly with reference to time-limited goals.

Although a host of authors has grappled with the problem of ordering and classifying the clinical phenomena of depression, considerable controversy persists. There seems to be agreement, however, that the term "depression" refers to "a broad spectrum of moods and behavior ranging from mild mood changes to the clinical syndrome" (Weissman, 1979). Included among the symptoms of depression are dysphoric mood, accompanied by loss of pleasure and interest; sleep and appetite disturbance; suicidal thoughts; loss of energy; and feelings of self-reproach. Various criteria are used to differentiate the depressive syndrome from other disorders (notably schizophrenia). The newly adopted DSM-III system of classification further requires that the symptoms should have lasted for at least a few weeks and that there must be evidence of impairment in social and personal functioning (American Psychiatric Association, 1980).

Depression is commonly differentiated from sadness, but both may be seen as fundamental reactions to the internal and external stresses that are a natural part of life. Thus, they may be counted among the common elements of human experience. It is, however, the relationship of this single element to the individual's total personality structure and function that determines whether "depression" is viewed as merely an appropriate and transient response or as a disturbance worthy of categorization as a major mental disorder. Although the presence of this specific symptom may reveal a great deal about a facet of a patient's pathology, it indicates relatively little about the healthy and adaptive resources of the individual in question (Knight, 1954; Waldhorn, 1960). It is these personal assets, in relation to the pathology, that may be a primary determinant of the individual's suitability for various forms of psychotherapeutic intervention. In this context, it is important to note that analytic authors tend to view depression in *longitudinal* and *dynamic* terms, whereas other theorists (notably behaviorally oriented authors) adopt a more circumscribed, symptom-oriented perspective. Arieti (1978), for example, differentiates his psychodynamic perspective from Beck's cognitive approach by stressing that a patient is not depressed because he or she has depressive thoughts; instead, there is evidence of a "*cognitive history* which to a considerable extent has been unconscious" (p. 8; emphasis added).

Arieti and Bemporad (1978), whose lucid treatise we take as the point of departure for the present discussion, propose a classification scheme involving two broad categories of depression that they term "primary" and "secondary" respectively (p. 61 ff.). These authors call attention to the fact that patients suffering from primary—that is, less severe—depression are more amenable to psychotherapy. Furthermore, it should be noted that patients in this group are seen as suffering from neurotic difficulties, of which depression is a concomitant. The significance of this point is that psychoanalytic psychotherapy in these as well as in other cases is not regarded as a "treatment for depression," but rather as an approach toward *strengthening the patient's adaptive capacities.* This basic working assumption further implies that as the patient gains greater strength in directing his or her life, symptoms such as depression will disappear. In short, psychoanalytic psychotherapy is aimed at changes in personality structure, rather than at the amelioration of symptoms.

Without attempting to retrace the evolution of psychoanalytic conceptions of depression, we summarize salient conclusions (for a more extensive discussion, see Bemporad, 1978):

(1) Depression is basically a problem of disturbed interpersonal relations. It highlights the close association between maintenance of self-esteem (an intrapsychic emphasis) and maintenance of a close, intimate relationship (an emphasis on "behavior" or "performance"). Concomitantly, depression is frequently seen in terms of systems theory, which stresses the *interactive* character of the problem in terms both of the person's past and present relationships with significant others.

(2) The predisposition and origin of depressive disorders is found in early childhood, notably in disappointments with significant others, which lead to pervasive ambivalence in all relationships (Arieti & Bemporad, 1978, pp. 23–24). These early experiences exert a lasting influence on the patient's life and typically are reinforced and exacerbated by current relationships with significant others.

(3) Under the influence of developments in structural theory and ego psychology, depression is increasingly seen as a problem in adaptive functioning. More specifically, it relates to the regulation of self-esteem (Fenichel, 1945) and reflects a disparity between the actual state of self and a desired ego ideal (Bemporad, 1978, p. 29). According to Bibring (1953), the person suffering from depression has experienced a severe blow to his or her self-esteem (e.g., disappointment or loss). This results in a conflict between actual or imaginary helplessness (an activation of a potent childhood state) and extremely high aspirations (e.g., aspirations for perfection, control, or love) which the person feels unable to fulfill. The problem is complicated by the fact that the original experience of deprivation or loss sets in motion an overwhelming rage that, because of the child's dependency, could not be directed outward and that is instead internalized (repressed) and directed against the self.

(4) Although this newer formulation appears to stay close to the clinical data, it does not uniquely define a depressive episode. As Bemporad points out (1978, p. 33), members of the cultural school

(e.g., Sullivan and Horney) have considered problems relating to regulation of self-esteem as central to almost all psychopathology. Therefore, difficulties of this kind appear to be a necessary but not a sufficient condition for explaining the phenomena of depression.

(5) If the foregoing conclusions are correct, they have critical implications for psychotherapy. In accordance with psychodynamic conceptualizations, the so-called mild depressions (which may be contrasted with all other conditions in which biochemical and genetic factors may play a more important part) are not a disease, syndrome, or specific disorder; instead, they are particular manifestations of "problems in living" with which all psychotherapists in the psychodynamic camp have been concerned. By the same token, depressives employ basically the same neurotic tactics and maneuvers as other patients. Thus, it follows that from the psychoanalytic perspective there is no special treatment for depressions of the kind under discussion, any more than there are special treatments for anxiety or a phobia. (We are disregarding relatively minor variations in technique that have been proposed over the years—e.g., avoidance of reassurance.) Instead, in all instances, the psychoanalytic therapist endeavors to strengthen the patient's adaptive capacities (i.e., to come to the aid of the patient's beleaguered ego). Depression, according to this view, is analogous to any other symptom—it signifies an adaptive failure resulting from inner conflicts. The goal of treatment, therefore, is to produce a better alignment of the conflicting strivings that the patient has learned to handle in a maladaptive manner.

For these reasons, the depressed patient, like all others who are seen as in need of and suitable for psychotherapeutic help, has difficulties in the areas of *autonomy* (independence, self-regulation) and *intimacy* (relatedness). As is true of other patients, depressives have not been given adequate emotional nurturance in childhood and thus have become unable to handle the demands for socialization that in their case have been experienced as extraordinarily harsh and severe.

It is already apparent that there are many ways in which a therapist can strengthen a patient's adaptive capacities (e.g., by giving reassurance, by providing guidance and counsel, and by promoting greater self-understanding through insight). However, in all instances there must be a human relationship in which an understanding, accepting, and empathic person partially gratifies the patient's wishes for dependency and succor. It remains an open question whether, beyond that, time-limited forms of dynamic psychotherapy can produce anything approximating a lasting reorganization of the patient's personality that might minimize the recurrence of depressive episodes and thus might serve a prophylactic function.

MODUS OPERANDI OF SHORT-TERM DYNAMIC PSYCHOTHERAPY

Although brief dynamic psychotherapy is often promoted as an innovative therapeutic approach, these newer treatment methods are firmly grounded in classical psychoanalytic principles. Whereas "psychoanalysis" is commonly associated with the notion of lengthy treatment and frequent therapy sessions, dynamically trained therapists would be compelled to agree with Gill's contention (1954) that such variables have little to do with the basic analytic tenets. In fact, in its inception, psychoanalysis was frequently of short duration, and the first successful cases of brief therapy have been credited to Freud (Sterba, 1951). However, as the analytic process became more focused on the technique of transference interpretation and the goal of structural personality change, the treatment process gradually lengthened. For many years, therefore, the only type of psychotherapy accorded credibility was that involving the prolonged working through of deep conflicts, and all procedures that were not the "pure gold" of analysis were depreciated. Since all legitimate therapy was long-term, its range of potential application was necessarily restricted.

In an attempt to offset what was viewed as the "stagnation" of the analytic treatment process, early theorists such as Ferenczi and Rank (1925), and later Alexander and French (1946), began to explore means whereby psychoanalytic principles could be preserved and applied more efficiently. Despite the significance of their respective theoretical contributions, these technical parameters failed to achieve support within the traditional analytic community, and thus had little impact on widespread clinical practice. Efforts to provide more expedient treatment alternatives, therefore, were largely dominated by the conservative, or crisis-intervention, school of therapy (e.g., Bellak & Small, 1965; Wolberg, 1965). This relatively atheoretical approach postulates that limited goals (i.e., the restoration of homeostasis) can be achieved in a very few sessions with primarily supportive measures such as reassurance and the giving of advice.

The renewed interest in short-term analytic treatment methods has been prompted by a desire to study the analytic process within a manageable time frame and by the increased realization of the need for broadening the scope of service delivery. David Malan (1976, 1979) and Peter Sifneos (1972, 1979), working independently in England and Boston, arrived nearly simultaneously at what has been termed the "radical" formulation of short-term dynamic principles: Longstanding neurotic patterns of behavior can be reversed through a time-limited psychotherapy that employs all the essential types of interpretation found in psychoanalysis. Other theorists—most notably Balint, Ornstein, and Balint (1972); Davanloo (1978); Horowitz (1976); and Mann (1973)—have reported similar results through the use of comparable procedures.[1]

Despite certain quantitative differences between classical psychoanalysis and time-limited approaches based on dynamic principles, the underlying assumptions are basically identical[2]:

(1) Patients always seek to achieve gratification by means they have learned in the past, and they present symptoms, problems in living, and so on, because learned patterns (including fantasies, fears, and misconceptions) are inappropriate, self-defeating, anachronistic, and generally maladaptive in their adult living. In Alexander and French's words (1946): "Every neurosis and every psychosis represents a failure of the ego in performing its function of securing adequate gratification for subjective needs under existing conditions" (p. viii). Thus, the task of any form of psychotherapy is to correct this failure of adjustment.

(2) Since these learned patterns are rooted in early significant relationships and their vicissitudes (e.g., deprivation, trauma), they can only be resolved within an interpersonal framework that in some ways resembles the earlier one but that is different from it in important respects. To the extent that a present-day relationship is experienced by the patient as similar to (reminiscent of) an earlier one, it will evoke the conflictual patterns of relatedness; conversely, to the extent that it is experienced by the patient as different, it can serve a therapeutic function (Alexander and French's concept of the "corrective emotional experience"). The more poignant the difference be-

1. Although most therapy belongs under the heading of "brief interventions," (Lorion, 1974), and many dynamically trained therapists treat cases that happen to be short-term in nature, the focus of this chapter is restricted to the "planned," brief, intensive approaches as developed by these major theorists.

2. This formulation is in substantial agreement with the point of view advanced by Alexander and French (1946). Their truly innovative, forward-looking book gains new and even greater significance in light of recent developments in this area.

tween the two forms of relatedness can be made—here, the so-called "transference neurosis" serves its unique function—the more incisive and radical the therapeutic change can become. Classical analysis differs from short-term dynamic psychotherapy solely in the degree to which the contrast is made vivid and explicit, worked through, and assimilated.

The foregoing is the transference paradigm, pure and simple. It follows that psychoanalytic psychotherapy, regardless of whether it is termed "classical analysis" or "brief psychotherapy," achieves results to the extent that it uses a "real" relationship between a patient and a therapist for the purpose of correcting patterns of relatedness traceable to the earlier ones that continue to be conflictual and therefore troublesome. Depending on the nature of the earlier difficulties, the extent to which they have interfered with the patient's maturation, and a host of other factors that have been extensively discussed in the literature and that represent prognostic indicators, psychotherapy may take varying amounts of time and varying therapeutic efforts; at times, it may be virtually impossible to effect the corrections that are needed and called for. However, no matter how brief or intensive the therapeutic effort may be, the basic formula remains the same: It is the utilization of an interpersonal relationship in the present to correct persistent difficulties created by an interpersonal relationship in the past. Whatever learning can be mediated by the therapeutic relationship—whether it is over a period of 3 months or 3 years—represents the therapeutic yield and thus the effectiveness of the psychotherapeutic effort. Difficulties in living that cannot be dealt with in this manner lie outside the province of psychoanalytic psychotherapy and cannot be remedied by its techniques.

Fundamentally, the technique for bringing about the necessary corrections has two major components:

(1) Therapists facilitate and encourage development of a viable interpersonal relationship between patients and themselves. This may lead to the so-called "transference neurosis" in classical psychoanalysis, or the patients may continue to experience the conflict as existing between themselves and other significant people in their lives, as is typically the case in brief dynamic psychotherapy.

(2) In both instances, the therapists, in addition to providing sympathetic understanding, emotional support, and so forth, seek to identify and correct maladaptive patterns of relatedness by helping the patients to appreciate their inutility.

To reiterate, it matters little whether the conflict centers around the patient–therapist relationship or whether the conflict is experienced with other significant figures in a patient's life. In either event, the therapist uses his or her position as a "good object" to produce corrections in the patient's self-esteem by appropriate therapeutic maneuvers. In analytic terms, the therapist comes to the aid of the patient's beleaguered ego, which means that he or she is strengthening the patient's adaptive resources. Insight is an appreciation of what one is doing wrong when one is doing it in the present (whether with the therapist or with other significant persons); therapy is thus successful to the extent that the therapist can bring maladaptive patterns into focus, and to the extent that the patient can experience with sufficient vividness their maladaptive character and utilize this appreciation to feel, think, and act differently (i.e., in more adaptive ways).[3]

The fact that classical psychoanalysis encourages the development of a transference neurosis, whereas brief dynamic psychotherapy relies heavily on a "real" relationship, does not contradict the foregoing assertions. All forms of psychotherapy—not only classical analysis or short-term dynamic psychotherapy—make effective use of a "real" relationship between two adults, which is, of course, heavily supported and made meaningful by the degree to which this relationship resembles and makes contact with what the patient has experienced in the way of "good relationships" with significant figures in the past. Classical analysis cannot dispense with this relationship any more than can other forms of therapy. Unless the patient can make effective use of a "good relationship," a serious contraindication for short-term dynamic therapy exists.

The preceding discussion does not answer the question of how the therapist can most effectively intervene in short-term dynamic psychotherapy; nor does it indicate what technical interventions are most propitious. It is apparent that the short-term therapist, like any other, brings to bear a combination of influences that summate into a therapeutic outcome. Moreover, considerable controversy exists among the proponents of various time-limited therapies regarding the most appropriate nuances of techniques to be applied in this setting. In

3. We share the view of most analytic writers that nothing is as convincing as something that is experienced directly with the therapist, but there are no systematic data to show that it is necessarily true. This is merely another challenging question for research.

general, however, short-term therapists seek to accomplish their aims through (1) refined technical operations and special modifications of procedures, and (2) improved methods for selecting patients who will be amenable to thse interventions. The certain common elements that appear integral to all time-limited approaches are now briefly summarized.

TECHNICAL OPERATIONS

TIME

Time is ultimately the variable that distinguishes the modern short-term dynamic approaches from traditional psychoanalytic practice. Nevertheless, the notion of time-limited treatment has loose denotative boundaries, as consensus has yet to be reached regarding the length of therapy that would demarcate the short- from the long-term process. In this literature, the term "brief" psychotherapy has been applied to therapeutic interventions lasting up to 40 sessions (a period that would hardly be considered "short-term" by therapists of many orientations). The brevity of the treatment process is considered by some to be an inverse function of the severity of the individual patient's pathology and the relative ambitiousness of the particular therapist's goals.

The concept of a time-limited dynamic treatment evokes the inevitable criticism that such abbreviated interventions must necessarily be "second-rate," or inferior to their long-term counterparts. Despite the pervasiveness of this assumption, existing empirical comparisons of treatment outcomes do not support this position (Butcher & Koss, 1978; Luborsky, Singer, & Luborsky, 1975). Indeed, many short-term therapists would assert that the imposition of a stringent time limitation actually serves to heighten the patient's emotional involvement and to facilitate the therapeutic endeavor. Setting an impending termination date at the outset of therapy may convey optimism to the patient, impart a feeling that significant progress can be made in a relatively short period of time, and thereby foster an important sense of mastery and independence. From another perspective, Rank (1925/1952) and subsequently Mann (1973) have suggested that knowledge of upcoming termination brings early developmental conflicts to the fore, pointing to the parallels between the pending end of the therapeutic relationship and the separation–individuation issues encountered at various developmental milestones. Thus, in this instance, successful resolution of separation anxiety may serve as a model for the mastery of other neurotic conflicts.

ACTIVE THERAPEUTIC STANCE

While traditional psychoanalysts are popularly characterized by their passivity, or attitude of "evenly suspended attention," short-term theorists concur that the limited time frame of this approach demands that therapists must be considerably more active, as well as calculated, in their evaluations, interventions, and goal setting. This *active therapeutic stance*—a critical factor that cuts across all time-limited approaches—has been conceptualized (Mendelsohn, 1978) as comprised of two basic dimensions: a therapeutic attitude or mental set (referred to as "active attention"), and a behavioral activity that is commonly termed "focusing."

Active Attention

In assessing the nature of the patient's difficulties and their dynamic implications, the short-term therapist must make maximal use of the information provided during the course of the intensive interview procedure and the therapy sessions. In this regard, the quality of the emerging therapeutic relationship supplies invaluable data concerning the nature of the patient's present and historical problems in relating to significant others, whereas the patient's responses to the therapist's tentative formulations are seen as important indications of the individual's psychological status and readiness for further interpretations. Therapeutic objectives must be identified early in the treatment process, and techniques must be optimally geared to the achievement of these relatively specific goals. Most essentially, the therapeutic attitude of active attention implies that techniques be applied flexibly, sensitively, and in ways most meaningful to the individual patient.

Focusing

The identification of a reasonably circumscribed therapeutic focus is of crucial importance in determining the hypothesized source of the patient's difficulties, and it serves as a valuable guidepost in time-limited treatment planning. This relatively specific dynamic focus has been described (Malan, 1976) as a link between the *acute* conflict that brings the patient into treatment and the *core* conflict that represents more pervasive attitudes and maladaptive patterns of behavior. Once this therapeutic focus has been delineated, it serves as a "red thread" or coherent theme guiding the therapist's interventions and narrowing the scope of the treatment. Through a process of "selective attention" and "selective neglect," the therapist purposefully directs the patient to central issues that highlight the major topics of the therapy, and actively discourages digressions from these salient themes. The time-limited technique of active focusing presents a vivid contrast to the traditional analytic atmosphere, in which the patient is given relative freedom to produce material and the transference is allowed to evolve gradually.

While short-term therapeutic approaches assign to the therapist a more active role than is typical in dynamically oriented therapy, it still remains important to enlist the patient's active participation in the therapeutic process. Failure to do so transforms the therapist into a "magical helper" and defeats the major strength of dynamic psychotherapy, that of fostering the patient's autonomy and sense of mastery. Thus, there must exist a fine balance of guiding the therapy without casting the patient into a dependent role.

VIGOROUS INTERPRETATION OF TRANSFERENCE

Central to the technique of short-term dynamic psychotherapy is the *active and vigorous interpretation of the transference.* The aims of this heavily interpretive process have been summarized by Malan (1976), following closely Menninger's concept (1973) of the "triangle of insight": "1) to clarify the nature of the defense, the anxiety and the impulse; 2) to clarify this in all three main areas: current, past, and transference; and 3) to make *links* among the three areas" (p. 260; emphasis added). Through making vivid the connection between the patient's historical past, the present life situation and current interpersonal relationships, and the transference relationship in the therapeutic situation, the ultimate goal—as in all analytic procedures—remains the achievement of insight. While some therapists (e.g., Alexander & French, 1946; Castelnuovo-Tedesco, 1975) strongly advise against the interpretation of negative transference in the time-limited setting, more recent theorists such as Davanloo (1978) and Sifneos (1979) see the early interpretation of negative transference reactions (often within the first interview) to be essential to therapeutic benefit, particularly with hostile, resistant patients.

SELECTION OF A SUITABLE PATIENT POPULATION

Perhaps the key variable accounting for the success of these time-limited approaches may be seen as the rigorous, systematic application of selection criteria: procedures designed to ensure that the resulting treatment population possesses the substantial personality resources (as well as the will) to withstand the frequently painful and always concentrated nature of the therapeutic interventions. In practice, this means that short-term therapists have tended to exclude the more difficult (resistant) patients, employing standards so stringent as to resemble closely those used to select candidates for analysis (cf. the review of the extensive literature on "analyzability" in Bachrach & Leaff, 1978). Short-term therapy patients, nevertheless, represent a relatively broad range of presenting pathology, and little attention is given to the identification or restriction of persons according to formal diagnostic categories. Considerable agreement exists with regard to the most important of these selection criteria:

(1) *Motivation for change* is perhaps the prime selection factor; only patients who are strongly committed to resolving their difficulties through insight (and who are willing to alter basic adaptational styles) are judged able to withstand the stress of this anxiety-provoking procedure and to derive eventual therapeutic benefit.

(2) A demonstrated ability to become involved in a *mutual, mature relationship* (which Sifneos, 1979, defines as a history of at least one significant "give-and-take" relationship) implies an ability for basic trust and a willingness to undergo the risks inherent in a therapeutic involvement. The patient's early interactions with the therapist, as well as historical data, are viewed as critical determinants of an individual's characteristic transference stance in therapy.

(3) Evidences of *ego strength* and adaptive capacities are considered critical; patients should be of at least average intelligence and should have demonstrated adequate adjustment in work, social, and educational realms.

(4) "*Psychological-mindedness*," a concept that loosely refers to the individual's capacity for introspection and ability to conceptualize

problems within an intrapsychic framework, signifies the degree to which the patient can accept and utilize insights into the factors underlying his or her maladaptive cognitions, feelings, and behaviors. Most short-term therapists evaluate this quality through the patient's response to tentative, trial interpretations during the initial interview procedures.

(5) The potential of short-term therapy candidates ultimately to appreciate the significance of their life circumstances is thought to be intimately related to their *affective involvement*, or capacity to express relevant emotions directly.

(6) In classical analysis, it is frequently necessary to expend considerable time and effort to bring a conflict into focus, whereas, for best results, the patient coming into brief therapy should experience *focal conflict.* In the absence of such a focal conflict, usually characterized by pronounced anxiety, distress, and suffering, brief dynamic therapy may have little chance of success. The opposite case consists of more diffuse characterological difficulties, which may indeed dictate long-term intensive work.

EMPIRICAL INVESTIGATIONS OF THE EFFICACY OF BRIEF DYNAMIC THERAPY

As stated previously, the major short-term dynamic theorists place primary emphasis on patients' ego resources and adaptive potential in selecting individuals appropriate for their brief and intensive procedures. If depression, like anxiety, is viewed as a component of numerous psychiatric disorders, then many of the patients treated by these approaches can be characterized as "depressed." However, depression per se is usually not the problem identified to be treated by short-term dynamic therapists, nor do their selection criteria typically make use of the standard diagnostic nomenclature. The current state of the research literature reflects this fact. No published studies of short-term dynamic therapy that focused on a patient population selected primarily on the basis of depression have been located. In addition, there are few existing investigations of short-term dynamic therapy performed by therapists with specific training in these techniques. Consequently, in an effort to assess the empirical evidence on the effectiveness of short-term dynamic psychotherapy with depressed patients, we have selected studies for review according to rather broad criteria. The subsequent examination of the empirical literature includes published studies investigating psychodynamically oriented therapy of brief duration (less than 6 months) with a patient population that can, in some manner, be identified as depressed (see Table 8.1). Finally, we address methodological weaknesses in the existing empirical literature that preclude firm statements regarding the unique efficacy of brief dynamic psychotherapy for the treatment of depression.

REPORTS OF TREATMENT EFFECTIVENESS

All of the prominent short-term dynamic theorists have reported success in treating depressed patients (e.g., Davanloo, 1978; Malan, 1976; Sifneos, 1972). These reports, however, consist mainly of individual case studies, and the effectiveness of these brief analytic procedures have not been examined in a controlled or comparative empirical manner. Despite their different technical emphases, the views of these short-term theorists are remarkably congruent with respect to the factors accounting for the success of their approaches. The achievement of therapeutic gain within this restricted time interval is generally credited to the careful assessment of potential patients and the use of highly focused technical interventions (see pp. 225–228). The existence of depression is not regarded by these authors as a contraindication to a patient's treatment, nor has depressive symptomatology been reported to be of significant prognostic value in predicting treatment outcome.

Of all the empirical studies reviewed, only one investigator (Stewart, 1972) selected his patients on the basis of their suitability for a time-limited dynamic approach. These specific criteria (e.g., positive response to trial interpretations, "relatability") were employed to select patients with the sufficiently "mature ego functioning" required to tolerate the anxiety and frustration of the therapeutic situation while still maintaining an alliance with the therapist. Of the 20 patients meeting these specifications, nearly half (45%) reported "depression" as their chief complaint. (Because of the emphasis on ego functioning in the selection process, chronicity was not considered a contraindication for treatment. These patients, therefore, reported symptomatology ranging from "lifelong recurrent depression" to more acute distress.) Following 6 months of individual dynamic psychotherapy, five of these patients were judged as improved, and four remained unchanged (according to the therapists' initial dynamic formulation of focal conflicts).

The effect of psychoanalytically oriented therapeutic interventions may be viewed more clearly in two studies in which depression was objectively assessed (Green, Gleser, Stone, & Seifert, 1975; Haskell, Pugatch, & McNair, 1969). Nevertheless, the patient populations under examination were not selected on the basis of either short-term dynamic criteria or their depressive symptomatology. Haskell *et al.* (1969) explored the response of 43 outpatients (47% of whom were diagnosed posttreatment as having a depressive reaction) to 12 sessions of time-limited therapy. Therapy focused on the conflicts engendered by impending termination and the central issues identified in the therapist's initial dynamic formulation. At termination, both therapists' and patients' ratings on the depression and distress scale of the Hopkins Symptom Rating Scale (HSRS) and patients' ratings of the depression mood factor of the Psychiatric Outpatient Mood Scale (POMS) had decreased significantly. In addition, significant positive changes were noted on ratings of global status made by the patient and therapist. Patient self-evaluations revealed that most of the therapeutic change occurred in the area of depressive symptomatology.

As part of a methodological investigation of the relationship among various outcome indices, Green *et al.* (1975) studied 50 patients experiencing acute stress reactions who were treated with a brief psychoanalytically oriented form of therapy for a maximum of six sessions. At the completion of therapy, 76% of these patients demonstrated improvement, 14% were unchanged, and 10% had deteriorated, as assessed by the Hamilton Rating Scale for Depression (HRSD). As a supplemental index of outcome, scores on the Symptom Checklist (SCL) were examined, although change on the depression index of this instrument was not reported independently. Patient improvement on these various subscales ranged from 72% to 82%.

DYNAMIC PSYCHOTHERAPY VERSUS MINIMAL-TREATMENT CONTROLS

In a series of studies exploring the effectiveness of time-limited treatment in emergency crisis clinics (Gottschalk, Fox, & Bates, 1973; Gottschalk, Mayerson, & Gottlieb, 1967), patients having serious

TABLE 8.1. Studies of Brief Dynamic Therapy with Depressed Patients

AUTHOR	POPULATION	TREATMENT LENGTH	OUTCOME CRITERIA	PRINCIPAL FINDINGS
REPORTS OF TREATMENT EFFECTIVENESS				
Stewart (1972)	Of 20 inpatients selected according to criteria for short-term dynamic therapy, 9 exhibited depression of varied severity.	4.9 months.	Therapist's clinical evaluation.	Depressive symptomatology decreased for 5 out of 9 patients.
Green, Gleser, Stone, & Seifert (1975)	50 nonpsychotic outpatients experiencing acute stress reactions.	6 months.	Hamilton Rating Scale for Depression (HRSD).	On HRSD: 76% improved, 14% were unchanged, 10% deteriorated.
			Symptom Checklist (SCL): Depression subscale.	Improvement on SCL subscales ranged from 72% to 82%.
Haskell, Pugatch, & McNair (1969)	43 outpatients; 47% diagnosed posttreatment as having depressive reactions.	8–16 sessions.	Hopkins Symptom Rating Scale (HSRS): Depression–Distress.	Significant improvement on HSRS depression as rated by patients and therapists.
			Psychiatric Outpatient Mood Scale (POMS): Depression Mood Factor.	Improvement in depression approached significance on POMS patient ratings.
DYNAMIC THERAPY VERSUS CONTROLS				
Gottschalk, Mayerson,	53 crisis-center patients exhibit-	Therapy group: 5.4 sessions.	Depression measured as a component of the	Treated patients showed greater improvement

& Gottlieb (1967)	ing primarily neurotic symptomatology.	Dropouts: 2.2 sessions.	Psychiatric Morbidity Scale (PMS).	than dropouts did.
Gottschalk, Fox, & Bates (1973)	68 crisis-center patients.	2.7 sessions.	Depression measured as a component of the PMS.	Treated patients and wait-list controls showed comparable improvement.
DYNAMIC THERAPY VERSUS OTHER FORMS OF PSYCHOTHERAPY				
Nichols (1974)	43 university counseling-center clients (primarily neurotics).	9 sessions.	Change on the sum of the MMPI scales of Depression, Psychasthenia, and Schizophrenia.	Brief psychoanalytic therapy resulted in greater reduction in the MMPI composite than did emotive therapy.
Sloane, Staples, Cristol, Yorkston, & Whipple (1975)	94 outpatients with elevations on at least one MMPI scale (two-thirds had elevations on Depression). Patients with severe depressions excluded.	13.7 sessions.	MMPI Depression scale.	Psychoanalytic therapy and behavior therapy resulted in significantly more improvement than did no treatment.
Strupp & Hadley (1979)	64 college students with elevated scores on MMPI Depression, Psychasthenia, and Social Introversion scales.	17–18 sessions.	MMPI Depression scale.	Patients receiving treatment by professional and lay therapists and a minimal contact group improved significantly. Improvement for the no-contact control was nonsignificant.

Continued

TABLE 8.1. *Continued.*

AUTHOR	POPULATION	TREATMENT LENGTH	OUTCOME CRITERIA	PRINCIPAL FINDINGS
			Therapists' and clinicians' depression ratings.	Patients treated by professional and lay therapists improved significantly on clinicians' assessment of depression. The patients of lay therapists improved significantly, according to the therapists' ratings.
DYNAMIC THERAPY VERSUS PHARMACOTHERAPY				
Daneman (1962)	195 outpatients diagnosed as having depressive reaction (primarily neurotic).	Biweekly for 1 to 12 months.	Depression symptom rating scale.	Imipramine plus psychotherapy resulted in more remissions than did a placebo plus psychotherapy condition.
Lesse (1978)	941 severely depressed ambulatory patients (75 received psychotherapy; 866 received either electroconvulsive therapy [ECT] or pharmacotherapy plus psychotherapy).	21 days.	Depression checklist.	Both ECT and pharmacotherapy plus psychotherapy resulted in greater improvement than did psychotherapy alone.

difficulty "coping with life stresses" were treated with Bellak and Small's brief dynamic technique (1965). The essential features that characterize this therapeutic strategy are an early formulation of the treatment focus; an emphasis on the precipitating stress ("narcissistic injury"); limited goals; and an avoidance of transference interpretations. Depression was measured as one component of the Psychiatric Morbidity Scale (PMS), which assesses symptoms; behaviors; current interpersonal problems and somatic complaints; and the degree to which each of these factors impairs functioning in vocational, domestic, and psychobiological areas.

In the initial investigation (Gottschalk *et al.*, 1967), 36 patients were treated by psychiatric resident therapists in weekly individual therapy lasting a maximum of six sessions. Psychoactive drugs were prescribed to some clients as an adjunctive therapeutic agent, and although the authors failed to control for this variable, prescriptions were reportedly "kept to a minimum." At the outcome assessment, 85% of the therapy patients were judged to be significantly improved on the PMS, 9% exhibited no change, and 6% had deteriorated. Of the early therapy dropouts (who served as the treatment controls), 57% showed improvement, 14% remained unchanged, and 29% had deteriorated. Using a variety of pretreatment and posttreatment personality measures, the authors concluded that the best predictors of outcome were pretreatment morbidity scores; that is, the greater the patient's initial disturbance, the less favorable the outcome. Providing empirical support for the views of short-term therapists, these authors found that the patients who displayed an interest in and capacity for satisfying interpersonal relationships were more likely to improve after 6 weeks of therapy.

In the second study, Gottschalk *et al.* (1973) compared treatment outcomes in 68 patients who were randomly assigned to either a waiting-list control or brief, crisis-oriented therapy. At the end of 6 weeks, there were no significant differences in the PMS scores of the two groups; rather, the investigators found that both groups had improved. (In evaluating these results, however, it must be considered that the extremely brief nature of this intervention—the mean number of treatment sessions was 2.7—may have resulted in minimal therapeutic impact.) As in the earlier investigation, pretherapy assessments of patients' ego resources and capacity for healthy relationships proved to be the most powerful predictors of treatment outcome.

DYNAMIC PSYCHOTHERAPY VERSUS OTHER BRIEF THERAPIES

Only three investigations dealt with the relative effectiveness of brief dynamic psychotherapy in reducing depressive symptomatology, as contrasted with the effectiveness of other psychotherapeutic approaches. Time-limited analytic techniques have been compared to behavior therapy (Sloane, Staples, Cristol, Yorkston, & Whipple, 1975) and cathartic procedures (Nichols, 1974), as well as to client-centered therapy and nonprofessional counseling (Strupp & Hadley, 1979).

In a short-term context, Nichols (1974) compared the effectiveness of two treatment approaches: cathartic therapy and an insight-oriented analytic technique. Patients were students at a major university, and their therapists were psychologists and psychiatrists on the staff of the campus health center. At termination of therapy, the insight-oriented approach resulted in a greater mean reduction of the sum of the Minnesota Multiphasic Personality Inventory (MMPI) scales of Depression, Psychasthenia, and Schizophrenia, although the effect of therapy on depression was not examined independently.

In a controlled study of treatment outcome (Sloane *et al.*, 1975), experienced therapists treated 94 outpatients using either behavioral techniques or psychodynamically oriented therapy (mean treatment sessions = 13.7). In examining their results, the authors concluded that although both procedures resulted in greater change than was evidenced in the no-treatment controls (waiting-list patients), these treatment approaches were least effective with depressed patients. It is important to note that of the control patients (who were selected on the basis of MMPI clinical-scale elevations), only the depressed group showed significant improvement at the conclusion of the waiting period. This finding highlights the self-limiting nature of some depressive symptomatology—a factor that may serve to confound the results of studies not utilizing the necessary control conditions.

As part of a large-scale investigation (Strupp & Hadley, 1979) that explored the relative contribution of technique and relationship factors to treatment outcome, 30 male patients ranging in age from 17 to 24 were treated in therapy for up to 25 sessions either by experienced therapists (experiential or analytic in orientation) or by college professors. The college professors had no formal training in psychotherapy, but were selected on the basis of their capacity for personal warmth and understanding. All patients had significant elevations on the Depression, Psychasthenia, and Social Introversion scales of the MMPI, as did the two comparison groups (a minimal-contact group, consisting of patients who completed the initial assessment procedures and were subsequently assigned to a waiting list; and a "silent" control group, comprised of persons who had elevations on the three "critical" MMPI scales but were not seeking therapy). At termination, patients comprising these relatively homogeneous patient groups experienced a significant reduction on the three MMPI scales—Depression, Psychasthenia, and Social Introversion. No between-group differences were found. On ratings of depressive symptomatology made by independent clinicians, the patient groups treated by therapists and college professors improved significantly more from intake to termination of therapy than did the minimal-treatment controls. Again, no between-treatment group differences were found. This study is notable for its attention to design and thorough assessment procedures; nevertheless, therapists were not specifically trained in short-term techniques, and they made few modifications in their basic procedures to fit the time constraint of 25 sessions.

DYNAMIC PSYCHOTHERAPY AND PHARMACOTHERAPY

Patients were selected primarily on the basis of depression in only those studies that concomitantly investigated the effects of dynamic psychotherapy and psychotropic medications. Daneman (1961) compared patients diagnosed as having a depressive reaction with two treatment procedures: imipramine plus psychotherapy, and placebo plus psychotherapy. Psychoanalytically oriented psychotherapy was offered on a twice-weekly basis, with a focus on "hostility directed toward the incorporated object image." Assessments of outcome were restricted to changes in depressive symptomatology as assessed by a symptom checklist. At the conclusion of 2 months of treatment, there was an 85% remission rate in the group receiving imipramine plus psychotherapy, as compared to a 12% remission rate in the group receiving the placebo plus psychotherapy. The value of this investigation, however, is severely limited, as the sole therapist in this investigation made all the ratings of therapeutic outcome, and the effects of psychotherapy and drugs were not examined independently. In this regard, it has been suggested that adjunctive pharmacotherapy may serve to detract from the psychotherapeutic process through the reduction of the patient's anxiety, depression, and related motivation for insight. Thus, it is conceivable that the administration of a placebo may also diminish the patient's motivation by fostering a "magical reliance" on what is perceived to be a biological treatment.

Lesse (1978) compared a group of 75 "severely depressed" ambulatory patients treated with psychoanalytically oriented techniques to comparable patients treated by either electroshock therapy ($n = 15$) or psychotherapy in combination with antidepressant drugs ($n = 851$). After several weeks of treatment, only 16% of the therapy patients had "good or excellent" results, compared with 86% of the electroshock patients and 83% of the patients receiving the combination of pharmacotherapy and insight-oriented techniques. Lesse concluded that psychotherapy alone should not be the treatment of choice for severely depressed patients, because it needlessly exposes them to "pain" and the risk of suicide. The author, however, stressed that drugs can never be regarded as the sole treatment for a psychological disturbance, since along with the medication, patients concurrently receive attention and interpersonal support. In treating severely depressed individuals, Lesse's recommendation is that psychotherapy should be ego-building and supportive initially, becoming increasingly intensive after the danger of suicide has passed. These conclusions and recommendations are similar to the observations of other short-term dynamic psychotherapists (e.g., Davanloo, 1978; Castelnuovo-Tedesco, 1975).

CONCEPTUAL AND METHODOLOGICAL CONSIDERATIONS

Although brief dynamic psychotherapy has been found effective in reducing depressive symptomatology, no definitive statement can be made regarding the unique effectiveness of short-term dynamic treatment approaches for the amelioration of depression. In fact, as evidenced by this review, the research on short-term dynamic approaches has not addressed this specific issue. Rather, these techniques have been applied to persons experiencing acute stress reactions (Gottschalk *et al.*, 1967, 1973; Green *et al.*, 1975); individuals exhibiting global distress syndrome (Sloane *et al.*, 1975; Strupp & Hadley, 1979); and patients selected on the basis of their appropriateness for short-term techniques (Davanloo, 1978; Malan, 1976; Sifneos, 1972; Stewart, 1972). Although most of these individuals manifested depressive symptomatology, patients were not selected on the basis of their depression, nor was change on depression isolated in many studies.

The majority of the studies reviewed failed to include more than a cursory description of the nature of the therapeutic approach, making it difficult to determine exactly what was being practiced under the rubric of "brief dynamic therapy" or to evaluate the results of these efforts accurately. Thus, it is likely that many of these therapies were dynamically oriented and brief (by virtue of the time frame of the investigation), although specialized techniques were not employed. In the Vanderbilt Project (Strupp, 1980-a, 1980-b, 1980-c), for example, several of the therapists were highly experienced and dynamically trained; however, none were considered experts in short-term therapy. Analyses of patient–therapist interactions in the Vanderbilt Project revealed that the psychodynamic therapists adhered to the psychoanalytic model of long-term intensive therapy (i.e., they assumed a passive–expectant stance, allowing the patient freedom to choose topics for discussion), rather than adapting their techniques to the abbreviated treatment period. Similarly, the description of the psychodynamic therapy employed in the Temple study (Sloane *et al.*, 1975) indicates that short-term techniques were not emphasized. Since principles of short-term dynamic psychotherapy were not systematically applied, a valid examination of this approach was not conducted.

In order to address the questions presented in this chapter, investigators must select patient populations according to criteria considered important for success with brief dynamic techniques, and they must also utilize traditional diagnostic schemes. Even in the study employing the most exacting selection criteria (Strupp & Hadley, 1979), the patients treated could not be considered homogeneous with regard to the standard diagnostic nomenclature. For example, patients in the Vanderbilt Project were selected on the basis of elevations on the MMPI Depression scale (with additional elevations on Psychasthenia and Social Introversion); nevertheless, these persons represented a very diverse group in terms of characterological styles and severity of pathology. In the Sloane *et al.* investigation (1975), over two-thirds of the patient sample had MMPI elevations on the Depression scale of greater than 77; however, less than one-tenth of these patients were diagnosed as depressive neuroses. Greater recognition must be given to the fact that depression is but one facet or manifestation of the larger personality constellation.

Several other methodological inadequacies lessen the informational value of existing investigations. Notably, many researchers have failed to include appropriate control or comparison groups in the design of their investigations (Green *et al.*, 1975; Haskell *et al.*, 1969), whereas others (Daneman, 1961) utilized treatment groups that did not allow conclusions to be drawn.

The question of therapists' experience level becomes crucial when viewed in the context of treating a depressed patient population. With these patients, extreme care and clinical sensitivity must be employed, particularly when the therapy is intense and "anxiety-provoking" (e.g., Sifneos, 1979). As Lambert, Bergin, and Collins (1977) have noted, negative effects are more likely to occur when therapy is conducted by inexperienced therapists and when the therapeutic process has not been closely planned. In our review, deterioration effects were noted in four investigations of brief therapy that employed relatively inexperienced therapists (Gottschalk *et al.*, 1967, 1973; Green *et al.*, 1975; Haskell *et al.*, 1969).

The brief-therapy literature (with the exception of Malan and recent work by Davanloo) has not been optimistic regarding the likelihood of radically changing deep-seated characterological problems. However, the impediments supposedly created by these more pervasive maladaptive patterns of behavior have not been systematically examined in the context of brief therapy. Generally, the focus of treatment and assessments of outcome in this literature have been directed to behavior, symptomatology, and day-to-day functioning, rather than to broader personality or characterological traits. This emphasis may be appropriate for short-term crisis-intervention procedures that have as their goal the relief of situationally determined anxiety and depression. To achieve a better understanding of the potential for change with the more radical short-term dynamic techniques, systematic comparisons and comprehensive assessments of diagnostic and outcome indices are indicated. Furthermore, long-term follow-up measures should be included, for these brief therapeutic interventions are frequently referred to as the "jumping-off point" from which more enduring and pervasive change may ensue.

CONCLUSIONS AND IMPLICATIONS

The preceding examination of the literature on time-limited dynamic psychotherapy for depression allows the following conclusions to be formulated.

FEW ADVANCES IN THE PSYCHODYNAMIC TREATMENT OF DEPRESSION

Psychoanalytic clinicians and theoreticians have provided important insights into the clinical aspects of depression. In particular, progress has been made in achieving a better understanding of the psychodynamics and developmental antecedents of depression, as well as of its meaning in the patient's current adaptation. These insights, however, have not been paralleled by comparable advances in the treatment of depression by psychoanalytic techniques. Although there are clearly multiple reasons for this inconsistency, the following observations seem germane.

Skepticism from Classical Psychoanalysts

Psychotherapy, of whatever description, has not proven notably successful in treating patients suffering from the most severe forms of depressions (e.g., manic–depressive disorders or psychotic depression). At the same time, through the renewed interest in the biologic and genetic bases of these disorders, progress has been made in developing pharmacological and somatic treatments, which for many patients in the "severe" category appear to be the treatments of choice. This leaves the large area of the so-called "mild" depressions (a misnomer, since patients suffering from these conditions are often seriously impaired, even though they do not require hospitalization). There are indications that the number of patients suffering from "mild" depression is increasing as the incidence of "classical" neuroses (hysteria, obsessive-compulsive syndrome, etc.) is declining. Thus, it might be expected that psychoanalytic authors have devoted considerable attention to the development of new psychotherapeutic approaches for these disorders. As we have noted, such has not been the case.[4]

For a number of years, there has been a certain interest on the part of psychodynamic therapists in developing time-limited forms of treatment, despite the tendency of the psychoanalytic establishment to view departures ("parameters") from the classical model of psychoanalysis with skepticism. This attitude has done much to retard progress. In more recent years, efforts by such authors as Malan, Sifneos, and Davanloo have emerged as major entries in the field of time-limited psychotherapy based on psychodynamic principles. However, as we have seen, these workers have not specifically addressed the development and application of time-limited forms of psychotherapy for depression.

Psychoanalytic Conceptualization of Depression

Perhaps the major reason for the lack of *specific* psychotherapeutic approaches to the treatment of depression is traceable to the psychoanalytic conceptualization of depression as a concomitant of a wide range of neurotic disorders, rather than as a clinical entity per se. Therefore, the contemporary trend in psychotherapy research (as well as in emerging government policy) to develop and test specific forms of psychotherapy for relatively specific disorders is basically antithetical to the psychoanalytic tradition. With the exception of various forms of crisis intervention (which lack a strong theoretical foundation), the thrust of psychotherapy from the psychoanalytic perspective has been to work toward strengthening the patient's adaptive capacities through modification of intrapsychic structures. These modifications are hypothesized to occur as the patient gains gradual insight into determinants of his or her unconscious conflicts. The goal of psychoanalytic psychotherapy, therefore, is not the direct

4. It should be recognized that currently prominent forms of psychotherapy for depression, such as Beck's cognitive-behavior therapy and Weissman's interpersonal psychotherapy, have clearly been influenced by psychoanalytic thinking, despite their respective special emphases.

modification of symptoms (of which depression is but one example), but the strengthening of the patient's adaptive capacities and ego resources. It is debatable whether this psychoanalytic goal is unique, because *any* psychotherapeutic approach that goes beyond simple reassurance or other measures of temporary relief may be seen as aimed in the same direction—that of modifying self-defeating and maladaptive cognitions and behavior. Therefore, successful psychoanalytic forms of interventions should result in behavioral as well as cognitive modifications, including changes in self-esteem, self-confidence, and coping skills. These changes may appear to be very similar to those attempted by other modern treatment approaches (e.g., Beck's cognitive therapy or Weissman's interpersonal therapy), although the therapeutic *techniques* are divergent. These considerations, as will be seen, have important implications for clinical practice as well as research.

NEED FOR CONSIDERATION OF PATIENT FACTORS

The crux of any form of psychotherapy consists of the *goals* it is designed to pursue and the *means* (techniques) by which these goals are to be achieved. These goals, of course, do not reflect only the therapist's priorities; they are at least equally determined by the patient's ability, commitment, and capacity to benefit from what the therapist has to offer. Thus, any possible therapeutic achievement is circumscribed by the *individual patient*, whose collaboration must be enlisted. With respect to techniques, it is inescapable that in most cases compromises must be made. Therapists as well as researchers have been insufficiently explicit on these points, which merit further elaboration.

Goals

There has been a tendency among the proponents of time-limited psychotherapy to pursue fairly ambitious goals. In particular, these authors are not interested in such relatively modest aims as alleviating a current episode of depression or temporarily raising the patient's morale; instead, they have worked toward more radical dynamic changes that are expected to prevent or minimize recurrence of the patient's neurotic difficulties. There is as yet scant empirical evidence that such changes do, in fact, occur.

The pursuit of any therapeutic goal, however, is crucially dependent upon the personal characteristics of the patient who enters therapy. The authors cited in this chapter have done much to elucidate this problem. Their solution has been to make the *selection of patients* for their particular form of therapy exceedingly stringent. By focusing on such factors as motivation, previous success in meeting life's challenges, presence of a focal conflict, and the ability to profit from interpretations, they have assigned considerable weight to the *personal qualities* of the patient. Much as classical analysts do, short-term therapists select patients whose character makeup, intelligence, psychological-mindedness, and other qualities allow them to become productive collaborators in the therapists' chosen approach; that is, they select "good learners."

This tendency to treat persons rather than impersonal syndromes has extremely important implications for the future of psychotherapy. By placing the stress on *who* can be treated rather than on *what* can be treated, time-limited forms of dynamic psychotherapy challenge the prevailing trend of grouping psychotherapy with most forms of medical treatment. In the latter, the *personality* of the patient is clearly of much less significance. It should be added that the weight of the empirical evidence emerging from psychotherapy research supports the view that successful treatment outcomes depend to a considerable extent upon the qualifications and personal characteristics brought by the patient to therapy.

It is also noteworthy that the stringent selection of patients for time-limited dynamic psychotherapy gives these approaches a distinctly elitist cast. These techniques, therefore, may be no more applicable to treating a broad spectrum of patients than is classical analysis. The preceding may suggest that those patients who meet the selection criteria have a greater capacity to heal themselves, and that they respond optimally to the therapeutic task as defined by these approaches.

While the stipulation of selection criteria has considerable clinical plausibility, no systematic studies have been performed to determine whether patients with lesser "qualifications" would fail to make significant therapeutic gains in time-limited treatment. There are probably no clear dividing lines, and the field (as well as society) would greatly benefit from efforts to define more sharply the limits of suitability, preferably with a view toward extending therapy to a larger group of patients.

Techniques

Short-term dynamic therapists, like their colleagues who subscribe to other approaches, have developed techniques that, in the view of the proponents, are uniquely effective. While their technical writings have considerable clinical and rational appeal, no convincing evidence has yet been presented to substantiate the claims. In particular, there are no rigorous comparative studies in which one technical approach has been pitted against others. In the absence of such demonstrations, and with the preponderance of the available evidence pointing to the overriding importance of patient, therapist, and interaction variables, it seems reasonable to adopt what might be called a "null position." This means that the success of psychotherapy in a given case depends not on specific techniques, but on the quality of the personal interaction between patient and therapist. The quality of the interaction, in turn, is a function of particular characteristics of the patient and the therapist. Given such a context, there are numerous ways in which patients can undergo a corrective learning experience that has the effect of helping them to overcome childhood traumas, to modify maladaptive patterns of relating to significant others, and to achieve greater self-realization. In short, there may be many ways to enable patients to assign *new meanings* to their life experiences and thereby to achieve therapeutic change.

Can the prime goals of achieving greater autonomy and more satisfying relationships be realized in time-limited psychotherapy? In particular, can therapists accelerate the learning process through special techniques? As we have indicated, dynamically oriented therapists interested in time-limited treatment have sought to achieve this goal through (1) stringent patient selection and (2) the pursuit of relatively specific (limited) goals by means of techniques considered uniquely effective with this patient group. However, even with "ideal" patients, there are undoubtedly limits to what can be accomplished in a given period of time. Although it may be true that these limits extend further than has hitherto been realized, they have not been systematically explored. Again, much will probably depend upon the individual patient, his or her previous mode of adaptation, the nature of the current disturbance, and similar factors. Furthermore, researchers and clinicians do not as yet possess adequate knowledge of what constitutes an "optimal" set of techniques.

The authors whose work we have reviewed in this chapter have generally adapted a rather "active" stance in the sense of vigorously pursuing those goals they have identified as desirable and feasible for a particular patient (Davanloo has coined the term "the relentless therapist"). This approach contrasts sharply with the traditional role of the analyst, whose defining characteristic has been patience and an abiding commitment to the proposition of letting the patient make his or her own self-discoveries. Critics of these short-term approaches may argue that inadequate attention has been directed at the process of *working through.* Freud has stressed that therapeutic learning takes time, that insights must be consolidated and assimilated by the patient, and that much learning occurs at a "silent" (unconscious) level.

There is as yet scant information on the length of the process required in an individual case, as well as on the factors facilitating or impeding its success. It *is* known that pervasive characterological maladaptations manifested by strong resistances tend to prolong the therapeutic process. Short-term therapists have dealt with this problem by selecting patients whose progress is predictably faster and by rejecting those who appear less suitable on these grounds. As we have noted, their judgment may be correct, but so far primary reliance has been placed on clinical impressions. Another implication relates to the best time to assess therapeutic change, which may not be at termination but six months or a year later. In sum, the short-term therapist may set a process in motion, but its fruition may occur considerably later.

Other questions relating to the therapist's "activity" are in need of further testing. Several contemporary short-term therapists (e.g., Davanloo and Sifneos) are highly confrontive in the sense of massing frontal attacks on the patient's defenses. Davanloo, for example, believes that such an approach has considerable promise, particularly with obsessional patients. Again, investigators lack precise data on such questions as the kinds of patients who respond positively to this approach; those patients who may respond negatively; long-term effects; and effectiveness of the treatment in comparison to that of other approaches. Furthermore, does a highly confrontative approach allow for the formation of a strongly positive therapeutic alliance? If the patient has a tendency to submit to powerful authority figures, can a confrontative therapist hope to strengthen the patient's self-determination instead of reinforcing the patient's wish for submission to a magical helper?

With regard to these issues, preliminary evidence has been obtained from the Vanderbilt Psychotherapy Project that therapists engaged in time-limited psychotherapy fail to deal optimally with *transference* as well as with *countertransference* problems. Perhaps because of the brevity of treatment and perhaps for other reasons, they tend to pay insufficient attention to negative transference reactions, particularly to the patient's negativism, hostility, and related resistances. Similarly, a common tendency for therapists to respond in kind to the patient's hostility and anger was observed. It may be possible for therapists to develop a keener awareness of these issues and to deal with them more adequately. However, there is also the possibility that the very nature of time-limited psychotherapy (particularly if the therapist elects to pursue a "dynamic focus" in a highly aggressive manner) precludes optimal therapeutic handling of these issues.[5] If this is true, there may be an inherent and irreconcilable antithesis between the objectives of time-related dynamic psychotherapy and the honored goal of open-ended psychoanalytic psychotherapy. The unquestionable merit of the latter is the therapist's consistent goal of working toward the resolution of transference problems, rather than capitalizing upon the patient's transferences. Thus, the therapist committed to the achievement of short-term goals may be in danger of compromising the basic goal of psychodynamic psychotherapy, that of helping the patient achieve greater autonomy and relatedness through softening and realigning his or her defensive structures in the context of a new human relationship

5. Problems of countertransference have received very little systematic attention in the literature on short-term dynamic therapy. A question must also be entertained concerning the degree to which personal charismatic qualities of particular short-term therapists interact synergistically with their preferred techniques. That is, treatment results may be as much (or more) a function of the individual therapist using the particular techniques as they are a function of the specific techniques themselves. This, in turn, raises questions concerning the extent to which particular techniques are effective in the hands of therapists with different therapeutic styles and personality characteristics.

with a benign helper. It must remain an open question whether and to what extent therapeutic pressures—applied to direct modifications of the patient's belief system, feelings, behavior, or defenses—are compatible with psychoanalytic tenets. The ultimate question facing therapists, researchers, and society may not be whether behavior change is possible, or what the optimal techniques might be for changing behavior, but rather what the *personal cost* to the patient undergoing change may be.

In the case of depression, it seems obvious that any technique—pharmacological or psychological—that promises to alleviate the patient's suffering and unhappiness deserves serious attention. Alleviating the patient's sense of demoralization and helplessness by any means may be a reasonable therapeutic goal. Ameliorating *current* interpersonal conflicts through insight by one form or another of time-limited psychotherapy may be another desirable step, but it, too, may not be enough. All of these approaches are geared to limited goals. Many patients want no radical changes or are unable to invest the effort in working toward radical changes. There can be no quarrel with limited objectives, provided that therapists learn to define and investigate the limits by appropriate empirical research. If depression is often not an "illness" but the product of complex problems in human adaptation, it is unlikely that panaceas are in the offing. This is not an admission of failure, but simply a recognition of reality. Educating legislators and the public at large as to what may realistically be expected from particular therapeutic interventions is another task that has as yet received inadequate attention. In sum, the review we have presented in this chapter leaves little doubt that much work remains to be done.

REFERENCES

Alexander, F., & French, T. M. *Psychoanalytic therapy.* New York: Ronald Press, 1946.

American Psychiatric Association. *Diagnostic and statistical manual of mental disorders* (3rd ed.). Washington, D.C.: Author, 1980.

Arieti, S. The basic questions and the psychological approach. In S. Arieti & J. Bemporad, *Severe and mild depression.* New York: Basic Books, 1978.

Arieti, S., & Bemporad, J. *Severe and mild depression.* New York: Basic Books, 1978.

Bachrach, H. M., & Leaff, L. A. "Analyzability": A systematic review of the clinical and quantitative literature. *Journal of the American Psychoanalytic Association*, 1978, *26*, 881–920.

Balint, M., Ornstein, P. H., & Balint, E. *Focal psychotherapy.* London: Tavistock, 1972.

Bellak, L., & Small, L. *Emergency psychotherapy and brief psychotherapy.* New York: Grune & Stratton, 1965.

Bemporad, J. Critical review of the major concepts of depression. In S. Arieti & J. Bemporad, *Severe and mild depression.* New York: Basic Books, 1978.

Bibring, E. The mechanism of depression. In P. Greenacre (Ed.), *Affective disorders.* New York: International Universities Press, 1953.

Butcher, J. N., & Koss, M. P. Research on brief and crisis-oriented psychotherapies. In S. L. Garfield & A. E. Bergin (Eds.), *Handbook of psychotherapy and behavior change: An empirical analysis.* New York: Wiley, 1978.

Castelnuovo-Tedesco, P. Brief psychotherapy. In S. Arieti (Ed.), *American handbook of psychiatry* (2nd ed., Vol. 5). New York: Basic Books, 1975.

Daneman, E. A. Imipramine in office management of depressive reactions (A double-blind study). *Diseases of the Nervous System,* 1961, *22*, 213–217.

Davanloo, H. *Basic principles and techniques in short-term dynamic psychotherapy.* New York: Spectrum, 1978.

Fenichel, O. *The psychoanalytic theory of neurosis.* New York: Norton, 1945.

Ferenczi, S., & Rank, O. [*Development of psychoanalysis*] (C. Newton, trans.). New York: Nervous and Mental Disease Publishing Co., 1925.

Gill, M. M. Psychoanalysis and exploratory psychotherapy. *Journal of the American Psychoanalytic Association*, 1954, *2*, 786–797.

Gottschalk, L. A., Fox, R. A., & Bates, D. E. A study of prediction and outcome in a mental health crisis clinic. *American Journal of Psychiatry*, 1973, *130*, 1107–1111.

Gottschalk, L. A., Mayerson, P., & Gottlieb, A. A. Prediction and evaluation of outcome in an emergency brief psychotherapy clinic. *Journal of Nervous and Mental Disease*, 1967, *144*, 77–96.

Green, B. L., Gleser, G. C., Stone, W. N., & Seifert, R. F. Relationships among diverse measures of psychotherapy outcome. *Journal of Consulting and Clinical Psychology*, 1975, *43*, 689–699.

Haskell, D. Pugatch, D., & McNair, D. M. Time-limited psychotherapy for whom? *Archives of General Psychiatry*, 1969, *21*, 546–552.

Horowitz, M. J. *Stress response syndromes.* New York: Jason Aronson, 1976.

Knight, R. P. An evaluation of psychotherapeutic techniques. In R. P. Knight & C. R. Friedman (Eds.), *Psychoanalytic psychiatry and psychology.* New York: International Universities Press, 1954.

Lambert, M. J., Bergin, E. A., & Collins, J. L. Therapist-induced deterioration in psychotherapy. In A. S. Gurman & A. M. Razin (Eds.), *Effective psychotherapy.* New York: Pergamon, 1977.

Lesse, S. Psychotherapy in combination with antidepressant drugs in severely depressed out-patients—20 year evaluation. *American Journal of Psychotherapy,* 1978, *32,* 48–73.

Lorion, R. P. Patient and therapist variables in the treatment of low-income patients. *Psychological Bulletin*, 1974, *81*, 344–354.

Luborsky, L., Singer, B., & Luborsky, L. Comparative studies of psychotherapies: Is it true that "Everybody has won and all must have prizes"? *Archives of General Psychiatry,* 1975, *32*, 995–1008.

Malan, D. H. *The frontier of brief psychotherapy.* New York: Plenum, 1976.

Malan, D. H. *Individual psychotherapy and the science of psychodynamics.* London: Butterworth, 1979.

Mann, J. *Time-limited psychotherapy.* Cambridge, Mass.: Harvard University Press, 1973.

Mendelson, M. *Psychoanalytic concepts of depression.* New York: Spectrum, 1974.

Mendelsohn, R. Critical factors in short-term psychotherapy. *Bulletin of the Menninger Clinic*, 1978, *42*, 133–149.

Menninger, K., & Holtzman, P. *Theory of psychoanalytic technique.* New York: Basic Books, 1973.

Nichols, M. P. Outcome of brief cathartic psychotherapy. *Journal of Consulting and Clinical Psychology*, 1974, *42*, 403–410.

Rank, O. *The trauma of birth.* New York: Robert Brunner, 1952. (Originally published, 1925.)

Sifneos, P. E. *Short-term psychotherapy and emotional crisis.* Cambridge, Mass.: Harvard University Press, 1972.

Sifneos, P. E. *Short-term psychotherapy: Evaluation and technique.* New York: Plenum, 1979.

Sloane, R. B., Staples, F. R., Cristol, A. H., Yorkston, N. J., & Whipple, K. *Psychotherapy versus behavior therapy.* Cambridge, Mass.: Harvard University Press, 1975.

Sterba, R. A case of brief psychotherapy by Sigmund Freud. *Psychoanalytic Review*, 1951, *38*, 75–80.

Stewart, H. Six months, fixed term, once weekly psychotherapy: A report on 20 cases with followups. *British Journal of Psychiatry*, 1972, *121*, 425–435.

Strupp, H. H. Success and failure in time-limited psychotherapy: A systematic comparison of two cases. *Archives of General Psychiatry*, 1980, *37*, 595–603. (a)

Strupp, H. H. Success and failure in time-limited psychotherapy: A systematic comparison of two cases (Comparison 2). *Archives of General Psychiatry*, 1980, *37*, 708–716. (b)

Strupp, H. H. Success and failure in time-limited psychotherapy: Further evidence (Comparison 4). *Archives of General Psychiatry*, 1980, *37*, 947–954. (c)

Strupp, H. H., & Hadley, S. W. Specific versus nonspecific factors in psychotherapy: A controlled study of outcome. *Archives of General Psychiatry*, 1979, *36*, 1125–1136.

Waldhorn, H. F. Assessment of analyzability: Technical and theoretical observations. *Psychoanalytic Quarterly*, 1960, *29*, 478–506.

Weissman, M. M. The psychological treatment of depression: Evidence for the efficacy of psychotherapy alone, in comparison to, and in combination with pharmacotherapy. *Archives of General Psychiatry*, 1979, *36*, 1261–1269.

Wolberg, L. *Short-term psychotherapy.* New York: Grune & Stratton, 1965.

9

PSYCHODYNAMIC THERAPY: CLINICAL APPLICATIONS

JOSEPH ZAIDEN

INTRODUCTION

The *affect* of depression (or sadness) is a universal, normal experience. All human beings feel depressed at some times in their lives, usually as a result of the loss of something valuable. This loss both induces emotional pain and lowers self-esteem. Persons who overcome such losses experience grief, detach themselves from the lost objects, and turn to new interests, all of which require time, energy, and a capacity to deal directly with loss. The *illness* of depression may ensue if there is an interruption of this process or if there is a disturbance in the capacity to deal directly with the pain. "Depression," the illness, refers to a clinical syndrome that is experienced by many fewer people than is "depression," the affect. However, the syndrome can be profoundly debilitating. This chapter focuses on the use of short-term dynamic psychotherapy with the syndrome of depression.

Following Franz Alexander's pioneering work, short-term dynamic psychotherapy (STDP) attracted little interest until the last two decades, when Davanloo, Malan, and Sifneos further developed, specified, applied, and began to test STDP techniques in various patient populations. Audiotape and videotape recordings have been produced that illustrate in detail various techniques and their application. Three international symposia on STDP have presented findings and ongoing research in this field. Davanloo heads the world's most sophisticated and extensive STDP unit, in Montreal; he has played a

Joseph Zaiden. Clinton County Mental Health Center, Shelby, North Carolina; private practice of short-term psychotherapy. Shelby, North Carolina.

critical role in organizing these symposia and in developing training methods, as well as in generating a data base for empirical research on STDP.

When I began using short-term techniques with depressed adults and children, I began with patients who had had multiple losses, poor ego strength, and questionable motivation. These patients would not pass selection criteria for this treatment (see below). While the degree of improvement was very limited, I was sufficiently encouraged to work more extensively with depressed patients. I found that poor response in these patients resulted, in part, from failure to utilize two assessment interviews properly. These sessions can be used to enhance patients' motivation. I also found that the therapist must help the patient to make early affectual connections to the lost object and to express some delayed grief during the early sessions. The latter appears to allow patients to experience a sense of relief and hope that brings an immediate increase in motivation with it.

Another factor leading to poor response in these first patients was the incomplete transference interpretations, particularly during the second and third stages of treatment (see below). Throughout these two stages previous losses with concomitant fears and regressive behavior are reenacted within the transference. I realized that it was essential to focus on past–present transference (PPT) linkages as soon as they arose in treatment. This focus on PPT allows patients to relive their losses and to work them through successfully in exchanges with, and in the relationship to, the therapist.

Resistances often appeared to rest on fears of abandonment and retaliation that were connected with previous losses. These resistances could be worked through in treatment by moving freely from feelings brought about by previous losses to those initiated by current losses, which reactivated these earlier feelings. Transferential interpretations allowed patients to make these linkages. They came to understand and express the feelings of inhibition, rage, and so forth, that were attached to the therapist as the treatment process was coming to an end. Thus, treatment moves freely from feelings of past losses to those currently felt through the transference toward the therapist and to current losses that have reactivated past feelings and caused the present decompensation. Before detailing the treatment methods, I present a brief review of various psychoanalytic concepts of depression.

PSYCHOANALYTIC CONCEPTS OF DEPRESSION

The original psychoanalytic description of depression evolved from a comparison of mourning and melancholia described by Abraham and retained by Freud. Abraham (1927) argued that ambivalence was basic to depression. He viewed love and hate as equally coexistent; depressed patients were unable to love, because when they loved, they hated. He stated that such patients were ambivalent both toward themselves and toward objects.

Freud (1917/1959, p. 243) extended this analysis and differentiated mourning from melancholia. He defined mourning as work and pain related to the loss of an external object. In melancholia, "the object has not perhaps actually died, but has been lost as an object of love, (e.g., a woman who has been jilted)" (1917/1959, p. 245). The ego is impoverished because object loss is transferred into ego loss. The free libidinal energy is not displaced to another object but withdrawn into the ego, which serves "to establish an identification of the ego with the abandoned object. The shadow of the object falls upon the ego and the ego is judged by the forsaken object" (1917/1959, p. 249). Thus, the ego is incapable of fulfilling its goals, although the goals remain as wanted and appropriate. There are also feelings of sadness, helplessness, and a general lowering of self-esteem. The attendant angry feelings are *not* turned outward, but are turned inward toward the lost, ambivalently loved, introjected object.

"Of the three preconditions of melancholia—loss of the object—ambivalence and regression of libido into the ego—the first two are also found in the obsessional self-reproaches arising after a death has occurred. We are thus led to the third factor as the main one responsible for the result. The conflict within the ego, which melancholia substitutes for the struggle over the object, must act like a painful wound" (Freud, 1917/1959, p. 258).

In the early 1920s, Abraham (1924/1927) emphasized the increased oral eroticism and frustrated oral cravings of the depressed patient. Both the ambivalence and the narcissism have an oral root. Further, he showed that the self-reproaches are internalized reproaches against the object, and vice versa.

Rado (1956) clarified the relationship between depression and self-esteem. He described depression as an abortive attempt to repair the failure to retain the love object. This failure leads to a regression to earlier dependent, aggressive behavior. The lost object is introjected into the loving, protective ego and into the punishing and protective superego.

Fenichel (1945) goes further and refers to depressed patients as "love addicts"—"unable to love actively, they passively need to be loved" (p. 358). He highlighted archaic regulation of self-esteem, which begins in infancy. To infants, milk or physical feeding is necessary for a feeling of well-being. Infants exhibit their omnipotence and demands by crying or screaming. When parents respond, this confirms the infants' omnipotence while allowing the infants to participate in their omnipotent giving. As they grow older, being loved is equated with a feeling of well-being. When they are not loved they become self-deprecating; when they are loved again, self-esteem returns. As the ego learns to anticipate the future and judge, it creates minor states of ego diminution as a precaution to total loss of narcissistic supplies. Still later in development, the superego takes over the regulation of self-esteem. Now doing right and being loved equals a feeling of well-being. The conscience creates states of ego diminution to warn against definitive loss of narcissistic supplies. When the conscience fails, the result is melancholia. "A severe depression represents the state into which the orally dependent individual gets when vital supplies are lacking. A slight depression is anticipation of this state for warning purposes" (Fenichel, 1945, p. 387). Whether the depression involves a severe or a slight loss of self-esteem is always a prominent issue. Fenichel defines the subjective formula as "I have lost everything; now the world is empty," if the loss of self-esteem is mainly due to a loss of external supplies; or "I have lost everything because I do not deserve anything," if the loss is mainly due to a loss of internal supplies from the superego (1945, p. 391). He believes that in severe depression the personality shifts completely from ego to superego function; the conscience becomes the personality. The ego is helpless and yields to the superego.

Bonime (1960) likewise differentiates between the severe and slight depression in his definition of the continuum. The depressive continuum moves from appropriate depressive affect through neurotic depression to psychotic depression. He points out that neurotic depressives are not totally depressed; they are individuals with some healthy needs and strivings.

> Basically, the depressive character develops in an environment in which the normal needs of a child for solicitous parents are unfulfilled; a milieu in which he is manipulated (often by aggrandizement), used, pushed, squelched, instead of having his realistic desires reasonably anticipated, reasonably respected, and reasonably nurtured. He may be doted on, ignored, competed with, abused, but whatever the form of neglect, oppression, oversolicitous confinement, or overt exploitation, the depressive is in reality deprived of a decently parented childhood. (Bonime, 1960, p. 195)

The result is that the depressive will do anything to attain his or her primary goal—having his or her narcissistic supplies replenished.

Bonime (1976) describes depressive characteristics as follows:

1. Manipulativeness. Depressives will manipulate anyone or any situation in order to be given to.
2. Aversion to influence. Any attempts to help or give to depressives are usually experienced as covert demands upon them. If they remain self-deprecating, they mask their resources and cannot use them. They function as if to say, "You can't make me live a full, productive life."
3. Unwillingness to give gratification. Depressives do not respond to others; thus, they do not allow anyone satisfaction from helping them.
4. Hostility. This is depressives' dependent, regressive way of expressing their anger, as if to say, "I will pay you back for not loving me."
5. Anxiety. Depressives are in a constant state of anxiety, because their isolated, insulated way of life is always on the verge of total failure; there is always the possibility that they cannot control the world with their depression.

In summary, the illness of depression involves a defensive system that is in a state of ruin or bankruptcy. Depression occurs in a person whose image and self-esteem are dependent upon the amount of love received from others. This type of functioning generally precedes superego development. Thus, such functioning indicates lack of superego development or severe regression. Review of the literature indicates the latter to be the cause of poor functioning. In depression, patients resort to very primitive, ineffectual defenses that leave them in a helpless state of surrender. Without some therapeutic intervention, they have no control over their painful struggle to learn, to love, and to work.

CRITERIA FOR PATIENT SELECTION

STDP begins by selecting patients who are likely to respond to the short-term approach. While there are as yet no conclusively agreed-upon guidelines for identifying such patients, the following criteria are suggested from clinical experience: the patient's ability to focus on a problem; the patient's response to interpretation; the patient's ability to make an affectual contact with the therapist; the patient's ability to tolerate anxiety and reenactment of depressive feelings; the patient's ability to make sacrifices; the patient's acceptance of the time limitation; and the absence of serious suicidal ideation. These criteria should be considered in detail.

ABILITY TO FOCUS

The patient's ability to focus on a particular problem is absolutely essential, as it lays the foundation for the joint search and resolution to be undertaken. During the selection process, the patient must define a specific problem that he or she believes is of primary concern. This problem focus should arise as a composite both of the patient's symptoms and reasons for seeking treatment, and of an assessment of other disturbances in functioning or other interpersonal relationships previously seen as unrelated. The patient must be able to focus discussion on the identified problem. This condition does not preclude patients who manifest appropriate and necessary resistances by trying to avoid some discussions of painful material. However, by the end of the evaluation session, both the patient and the therapist should have clarified and agreed upon the focal conflict.

Consider the "Case of the Pending Divorce." This 36-year-old depressed male stated that he was unable to function properly in many areas and that his wife had asked for a divorce. He was both seductive and rejecting with women, and fearful and subservient toward men. In the first session, his only concern was the pending divorce. The therapist confronted with him the question, "Why are you here? Is it not a fact that you've come here as if sent by your wife?" The patient was surprised and unable to respond.

During the second assessment session, he began to discuss his family. Upon being asked whom he resembled most, his mother or his father, he became confused and began to stutter, "Mother—father—I don't know." After further discussion, he stated, "I don't know who I am or what I want—this is what I want to work on. I am here for myself."

The dynamic origins of the focus must be established during the selection process. On occasions, patients present two foci, as in the above example. In such instances, the two foci are often closely interrelated. Thus, a patient's difficulty in relating to women indicates unresolved conflicts with the mother, while a concurrent difficulty in finding meaning and satisfaction in work may indicate that the dynamic root is retaliatory fears relating to a competitive self-defeating pattern developed in the relationship with the father.

RESPONSE TO INTERPRETATION

Response to interpretation is another clue as to whether the patient can become involved with the therapist. If the patient responds affectively or elaborates verbally on interpretations, he or she is receptive to intervention. If these responses are not evident, the patient is probably too well defended or insulated to acknowledge any feelings and deal directly with the pain. The treatment process is an interference in the psychological system of the patient; a patient who is unable to accept any interference is unable to use the treatment process to deal with his or her problems.

ABILITY TO MAKE AFFECTUAL CONTACT

The patient must be able to make affectual contact with the therapist, since the basis of treatment is the transferential relationship between patient and therapist. If patients have not had previous meaningful relationships in their lives, they will be unable to develop the needed transferential relationship with the therapist. If they have had meaningful relationships, they can develop a relationship with the therapist that will allow them to replace the bad introjected object with a new, good one. Previous meaningful relationships in the lives of patients indicate that they have been able to reach out to others in the past and have been able to respond to others reaching out to them.

It is important to assess whether the patient is still able to reach out or to respond to others reaching out. Has the patient withdrawn from all contact with others? Does the patient show a lack of interest in involvement with others? How is the patient reaching out to object's If the patient is still reaching out, early parenting has been there, and replacement of the bad introjected object is possible. The therapist becomes the new, good object.

Evidence of meaningful relationship is found in the life histories of patients and in affectual responses to the therapist. The affectual contact is demonstrated by crying, showing anger, expressing disbelief, or giving any tangible sign of a new insight. A new insight is any feeling and/or information that is meaningfully tied together with other information for the first time. This new insight should bring an increased interest and even an element of surprise to the patient. If this does occur, then the patient begins to develop a sense that he can work conjointly with someone on problems that have seemed insoluble in the past. New hope is felt by both patient and therapist as the partnership becomes apparent. A patient who cannot interact in this manner during the selection process surely will be unable to do so during any other sessions, when the material and interpretations might be more emotionally laden.

ABILITY TO TOLERATE ANXIETY AND REENACTMENT

Patients should be able to tolerate anxiety and reenactment of depressive feelings during the assessment without displaying evidence of regression or decompensations, since STDP is an anxiety-provoking treatment. The therapist must make a definitive evaluation of the patient's ego capacity during the evaluation.

Consider the man, age 45, who gave a history of an injury that had lasted a year and that had prevented him from working the last 8 months. During this period, he experienced depressive feelings, suicidal thoughts, anxiety attacks related to fear of death, and a profound fear of institutionalization. Although he was married, he was openly having an affair.

During the assessment interview, he became anxious when asked about his need to punish his wife by having an affair with her best friend. He became sweaty, stared out the window, and began to hyperventilate. When confronted with the fact that he was avoiding me, running away from the interviewer the same way he stayed home with the injury to avoid fear of failure on the job, he became physically more anxious but remained. After I described to the patient his actual physical feelings and suggested that he was reexperiencing the same fears of failure in work with me, he began to try to control his breathing. He quieted down and acknowledged his fear of getting close to anyone and his mistrust of everyone.

Suspiciousness and mistrust per se are not contraindications, but they must be differentiated from symptoms of a paranoid personality. Often these patients show mistrust at the service of past and current familial experiences. In the above example, the therapist needed to assess the patient's ability to tolerate and respond to an interpretative technique. If his ego had been too fragile for this, STDP would not have been advised; long-term treatment would have been the choice.

Previous and/or current familial experiences have often led to injury. Patients fear repetition of this injury in another interpersonal relationship, and may therefore be mistrustful. The assessment should clarify this by confronting the patient about previous futile and painful experiences that have led to withdrawal and mistrust. Initially, patients will bring these distorted expectations to the patient–therapist relationship.

Consider a patient with a 3-year history of depression, profound feelings of isolation, and marital problems, who came to assessment stating that he had very few if any friends. He explained that whenever he met someone new, he would scrutinize him, trying to find his flaws. Upon finding flaws, he then had reasons to look down upon and reject the person.

He then asked if he could smoke, to which I replied, "No." He then asked why I kept on my desk an ashtray, all the while smiling slightly. I asked him his thoughts on this, to which he replied, "Do you do it to tease people? If not, why don't you put it away?" I replied, "Are you suggesting I set it there specifically to tease you? Are you already looking for my flaws, so that, like your acquaintances, I will meet the same fate—your rejection? So even as you start a possible contract with me, you are setting up a situation that would lead to failure again?"

The patient turned red, smiled uncomfortably, looked at me directly for the first time and said, "I guess I don't trust you." This response pattern suggests that the patient did have sufficient ego strength to participate in STDP.

ABILITY TO MAKE SACRIFICES

Patients must be able to invest in the treatment process and in themselves. Are patients willing to arrange their schedules to make appointments? To accept some inconvenience in traveling to see the therapist? Possibly to give up some other pleasures or necessities for a period of time? To pay for the treatment?

Patients who are unwilling to be even a little inconvenienced physically and/or financially are persons who are unable to make investments in themselves; such persons are unable to deal directly with problems and are very poor candidates for STDP or any other treatment. On the other hand, some may be too willing to give up too much. Making an extreme sacrifice may be a way to avoid involvement, a way of sabotaging the treatment process.

ACCEPTANCE OF TIME LIMITATION

The patient must accept the time limitation in STDP. Patients will often resist working as long as the therapist will allow it. The therapist must assess patients' feelings and reservations about the time limitation. Are reservations appropriate, or do they indicate patients' lack of faith in themselves to do the work or a lack of trust in the therapist? Are they related to fears about an abrupt, inappropriate, or painful termination? A patient's refusal to accept the time limitation despite reservations is a lack of commitment to work on the problem.

ABSENCE OF SERIOUS SUICIDAL IDEATION

Appropriate patients will not have current indications of serious suicidal ideation. The therapist assesses the level of depression before beginning treatment by a mental status examination. Serious suicidal ideation precludes the patient's emotional availability to this anxiety-provoking treatment. Serious suicidal ideation includes statements about self-harm that describe intent, purpose, and real meaning. The provocation of any additional anxiety may precipitate the acting out of these thoughts.

If the patient has had suicidal ideation precipitated by a real event in the past, but has not acted on these thoughts, the therapist must discuss these previous events directly to clarify whether and how those thoughts and feelings in the past have been resolved. Any residue or ruminative suicidal thinking without clear external precipitants is a contraindication to this treatment.

Patients must meet the above criteria to be selected for STDP. If one criterion is not fully met by a particular patient, there must be an apparent, dynamic reason for this that the therapist believes will not profoundly interfere with the course of treatment. If the dynamic reason for this is part of the focal conflict, then the patient can be accepted, as it is a problem to be resolved. However, if patients are unable to meet criteria in any other ways, they are better treated with other methods.

EVALUATION AND TREATMENT

While the symptom picture of depression may include sadness, loss of interest in the future, reduction of initiative in social and occupational pursuits, somatic complaints, agitation, feelings of helplessness and loneliness, self-depreciation, social withdrawal, and possible self-destructive ideation, it must be recalled that "one cannot measure psychopathology in terms of immediate symptomatology. A patient's distress and symptoms should be understood and evaluated in light of his developmental implications" (Bonime, 1976). These implications can be defined only by a review of the patient's life history. This review is undertaken with the patient during the evaluation process. Thus, evaluation includes both history taking and the initiation of a therapeutic alliance with the potential patient.

HISTORY TAKING

History taking increases patients' involvement in the psychotherapeutic process. By summarizing and giving factual information about their lives, patients become involved in thinking about the reality and the fantasized memories of what has been given or denied to them. They evaluate their important human relationships; gain an overview of past experiences (good and/or bad); and discuss old conflicts, especially those that have been reactivated by the current crisis. The therapist helps patients to express and clarify these facts, define relationships, and begin the cognitive recollection of affects that were or should have been present with these events. The therapist must gently but firmly focus patients on areas that they repeatedly present, in order to reconstruct the historical determinants of the patients' present difficulties.

History taking includes detailed discussion of why a patient seeks treatment now. The therapist evaluates the levels of regression and fixation to delineate the developmental failure that caused the trauma and the course of illness. By the end of evaluation, the focal conflict should be apparent to both therapist and patient.

As an illustration, consider the "Case of the Isolated Man." This 45-year-old man suffered from a depressive illness that he defined as lifelong. He had previously been in treatment for six sessions, which he had terminated because the therapy had not made him feel better. This time, he came to treatment at the suggestion of a colleague at work. The patient identified his problems as basically manifestations of "midlife crisis." "I have no satisfactions. What I expect does not happen in reality."

During the first evaluation interview, he was vague; he talked a great deal but volunteered very little real information. He prefaced each statement with qualifying words such as "basically," "generally," "perhaps," "maybe," "logically," "I guess." He was an only child, and his mother had been hospitalized for several years when he was 5 years of age, during which time his father had taken care of him. The patient married at age 27 and divorced at age 34. The marriage followed a 3-year courtship and pressure from his girlfriend: "She gave me an ultimatum; I guess she asked for a commitment. I gave in because she caught me with my guard down."

The patient was dissatisfied with his job, which he felt was "at a dead end." He suffered from insomnia and experienced "general feelings of being lost." He reported two previous depressive episodes, one at age 27 when he was being pressured into marriage, and another at age 35, the year following his divorce.

Throughout evaluation, he was detached and uninvolved. His manner of communication forced me to take from him, instead of permitting a mutually giving discussion. To determine whether this patient was a suitable candidate for STDP, I had to test his degree of detachment. I asked him if he always communicated in such a detached, vague manner. He frowned and stated that he was confused and that he did not understand the question. I gave him specific examples from our interview of how I had to extract information from him, how he prefaced his statements with qualifiers, and how he had not shown any kind of emotion at any time. He began to squirm in his chair. I asked if our work would be "basically general or maybe something else? What will we accomplish at the end of our work? Perhaps a general and a superficial result?" The patient quietly said, "I don't know. Nothing, I guess." These limited affectual responses were a direct response to my challenging his defensive manner of relating. They indicated that he was able to allow some intervention and experience some feelings. I then told him to think about specific problematic areas and to be prepared to discuss them in detail next time. The patient agreed but was still frowning and squirming. He then paid for the session but insisted upon a receipt, which I viewed as an indication of his ambivalence about treatment, his mistrust of me, and his unexpressed anger.

At the beginning of the second evaluation interview, he reported that he felt very unsure about keeping the appointment and that he had spent the week wondering about whether to return. He said he was unaware that he was "so detached and vague." While unable to say what this meant to him, he did say that the previous interview helped him identify two areas that were problematic: "my difficulty in expressing love," and the fact that "I'm not effective in work, I'm not totally involved." When asked when these areas first became problematic, he immediately discussed the history of each problem and volunteered specific information (e.g., dates, ages). He talked about his relationship with his parents in a more definitive, interested manner, occasionally acknowledging his use of vague statements with much surprise and displeasure.

He produced three powerful early memories: the occurrence of a hurricane at the time that his mother was hospitalized; a teacher's expression of sorrow about his plight; and a reunion at age 12 with his mother when she was permanently discharged from the hospital. When it was pointed out to the patient that all his early memories were related to his mother and his feelings about her leaving or returning, he choked up and became quiet. When asked what he was feeling, he stated that the feelings he experienced when he talked about his mother were the same as the ones he had experienced when he had talked to his former wife a month earlier and realized that he "loved and lost her." He became teary when stating this; he then cried heavily. He was able to connect this to his problem with women, his fear of committing himself to them, his fear of committing himself to work, and his fear that "maybe I won't get what I want" from the treatment process. The patient was confronted with these questions: "Have you established your expectations for failure even before we begin? Do you think this relationship will get you the same poor results you obtained in the past? Why do you want to continue your suffering?" He cried again and said "I guess not."

Thus, the central reason for the patient's depression was brought into focus in two evaluation interviews. Old memories and conflicts about his mother were reviewed; he realized that he displaced his veiled anger onto other women. His feeling of fear of rejection prevented him from making a commitment to anything: women, his job, and life in general. The patient's defensive system was set up to establish distance and to reject before being rejected.

History taking provides an assessment of the development and the adaptive capacities of the ego and the superego, as well as of the levels of regression. Ego development and adaptation are inferred from the patient's past and current object relationships, motivation, affectual responses, intelligence, response to interpretation, and defensive pattern. A greater capacity for human relationships implies a better potential for developing a transferential relationship with the therapist. The way in which patients interact with the therapist is not different from the way in which they interact with significant others in their lives. The transferential relationship provides an opportunity to rework relationships. Patients' activity and emotional involvement in these initial sessions clarify their motivation for treatment and their ability to deal directly with the concomitant emotions. It is important to understand the kinds of defenses and the levels at which these defenses are used if there is to be a planned, dynamic intervention. The degree of aggression and guilt are extremely important as indications of whether a patient harbors any current self-destructive impulses.

INITIATION OF THE THERAPEUTIC ALLIANCE

Throughout both evaluation and treatment, patients move on a continuum from detachment to therapeutic alliance. Detachment, or the maintenance of an aloof, withdrawn position, sets up a defensive wall that prevents any sharing of feelings, protects the patient from therapeutic interpretations, and is often associated with intellectualizations about personal involvement. The therapeutic alliance begins when patient express feelings to, and explore them with, the therapist. This affectual alliance progressively grows to pervade the sessions, while detachment progressively diminishes.

The "Case of the Isolated Man" illustrates movement on this continuum during evaluation. Detachment dominated the first session, while the affectual alliance began in the second session, as evidenced by the patient's changes in body posture and the tears that followed gentle confrontation by the therapist.

The actual treatment process is a continuation of the work that begins during evaluation. The therapist must maintain the therapeutic focus that he and the patient have agreed upon. While maintaining this focus, the therapist helps the patient to move from a position of defensive withdrawal toward a therapeutic working alliance, which itself facilitates maintenance of the focus. The therapist utilizes positive transference and quickly interprets any negative transference.

This continual movement from detachment to alliance is illustrated by excerpts from sessions of the "Isolated Man."

Session 3

PATIENT: My mother left for the hospital twice, not once.

[*At this point, the patient reiterates information that has been thoroughly discussed in the previous interviews with no new insights. There is a long pause.*]

THERAPIST: Have you had any dreams?

PATIENT: (*Long pause.*) Yes. (*Pause.*) I was somehow in the air falling into a swimming pool. The pool was full of mud instead of water. There were crocodiles in the pool chasing me. I was struggling to get to the edge. People were there—relatives, my mother, father, grandmother. My mother pulled me out.

THERAPIST: What are your thoughts about this dream?

PATIENT: Well (*pause*), I feel insecure and fear some kind of injury or death. My mother and father try to rescue me. (*Pause.*) I had this dream before; the first time was immediately after my mother's first hospitalization.

[*At this point the patient seems very uncomfortable; he squirms in his chair and looks around the room, but says nothing.*]

PATIENT: When she came back it wasn't like she was with me. I was frightened . . . ah . . . confused that she came back. She was frail and bent over. (*The patient's voice suddenly gets louder.*) Doctor, I just remembered something. When I was 13, a boy and I fell off a cliff. I got a compound fracture of my leg. I was on vacation with my mother. I just sat in our country house with her. That time we were close in our relationship.

THERAPIST: That was after she was home permanently?

PATIENT: Yes.

THERAPIST: Your mother had TB?

PATIENT: Yes.

THERAPIST: Do you know what it is?

PATIENT: Yes, a disease.

THERAPIST: Do you know how it is contracted? (*The patient looks at therapist blankly.*) It is contracted through the mouth and nose. Do you know that if she had kissed you when she had active TB, you could have contracted the disease?

PATIENT: (*Stares at the therapist; he becomes flushed and then pale.*) I never realized it.

THERAPIST: But you are an intelligent man, you're fond of biology; why did this never occur to you? (*The patient sobs heavily for a few minutes as grief to appropriate object emerges.*)

THERAPIST: Why are you crying?

PATIENT: The realization that her expression of love was not there because of TB. (*The patient continues to cry.*) You know, I was never comfortable with physical contact at home. I have a tendency to be unphysical. (*The patient becomes more composed but still seems uncomfortable.*) In the dream, the mud reminds me of the quicksand that I saw in the movies. I remembered being terrified of sinking and disappearing. I was afraid I would be swallowed up in the mud like in quicksand. I remember struggling in the pool to get to the edge; people were urging me on. Now, sometimes, in the morning, I have fears like when I am afraid to be swallowed up in the mud. I'm afraid of something ominous in the future—scary feelings tied up with my career thing. I fear an economic helplessness, like I am at the mercy of the world and made to do things I don't want to do. [*Realization that his mother could have loved him, and also of his fears of being alone and vulnerable.*]

THERAPIST: What do you think of these fears?

PATIENT: (*Long pause. The patient again becomes flushed and choked up.*) Maybe it has to do with my *fear commitment.*

[*At this point, the patient talks about his fear of real involvement with women and his career. He discusses the fact that, even as he was planning his marriage, he was thinking of the necessary steps to take should he get divorced. Note that he goes back to the initial two foci of treatment.*]

[*The therapist accidentally knocks a piece of paper to the floor. The patient, normally slow-moving, quickly jumps up to pick up the paper. This transferential gesture is immediately confronted.*]

THERAPIST: You moved fast to pick up my paper.

PATIENT: What about it?

THERAPIST: What made you do that?

PATIENT: (*Chuckles.*) I'm being cooperative, polite; it's the thing to do.

THERAPIST: What need do you have to be cooperative?

PATIENT: (*Frowns.*) Don't make so much of this. I want to cooperate with you.

THERAPIST: "Cooperate"—what does this mean? (*The patient looks puzzled and doesn't answer.*) In the first session you spent 10 minutes asking for a receipt, although I told you I would bill you. You wouldn't leave until I took the money and gave you a receipt. How come [you're] so cooperative now?

PATIENT: (*Laughs.*) I didn't think of that. I remember. I don't know why now. [*He knows exactly why—he was not coming back for a second session.*]

THERAPIST: Are you afraid of what can happen if you don't cooperate?

PATIENT: Perhaps. Maybe. You could disapprove.

THERAPIST: What does "cooperate" mean?

PATIENT: I don't understand.

THERAPIST: How did you feel in that first session?

PATIENT: Very far away, distant.

THERAPIST: And now?

PATIENT: Not so distant.

THERAPIST: Not so distant? Since that session we have talked about many things, and you have allowed yourself to experience a lot of feeling with me. Maybe not so distant is *close.*

PATIENT: Yes (*softly*).

THERAPIST: What happens if I disapprove?

PATIENT: You could terminate?

[*Note that the patient makes the connection that "too close" may be followed by leaving and hurt.*]

THERAPIST: Maybe you've decided you want something here. You then become subservient and pick up papers at my feet? Is this the way you get close to people—become subservient?

PATIENT: Reminds me of when Mother left. Father . . . (*The patient starts to cry.*)

[*The patient makes the link between present and past with present and past appropriate affect.*]

THERAPIST: Why are you crying?

PATIENT: There are so many other times when I demean myself. I didn't know any other way.

[*The remainder of the interview focused on the other situations in which he demeaned himself to get close to men and women.*]

A therapeutic alliance is evident in this session. The patient shared information, openly expressed emotion, and responded to interpretations. The interview focused on closeness, which was dealt with transferentially.

In the fourth session, the patient's emergent resistance can be seen. His vague manner of communicating became identical to that of the first assessment session.

Session 4

PATIENT: I wanted to ask you something of the nature of this kind of treatment, ah . . . if you wouldn't mind commenting, ah . . .

THERAPIST: Yes

PATIENT: Ah . . . which would be true for any kind of psychotherapy, I guess. Ah . . . through what means is, ah, is a kind of improvement on elimination of difficulties realized? I mean, ah . . . it . . . I'm now beginning to find out certain things about myself. Now how does that ultimately change me? I mean, suppose I just tuck them away in the back of my mind, or do I . . . ? Ah . . . does it change me more or less automatically, or do I (*pause*) do I bring these things to bear, ah . . . upon my (*pause*) future ah . . . situations, or do I have to work at that, or, or, ah . . . I'm just curious how, how, ah . . . a cure, or that's perhaps too strong a word. But, how is the (*pause*) how is the change in my behavior ultimately effected, would you say?

THERAPIST: Why don't you yourself try to give some answers to your own questions? What do you think thus far from what you, ah . . . have learned if anything here and from your past life experiences? What are your thoughts on this? Because you've touched a number of areas.

PATIENT: Just now you mean? Well (*pause*), I don't know. I realize that I can have a rather powerful experience here and yet . . . a few days later, ah . . . I appear to be my old self—that is, I spend too much time thinking about it after a certain point. I may be different at this point, but I don't know, and I'm just curious how, how that works, ah . . . or if it works, or should I be able to know the difference? Ah . . .

THERAPIST: Well, what do you think? An . . . (*pause*), what is your feeling now? You must have some thoughts about something specific, perhaps, this week?

PATIENT: (*Shakes head, begins to say "No."*) Yeah. I've been trying . . . it's been a little hard for me to focus on them this week, and that's one reason that, that, ah . . . this question came to my mind. I know . . .

THERAPIST: What has been hard for you to focus on?

PATIENT: Well, usually before I come up here or on the way, I'm, I'm . . . I try to think of things that I'm going to be concerned with and, and, ah . . . kind of review what has happened and all that kind of thing. And I noticed today it's a little difficult for me to get at it. It seems a little further away than usual. And, ah . . .

THERAPIST: Does this remind you of anything? The way that you feel today about being further away?

PATIENT: Not especially. I'm not aware of it.

THERAPIST: You—you understand my question?

PATIENT: (*hesitating*) Are . . . are you referring to the idea of being detached, possibly?

THERAPIST: I don't know. (*Pause.*) You used the words "further away."

PATIENT: What I mean is that it's hard for me to focus, or I don't feel as close [to] these emotional things as I did, say, a couple of times in the past when I was here, you know?

[*To the patient, "focus" represents achieving closeness. He and the therapist have agreed to focus; "not focusing" means affectual detachment.*]

THERAPIST: What do you think about the fact that today you feel further away? That means that this week you had trouble looking into the material that you worked with last week.

PATIENT: I had trouble, ah . . . I just feel a little removed from it, that, ah . . . it seems more distant from my concern right now, and I don't exactly know why.

The patient's language suggests that he was defensive, confused, and withdrawn from any feelings related to the primary loss. He was unable to be specific or focused. Having decided that he was vulnerable, he pushed back to his earlier isolation defense. Having gotten too close in the previous session, he began the stage of "treatment resistance" (see below). His behavior was more akin to his behavior in the first evaluation interview. He was resistive and nonresponsive to any attempt by the therapist to intervene or get close to him through this session.

In the sixth session, the patient demonstrated a renewed involvement in the therapeutic process.

Session 6

PATIENT: Are you asking me to figure out . . . ?

THERAPIST: Isn't that what you're here for—to figure out things that you never wanted to look at, or looked at on the surface?

PATIENT: Okay, all right; now that I understand you, I'm willing to pursue it.

THERAPIST: So, clearly you balked at the fact that [your] mother could pull away your protection.

PATIENT: That's what was so heartbreaking to me, that she was doing everything she shouldn't have been doing—practically killing herself on my behalf.

THERAPIST: But her heart was in the right place each time, as you had told me.

PATIENT: Right.

THERAPIST: She may have made the most wise decision in the world, but the feeling and the caring were never in question?

PATIENT: I never realized that as fully, and it just came over me.

THERAPIST: It seems that even after she is well, instead of pulling away as some people do, it seems your mother makes another move toward you.

PATIENT: But there was no touching that I recall especially. I mean it wasn't one of those hugging, touching sort of things. (*Pause.*)

THERAPIST: The closeness that you remember in those summer vacations, was it bilateral? The question is, did she come over to you and did you pull away? Or she wasn't coming over to you?

PATIENT: What is that again?

THERAPIST: The question was, who was pulling away from whom?

PATIENT: At what point?

THERAPIST: Your teens.

PATIENT: Pulling away. I think what you're getting at is, you are suggesting that I was pulling away?

THERAPIST: I don't know. How am I suggesting?

PATIENT: By "pulling away," you mean not offering physical . . . okay.

THERAPIST: Then she comes back when you are 11. So you have 2 years, something is missing, then she was with you about 2 years or 3, and then as soon as you are getting [it] established that she is staying, she goes away all over again.

PATIENT: I think that's significant, though, about this business of pulling away and being close, because the fact that maybe I wasn't—I don't remember this, but it's possible that I wasn't convinced that she was really there for good anymore.

THERAPIST: You don't have any memories of that?

PATIENT: No, but I do remember at times in my childhood feeling that she was almost a stranger. One time I remember that she came home. I don't remember at what point that was, and, like, I hardly . . . she was practically a stranger. I didn't quite know who she was, almost. But I had a sort of . . . it was very tentative, you know, like "Hello" almost.

[*The remainder of the session focused on the patient's relationships with women and displacement of his veiled anger toward them.*]

TECHNIQUE

"Technique" refers to the method of using specific details in a particular way to accomplish a desired goal. While the evaluation process is aimed at delineating the degree of pathology and the appropriateness of STDP, treatment is aimed at resolving the circumscribed conflicts that have caused the depression. Specific techniques are used to explore, interpret the transference, confront, and clarify. These techniques are designed to clarify the conflicts and defenses and to help the patient discover how current daily conflicts relate to similar conflicts in the past. In addition, through evocative, direct questioning, the therapist helps the patient out of his or her passive, helpless interaction in dealing with the patient–therapist relationship. Exploration of the transferential relationship allows the patient to identify patterns in interpersonal relationships; to break this pattern, the therapist empathetically listens to the patient's problems and thus plants the seeds of worthiness in the patient. This method breaks the cycle of helplessness, failure, and despair in depressed patients. Finally, the therapeutic relationship allows the patient to focus totally on his or her problems. As the patient works with the therapist to resolve problems, changes in self-attitudes and personality ensue.

FOUR PHASES OF TREATMENT

The treatment process can be divided into four phases: "primary resistance," "treatment resistance," "termination resistance," and "termination resolution."

The initial stage, primary resistance, consists of resistance shown by the patient as a defense against the primary loss. The patient struggles against both intellectual and emotional recognition of the pain of the initial parental separation and the ambivalence toward his or her parents. The work of this stage is (1) continued assessment of the degree of primary defensiveness; (2) challenging of the defenses covering the primary loss; and (3) clarification of the ambivalence. The critical techniques include transference interpretations, activity, and concentration on focus. Primary resistance opens the neurosis, which is then clarified with these techniques. During this period, distancing is typically the patient's primary defense. Distancing may be attempted in different ways; however, the purpose is always to maintain the chasm between the patient and the therapist, thereby preventing painful repetition of the initial parental involvement and loss.

Interactions between patient and therapist must be challenged and completely understood. The patient must begin in this phase to face the pain and reality of his or her vulnerability directly, instead of protecting it to the point of isolation. The constant activity of the therapist in the form of direct questioning, clarifying content and interaction, and maintaining the focus provide the foundation upon which the therapist can solicitously challenge the patient. The challenging of defenses is possible only if there is a therapeutic alliance, and the transference interpretations evoke a positive abreactive experience. The challenging of defenses without the development of a therapeutic alliance is a destructive attack on the patient and must always be avoided.

The second stage, treatment resistance, occurs as the therapist challenges the patient's primary defenses. The patient becomes fearful and begins to resist the process itself. The mobilization of this secondary defense to treatment is necessary in order for the process to be effective. The patient is afraid of exposure to the newly cathected therapist and a reenactment of the early loss with concomitant feelings. The therapist must actively challenge, confront, and clarify the situation. Most importantly, interpretations of past and present behavior patterns must be provided. These behavior patterns are foundations of self-defeat; thus, patients learn that they are the powerful victims who control their own defeats. As patients experience the continuum of resistance—from small annoyances to greater angers—in the transferential situation, they will try to repress the feelings as they have done previously. The therapist must not allow denial or repression of feelings to be reentrenched. Patients do not experience retaliation for their anger; instead, there is active encouragement to look and explore. Uncovering occurs in a gentle manner, with further clarification of the fear of retaliation as it relates to current people in the patients' lives. Thus, patients receive a corrective emotional experience. The expression of anger by patients must be focused and directed at a source. Aimless expression of anger is synonymous with untargeted rage. If there is no external target, the rage is turned in, and thus the depression is directed inward also. Therefore, the therapist's modulation and direction of anger through the therapeutic alliance is of primary importance. The techniques to be used in dealing with this anger and resistance are (1) interpreting every avoidance of feeling toward the therapist; and (2) focusing with patients on why they are there and reminding them of their part of the contract to do work. The confrontations and/or interpretations help patients to repair the fantasized anger with the parents by working through the transferential anger with the therapist. Patients learn that feelings can be expressed in an appropriate way to the right object without retaliation, termination, or loss. Thus, reenactment of the parental neurosis is not necessary.

The third stage, termination resistance, occurs as soon as a patient senses the impending termination. A remobilization of early defenses against loss ensues, and sometimes a recurrence of symptoms may result. The patient may experience a new crisis that is a reenactment of past neurotic failures. That patient begins to pull back from recently achieved interpersonal relationships into a renewed isolation.

The first signs generally occur near the middle of treatment. Patients begin to express doubts about their progress and/or the ability of the therapist to help; they defensively try to maneuver the therapist, and they express their anger in an indirect fashion.

The following excerpt illustrates termination resistance. The therapist arrived 15 minutes late for the session.

PATIENT: Tough night, huh, Doc?

THERAPIST: What do you mean?

PATIENT: Come on, don't give me an argument.

THERAPIST: I'm late. How did you feel when you realized I would be . . .

PATIENT: I didn't think about it; I didn't get angry or anything.

THERAPIST: Not angry about my being late? But you said, "Don't give me an argument."

PATIENT: That's an expression. It means nothing.

THERAPIST: Nothing? "Anger," "argument,"—your words. Your words, but you put them in my mouth by telling me not to be angry. You were on time. I was late. Who has reason to be angry?

PATIENT: Why get angry? Sometimes . . .

THERAPIST: No, no. Who has reason to be angry?

PATIENT: I guess I do.

THERAPIST: How do you feel now?

PATIENT: Now, I'm getting annoyed . . .

THERAPIST: Only annoyed?

PATIENT: Okay, very annoyed. I just made a little comment and you make a big deal . . .

THERAPIST: I make a big deal. What do you make it, a little deal? What are your feelings?

Finally, the patient openly expressed that he was angry with the therapist for being late; this led to a discussion of his fears that the therapist would not show up at all, but would abandon him. Interpretations were made that helped him to understand that this pattern of defensive maneuvering was his usual way of dealing with anger. His fear of abandonment was further connected to the reality that the treatment was half finished.

If anger is present but not dealt with, both treatment and termination will be prolonged. The therapist should directly and quickly confront the quality and timing of the defensive maneuvering at the onset of crisis. The work of the therapist is to bring feelings related to previous losses and current relationships into focus, in order to show that a similar pattern is being reenacted in the transference. In the case just cited, the patient was pushing the therapist away, thereby invoking failure. The therapist showed the patient how his maneuvering defeated the treatment and helped him to understand that defeating treatment and the therapist would be defeating himself.

Termination resolution is the fourth phase. If the therapist does not manage transference interpretations effectively during treatment, transference resistance will ensue during termination. When both patient and therapist begin to feel that treatment needs to be prolonged, transference resistance should be strongly suspected.

The transference defense of submissiveness (the helplessness of a little child) can be used to revert the therapist–patient relationship into a paralytic parent–child deadlock. The therapist must actively confront the patient with attempts to employ submissiveness.

If a deadlock occurs in the final stage, the patient will return to earlier narcissistic omnipotence. This position will reinforce the neurosis. Such patients will become more omnipotent, with greater conviction now of their pathological uniqueness, reinforced in their feelings of destructive power over themselves and others. In essence, they have "killed" again—before, the parent; now, the therapist—but the latter cements their hopeless position. If termination resolution is successful, a reenactment in the person of the therapist is often seen. The patient now identifies the loss of the therapist, grieves over it, and connects it clearly to earlier parental losses; however, for the first time, it is a different termination, a nonambivalent one.

The following excerpts from the "Case of the Victim" exemplify the stages of treatment and specific therapeutic techniques. During evaluation, this 38-year-old married father of one stated, "I have a lot of problems coping; I am getting more depressed; I am not thinking clearly, not dealing with things well on my job; I am never happy; I don't smile. Why do things upset me so much?" He had sleep problems, was drinking heavily, and had just terminated an affair of 8 months' duration. He stated that he rarely got angry. To him, anger meant a long-term thing. He stated that anger ended relationships. In all the years of marriage, he never expressed anger, although he was easily frustrated at the time of assessment.

At age 13, his father had accused him of an unforgivable betrayal. When he was 16, his parents had separated. His mother had died of advanced muscular illness. His father had died of a heart attack when he was aged 21, after which the patient had left college. At work, 3 years later, he had met a boss who was "like a father" to him. The patient's conflict over departure from the job and an affair with a secretary had led to decompensation. He had quit his job and taken a poor temporary position. He had meaningful relationships with his two older siblings and his former boss, although he had no friends. He felt that his problems were centered around his masculinity and his relationships with women.

FIRST STAGE OF TREATMENT: PRIMARY RESISTANCE

During the 14th session, something happened to the tape recorder. When I reached to press the button, the patient asked what I was doing.

PATIENT: Okay, I'll put on another show next week.

THERAPIST: You feel you are putting on a show?

PATIENT: This bothers me.

THERAPIST: How does this bother you? Why did you agree to it if it bothers you?

PATIENT: Because if it may help, then I'll get used to it.

THERAPIST: What bothers you about it?

PATIENT: I don't like the way I sound on tape.

THERAPIST: How do you think you sound?

PATIENT: I once had a very bad experience with the tape recorder at school, and I messed up the tape. So I basically don't like talking into the tape.

[*Here the patient is suggesting that he'll fail in therapy. He's afraid of being exposed in treatment.*]

THERAPIST: Because you think you are gong to mess it up again?

PATIENT: I don't like the way I sound on it, and I think I could mess it up.

THERAPIST: The sound doesn't please you?

PATIENT: No.

THERAPIST: It doesn't live up to the expectations of how it should sound?

PATIENT: Yes.

THERAPIST: Is that the only reason the tape recorder bothers you?

PATIENT: It's the only reason I feel.

THERAPIST: Then why did you say "I'll do another show" and then smile?

PATIENT: Well it's sort of like a show—the tape . . .

THERAPIST: On stage? Do you feel you are being used?

PATIENT: No, I think that is a little farfetched.

THERAPIST: We can stop it any time you want.

PATIENT: Well maybe it will be interesting; so far, there have been a lot of things I didn't want to discuss, but we did and it seemed to have helped me. So if you think it will help, I'm trusting you; but it still makes me uncomfortable.

[*Here the patient is still experiencing some feelings of being used and some mistrust.*]

THERAPIST: Okay, let's go back to where we were.

PATIENT: Back to my mother; I think that's where we were. You asked me how did I feel when I first came here. I don't know. It was interesting to me that the first time I came here I talked about my father, and several sessions later I still hadn't spoken about my mother at all. And before I came here, I always analyzed the problems that I didn't think she was a great mother. I felt that she had problems, and I felt that I may have disliked her or even hated her. At times I felt this. But, looking back, there are times when I don't remember her being in my mind. I have trouble remembering her except when she was sick. I can't remember her physically.

THERAPIST: Are you saying you don't remember the good times and closeness with your mother?

PATIENT: Yes, I remember situations, but the first thing that always flashes into my mind is when she was sick.

THERAPIST: Let's go back. With your father, you said that you had feelings for him that you knew all along; your anger with him wouldn't allow you to express the feelings and the loss of him. Then you did express this—in the first few sessions you cried for him. With [your] mother, you're telling me that before you came you had some questions about her as a mother, but at the same time you remember little bits of the close relationship between you and her. You can't remember her physically, only the highlight of her sickness?

PATIENT: Well, I remember her, her large breasts, but I can't picture her as a full person. I remember parts, like I remember she had nice hands . . . but no total picture. I remember going shopping with her and how I used to follow her around when she listened to the soap operas as she dusted and cleaned; taking walks with her and going to Woolworth's, and she bought me things.

THERAPIST: What do you remember most, good times or bad times?

PATIENT: (*Sighs.*) You mean when I walked in here? (*Pause.*) I think . . . I felt resentment toward her for the position she put me in with my father. She said to me in a conversation while she was dying . . . (*Sighs.*) Once especially, Patty and I were there, she said, "I know what will happen after I die; you'll all go there and live with your father and that woman." I said, "No, I won't." And she said that I would. It was as if she said, "I don't want you to," or maybe it's what I read into it.

THERAPIST: Had you thought that out before?

PATIENT: No, I hadn't thought of this before.

THERAPIST: She gave you a deathbed statement.

PATIENT: Yes, almost. The last lucid words she said [were]—my sister and I were at the house with her; we picked her up and carried her to the bed. (*Sounds choked up and looks sad.*)

THERAPIST: How do you feel now?

PATIENT: Uncomfortable and sad.

THERAPIST: Do you feel like crying?

PATIENT: A little bit.

THERAPIST: What makes you hold it back?

[*The therapist helps the patient experience and remember the grief.*]

PATIENT: I don't know; this stuff was so bizarre!

THERAPIST: Okay, tell me what's bizarre.

PATIENT: To me it was bizarre, that she would ask me to do that.

THERAPIST: Why?

PATIENT: That's leaving somebody some legacy.

THERAPIST: The legacy was what?

PATIENT: "Don't let your father be happy. And don't you be happy." (*Pause.*) The last thing she said before she went to the hospital (*sighs loudly*), she sat up in bed and said, "My God, my son, what have I done to you." That was the last thing.

THERAPIST: What do you think she meant by that comment?

[*The patient is coming to an awareness of his mother's control over his life.*]

PATIENT: Well, initially I remember looking at her and thought she meant because of what I was seeing, seeing her dying of that illness, but now I think she realized what she had done, what position she had put me in. You know she was a very bright woman. She may not have been completely balanced at that point . . .

THERAPIST: Then her last statement was apologizing for what had taken place in the relationship with your father?

(*The patient is softly crying.*)

THERAPIST: You didn't see it that way before.

[*As the patient's ambivalent feelings toward his mother surface, grieving begins.*]

PATIENT: Well . . . (*Has difficulty talking.*)

THERAPIST: This is the first time you see this now? You saw the legacy of continuing the war with [your] father and keeping [your] father away . . .

PATIENT: What I think I really saw was the pain it also must have caused her, she didn't know what she was doing. For someone to say that, the last thing; she knew she was dying, it was over . . . I just saw the pain, I didn't read deeper into it . . . just thought, look what happened over the last 9 months since she had been dying.

THERAPIST: You never looked at the significance of what was being said to you? What was she telling you? What was the real legacy?

PATIENT: (*Is restless in his seat and looking down at the floor; he sighs loudly; there is a long pause.*) She told me to be angry with him; she told me to pay him back for her.

[*The patient views himself as an avenger for his mother.*]

THERAPIST: Let's look at the words again. She said to you, "As soon as I die, you and your sister will go and live with him and that other woman." How did she feel about the fact that he took up with that other woman?

PATIENT: Well, everything was jumbled up. She made like she couldn't function at all when he left.

THERAPIST: Did she resent the other woman?

PATIENT: Oh, yeah. I remember her calling the other woman and having arguments, etc. The other woman called the house . . .

THERAPIST: For someone who was not interested in your father, why was she bothering with the other woman?

PATIENT: Did I say she wasn't interested in my father? She was . . .

THERAPIST: It sounds like the fire was still burning.

PATIENT: She was definitely interested. It was like she just destroyed herself after.

THERAPIST: What was your mother asking you and your sisters? Was she addressing the three of you or just you when she made her deathbed statements?

PATIENT: My sister Marcia wasn't there, just Patty and I. (*Long pause.*) She was telling me that I don't love her?

THERAPIST: Oh! She was questioning the love for her from both of you. Look at the phrasing. Do you understand what I'm saying? Was she asking you to be loyal to her to the end? Doesn't that have the sound of a pretty powerful love affair?

PATIENT: Loyal? For me to be loyal to her . . . to the end? To the end of what, the end of her life?

THERAPIST: If you only were with her as long as you had to be because of necessity, not because you cared for her, and the minute she died you would run to somebody else, that means that your love for her was questionable and would break the minute she died. She was asking you, really, "How much do you really love me?" What does that mean? Was the anger there?

PATIENT: Of course, of course.

THERAPIST: She was questioning whether you truly loved her because she was sick or for herself. She wanted to know if you stayed with her because you felt sorry for her or because you truly loved her. She was asking, would you be loyal to her at the expense of your relationship with [your] father. Do you understand?

(*The patient nods his head "Yes." He has difficulty talking.*)

THERAPIST: What she says to you, "What have I done to you, my son," you interpret that to mean what?

PATIENT: Well, initially, I thought she was saying that I was stuck there and had to take care of her . . .

THERAPIST: But she didn't say "my daughter?"

PATIENT: No, only to me . . .

THERAPIST: Why only to you? Your sister was there.

PATIENT: I don't know . . . I don't know.

THERAPIST: How did the girls relate to your father?

PATIENT: (*Sighs loudly.*) Well, Patty was subservient, always trying to please him. Marcia stood up to him.

THERAPIST: When [your] mother died, did they want to move [in] with [your] father?

PATIENT: Patty did.

THERAPIST: And Marcia?

PATIENT: I feel angry at Patty saying that; just now, I felt angry with her.

THERAPIST: Why, what do you mean? What made you feel angry towards Patty?

PATIENT: Because Patty had a history of that. I don't think Patty was loyal.

THERAPIST: Loyal to whom?

PATIENT: To my mother. I think her loyalties lie completely with my father. Marcia stood up to him; because she didn't cut him down, it was okay.

THERAPIST: So the girls' relationship with your father [was] slightly better than your relationship with your father?

PATIENT: A lot better than mine after my mother died. They still communicated with him.

THERAPIST: Okay, then, think about it; when your mother said, "What have I done to you, my son," what did she mean? Is it any clearer now?

PATIENT: She broke me away from my father.

THERAPIST: Why?

PATIENT: She wanted to hurt him for some reason.

THERAPIST: Why would she say that? Why would she close up by saying that to you? What was the message by telling you that?

(*The patient does not respond. There is a long pause.*)

THERAPIST: You don't understand?

PATIENT: "Don't be angry with him; I'm sorry I did this"?

[*Note that the patient is clarifying historical misconception.*]

THERAPIST: Well, what other answer do you have? What other interpretation do you have? She didn't say "the girls"? The words are very clear.

(*The patient does not answer and seems very uncomfortable.*)

THERAPIST: I'm staying with this for a while because this is something that you have thought about for a number of years, and it is the first time that you have looked at the feelings behind the words and your feelings.

PATIENT: I think she was saying to me that she was sorry that she did that. If she had time to explain it—she thought, "Oh my God, I'm dying and I don't have time to explain."

THERAPIST: Have you ever heard of the death statement? When someone makes a death statement, that's considered what in court?

(*The patient shrugs.*)

THERAPIST: The strongest statement that you can bring to court is the final statement of the person, which is called the death statement. You didn't know that?

PATIENT: I don't know what you mean.

[*Slim resistance; the therapist makes a composite of the mother's apparently contradictory statement.*]

THERAPIST: When someone is going to die and they make a death statement, the courts place a high priority upon it; it is a very significant statement. It is a confession. [Your] mother first asked for your reassurance of your love. She was saying that she loved you and she needed you. Then she turned to you as a son and [said], "What have I done to you?" She had put you in the middle of the struggle: if you went to Father, you betrayed Mother; if you totally committed yourself to Mother, you would lose Father. Your guilt would keep you forever away from your father, because you had to continue the legacy of Mother.

PATIENT: (*tearfully*) I understand. I really wanted to move [in] with Father, because I was alone too.

[*Note that his ambivalence has begun to clear as he begins to empathize and identify with the father.*]

THERAPIST: Of course you did. It seems that's what you wanted the most, but how could you do it? Because of your own grief, you only heard the anger to [your] father at the time your mother made her statement. But you never heard her say, "I'm a foolish woman and I have no right to do this to you." She said she was sorry for what she had done to you. She told you to go back with your father and make some peace with him. But how could you hear two contradictory messages?

(*The patient is very quietly crying.*)

THERAPIST: You loved them both and they loved you; [your] mother loved you almost exclusively. Your own attraction to mother and anger to father couldn't allow you to understand and love both, you had to choose with guilt and despair. You were caught in a trap and have forever punished yourself out of guilt.

PATIENT: I understand the pattern.

THERAPIST: With your wife, another woman, your boss, your father?

PATIENT: The same thing over and over; we talked about this pattern before.

THERAPIST: You seem close to tears again.

PATIENT: Yes, I guess I'm crying again. It's so long . . .

THERAPIST: You never told me about the comment from your mother before.

PATIENT: No, I don't think I ever mentioned it to my sisters either. I think I was all tied up in the anger; I was angry with my sister. I misread the whole thing. I never looked at it. I isolated myself from everyone, my sisters, friends—I took everything on my shoulders and I couldn't carry it.

[*He acknowledges the tie with the past and his freedom to do differently.*]

THERAPIST: That's an untenable position.

PATIENT: Then 3 years later he dies. So I was really *successful* in what she told me to do, because I isolated myself from him too. Maybe that's why I felt relief after he died? I didn't have to live it any more. [*He expresses no grief.*]

[*His success was to make himself a victim.*]

THERAPIST: Could you have felt the relief?

PATIENT: Well, initially I felt . . . I don't know.

THERAPIST: With [your] mother?

PATIENT: I felt some relief too. [*He expresses no grief.*]

THERAPIST: And that made you feel guilty?

PATIENT: Yes.

THERAPIST: Remember when you first came here, you cried for your father? There really was a great deal of love between both of you.

PATIENT: (*Sighs loudly.*) Yes, I think about that today; it was intense. Now I'm grown and I have a family, and I've accomplished things he would like to have seen me accomplish. I'm a lot like him, which would have made him very happy. There are times when I'm riding along on the road and I pretend he's setting next to me . . . A lot was jammed into that time period. We never resolved the problem.

THERAPIST: You feel like crying now?

PATIENT: Yes. (*Cries a little.*) I think on it; it could have been resolved. We would have been able to talk more as *equals*.

THERAPIST: When you brought your wife here, you said it felt good because you felt I approved of her and it was like your father approved?

PATIENT: (*still crying softly*) Yes, I miss that part a great deal. If he were . . .

[*The remainder of this session focused on the patient's understanding of the sessions and his feelings about it. The patient had difficulty ending the session.*]

SECOND STAGE OF TREATMENT: TREATMENT RESISTANCE

The 16th session with this patient illustrates the second stage of treatment. The therapist's upcoming vacation rekindles feelings that the patient regresses to; he revives the "I need you" of past losses.

THERAPIST: We should clarify the appointment. That means that there are 3 weeks we won't see each other.

PATIENT: That really bothers me.

THERAPIST: How does it bother you?

PATIENT: I tell you—last session I told, or at least I think I told you—I thought it was a good session. At the end of the session, I asked you what you thought and I didn't think too much about it, but then I had a very bad week. I realized *I didn't get any feedback from you at all*, and that bothered me. I guess because I did all the talking . . . I guess that's what I'm supposed to do . . . all the working, supposedly, but I'm still not sure whether I'm right or wrong about some of the conclusions I made.

THERAPIST: Which ones? What do you mean?

PATIENT: Well, in terms of the other sessions that we had, there was more give and take between the two of us, and we had very little give in terms of comments and in terms of *steering me in a direction*.

THERAPIST: Then the notion that you have is that I should be steering you?

PATIENT: Well, not so much . . .

THERAPIST: What should you be doing while I'm steering you?

PATIENT: I should be thinking about it.

THERAPIST: Should you be following the guy who's at the steering wheel?

PATIENT: Well, not necessarily; we have changed directions other times. Even though you didn't steer me, but made comments, and we've gone back to things that were bothering me. You know, and I just felt that . . . *I felt a little like you; you know, last session, there was no sense in being here.*

THERAPIST: You mean you would rather not be here?

PATIENT: (*hesitantly*) No, but I think I got more out of the other sessions.

THERAPIST: Then your expectations are that when you come here, you must get a great deal out of me.

PATIENT: Not a great deal, but I would like more back-and-forth discussion.

THERAPIST: Could there have been a reason why last week was not as productive as you would have liked it to have been?

PATIENT: Maybe because I completely directed it.

[*Here the patient implies that if he takes charge, failure will follow.*]

THERAPIST: But you were not getting as much result as you wanted?

PATIENT: Excuse me?

THERAPIST: You directed it, but didn't get as much result as you wanted.

PATIENT: (*After a long pause.*) Yeah, well, if I directed it, usually the things you stop me at are things that I'm blocking in some way or that I'm not seeing properly. You didn't stop me at all, so these are obviously things that I . . .

THERAPIST: (*interrupting*) Last week I didn't run the session. Why do you let me run the sessions? (*Long pause.*)

PATIENT: But I'm coming to you for direction, to help me find a direction.

THERAPIST: You are the one who does all the finding and moving; all I do, as you correctly pointed out, is if I see something that looks like a block—for example, if there is feeling emerging and you begin to stop it or I think you are stopping it—I mention it, but you are the one who comes up with the feeling.

PATIENT: (*interrupting*) All right, all right . . .

THERAPIST: How do I know you are gong to come up with the feelings?

PATIENT: Okay, you're saying that the last session you didn't see that I was blocking anything or you didn't feel that I was blocking anything.

THERAPIST: Whenever I feel there is a block that interferes with our work, or whenever I can see it, I point it out to you.

[*Next, the patient brings into his awareness the reasons for his regressions.*]

PATIENT: Okay, I see. (*Pause.*) Let me tell you the other thing that bothered me—from the last session I mean. The fact that it looks to me as if we're coming to the end of the visits here; in terms of *you ending.*

THERAPIST: How is that?

PATIENT: Well, you didn't show concern about the missing of the 3 weeks or 4 weeks.

THERAPIST: "Concern"—what do you mean by that?

PATIENT: Well, I don't think you asked if I wanted to seek other visits or not. I mean because of the time you are missing. After all, it is a 3-week time period.

THERAPIST: I don't follow what you mean.

PATIENT: Well, I'll be away, you'll be away—Okay?

THERAPIST: Yes.

PATIENT: So if this was our *last visit* and we would not have one for Friday, I would not see you for almost one full month. I think it's a long period of time. All right? And I'd say there was no concern on your part. You never show any; you leave it for me to show concern. Well I'm concerned about it so *I'm telling you that now.* (*Patient's tone of voice is angered.*)

[*The patient transferentially reenacts his feelings about the loss of his father. He repairs these feelings with "I care for you," said in anger.*]

THERAPIST: You never think of the something your wife had suggested—you never call me.

PATIENT: Yeah, she suggested I call you this week too, because I had a very bad week. She said, "Why don't you call?" And I said, "Well, I'm going to see him Monday."

THERAPIST: Why didn't you call?

PATIENT: Well, I sort of felt that I had the situation in hand well enough, though I was depressed.

THERAPIST: Were you aware of what was making you depressed?

PATIENT: Yeah, I think I was aware of quite a few things. That situation with the boss depressed me, the fact that I didn't stick to my guns. I have an important position and here I was pulling out the pins. The fact I'm going to be dealing with this guy all the time is going to be terrible. He tells me about a trip we have to take; he gives me a date and I plan everything out; and then he calls me later and tells me the time has changed, but he calls at the last minute and I can't change other appointments. So I make plans to leave early and return to New York because there is an important appointment that I can't possibly change. I know it's wrong for me to leave early, because I should meet these people who are important to the business, so I just explained to his partner and told her to tell him. All arrangements were made; it was all planned, then at 4:55 when I'm leaving he asks if I can stay until 6:30. I told him no, that I had an appointment I could not cancel. I told him I had a doctor's appointment that I absolutely couldn't break. I told him that if he had told me earlier that I possibly could have rearranged things. I was leaving to come here and this was the day before the big problem with my boss. I was proud of myself for telling him no. I thought this would teach the guy. I think this whole thing brought on the problem the next morning, or it seemed to. First he called me in and said he was up all night because it bothered him that I had to go to the doctor; and how would I feel if I had just hired a sales manager and asked him to stay late and he told me he was going to a doctor?

I told him I would probably be understanding of his going to the doctor and try to give him more warning beforehand. And when I told him I was seeing a psychiatrist and it was a very hard appointment to break, I felt a little uncomfortable—well, because whether I should say that to a new employer. But he's the kind of guy who has seen just about everything so . . .

[*This vignette shows rage displaced from the therapist onto his boss. The patient is attempting to set up the sabotage, "I am a sick little boy. You're going away. I'll get myself fired because I come here."*]

THERAPIST: But it worried you?

PATIENT: It worried me a little bit. I was worried not that he would think anything in terms of me being a nut, but in terms of disclosing my private information to him, which I said I wasn't going to do anymore.

THERAPIST: Why did you tell him that?

PATIENT: Because I was scared again. When they had me in there, the guy scared me, and it looked like they were going to say, "You're fired."

THERAPIST: If in the original contract you had told him that you made commitments and would have to leave promptly at 5:00 one day a week, would you have had to divulge your private business?

PATIENT: Well . . . (*Hunches shoulders.*)

THERAPIST: The real question is, if it was important to your business, what prevented you from calling and asking if the appointment could be changed?

[*Here the therapist sets the stage for a corrective emotional experience.*]

PATIENT: With you?

THERAPIST: Yes.

PATIENT: Well, that's true; I could have asked, but I didn't want to.

THERAPIST: Why?

PATIENT: I didn't want to. I wanted to come here at 6:00; that's our appointment and that's the time I wanted to come.

THERAPIST: Okay, but what about what I'm asking you?

PATIENT: Yes, I had alternatives and I didn't think of them . . .

THERAPIST: What prevented you from thinking of the alternatives?

PATIENT: I wanted to see you, number 1; number 2, this time I wanted to construct it properly, lay the ground rules properly in terms of how the guy treated me.

THERAPIST: Would you have felt free to call me and change the appointment?

PATIENT: I would have been upset.

THERAPIST: Why?

PATIENT: Well the fact that I was coming here, and the expectations that were made about coming back here . . .

THERAPIST: Maybe I would have been able to see you later on in the evening.

PATIENT: Well, that's true; I guess I should have explored that. The guy did say "Well, why don't you call him and see him at 7?" He did say that. (*Pause.*) I'm saying he may be right.

THERAPIST: The question that I'm asking you is, how do you feel if you have to change or cancel an appointment with me?

[*The therapist is directing the patient to place his feelings upon the therapist.*]

PATIENT: (*Long pause.*) Well, there are a couple of things: The ground rules here were if I don't show for an appointment, I have to pay anyway.

THERAPIST: If you have good reason there is no way that I would charge you. If you are sick, I would not charge you.

PATIENT: Yeah, but an hour before?

THERAPIST: If it is something important to your job or family; do you not consider that important? I would trust the importance to you.

[*The therapist establishes the corrective experience.*]

PATIENT: Yes, it's important, but I don't want to make it as important.

THERAPIST: Why?

PATIENT: (*softly*) I just don't want to . . . I don't want to ask for help. Maybe, I, I . . . I know this has got to end, and I don't want to get that dependent, either. (*Long pause.*) I think I underestimate how I feel, like I have painful hemorrhoids for 10 years . . .

THERAPIST: How would you feel about calling me and telling me anything?

PATIENT: Well, I just don't call, obviously, and there are times when I want to.

THERAPIST: Does this remind you of any other situation when you wanted to call but didn't?

PATIENT: My father, sure.

THERAPIST: How is that?

PATIENT: During the war [*referring to the war between himself and his father*].

THERAPIST: Tell me about it.

PATIENT: Well, I needed plenty of help. I was going to school; my mother had just died; I was totally alone. I had money problems with paying for school—sure, I would have liked to call.

[*The patient makes his own link between present, past, and therapist. He confirms the past inhibition about calling his father displaced to the therapist.*]

THERAPIST: What prevented you?

PATIENT: We had a war. I was angry with him.

THERAPIST: What would it have meant if you had called?

PATIENT: It would have meant that I gave in; that it was a betrayal to my mother.

THERAPIST: You said "betrayal," "war," "giving in," and you say to me, "I don't want to become that dependent." (*Long pause.*) So you needed your father, yet you couldn't call your father?

PATIENT: I could have called, but I didn't call him. Sure, I needed him. All I had to do was call him, and he would have been there.

THERAPIST: You needed Dr. Zaiden and you couldn't call Dr. Zaiden?

PATIENT: I stopped myself. But you're here.

THERAPIST: But your father was there.

PATIENT: And I was at war, that's right! But we shouldn't be at war where I can't call you.

THERAPIST: Okay, what about that? (*Long pause.*)

PATIENT: There's something I'm totally confused—no, I'm not totally confused but I see what you're saying, I see what I'm saying. This thing about calling you—I'm trying to relate it back to other people. I don't call anybody to help me. I started to call Carol's father since I've been coming here . . .

THERAPIST: What about Carol [*the patient's wife*]?

PATIENT: I never had to ask; she just gave to me. It's different.

THERAPIST: Yes, it's a big difference between what somebody gives you and what you get because you ask and say you need.

PATIENT: I don't think I ask *Carol* for too much; before, I didn't ask. I can ask her now . . .

THERAPIST: And you had a bad week and you couldn't call me. How did you feel when you had a bad time during the "war" and you couldn't call your father?

PATIENT: Poorly.

THERAPIST: Do you think there could be a quiet war going on between you and me?

PATIENT: It could be (*almost inaudible*).

THERAPIST: In this quiet war are you afraid to subjugate yourself to me?

PATIENT: It could be. (*Sighs loudly.*)

THERAPIST: Subjugation or assertion!

PATIENT: I didn't get that part.

THERAPIST: One can be a little boy and subjugate himself, or one can be a man and assertively define his own territory and define the contract of the relationship, as you did with your boss at first and we did here.

(*The patient changes the subject; he begins to talk about disliking the work he does and complains about how difficult it is to make a career change.*)

THERAPIST: You're avoiding looking at something, aren't you?

PATIENT: (*Sighs.*) Yes, my father.

THERAPIST: It's easier to move to some other territory than for us to work on this? But this is what we are here for, to work on these problems. If you need to call me and you don't then aren't we in the same situation like you and your father?

(*The patient becomes physically quiet.*)

THERAPIST: How did you feel about my being away for 3 weeks?

PATIENT: I'm sure that's what was upsetting me.

THERAPIST: You didn't tell me that last week. What are you doing?

PATIENT: Trying to push it all away.

THERAPIST: Like with your father?

PATIENT: Yes.

THERAPIST: So you wanted to be with your father and you suffered instead of calling him. And with me? When you don't call me . . .

PATIENT: It's the same.

THIRD STAGE OF TREATMENT: TERMINATION RESISTANCE

Termination resistance, the third stage of treatment, is evident in the desire expressed by the patient in the 19th interview to slow down so that he would not have to face termination.

PATIENT: I was 14 years old, I was lying around. My father pushed me to get a job.

THERAPIST: Why do you think he was pushing you then?

PATIENT: I was very small. I was worried. I was always like that. I worried when I did go for jobs, that I won't measure up as a man.

THERAPIST: How did you feel at the time he was pushing you?

PATIENT: I was angry with him. I felt that he was using me. I wasn't ready, but he got me the job. *He directed me*; I didn't go out looking for the job.

THERAPIST: Is it because he got you the job that you didn't show any anger at the time? Otherwise he wouldn't have directed you.

PATIENT: I didn't have that much contact with him.

THERAPIST: How could he direct you?

PATIENT: He did *direct me* along to a certain extent, but he just jumped too fast. Maybe if he had waited—I was small and needed more time to face these situations.

[*The patient is saying that the therapist should not push him out as his father did. He wants the therapist to let him stay in treatment longer.*]

THERAPIST: Are you saying what you need right now is your father pushing you to get yourself a job?

PATIENT: Yes, I need somebody *pushing me.* I need *time* to face these situations.

THERAPIST: That's what you are asking me to do?

PATIENT: No, that's what confuses me about myself. Is it because I am too comfortable or looking for the right thing? I don't want to fall into that trap again. At the same time I wonder if I would be looking *harder* if someone was *pushing me.*

THERAPIST: Are you asking me to push you?

PATIENT: Yes, I could be in the way I am asking today. I guess I am asking for an option.

THERAPIST: The last three times you have been here you asked me to push you.

PATIENT: Bill pushed me. He always told me who was looking for somebody to hire me.

THERAPIST: Do you want me to push you like your father?

PATIENT: (*in a very subdued voice*) In some aspects, *not all the time.*

THERAPIST: How are you going to feel when we terminate the treatment if in some ways I have become your father?

PATIENT: I am going to feel poorly unless I solve *all* these things in my head.

THERAPIST: So if you don't solve *all* the things, how are you going to terminate with me? Have you noticed your usage of the word "all"?

PATIENT: Yes, I know what you are saying "all."

THERAPIST: I am saying "all"?

PATIENT: No, I am saying "all." I guess by saying it, I am setting it up for a failure.

THERAPIST: Certainly if the issue of your getting a job continues to dominate the session, we will not be able to solve the things we set out to do in our contract. If we fail in our goal, would you say at the end [that] you need somebody pushing you *at all times* for you to be effective? When Bill left the job years back, what happened?

PATIENT: I found for myself that I couldn't do it alone. I fell apart.

THERAPIST: If you remember, you never felt that you deserved the raises he gave you—that your own worth was not at the service of your own value. It was what Bill would hand down to you because he likes you. When he left, what did you have?

PATIENT: Nothing.

THERAPIST: Isn't that what you are trying to reenact with me in our work here? So if you put me in charge and we have this superior–inferior relation, isn't that what you will continue to do in other relationships in your life—thus prefacing your relationships with the insinuation, "I am worthless, treat me accordingly"?

During termination resistance and termination resolution, patients become aware of the displacement of anger from a significant parent to current love objects. They abstract their sadness and grief at having used these people (spouses, children) as unwitting victims.

This is a necessary component that clarifies their present interpersonal relations; extreme emotional behavior (explosiveness or passivity) ceases. New feelings for loved ones are felt spontaneously without undue transferential burden or overreaction. Near the end of his treatment, the patient followed here no longer needed to be a father to his sisters, or, conversely, a child to them. He began to act and feel like a brother. He also now recaptured a sister. He stopped being the seducer and the angry father to his wife. He became an equal partner and regained another partner (his wife), whom he can accept now as a woman in her own right.

Instead of overidentifying with his son and thus activating the competitive hidden negatives (doing what he felt consciously was the opposite of his father, while unconsciously repeating his negative perception of his father's neurosis), he now became free to be a father to his son. He could begin to change his behavior to men from alternating between abject submission or transferential explosions, and thus could eliminate the self-defeating components (getting fired, etc.). He could now be a worker who could assert himself to a boss; he could relate man-to-man without declaring war. The following vignettes near the end of treatment, from the 26th and 28th interviews, illustrate these conclusions.

THERAPIST: Oh! Your mind went blank?

PATIENT: No! I was thinking about my wife and my son.

THERAPIST: What about your wife and son?

PATIENT: Because something bothered me last night.

THERAPIST: What bothered you last night?

PATIENT: My son hasn't been going to sleep early since I have been coming here. I told my wife that we have to have time for ourselves, and he has to know that he has his world and we have ours. He is a child and when it's 8:30 or whatever time he goes to his room, because we have no privacy. Besides when I don't work I am not tired at 10:30 anyway, and if I want to have any sex I want to have it before 10:30 or 11:00 or before he finally decides in his mind he wants to go to sleep. So I said he will have to go in [to bed] at 9:00. So he came out of his bath and I told him it was bedtime, and at 9:00 he goes in. And he was watching the clock and he knew that I said it and he went in, and she always carries him in and she played in the bedroom with him. I was really angry with her. So I said to her, "For Christ's sake, I told him to go to bed at 9:00 because we don't have any privacy, and you go in from 9:00–9:30 and you played with him. And to carry the stuff further, you know I wanted your company, and you go when you are with him all day, and he is getting exactly what he wants anyways at bedtime. He wants to be with his mother and you are giving it to him." It annoys me because I do see the situation and it's a repeat.

THERAPIST: And if you hadn't looked at these things, you would have done these things? You would have allowed her and him to continue with this relationship?

PATIENT: It's not good.

[*This vignette, at the end of treatment, illustrates the patient's conscious awareness of his depression. He finally buries his parents and their neurosis, and recaptures their love for him and other positive qualities. He sees their control over him in the past years and acknowledges his new freedom.*]

(*Patient has been tied up in traffic.*)

PATIENT: Thank you for seeing me. I am all screwed up today (*in a despondent voice*). Really. Last night I got up around 4:30 A.M. I thought it was morning. (*Sigh.*) I got up like a jolt. I felt I was totally out of control of everything and, ah, ah . . . (*sighs again*). And then I woke my wife up. [I told her,] "Look, I feel lousy," which is something I would never have done before [and] which I have learned here. She got up and came downstairs. We had a long discussion about all kinds of things. I was worried I was losing my job. (*He just got the job.*) Ah . . . talking to her, things began to take shape . . . ah . . . much the way I talk out when I see you. We talked for about 2½ hours or 3 hours. I felt okay this morning.

THERAPIST: You haven't told me what actually happened.

PATIENT: In what woke me up? (*Sighs again.*) I woke up and said, "I am going to get fired." [*He had lied in the job application.*]

THERAPIST: Was it a dream?

PATIENT: I am not sure. I must have been going over the things that happened that day. Things that I discussed with you about the boss asking me to stay late, like it happened in the previous job where I got fired. Last night I had to go to the dentist. My cap was falling out, and I had told my boss three days before [that] I had to go to the dentist. I asked him if it was possible even if I had to come in earlier another day. (*Sighs.*) "Oh, Christ! No, I would like you to stay so as to help that guy finish the job." I stayed a half hour extra and I was late for the dentist. So I felt guilty about that—well, here I am sabotaging it again, etc. That's why I think I had the dream. I woke up with a tremendous anxiety, like the whole world was falling apart again. I just didn't know which way to go. I got focus again when I spoke to her [*his wife*]. I felt good about that at least. I handled it. I didn't let it ride. I spoke and I got it out and I spoke to her. I talked about business (*pause*) with her as well . . .

THERAPIST: Do you do that with her normally?

PATIENT: No, as we went over it before here. I wouldn't normally wake her, like; she wasn't too choked up, it took her about 15 to 20 minutes. I don't blame her; it was in the middle of the night. Normally I would have said, "Oh, why wake her, she can't help."

THERAPIST: Do you normally discuss business with her during the day hours?

PATIENT: Do I normally discuss—yeah.

THERAPIST: Then she has been a "person" for many years?

PATIENT: That I could talk to, yeah. And (*pause*) I spoke to her about our relationship with our son, about our relationship, how she should go for some counseling; she could see things and things we discussed here.

THERAPIST: You didn't discuss this before that day?

PATIENT: No! Just last night.

THERAPIST: The night before you come to see me.

PATIENT: Right, which I tied all that into. I was trying to see if there was any relationship at all . . . ah . . . (*Pause.*) I would imagine there is a relationship. I am not sure.

THERAPIST: You didn't think there was a relationship?

PATIENT: Coming to see you? (*Pause.*) Yes. I am sure of it. It's a traumatic thing for me.

THERAPIST: What's traumatic?

PATIENT: Well, about this relationship. It's as we discussed last time; I know it's something that has to be done. I . . . ah, ah . . .

THERAPIST: What did you think of last week's session?

PATIENT: I mentioned that to my wife. The main thing I thought about last week's session was that you were a very kind person (*pause*) in terms that you helped me, and I realized that I saw my parents . . . ah . . . the first time I was aware consciously that I found something important, that I started to cry. I cried for them, and you asked me who I was crying for. I don't think I ever cried for them before.

THERAPIST: Did you cry for them?

PATIENT: I was crying for myself, I think, or maybe I was crying for them and I didn't realize it because it's the first time I recognized it. (*Sighs, pause.*) And the realization of their death, it's something I have to live with and also the point that they are still with me.

THERAPIST: That realization had not really dawned on you as it did the last time you were here.

PATIENT: Ah . . . no.

THERAPIST: That they had not been dead?

PATIENT: Well, it's not so much that they hadn't been dead, but I realized during the last session (*pause*) I realized (*pause*) then I mentioned it to my wife last night. It must have been my relationship with her . . . (*pause*) how much control they still had in my life, until I came here. And how much control they still do unless I realize it, unless I try to become me instead of trying to be other things.

THERAPIST: Is it almost as if you buried yourself with them?

PATIENT: Oh! Sure, but, you know, the fact it was a happy thing, knowing that I am not buried with them and that I can still remember them well and not be dead with them . . . ah . . . then I don't. I owe it to nobody to do that, in terms of loyalty to myself, which we brought up in the last session.

FOURTH STAGE OF TREATMENT: FINAL RESOLUTION OF TERMINATION

During the final stage of treatment, patients should be able to express their feelings directly with little fear and guilt. Previously, these feelings have been felt in extremes and not expressed because of the fear of their finality and doom.

During the last part of the treatment, patients see more and more, and in a more natural fashion. Their ability to feel and act automatically is revived; their censors are no longer holding them back. Now, one sentence clears things up. They feel a new sense of mastery never felt before (sometimes perplexing). Their self-confidence is enhanced. This does not mean, of course, that all doubts are removed. Patients will say, "Now, I know when things start not going well. I get this feeling that tells me something is not right. I then proceed, to see what I am avoiding, and find that I have tried again to be dishonest with my feelings. I then look at myself and can be honest with what I am and what I want."

As a result of the resolution of the parental ambivalence, patients can now differentiate between real and imaginary memories and feelings. The work of therapy at this point is the final clarification and proper expression of both real and fantasized rage through the transferential patient–therapist relationship. This process now brings free mobilization of affect; prior to this, feelings have been protectively held through the many defenses that first brought the patients to treatment. The mobilization of affect allows a patient to feel and express emotion toward the proper object without guilt or repression. This reignites an affectual format and brings back the original love bond to the significant parent. The recathection of love to the parent now allows the patient to freely grieve the loss. Now, there is no significant ambivalence to the self or others. Patients can now like themselves, feel themselves worthy. Their sense of worth is generally seen in an immediate need to help others.

The father of the patient under discussion died in an imagined state of "war" on the patient's part; the patient continued to suffer after his loss with no peace of mind. The patient's achievement of peace and reestablishment of a new closeness to a brother-in-law represented a symbolic reparation with his father. The brother-in-law was married to his sister Marcia, who he said became the mother after the father's death.

When the brother-in-law got hurt, the patient experienced an overflow of grief and concern; he cried, dreamed, and insisted on going to help the injured man. This overflow of emotion was transferential, and the patient was able to recognize it consciously and to tie it in with his father.

This led to his comments of "He is a big, strapping, strong guy, who was hurt, who needed my help." For the first time, the patient was at peace and recognized his worth. Prior to this, he felt small, unloved, not accepted or needed. The strong brother-in-law represented a strong father, but now the patient was no longer questioning his maleness. He said, "He leaned on me. He needed me. I felt and showed concern freely. Father has forgiven me. I am a man, and I am free to relate to other men directly and honestly." Now follows the vignette that illustrates the above comments:

THERAPIST: How do you feel about me?

PATIENT: What do you mean? Today? You mean . . .

THERAPIST: All the time.

PATIENT: All the time?

THERAPIST: In these sessions.

PATIENT: I feel kindly towards you.

THERAPIST: What makes you feel kindly towards me?

PATIENT: Well, you know, I think that . . . ah . . . (*pause*) from a doctor's standpoint, you are breaking this off properly, and I think I feel an insight from you that is very kind, and you relate very well and have done very well; but you relate back to that human level. I think you relate to people's pain and I have pain, so make that general. You're a kindly person.

THERAPIST: You feel affection towards me?

PATIENT: Yeah!

THERAPIST: Do you feel uncomfortable about that?

PATIENT: No, relating—we talked about that yesterday with other men. No, I see myself opening up now to other men, starting to get friends.

[*Fear of closeness was fear of disapproval by the male therapist. He connects it with open and freer relations with men.*]

THERAPIST: Was there a time you felt concern about getting close to me?

PATIENT: Oh, yeah, I am sure, and I am sure I am not totally close to you; there are things I hold back.

THERAPIST: No, I don't mean about your telling me everything. But that you felt close?

PATIENT: Oh, sure, yes.

THERAPIST: Was that something that . . .

PATIENT: No, I knew that this thing was going to terminate. Number one, it would have to, as other relationships have terminated —meaning my mother and my father—so that it was only help for a time, until I started to understand that the help you and I could talk about a problem and you may not be able to help me with the specific problem, like you said, "You handled that with your attorney." But as problems arose, I would be able to go to the right people for specific help.

THERAPIST: Are you saying that you now know that you can carry what you have gained here?

PATIENT: I do see that I know that. As a doctor you do want to hear that, I am sure, and I do see that in a lot of different ways.

My brother-in-law got hurt. I was worried about him all day long yesterday. I would never—I would call my sister to ask how he is. I would never tell him, "Hey, I was worried about you all day."

THERAPIST: You would call her and tell her that you were worried about him?

PATIENT: You are right! I wouldn't have it on his relationship, on a man relationship, you know. Think I was dreaming about him, too. I was upset in the dream. He cut his head open at the swimming pool, uh!

THERAPIST: You were upset about him being seriously hurt?

PATIENT: I was very touched. My sister called me from the hospital, and this is something I don't understand, either. All their friends were there, and she called me to let me know he hurt himself at the club. Ah . . . that was Sunday . . . ah . . . (*pause*), and he is okay. She is in the hospital and she's got 3 or 4 friends with her from the club. In the old days, I would have said, "Oh, you got your goddamned friends with you," and be angry. They didn't call me first, and that kind of thing, and instead, you know, I said, "Let me come over." She said, "Okay, you don't need to." I said, "Let me come over and I will take a ride over." She says, "Okay, could you bring him a shirt?"

THERAPIST: That's the oldest sister?

PATIENT: Yeah. "Could you bring him a shirt?" So, I said, "Yes, I will bring him a shirt." He was in his bathing suit. So I came in with a shirt, and all his friends were sitting there. You know . . . ah . . . I handed her the shirt. A brand-new shirt and she joked about it, a little bit about it, and I sat with her and the kids were there. Uh! I did realize the kids were there and they seemed happy to see me, and it made me feel good. You know, for my worth, they seemed a little calmer when I got there. The both kids ran over right away with their mother sitting there. They felt a little more relaxed. And then my brother-in-law came out. He was really woozy and he's a big strapping strong guy, and you know (*pause*) we walked outside and a couple of his friends were there. One man friend and two women friends were there. When we walked out he started to teeter a little bit. He leaned on me and, you know, I felt so terrible, and he didn't even question all the people there, and he asked me where my car was and he just got into my car. And I was very touched by it, because he was really whacked out by it and he wanted to get into my car. My sister had her car, and he didn't want to go with her or the kids. He didn't ask where is my sister's car or where Marcia was.

THERAPIST: Why did he go in your car?

PATIENT: I guess he showed me something that he cares for me and he wanted me.

THERAPIST: So did you?

PATIENT: Yeah, I drove him home.

THERAPIST: You opened the door and he jumped right in?

PATIENT: Yeah!

THERAPIST: Then that means, after all these years, perhaps he wanted to go into the door without realizing you were closing the doors.

PATIENT: I didn't know it then.

THERAPIST: But you realize it now with me.

PATIENT: Yeah, I do.

THERAPIST: There is a certain tenderness coming through in you. Do you like it? Is it you?

PATIENT: Yes, it's me.

THERAPIST: So are you the shark or the dolphin?

PATIENT: I don't know that's a business relationship.

THERAPIST: No, I am not talking about business relationships.

PATIENT: No, in that I can be the dolphin for sure.

THERAPIST: See, because your feelings are your strong nose.

PATIENT: These people are never going to hurt me unless I hurt them, especially if I teach them by showing them and speaking to them. And they will talk back to me.

THERAPIST: Then all the world can be opened to you in human relationships.

At the final resolution of termination, patients are able to think and feel in a homeostatic fashion. No secondary censor is present, thus; there is less waste of energy. The remobilization of new parts of the self frees energy for better resolution of problems and goal seeking. This is absolutely necessary for patients to terminate treatment satisfactorily and to resolve further conflicts in the examination of remnants of past neurotic drives and defenses. Patients' improved relationships with others lead to contacts with less or no seduction, no manipulation, and no need to be submissive.

Patients have now integrated their parents with the negative and positive aspects in proper perspective. The kaleidoscopic view of the parents prior to integration leads to the neurotic, distorted images. They cannot see the parents as a whole, for then they would be "betrayers, incesters, murderers." The development of the defensive systems of seeing the parents in parts has helped the patients to maintain their sanity. The mosaic view that develops as a result of integration of the parents allows patients to see the whole images with shades of grays and blues in addition to black and white, all acceptable as parts to make up the whole.

The development of the whole images has been done through the therapist's use of the following techniques:

1. Transference interpretations used to pull out each layer of hurt and defensiveness, with the primary concern that a patient doesn't run away in panic.

2. Open, direct confrontation of verbalizations and reactions, without seduction or punitive responses.

3. Refusal to allow the patient to "seduce" him or defeat ("kill") the therapy. This breaks the back of the negative omnipotence through transference.

4. Assistance to patients in putting together all the anatomical and emotional pieces of their conflicts.

The resolution of therapy is resolution of ambivalence; it occurs when the therapist has helped the patient to coordinate both emotional arms and to use them homeostatically. The patient's ambivalence to past love objects has greatly diminished, allowing him or her to more freely express emotions of love and anger to past objects, to the therapist, and to current significant others. He or she can separate without hate and maintain positive feelings; thus treatment is finished. The emotional arms, prior to this, function independently. The left hand, the sinistral, gives its name to the term "sinister"; it can maim or kill. The right hand is historically good; the good eventually sit at "the right hand of God," which is loving and protective. Thus, the conflicting feelings in an embrace can surround another in love or can destroy. In therapy, both sides must be uncovered and understood. When the conflict is understood both intellectually and emotionally, homeostatic functioning occurs, and treatment is over. The embrace now is wholesome.

The following interviews symbolize the working through of the final resolution for the patient under discussion. The patient had had, since the age of 11, recurrent nightmares about the hydrogen bomb exploding and constant fears of nuclear explosions and missiles. The dream represented the extremes (total extermination to all; death to him and his father; a symbolic end to his world). The patient had been carrying and suffering from a "ticking bomb" (a bomb inside himself that could explode anytime). When he perceived that he would soon be in the last session (one more was left), he had a dream that the bomb exploded. It killed no one; he felt relieved. The war was over for him. He was safe and free. (The solving dream verifies change at the unconscious level.) The termination with the therapist did not lead to his being attacked, but to a peaceful, new therapeutic termination.

The following vignette from the 29th interview illustrates the dream.

THERAPIST: How do you feel about termination?

PATIENT: I don't feel good about it.

THERAPIST: Tell me about it.

PATIENT: Well, I mean, it took me a long time to get here to therapy. It's 3 weeks since the last visit. I didn't want to break off coming here, and I realize that, and I'm uptight about it.

THERAPIST: Have you given it some thought?

PATIENT: I've given it a lot of thought; but not a lot of conscious thought . . . ah . . . even in terms of whether I'd be able to continue this on my own. I've been again on and off the depression, and so forth.

THERAPIST: Tell me about it.

PATIENT: Well, when I was away last week, I called my wife on Sunday night . . . ah . . . it was okay. Monday night I really felt distraught. I told her I really felt lousy; I didn't know what it was. Then, I went to sleep and I had a dream again.

THERAPIST: What was the dream?

PATIENT: Ah . . . the dream was that an atomic bomb went off, and I guess that, the way I analyze it, was probably the extreme. And, you know, I saw the mushroom, and you know, nothing happened, and I woke up.

THERAPIST: Anything else besides the mushroom?

PATIENT: (*Pause.*) Ah, what I was dreaming in relation to . . . there must have been other things, because there's something I remember right now. And then I woke up and I felt a little better, as if I'd solved something so in terms of relating it. Then I got looking at the extreme. Now, I solved the problem even though I had the anxiety, whatever it was. I felt better after the dream; evidently it solved something while I was sleeping.

THERAPIST: You don't remember anything more of the dream?

PATIENT: I woke up at 5:00 in the morning in the hotel room. I was up an hour and I'm surprised that I went back to sleep. I normally don't. I felt relieved, sort of the anxiety was not there.

THERAPIST: What happened when you woke up?

PATIENT: What I think happened was it was more of my own therapy session.

THERAPIST: Tell me about it.

PATIENT: I guess I have some sort of anxiety, and I was trying to solve it during my sleep. I must have solved it while I was sleeping.

In those other times in the past, I woke up. I felt a strong anxiety. In this last dream, I felt relaxed–not relaxed, but [as] if there was something that I had solved.

THERAPIST: What did you think about when you woke up?

PATIENT: All I could remember about the atomic bomb dream was that I woke and I was all right and then I went back to sleep.

THERAPIST: Is this a dream you've ever had before?

PATIENT: Yeah, I've always been frightened of that.

THERAPIST: Of what?

PATIENT: Of bombs, the atomic bomb.

THERAPIST: Oh, yes. Since you were a child, you mean?

PATIENT: Yeah, I was thinking of that the other day.

THERAPIST: Yes.

PATIENT: When they had the first atomic bomb test, my father had told me to watch it on television, something that I would remember. I always had a fear of that. In '56, the one day they did it on television. The hydrogen bomb. I don't know why that sticks in my head. '56 but, maybe, it was earlier.

THERAPIST: You mean the H-bomb?

PATIENT: All these years, I've been frightened as they've been developing the missiles.

THERAPIST: Was it a frightening experience? Or did you have nightmares too?

PATIENT: A little of both. I would consciously think of the missiles crisis and the Kennedy thing.

THERAPIST: What was your fear?

PATIENT: That someone would drop a bomb on us, and it would destroy mankind.

THERAPIST: Have you had this dream before with people getting killed with the atomic bomb? How did the dreams end?

PATIENT: Oh, I see. If I die, and now you want to see the difference in them. Very interesting. I can see how that would make a difference. I probably died in them. I had a conscious fear, as well as an unconscious fear. I had problems falling asleep thinking about it, but it would be that probably they dropped the bomb and everybody died, and here this time they dropped the bomb and nothing happened.

THERAPIST: You've had this dream in which everybody died before you died?

PATIENT: Yes, since I was 11. We were having problems.

THERAPIST: Does this dream have any connection to what we have been talking about the last time you were here?

PATIENT: Well, ending the sessions. I had the fear of that and that's an end, too.

THERAPIST: As you said before, [the fear] is an extreme. Yet you feel relieved after the dream. What brought the relief?

PATIENT: The understanding of the fact that I try not to look at extremes any more when ending the relationships.

This excerpt from the 30th session (the last) illustrates the patient's final sense of being at peace with himself.

PATIENT: I am sorry I am late. (*Sighs.*) Last time, when I first left you—what was it, 4 weeks ago? What was it? The first week or two (*sighs*) [were] rough. The last 2 weeks have been pretty good. I would say it is because the business situation is getting better, but the fact is, I am handling things a lot better. At the same time, that may be when the business situation is better.

THERAPIST: How's that?

PATIENT: Well, I am still on the same job, but I have had other job offers, and things are getting better. It doesn't seem to have affected me as deeply. I still have the same business problems, but I seem to be able to turn it off better at the end of the day. I don't like to travel, but I haven't been getting depressed on the road. A little bit I will, then I will talk to myself and I seem to get out of it. I haven't been having extremes either from the highs. (*Sighs.*) Last week something happened with the job. I was riding home and in the past I would have been ecstatic over it, but I was mildly content, I wasn't overjoyed, and I wasn't even thinking about the day afterwards. When I started to think about it I had it all down. Now I can see the negatives of a situation as well as the positives.

THERAPIST: Mm, mm. Is Patty intimated by the fact that you are concluding this week?

PATIENT: Oh, yes, I am having a tug of war with her. The tug of war is I will not allow her to affect my life and my wife, certainly in [the way in] which she was affecting my thoughts; and I stopped that completely without being unkind, and (*coughing*) it's confusing her terribly.

THERAPIST: Do you know what you are saying?

PATIENT: Yeah, I've broken off and decided I was going to be a man and do my own thing.

THERAPIST: What were you doing with her before?

PATIENT: I was listening to her and [she was] telling me what to do. I was a son to her; I was all kinds of things to her. She could maneuver me, and I didn't know how to stop her.

THERAPIST: You could say no.

PATIENT: Say no!

THERAPIST: Which she couldn't say.

PATIENT: She is unbelievable. She was going over to my other sister's house and had stopped at my house and there was something she was very annoyed at. I said, "Patty, you want something to eat?" "Uh—no." I said, "You're not hungry?" "I am on a diet. The pills are affecting my weight," and she left. I went over to my other sister's house, and the two of them are sitting there, and she was there eating. So I said, "Patty, you just told me over at my house you were watching your weight," and my other sister Marcia said to me, "What is this, pick-on-Patty day?" And I said to her, "When you stop being Patty's mother and my mother, you will be a lot happier. I refuse to accept this anymore." And I walked out of the house (*coughing again*) and went to watch my nephew play football.

THERAPIST: Did you have a good time?

PATIENT: (*coughing again*) No! I was pissed off. I said to my brother-in-law . . . (*Gets into a fit of coughing.*)

THERAPIST: There is something there you can't swallow.

PATIENT: Then my sister came to me, she came to the game.

THERAPIST: Were you still angry?

PATIENT: Yes, I was angry. I think straight normal angry. I had a right to be angry, I was really angry—frustrated, angry—that they could keep repeating the same thing, and I put a stop to it.

THERAPIST: You stopped the game?

PATIENT: Yes! I stopped the game. My old sister keeps looking at me as if saying, "What the hell has happened?", you know?

THERAPIST: She was never in treatment?

PATIENT: No! She wouldn't even consider it. I spoke to her.

THERAPIST: You think she needs it?

PATIENT: I don't think this can hurt anybody. I think it's helpful to anybody, I really do.

THERAPIST: At the same time, the relationship can be helped by your not playing the game. That in itself is very beneficial, like you have seen with your own son.

PATIENT: Yes, but without having put another load on me, I can be helpful. I am being honest showing them the way. My sister Marcia came over to me and apologized—Oh, God, she never apologizes. The other one came took my son home. He had gone in his pants. I don't know what's doing there. I was angry, but I knew exactly why I was angry, and I felt great. I couldn't stand them ganging up on me like when we were children. And they went to my mother and told on me, it's over. Which was a repeat.

THERAPIST: This, in essence, clarifying your human relationships, specifically with your sister Marcia. You couldn't deal with your brother-in-law until you dealt with your relationship with your sister.

PATIENT: Right, exactly, for which she's my mother, so I understand both of them. You understand I love my mother, but I was setting my sister up, because we were set up that day; we set it up that way.

THERAPIST: You are not afraid of your feelings any more?

PATIENT: No, I am still, ah . . . (*pause*), not afraid of them but what I have come to do with them—ah ha, coming to do which is good. That when I have a bad feeling in my gut, I don't go back through the mother thing or father thing, but I know immediately something is wrong. I stop and try to correct what's in my gut, because I know I have done something wrong.

THERAPIST: The way you are—basically you know what you are.

PATIENT: I am a person, a pretty nice person, and if I follow the way I feel, then I am a pretty nice person. I am not better than anybody, but I am a pretty nice person by himself.

THERAPIST: Are you saying you have made peace with your feelings?

PATIENT: Yes, I think exactly that.

CONCLUSION

In the treatment of this patient, the four different stages of treatment can be detected: primary resistance, treatment resistance, termination resistance, and termination resolution.

The first stage challenges the defenses covering patients' primary lost objects and reconstructs historically the real and imaginary losses. In doing this, it dispells the misconceptions and thus the inappropriate affectual feelings toward significant lost ones.

Ambivalent negative feelings are clarified and expressed. Now emerge the real positive feelings to past significant lost objects. In essence, the lost objects are recathected. Now the recathected positive feelings toward the lost objects become a positive introject to substitute for the negative and totally ambivalent introject that prevailed before. Patients now can and must, with the therapist, relieve the love objects in treatment and accept clearly the significance of their loss. This leads to the patients' improved sense of self-worth and thus allows patients to gain the necessary strength and new hope. They can, now that the fears, guilt, and retaliatory feelings have diminished, begin the painful uncovering and deal with the fears of new exposure to the therapist. This heralds the second stage, that of treatment resistance.

Patients have now cathected the therapist; the therapist is a now helpful ally, who has helped them feel and see something that has opened up new solutions to their suffering. Very quickly, these patients now feel some of the same feelings that were attached to the original lost objects toward the therapist. It leads to renewed fears of loss and punishment and to the beginning of concern about an impending termination with the therapist.

The newly freed libidinal energy allows patients to be able to think and feel more clearly and thus to increase motivation. The latter factors should allow patients to tolerate the challenging of their newly formed defenses, which have the same roots, of course, as the primary defenses. I emphasize that the newly formed therapeutic alliance is the ingredient that allows patients to continue to work. If it is not present, patients will become more resistive, and this will enhance their early primary defenses. At this point, the transference linkages are used more frequently. Confrontations should be of this type: "You are here for a purpose. *We* (you and I) have to do something *together*, and *you* are trying to reenact the patterns of *your* previous interpersonal failures here, by stopping your work with *me* and failing again."

Patients begin to free past repressed emotions of rage in disappointment now felt toward the therapist. Technically, every sign of repressed feeling must now be brought forth by the therapist to conscious awareness. Common signs are irritation expressed when the therapist is late and annoyance felt at the therapist's frequent questioning of certain areas that patients want to defend against. The confrontation of the repression of these feelings toward the therapist will allow patients to reexperience the fears of retaliation and the connection to past parental lost objects. The corrective emotional experience takes place. The therapist does not attack, does not seduce, does not destroy; but neither does he join the patients' resistance. Patients again feel a renewed sense of confidence in themselves and the therapist, which further enhances the therapeutic alliance.

The now openly expressed feelings open up the past repressed feelings, making the past–present linkages between feelings possible. In freeing the present feelings toward the therapist, patients free the past feelings toward the primary lost objects. Patients are now freed in the past and in the present, and this allows them to see and feel that none of their previous fears have become realities.

In the third stage, the stage of termination resistance, patients in essence reenact with the therapist their earlier feelings of loss and abandonment. The abreactions of these feelings in treatment, and the recapturing and tying of these feelings to similar past feelings of loss, are crucial.

Patients can see now that their depression was rooted in the ambivalent lost object and that they have tried to reenact this attachment with the therapist. At this point, there may be symptom reappearance, regression, and the unexpressed or expressed wish to stop treatment before the therapist "pushes me away." In this stage, patients see that their depression is tied to their previous need to bury themselves with the lost objects. And in this situation, if they now fail and stop treatment, they will make the therapist fail and themselves fail, thus repeating the burial now of both patient and therapist. Confrontation of this urge to fail, using past–present linkages, is used as the urge arises in treatment.

The fourth stage of treatment is that of termination resolution. At this point, ambivalence toward the past loved objects should be greatly diminished. Love and anger are freed, and they are expressed more readily and less guiltily to the past objects, to the therapist, and to currently significant others. Patients are now in command of their feelings. They are now free because they have repaired their relationships with those significant ones in the past. They can separate from them appropriately, without hate, and they can maintain positive memories and reject the neurotic components of past relationships. They are now free to identify with nonambivalent objects. They deal with the current others and seek out identification with nonambivalent objects. Patients will give examples that clearly indicate that emotional insight has been acquired. Their dreams will have changed. If these were recurrent dreams, they have ceased. In dealings with significant people, both vertical and horizontal (vertical dealings are those with parents and children; horizontal dealings are those with the rest of the world), they express themselves and their feelings clearly and without hesitation. Even their syntax should improve as the hesitation and doubts disappear. They speak of a sense of peace and a sense of a new, different, peaceful termination with the therapist. The term "termination" now connotes not a sense of superiority–inferiority, but a sense of parity. Two people who have worked together can now go different ways. Predominantly positive feelings end this relationship; it is a different kind of termination.

ACKNOWLEDGMENT

I would like to give special thanks to Rozetta Wilmore, a most sensitive and perceptive short-term therapist, who collaborated with me in preparing this chapter.

REFERENCES

Abraham, K. Notes on the psychoanalytic investigation and treatment of manic-depressive insanity. In *Selected papers of Karl Abraham.* London: Hogarth Press, 1927.

Abraham, K. A short study of the development of the libido, viewed in the light of mental disorders. In *Selected papers of Karl Abraham.* London: Hogarth Press, 1927. (Originally published, 1924.)

Bonime, W. Depression as a practice: Dynamic and therapeutic considerations. *Comprehensive Psychiatry*, 1960, *1*, 194–198.

Bonime, W. The psychodynamics of neurotic depression. *Journal of the American Academy of Psychoanalysis*, 1976, *4*(3), 301–326.

Davanloo, H. *Basic principles and techniques in short-term dynamic psychotherapy.* New York: S. P. Medical & Scientific Books, 1976.

Fenichel, O. *The psychoanalytic theory of neurosis.* New York: Norton, 1945.

Freud, S. Mourning and melancholia. In *Collected Papers* (Vol. 4). New York: Basic Books, 1959. (Originally published, 1917.)

Malan, D. H. *A study of brief psychotherapy.* New York: Plenum, 1963.

Rado, S. The problem of melancholia. In *Psychoanalysis of behavior: Collected papers* (Vols. 1 & 2). New York: Grune & Stratton, 1956.

Sifneos, P. *Short-term psychotherapy and emotional crisis.* Cambridge, Mass.: Harvard University Press, 1972.

10

THE FOCUS IN BRIEF PSYCHOTHERAPY: A CROSS-FERTILIZATION BETWEEN RESEARCH AND PRACTICE

ANTHONY RYLE

DIFFERING NEEDS OF RESEARCH AND THERAPY

Among the difficulties that have beset research into nonbehavioral forms of psychotherapy is the apparent incompatibility between the needs of research and therapy. Psychotherapy has been seen as essentially nondirective, exploratory, and open-ended, using means that are idiosyncratic to the therapist to pursue problems that are idiosyncratic to the patient or client; the process retains something mysterious, creative, and inaccessible. Research, on the other hand, has demanded defined, precisely described phenomena, procedures, and goals, preferably accessible to measurement by generalizable standard techniques. Nonetheless, modifications in attitudes of therapists and their methods, and changes in the assumptions guiding researchers, have recently narrowed the gap between these two pursuits.

The research problems facing anyone wishing to investigate any questions more specific than the (almost meaningless) general question "Does psychotherapy work?" are formidable. They include the development of means of describing, categorizing, and measuring the therapeutic input; ways of classifying and measuring patients and their problems; and ways of defining and demonstrating, preferably in quantifiable forms, the changes produced. The innate difficulties of

Anthony Ryle. University Health Service, The University of Sussex, Falmer, Brighton, Sussex, England.

all these procedures have been compounded by the inferiority feelings of researchers in this field, who have tended to follow research designs appropriate to quite different forms of intervention, notably drug trials. In my view, the variables that are difficult to control and that make even drug trials difficult to design—namely, placebo effects, observer influence, and relevant but immeasurable differences in subjects and therapists—may possibly influence the effects of psychotherapy and cannot be ignored in the design of comparative trials of psychotherapy. The currently fashionable attempts to standardize therapist behavior through the specification of procedures in treatment manuals threaten, on the other hand, to distort and maim, in the name of research, the subtle individual sensitivity and differential responsiveness that are likely to prove to be among the most effective components in the work of successful therapists.

WHICH THERAPIES WORK WITH WHICH PATIENTS?

These are difficulties to be overcome in the future, I suspect more through the development of better modes of process analysis than through attempts to predetermine the process; but, meanwhile, the field still awaits more fine-grained and relevant measures of outcome with which to measure the effects of different inputs. It is to this area, which seems of prior importance, that my own interests have been largely confined. The largely unhelpful influence of drug-trial design is also apparent here, with a heavy reliance being put on applying standard measuring techniques to more or less heterogeneous groups of patients. Crude measures of this sort have shown reasonably satisfactorily that such groups of patients, treated by various therapists and therapies, do improve more than, or more quickly than, untreated patients do. Beyond this rather limited conclusion, however, progress has only come from far more detailed studies, often of single cases.

The emergence of the single-case study as a respectable scientific enterprise is of fairly recent date (Shapiro, 1966). The movement toward its acceptance has been accelerated by the considerable growth in the use of behavioral methods in recent years, because such methods depend upon the careful construction of individual profiles that delineate the areas of difficulties and the goals of treatment for each patient; these goals, in turn, are often broken down into a series of subgoals, and the serial attainment of these is assessed in the course of treatment. In this way, detailed records of relevant change become an essential component of the therapeutic process. Investigators meet here, mercifully, the convergence of, rather than the conflict between, the needs of therapy and of research.

There are, however, many reasons for dissatisfaction with an exclusively behavioral account of neurotic problems. Both traditional medical nosologies and psychodynamic formulations offer important additional understandings. Dynamic therapists have been largely unconcerned with treatment goals described in symptomatic terms, believing that the resolution of underlying conflicts and the modification of personality structure are the proper concerns of all but the most superficial therapies. They have not, however, been able to ignore the evidence of their rivals as to the value of identifying a clear focus for short-term intervention. The forms in which the focus for treatment has been articulated by dynamic therapists remain, however, somewhat vague. The difficulties experienced by the psychoanalysts in defining the goal and focus of their therapy was partly responsible for the inconclusive results of an attempted controlled trial of analytical psychotherapy versus eclectic management (Balfour, Candy, Cawley, Hildebrand, Malan, Marks, & Wilson, 1972). Malan (1976) has observed that deep psychoanalytic formulations about a case produce very low agreement between different observers, while superficial formulations have very little explanatory value. It is unclear how explicitly workers in the psychoanalytic tradition who are active in short-term therapy (Malan, 1976; Sifneos, 1972) share the focus of their work with their patients, although in the work of behavioral and cognitive therapists, this sharing of the goal and an essentially problem-oriented approach has seemed to be a valuable aspect of the therapy, contributing to patients' sense of participation in the process of their own cures.

While psychoanalysts have found it difficult to specify satisfactorily the goals and focus of their intervention, it is clear that the simplification represented by a behavioral-profile diagnosis is unsatisfactory. The recent growth of interest in cognitive psychotherapy, and the recognition by influential behaviorists such as Bandura (1977a) and Lazarus (1970) of the central importance of the cognitive changes produced by treatment, bear witness to a major shift in attention among nonanalytic psychotherapists toward central processes. This shift has been, to some degree, matched by a growing concern among some psychoanalysts (e.g., Klein, 1970) to revise the complex, contradictory, overzealously defended and maintained theoretical constructions of orthodox psychoanalysis. In the growing middle ground defined by these shifts, there emerges for the first time the possibility of a common language for the psychotherapies (Ryle, 1978, in press). Out of this common language comes the possibility of determining the focus and goals of psychotherapy in ways that are as specific as those used by the behaviorists, yet that pay proper attention and respect to the more complicated processes described by those working in the dynamic tradition. The work described in the rest of this chapter offers a contribution to this task.

A NEW SYNTHESIS OF THERAPIES

The approach offered, although convergent with the general trends outlined above, had a more specific origin in a program of research on individual, marital, and group therapy, using varieties of repertory grid techniques (see Ryle, 1975). Most of this work consisted of small-scale studies of individuals, couples, or small groups, treated with interpretive psychotherapy along lines derived from psychoanalytic (particularly object-relations) theory. The task of relating the process of therapy and the concepts of psychoanalysis to the findings derived from repertory grid technique (which are expressed essentially in cognitive terms) required an explicit act of translation. This task, in turn, generated an increasing impatience with aspects of psychoanalytic theory and its language, and an increasingly strong conviction that the proper attention paid by psychoanalytic theory to development; to mental structures; to conflict; and to the historically determined distortions of and limits upon perception, memory, and behavior that underlie neurosis could be more accessibly and more adequately restated in very different forms, using terms derived from or consonant with the current understandings of cognitive psychology.

The task of therapy is to identify the ways in which and the extent to which individuals are responsible for their suffering, and to help them change. The puzzle about neurotic behavior is that neurotic individuals, even though they dislike the symptoms, behaviors, and beliefs that they suffer from, and even when they can fully accept the degree to which they are responsible for them, have great difficulty in changing. Treatment processes involve the accurate identification of feelings and behaviors; the restoration of a sense of self-efficacy (Bandura, 1977b); and the revision of those beliefs, assumptions, and behaviors that maintain or exacerbate the difficulties.

Behavioral treatment concentrates on breaking maladaptive, self-maintaining behaviors; cognitive therapy concentrates upon the correction of maladaptive beliefs and thought processes, especially those referring to the self; psychoanalysis aims to restructure the personality, to identify and reduce intrapsychic conflict, and to extend the role of those processes mediating between the inner world of needs and the outer world of reality. In the synthetic view offered here, these different approaches are combined in a form providing a definition of the focus and goals of therapy that can at once aid the process of therapy and provide a basis for measuring its success.

The procedure (described in Ryle, 1979a) is based on the formulation, after clinical assessment and the use of repertory grid testing, of target problems in the shape of symptoms, unwanted behaviors, and maladaptive assumptions about the self, as well as the formulation of target dilemmas, traps, and snags. The attainment of change in respect of target problems is rated serially by the patient on target problem rating scales (TPRSs), and the resolution of dilemmas, traps, and snags (to be defined below) is similarly rated on dilemma, trap, and snag rating scales (DTSRSs). For research purposes, the improvement obtained in these respects can be matched to other measures—for example, measures of symptomatology, of social adjustment, and of change in repertory grid measures indicating cognitive reorganization. The desired direction of these can be specified at the start of treatment. Preliminary studies using such measures have been completed (Ryle, 1979b, 1980).

The definition of target problems is relatively simple. Essentially, they represent the agreed goals of therapy described in a way that is acceptable to patient and therapist. Target problems may be simple symptoms (e.g., recurrent depressions, or psychosomatic abdominal pain), in which case the reduction or loss of symptoms would be the goal, but they may usefully include negative self-descriptions or nonadaptive self-referent attitudes, such as undue self-criticism or a tendency to accept unreasonable demands from others. These formulations do not usually go beyond a patient's own definition of his or her problems. The dilemma, trap, and snag (DTS) formulations, on the other hand, represent a preliminary hypothesis about underlying mental and behavioral processes of which the patient is frequently incompletely aware.

DILEMMAS, TRAPS, AND SNAGS[1]

The dynamic therapist will wish to discern and modify the beliefs, assumptions, fantasies, and defensive modes underlying the patient's problems. This process leads to a reframing or redefinition of the problem, and the redefinition must be shared with the patient in terms acceptable to him or her. Just as an interpretation, to be of use to the patient, must not jump too far ahead of his or her understanding, so this redefinition needs to be described at an appropriate level of abstraction. In practice, this means that the therapist should be able to offer to the patient a preliminary formulation of what underlies his or her difficulties. For the psychotherapy patient, this involves linking together in new ways what he or she has communicated; these ways must point out how the patient's perceptions and understandings of the world and his or her behavior in it cause or maintain his or her difficulties. This establishes the general point that the focus of attention is the patient's perceptions and understandings, and, beyond this, it will suggest specific attention to particular relevant issues. The focus of therapy, in this sense, represents a set of agreed provisional hypotheses, limited inevitably and, in the case of brief psychotherapy, appropriately, by the patient's ability to understand what the therapist proposes. These same limitations will affect the scope of the subsequent therapeutic work, but the initial focus need not prejudge the course of that work.

The therapist's redefinition of the problem, in terms of underlying mental processes, provides a basis for the extension of the goals of therapy, which now include the achievement of necessary cognitive changes in those areas related to the patient's difficulties. These goals can, in turn, form the basis for serial ratings of change.

It is proposed here that neurotic difficulties, and the patient's inability to change, are related to the terms in which he or she construes his or her world, and that these terms can be usefully conceptualized as "dilemmas," "traps," and "snags." While the patient can only see possible action in terms of his or her dilemmas,

1. This section of the chapter is based upon Ryle (1979a).

while his or her interactions with others are mutually maintained in terms of traps, or while change has or is felt to have snags, the possibility of change is slight. The degree to which these terms are known to the patient or the degree to which he or she can be made aware of them will vary. The first task of dynamic therapy is to extend such understanding; once these formulations are understood by the patient, they can become both an appropriate focus for therapy and a basis for serial target problem ratings.

Dilemmas can be expressed in the form of "either–or" (false dichotomies that restrict the range of choice) or of "if–then" (false assumptions of association that similarly inhibit change). Two common dilemmas could be expressed as follows: (1) "In relationships, I am *either* close to someone and feel smothered, *or* I am cut off and feel lonely"; this predicament is illustrated by the tale of the two porcupines on the cold mountainside going endlessly to and fro between coldness apart and pain together. (2) "I feel that *if* I am masculine, *then* I have to be insensitive." Another form of dilemma has been illustrated by Rowe (1970): A chronically depressed patient was shown to be trapped in a construction whereby her choice was *either* being depressed and humane *or* being a destructive and unpleasant person. In general, nonadaptive beliefs and behaviors are often persisted in because the apparent alternatives are seen as equally or more undesirable.

Traps are usually the result of relating to others in terms based upon complementary dilemmas. Marital and family therapists are particularly concerned with these circular mechanisms. Individual traps can be formulated in terms such as the following: "I am unduly accommodating to others; the result of this is that I often feel abused or invaded by them; this leads to me being irritable or unreasonably angry; as a result of this, I become guilty, and this makes me unduly accommodating to others. . . ." In this case, a faulty perception of interpersonal options (*either* abuse *or* be abused) leads to behavior that confirms the perception. A partner sharing the same dilemma will further reinforce it.

An important obstacle to change may be the consequences anticipated as a result of such change, and the word "snag" is used in the sense "I want to change, but the snag is . . ."; it also stands for "Subtle Negative Aspects of Goals." These consequences may be the actual responses of others, or the expectation of their responses, or the acting as if such responses would follow, even though the expectation is known to be without real foundation. It can also be the case that the feared consequence may be deduced by the therapist, but not consciously known by the patient. Ezriel (1950) has emphasized the importance of interpreting the feared consequences of the avoided response in group therapy. The consequences of change for the patient may only become apparent as the change takes place, but careful enquiry will often reveal that they are anticipated (Haley, 1963; Tschudi, 1977). Too exclusive preoccupation with the infantile origins of neurosis and with intrapsychic rather than interpersonal processes may have led to the neglect of such enquiries by those working in the psychoanalytic tradition, and the concepts of resistance and of secondary gain provide only a partial account of them.

An example of a snag could be that of an agoraphobic patient in treatment, who relapses because the implications of recovery turn out to include the neurotic illness of her spouse (Hafner, 1977). Often, however, the consciously or unconsciously feared implications of change are largely "fantasy," as in the common Oedipal fears of young adults, which can limit assertion or prohibit success "as if" these would be damaging to, or would provoke revenge from, parents. In such cases, the treatment goal must be to recognize and then discard the falsely construed implication, a process that may require testing out of the reality and magnitude of the feared outcome—actually in the world, and/or with the therapist in the transference.

Once the patient's dilemmas, traps, and snags can be identified, the reports brought to therapy sessions and the processes of those sessions can be usefully related to these underlying formulations, which, if correctly identified, will have extensive explanatory power. The resolution of the dilemmas, traps, and snags becomes the goal of treatment and the basis of a modified form of target problem rating, whereby the patient indicates how far he or she feels he or she is still governed by the terms set out in these formulations. The therapist can rate his judgment of this independently.

Six main groups of problems were identified in a survey of 25 current or recent psychotherapy patients, treated by the author. The groups are listed below; most individuals showed problems in more than one group. Individuals, of course, expressed these in idiosyncratic terms.

1. Distant or in-danger dilemmas: *either* isolated *or* at risk. Emotional closeness provokes fears of loss of self or damage to self.

2. Dyadic control dilemmas: *either* controlled *or* controlling; *either* powerfully giving *or* helplessly receiving.

3. (a) Must–won't dilemmas: Obligations, or plans, or intentions experienced as obligations, are responded to by resentful compliance or are blocked or sabotaged, with the loss of the sense of being able to choose or want. This is often associated with

3. (b) Problems of access to feelings and of self-control, experienced as having to be *either* in tight control of behavior and feelings *or* in chaos.

4. Instrumental–expressive dilemmas: These are usually experienced in relation to sex roles, the person feeling forced to choose between strength and sensitivity or between thought and feeling.

5. Traps: Traps are usually the acting out of dilemmas with others, who maintain the system by playing the complementary role in the dilemma. Any of the above dilemmas may be involved.

6. Snags: The common pattern here is of feared consequences for, or from, a parent or sexual partner.

The dilemmas listed above can be directly related to formulations derived from psychoanalysis (e.g., Erikson, 1959; Mahler, Pine, & Bergman, 1975). Thus, Nos. 1 and 2 can be seen to relate to the issues of separation, individuation, basic trust, and the oral stage; No. 3 to autonomy versus shame and doubt, and the anal stage; and No. 4 to the Oedipal stage. The order in which they are listed follows early to late stages of infantile development; their intensity and pervasiveness varies greatly. The first dilemma, for example, can present in an extreme form in a schizoid or in a mild form as part of a more or less normal adolescent identity crisis. Traps, in psychoanalytic terms, would represent interpersonal manifestation of intrapsychic processes, in particular of the more primitive defenses of splitting and projective identification; snags would be related to fantasy and to ego defenses against both id and superego forces. Psychoanalytic theory would postulate that more severe difficulty reflects earlier infantile conflicts and more rigid and generalized defenses; in practice, the judgment of the infantile stage is based on the intensity and extent to which behavior and experience are restricted.

The description of neurotic difficulty in the terms suggested here does not conflict with the psychoanalytic model. It differs in that it aims only to give an account of process and not of genesis, and hence uses a language that is simple and accessible to patients. In any case, to accept that the origins of these patterns are to be found in infantile modes of conceptualization and relationship does not imply that this explanation need be communicated to the patient. Such explanations are not necessarily helpful, for interpretation of the origins of a problem can represent, as Hurvitz (1975) argues, a terminal hypothesis with no implication for change or action; patients are more helped by instrumental hypotheses indicating possible alternative paths. When the patient's problem is described as being limited within a dilemma, caught in an interpersonal trap, or blocked by a snag, the goal of treatment is clearly *to achieve a change in the terms through which his or her experience is construed.* How this change is to be achieved is not predetermined by the formulation; interpretive, rational-emotive, cognitive, behavioral, individual, conjoint, family, or group methods of therapy, or magic, may all be effective; and more than one approach may be employed.

SUCCESS OF THE DTS APPROACH

The initial aim of this approach was to make the goals of dynamic psychotherapy more accessible and measurable, and preliminary work suggests that this aim has been achieved. Most patients rate improvement on most TPRSs and DTSRSs, and those cognitive changes related to the DTSs that are manifest in repertory grid features (notably construct correlations indicating the "implicit interpersonal theories" governing patients' relationship with themselves and others) usually change in the course of therapy in the desired direction. For example (Ryle, 1979b), a depressed patient had a dilemma that was summarized as "if looking after, then submitting." She rated herself as improved in respect of this dilemma (by 7 mm out of the possible 20 mm on a visual analogue scale). Repeat testing by repertory grid showed an increase in the correlation of "looks after" with "controls" (from .25 to .60) and a decrease in the correlation between "looks after" and "gives in to" (from .72 to .51). (See also Ryle, 1980.)

As well as achieving the research aim, however, this work has had the effect of accelerating changes in my clinical approach in the direction of greater eclecticism and greater activity. By breaking down goals and problems into more or less discrete entities, a more flexible and individually tailored treatment program has become possible—the choice of treatment being determined both by patients' problems and by their attitudes to and capacity for different kinds of therapeutic work. I still place much reliance on a basically interpretive mode, linking past history to current difficulties and linking both to manifestations in the transference, but I usually link such interpretations to the DTS formulations. This is particularly apposite in respect of the common dyadic control and instrumental–expressive dilemmas, where origins in parental relationships and repetitions in the transference are clear, and in the case of snags, which are frequently manifest in the form of negative therapeutic reactions. Specific symptoms may be approached by a purely behavioral method (e.g., the use of paradoxical inhibition in panic attacks may precede or obviate the need for understanding the source of these attacks), but behavioral means will usually be used in relation to the explanations expressed in DTS formulations. For example, in the common placation trap, assertion will be encouraged not as a general principle, but in specific relation to the processes maintaining low self-esteem, which can be summarized as follows: Low self-esteem causes placatory behavior; placatory behavior results in being abused; being abused leads to resentment, depression, or temper tantrums; these provoke rejection by self or others, with resulting low self-esteem.

Beck's method (1976) of teaching patients how to monitor and subsequently to block dysfunctional depressive thinking can be extended to other forms of patient symptomatology and behavior—for example, to other mood changes besides depression, or to the binge eating of anorectic patients. This represents the extension of the concept of the "trap" to cover thoughts and private acts.

Introducing these additional treatment methods requires more precise consideration of the issues of therapy than is demanded by the conventional reflective, relatively inactive dynamic approach, and it involves more direct suggestion and instruction. The patient is similarly called upon to do more individual homework. It is my impression that these changes are beneficial in the context of brief therapy. While the transference is a hardy plant and will still flourish and be manifest, some forms of it—notably, its regressive, idealizing, and persecutory aspects—are less likely to be generated by this approach, for the more visible and active therapist is making less claim to omniscience and is maintaining less control than is the conventional blank-screen analyst. The extent to which this way of conceptualizing therapy will be helpful in longer-term treatment; the number of patients who require therapist inactivity in order to discover or recover their capacity to change; the number of patients who need the analytically engendered transference illness in order to recover from their problems—all remain uncertain. But it is my conviction that the approach has accelerated and improved the effects of my own short-term work, which, in common with many writers (e.g., Malan), I believe can be suitable for some patients with serious and long-standing difficulties.

In presenting this account of work that is in many respects far from complete (a fuller account will be found in Ryle, in press), my aim has been to demonstrate at least the stable and fruitful cohabitation, if not the marriage, of psychotherapy and research. My own search for a more accurate conceptualization of the focus and goals of therapy grew out of the requirements of research, but it has also enabled me to set up better conditions for the practice of therapy. Moreover, it has reinforced my conviction that many of the conflicts and contradictions in the field of psychotherapy and research can be resolved. In closing, I would like to apply the arguments of this paper to that issue. Kelly (1955) did patients, or clients, the honor of allowing them similar cognitive processes to those characterizing therapists and scientists; in the same way, perhaps, as therapists and scientists, we should allow ourselves the same problems, difficulties, and solutions as patients. We, too, are often intellectually limited by dilemmas (e.g., the restrictive paradigms of Kuhn, 1962) or trapped in sterile debates that serve only to confirm our own restricted positions; if we would change, we are often faced with snags in the form of negative institutional responses or threats to professional identity. The existence of a common ground and a common language for therapies of different theoretical origins, and the availability of this shared framework to clinical work and to research, may offer aid in the resolution of these difficulties.

REFERENCES

Bandura, A. *Social learning theory*. Englewood Cliffs, N.J.: Prentice-Hall, 1977. (a)

Bandura, A. Self-efficacy: Towards a unifying theory of behavioral change. *Psychological Review*, 1977, *84*, 191–215. (b)

Beck, A. T. *Cognitive therapy and the emotional disorders.* New York: International Universities Press, 1976.

Candy, J., Balfour, H. G., Cawley, R. H., Hildebrand, H. R., Malan, D. H., Marks, I. M., & Wilson, J. A feasibility study for a controlled trial of psychotherapy. *Psychological Medicine*, 1972, *2*, 345–362.

Erikson, E. Identity and the life cycle. *Psychological Issues*, 1959, *1* (Whole issue).

Ezriel, H. A psychoanalytic approach to group therapy. *British Journal of Medical Psychology*, 1950, *23*, 59–74.

Hafner, R. J. The husbands of agoraphobic women and their influence on treatment outcome. *British Journal of Psychiatry*, 1977, *131*, 289–294.

Haley, J. *Strategies of psychotherapy.* New York: Grune & Stratton, 1963.

Hurvitz, N. Interaction hypotheses in marriage counseling. In A. S. Gurman & D. G. Rice (Eds.), *Couples in conflict: New direction in marital counseling.* New York: Jason Aronson, 1975.

Kelly, G. *The psychology of personal constructs.* New York: Norton, 1955.

Klein, G. S. *Perception, motives and personality.* New York: Knopf, 1970.

Kuhn, T. S. *The structure of scientific revolutions.* Chicago: University of Chicago Press, 1962.

Lazarus, A. A. *Behavior therapy and beyond.* New York: McGraw-Hill, 1970.

Mahler, M. S., Pine, F., & Bergman, A. *The psychological birth of the human infant.* London: Hutchinson, 1975.

Malan, D. H. *The frontier of brief psychotherapy.* London: Hutchinson, 1976.

Rowe, D. Poor prognosis in a case of depression as predicted by the repertory grid. *British Journal of Psychiatry*, 1970, *119*, 319–321.

Ryle, A. *Frames and cages: The repertory grid approach to human understanding.* Falmer, Brighton, England: Sussex University Press, 1975; New York: International Universities Press, 1975.

Ryle, A. A common language for the psychotherapies. *British Journal of Psychiatry*, 1978, *132*, 585–594.

Ryle, A. The focus in brief interpretive psychotherapy: Dilemmas, traps, and snags as target problems. *British Journal of Psychiatry*, 1979, *134*, 46–54. (a)

Ryle, A. Defining goals and assessing change in brief psychotherapy: A pilot study using target ratings and the dyad grid. *British Journal of Medical Psychology*, 1979, *52*, 223–233. (b)

Ryle, A. Some measures of goal attainment in focused, integrated active psychotherapy: A study of fifteen cases. *British Journal of Psychiatry*, 1980, *137*, 475–486.

Ryle, A. *Psychotherapy: A cognitive interpretation of theory and practice.* London: Academic Press, in press.

Shapiro, M. S. The single case in clinical psychological research. *Journal of General Psychology*, 1966, *74*, 3–23.

Sifneos, P. E. *Short-term psychotherapy and emotional crisis.* Cambridge, Mass.: Harvard University Press, 1972.

Tschudi, F. Loaded and honest questions: A construct theory view of symptoms and therapy. In D. Bannister (Ed.), *New perspectives in personal construct theory.* London: Academic Press, 1977.

CONCLUSION

As noted in Chapter 1, the affective disorders are indeed heterogeneous with regard to biology, genetics, pharmacological response patterns, and psychotherapeutic response patterns. Subsequent chapters in this volume have emphasized different theoretical and practical approaches to the treatment of at least some patients with affective disorders. Whether researchers and clinicians wish to emphasize measurable behaviors, interpersonal roles, cognitions and silent assumptions, or unconscious drives and defenses, they are still left with the question: For which patient is which of, or are all of, these psychotherapeutic approaches most appropriate? Chapter 10 has commented on common problems encountered in the conduct of psychotherapy, whether by behavioral, interpersonal, cognitive, or psychodynamic practitioners.

As is often the case, as a few answers are gathered, many more pertinent questions can now be formulated. What particular types of depression are most responsive to psychotherapy? Are there particular personality types that make a specific psychotherapeutic package more or less acceptable? Which therapies are most effective at reducing the symptoms? Do therapies differ in their ability to provide prophylaxis against subsequent episodes of depression?

In addition to questions about indications and contraindications, further evidence is clearly needed with regard to the overall effectiveness of each of these four approaches. Do they differ from one another with regard to the overall symptom-reducing or prophylactic effect? Is one psychotherapeutic approach better for one type of depression, whereas perhaps another is more suited for different types of depression? Are there particular contraindications to any psychotherapeutic approach? Why is it that some patients fail to respond to the psychotherapeutic package? Are there particular active ingredients that can be distilled from each of the treatments proposed? Do these active ingredients differ, depending upon the type of depression or type of personality?

Additional technical questions are extremely important, especially to clinical practice. Does the frequency of the psychotherapeutic sessions matter? Are "booster" sessions following termination of particular value with one approach or another, or in particular types of depression? How much further therapeutic change will occur after the termination of any one of these psychotherapies?

Furthermore, the relationship of psychotherapy to medication in the affective disorders is still somewhat unclear. Are there patients who require a combination of treatments, meaning both chemotherapy and psychotherapy? Which patients will respond to either of these treatments alone? While many clinicians may continue to believe that medication will interfere with psychotherapy, research evidence that this is true has not been accrued. In fact, evidence to the contrary is available now.

Finally, which patients are most suited for long-term as opposed to short-term psychotherapy? Should important others in the patients' social systems be involved more frequently in the course of one or more of these therapies? Would this add to efficacy? Are there particular patient groups for whom technical innovations must be created? For example, do patients from lower socioeconomic classes require modifications of any of the techniques proposed?

Psychotherapy is an expensive and time-consuming process. The available evidence would suggest that in many patients with depression, psychotherapeutic treatments may well be effective, at least in terms of symptom reduction. If an equivalent amount of symptom reduction can be obtained with medication alone, then the cost–benefit equation would argue that medication will replace psychotherapies in the long run in the treatment of these disorders. What medications cannot do, however, is to provide prophylaxis once they are discontinued. While hopes abound that psychotherapeutic methods will teach patients skills or techniques that they can use to prevent subsequent episodes of depression, or will change attitudes, assumptions, or drives that predispose to depression, these hopes are not yet documented by empirical research. Should the prophylactic effects of psychotherapy be documented, then the cost–benefit argument for psychotherapy would be much more strongly made.

It is possible, from the work of psychotherapists of various persuasions, that specific hypotheses could be formed with regard to the kinds of developmental experiences that may contribute to vulnerability to depression. While research into these predisposing factors is at a very rudimentary phase, further efforts in this direction may well be of substantial benefit. Medical science has rarely significantly reduced the impact of a set of disorders in the population without being able to offer some methods of primary prevention. Perhaps the insights offered by therapists of the affective disorders can provide clues to researchers for subsequent study of such factors.

It is obvious that the number of questions of both practical and theoretical significance is indeed large. However, the relevance of these questions to the treatment and prevention of the affective disorders is unarguable. Pursuit of these questions is a time-consuming and costly process. However, the ultimate benefits to patients with depression, as well as to those who live with, work, and are otherwise influenced by those with depression, are also unarguable.

Recent developments with regard to biological markers for the affective disorders offer an important opportunity for future psychotherapy research. Are there biological markers that predict response or nonresponse to psychotherapy? Does psychotherapy itself produce biological changes that can be measured with our new technologies? Are there specific psychological measures or markers that might either identify patients who, as a group, are responsive to psychotherapies, or identify patients for whom a particular therapeutic approach is most suited?

In weighing the costs and benefits of pursuing answers to the above questions, the general population and its governmental representatives, as well as those from the private sector, must become more aware of the advances that have recently been made in the area of psychotherapy for the depressions; they must also be made more aware of the significance that answers to these new questions might have in terms of relieving suffering and developing further knowledge.

AUTHOR INDEX

SUBJECT INDEX